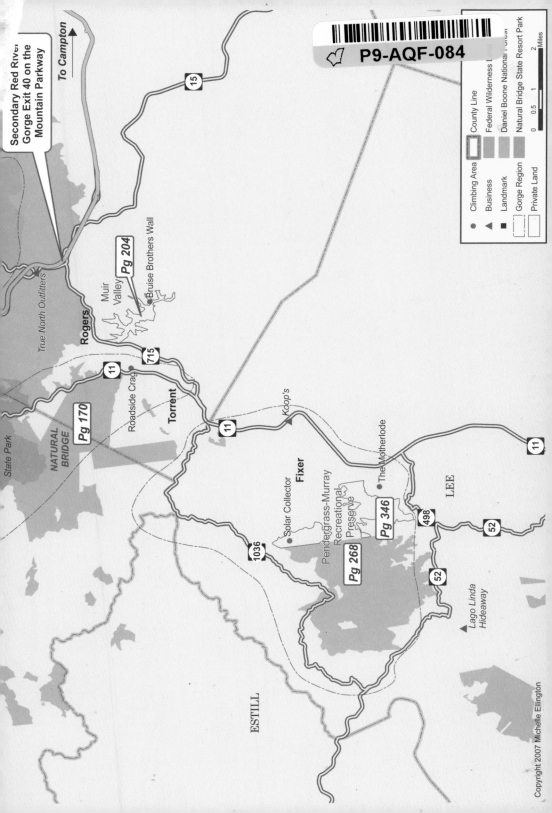

Secondary Red River
Gorge Exit 40 on the
Mountain Parkway

To Campton

True North Outfitters

Rogers

Muir
Valley

Bruise Brothers Wall

Pg 204

15

715

11

Roadside Crag

Torrent

Pg 170

NATURAL
BRIDGE

State Park

Koop's

Fixer

Solar Collector

The Motherlode

Pendergrass-Murray
Recreational
Preserve

Pg 346

Pg 268

498

LEE

52

1036

52

Lago Linda
Hideaway

ESTILL

Legend

● Climbing Area   County Line
▲ Business   Federal Wilderness [Area]
■ Landmark   Daniel Boone National [Forest]
                        Natural Bridge State Resort Park
                        Gorge Region
                        Private Land

0   0.5   1   2
          Miles

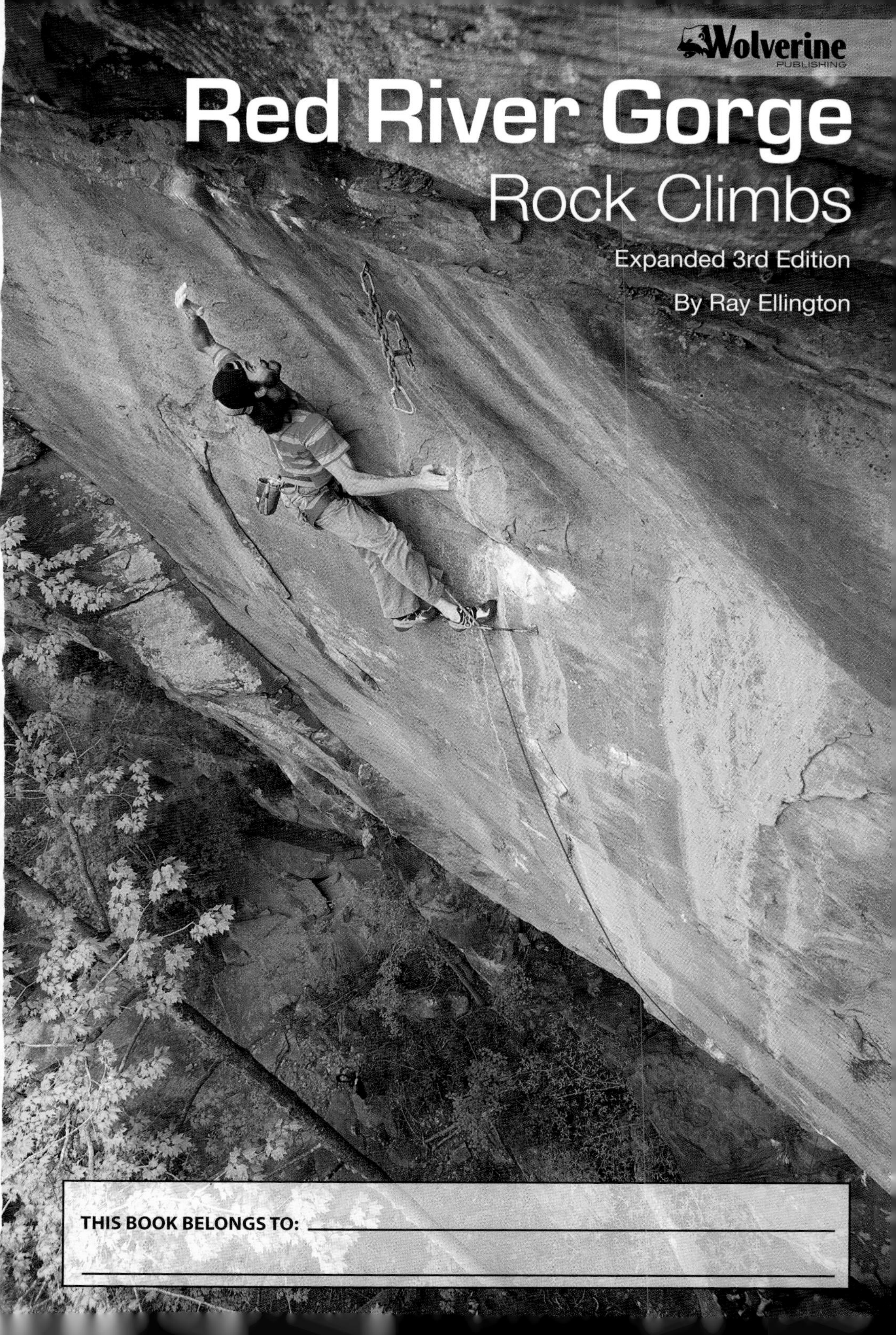

Wolverine
PUBLISHING

Red River Gorge
Rock Climbs

Expanded 3rd Edition

By Ray Ellington

THIS BOOK BELONGS TO: ______________________

____

RED RIVER GORGE ROCK CLIMBS
Third Edition
Author: Ray Ellington.
Maps: Michelle Ellington
Photographs: Ray Ellington, unless otherwise credited.
Published and distributed by Wolverine Publishing, LLC.

Cover photo:
Chris Sharma on *50 Words For Pump* 5.14c. Bob Marley Crag, page 336. Photo Keith Ladzinsky.

Opening page photo:
Peter McDermott on *Brilliant Orange* 5.13a, Gold Coast, page 282. Photo: Dawn Kish.

International Standard Book Number:
ISBN: 978-0-9826154-2-3

Wolverine Publishing is continually expanding its range of guidebooks. If you have a manuscript or idea for a book, or would like to find out more about our company and publications, contact:
Dave Pegg
Wolverine Publishing
1491 County Road 237
Silt, CO 81652
970-876-0268
dave@wolverinepublishing.com
www.wolverinepublishing.com

Printed in China

USING THIS BOOK

This a comprehensive guide to the roped climbing, both traditional and sport, in the Red River Gorge. It is not a comprehensive bouldering guide, although we have listed classic boulder problems at established crags. Routes are rated for difficulty using the Yosemite Decimal System and for quality using a 5-star scale. The only convention that isn't standard is the use of color to differentiate routes:

1 Blue denotes a sport climb. Blue routes can be led with a rack of quickdraws only.

2 Red denotes a traditional climb. It also denotes a mixed or aid climb. Red routes require the leader to carry and place natural protection devices.

3 Green denotes a boulder problem.

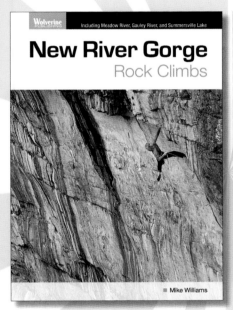
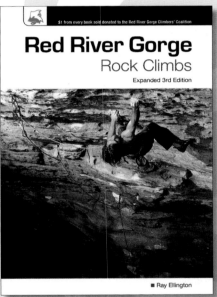

ON THE EDGE

Jason Forrester sends Rebar, 5.11a, Gold Coast. Trains at Rocksport.

ROCKSPORT

WARNING

DO NOT USE THIS GUIDEBOOK UNLESS YOU READ AND AGREE TO THE FOLLOWING:

Rock climbing is a dangerous sport that can result in death, paralysis or serious injury.

This book is intended as a reference tool for advanced/expert climbers. The activity and the terrain it describes can be or is extremely dangerous and requires a high degree of ability and experience to negotiate. This book is not intended for inexperienced or novice climbers, nor is it intended as an instructional manual. If you are unsure of your ability to handle any circumstances that may arise, employ the services of a professional instructor or guide.

This book relies upon information and opinions provided by others that may not be accurate. Opinions concerning the technical difficulties, ratings of climbs, and protection or lack thereof are subjective and may differ from yours and others opinions. Ratings may differ from area to area, holds may break, fixed protection may fail, fall out or be missing, and weather may deteriorate, these and other factors, such as rock fall, inadequate or faulty protection, etc., may all increase the danger of a climbing route and may contribute to the climb being other than as described in the book. Furthermore, errors may be made during the editing, designing, proofing, and printing of this book. Thus, the information in this book is unverified, and the authors and publisher cannot guarantee its accuracy. Numerous hazards exist that are not described in this book. Climbing on any terrain described in this book, regardless of its description or rating, may result in your death, paralysis or injury.

Do not use this book unless you are a skilled and experienced climber who understands and accepts the risks of rock climbing. If you choose to use any information in this book to plan, attempt, or climb a particular route, you do so at your own risk. Please take all precautions and use your own ability, evaluation, and judgment to assess the risks of your chosen climb, rather than relying on the information in this book.

THE AUTHORS AND PUBLISHER MAKE NO REPRESENTATIONS OR WARRANTIES, EXPRESSED OR IMPLIED, OF ANY KIND REGARDING THE CONTENTS OF THIS BOOK, AND EXPRESSLY DISCLAIM ANY AND ALL REPRESENTATIONS OR WARRANTIES REGARDING THE CONTENTS OF THIS BOOK, INCLUDING, WITHOUT LIMITATION, THE ACCURACY OR RELIABILITY OF INFORMATION CONTAINED HEREIN. WARRANTIES OF FITNESS FOR A PARTICULAR PURPOSE AND/OR MERCHANTABILITY ARE EXPRESSLY DISCLAIMED.

THE USER ASSUMES ALL RISKS ASSOCIATED WITH THE USE OF THIS BOOK INCLUDING, WITHOUT LIMITATION, ALL RISKS ASSOCIATED WITH ROCK CLIMBING.

RED RIVER OUTDOORS

for all your adventure needs

- cabin rentals
- climbing guide service and instruction
- paintball
- mountain bike rental
- canoe/kayak rental
- wedding packages

41

243

280

338

CONTENTS ──

PEOPLE

NORTHERN GORGE 94

MIDDLE GORGE 108

UPPER GORGE 130

EASTERN GORGE 140

TUNNEL RIDGE ROAD 166

NATURAL BRIDGE 170

Red River Gorge Rock Climbs app

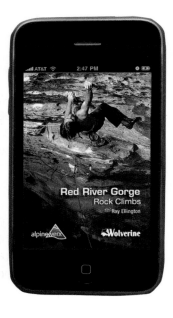

Explore the entire content of an 1800 route (400-page printed) guide with a few taps using touchable lists, maps, photos, and topos.

Search and sort routes that meet your search criteria: sport, trad, difficulty, star rating, area.

TickList the climbs you want to do.

Log the climbs you send and your progress on projects.

Navigate complex terrain in real time using embedded maps and GPS.

FOREWORD

By Bill Ramsey

It was an unusually hot day in late May in 1991. I was enjoying a rest day from climbing with some friends, swimming and jumping off of bridges at the New River Gorge. This was during my one and only climbing trip of the year, and although I had started climbing 15 years earlier, I was being introduced to a new dimension of it – something called "sport climbing." My comrades were Steve Downes, a fellow climber/philosophy professor, and two local rock stars named Doug Reed and Porter Jarrard. As I grabbed another beer out of the cooler, the conversation turned to future plans. Porter casually stated that he was going to spend much of the following year bolting new routes at a major climbing area just outside of Lexington, Kentucky. When I told him that I'd never heard of climbing in Kentucky, he turned and said with a classic Porter grin: "Trust me, you will."

No kidding. During the next few years, while I focused on writing and teaching at Notre Dame, reports would percolate up from Kentucky about wildly steep routes on good rock covered in pockets and edges. Eventually, I checked the map and saw that the Red River Gorge was "only" 400 miles away. I talked a ND graduate student into a three-day

Bill Ramsey on *The Return of Darth Moll*, The Dark Side. Photo Hugh Loeffler.

exploratory road trip to the Red. What we found would eventually change the direction of my life.

The climbing I discovered was so brilliant and fun that I started making a point of driving to the Red every other month. Soon this became a once- or twice-a-month affair. Before long, I found myself making the seven-hour drive every weekend – often connecting with partners from Chicago, Indianapolis, or with locals from Lexington. My eventual return to what can be characterized as full-blown "obsession-driven" climbing was partly the manifestation of something in my life-blood – having started at 17 with my father, I had experienced an emptiness since withdrawing from the sport to pursue an academic career. But I was also being pulled back by something external – something that had to do with the wonders of Corbin sandstone and people like Porter who knew how to turn it into a playground.

Religious philosophers often point to signs of "intelligent design" in the natural world as proof of God's existence – arguments that I generally scoff at. But the nature of the climbing at the Red sometimes makes me wonder. When one is desperately making a blind reach, it is not uncommon to find a natural pocket that is exactly where it needs to be and that perfectly fits the human hand, complete with a mini-pocket for the thumb. The overall quality of the rock, the diversity of the holds, the continual steepness that makes for clean falls and athletic moves – all of these contribute to the sense that if one could actually construct an outdoor cliff with real rock, this is what it would be like. Climbs considered "bad" here would be four-star classics at most places.

Which is not to say everybody loves Red. The most common complaint is that the routes are all mindless jug-hauls. This might have something to do with the fact that the first question most visitors ask upon arriving is, "Where are the mindless jug-hauls?" This is a bit like spending a week bouldering in Yosemite, and then whining that there are no long routes. The second criticism concerns the "down-home" culture of the folks that inhabit the surrounding countryside. While the local economy is indeed impoverished and there are a few bad apples, the people in this region are no less friendly than the ranchers around Rifle, or the farmers next to Smith Rock. Big surprise – the rural location of most rock-climbing areas tends to make the surrounding culture ... well, rural.

My re-discovered love of climbing wasn't due to just the geological aspects of the Red. The collection of dedicated and colorful characters who climb here offers kinship that is both welcome and welcoming. It is one of the few places where large factions of sport climbers and traditional climbers not only manage to coexist, but extend to one another a degree of mutual admiration. It is a place that spawned brilliant climbing prodigies like Katie Brown and David Hume, who set an example of grace and achievement, with no ego. The word that best describes the people here is "generous." This comes in many forms, including the hospitality of Miguel, who runs one of the friendliest climber campgrounds in the world. It includes the magnanimous efforts of route-developers like Porter, Hugh Loffler, Chris Martin, and Terry Kindred – folks who do all the hard work and often let others, like myself, receive the glory. It includes the energy Ray Ellington and others devote to maintaining an incredibly informative website that helps provide cohesion (and some useful friction) to those who climb here. And, of course, it includes the incredible devotion to access demonstrated by people like Shannon Stuart-Smith, the RRGCC, and Rick Weber – people who are responsible for the largest amount of climber-owned real estate in the country. The best way to thank these and others is by passing it on – by making an effort to give back as much to the land and the cliffs and your fellow climbers as you wind up taking. Considering just how much the Red has given me, I know I won't be able to fully reciprocate. But I am going to try.

HOW WE DO

Kris Hampton, aka "Odub", has been climbing in the Red for 13 years. He has done many first ascents and several of his photographs appear in this book. Kris grew up listening to hip-hop and has been rapping since 1990, and before long started mixing his love for climbing with his skill for rapping. The result is some unique lyrics ("I've got 99 problems but this pitch ain't one"). More music from Odub, including the following rap, can be found at www.odubmusic.com.

Some clip bolts, some place cams
Sandy holds, sweaty jams
Giant jugs, can't understand
How you got so pumped you can't squeeze your hands
Over-grip, start to slip
Big sloper, fingertip crimp
And you know if you go, you're hosed
This is soft sandstone, will your pieces blow?
Big steep wall, long jug haul
Bolts run out, all clean fall
Brave ego been called off cuz
It's the biggest holds that you'll ever fall off of
Not a tall wall but, your forearms flamin'
Next day at Miguel's, sore arm complainin'
Don't bring your crashpad kid, cuz fact is
No boulders here, cuz we don't need the practice.

Motherlode, cheater stone
Stick clip army, grid of bolts
Roadside Crag, 44 bags
waitin' in line for the same climb, Dag!
Torrent Falls, *Bare Metal Teen*
Hardest 12a that you ever seen
Sky Bridge Ridge, world's best pitch
Go ahead try it: get *Inhibited*
Now the Red doesn't look like a river at all
Unless you happen to catch it after heavy rainfall
Visit in the summer, you won't get pity
If your ass passes out from the thick humidity
Gotta dodge the wolfspiders in every dihedral
That path through the rhodos...who knows where it leads ya?
Red River Gorge, I ain't said the worst
But I wouldn't trade it for another place on Earth.

INTRODUCTION

Ray Ellington

Winding through the poverty stricken town of Nada, my car is chased by a pack of stray dogs. My own dogs hang their heads out of the window breathing in the fresh air of the Appalachian foothills. Sandstone cliffs peek through thickets of rhododendrons and the occasional tree masquerades as a splitter finger crack, causing me to turn my head and almost lose control. I sneak my SUV up to the blind corner before the one-lane Nada tunnel, looking for oncoming headlights. On the other side of the tunnel, I drive beneath the intimidating overhang of *Black Death* and envision Greg Smith, the first ascentionist, in 1984 out on the sharp end with minimal protection clawing through the topout while his friends cheer him on from below. They stand in the middle of the road wearing their Hugh Herr and Wild Things climbing tights, oblivious to the threat of approaching vehicles. Passing Military Wall, I imagine Porter Jarrard pulling up to the parking lot in 1990 with a fully charged Hilti, his whirlwind energy unleashed on the cliff, establishing so many classic climbs in such a short period of time.

Then I round the corner and see the massive block of Raven's Rock. It still sends a chill down my spine, just as it did when I first laid eyes on it. Then, not even aware of rock climbing, my friend Eric Siemer and I

Crouching Tiger, Hidden Dragon, Pistol Ridge.
Photo Kris Hampton.

would escape the city every Friday night after work and make the two and a half hour drive from Cincinnati for a heavy dose of our newfound love of the wilderness. Army duffle bags full of jeans, knives, cotton hooded sweatshirts, Mag lights, and, most importantly, a fifth of Jack Daniels and a few warm Cokes. Crossing the steel bridge, I see a couple of canoes floating down the Red River, the water appearing an almost fluorescent green, and I drive past the turnoff where 77 heads up to Fortress Wall, where I had my first encounter with traditional climbing nearly 13 years ago.

Today I am heading to the Small Walls, which are, ironically, the largest walls in the Red, to repeat a climb called *The Quest*. During the past month I have gone nowhere but a single crag to work on a single route and I need a break. *The Quest* will take me high above the Red River, the crowds, and the tourist traffic. *The Quest* will offer silence, exposure, serenity, and occasional moments of fear. It is the medicine I need to get back to my roots and experience the things I love most about the Red.

The Red is an incredible climbing destination. The amount and variety of rock it offers is almost impossible to imagine. Not only will you find some of the finest sport climbing in the world, but also flaring offwidths, overhanging fist cracks, thin dihedrals, and splitter finger cracks. The combination makes it the best all-round destination area in the country.

But there's more to the Red than just the climbing. It is also a lush forest rich with plant life, a wild and scenic river, a protected wilderness area, and an opportunity to hike for miles and not hear a single voice besides your partner's. I'm excited to be able to share my passion for the Red River Gorge with you through this book. Whether it be bushwacking through thick rhodos in search of that unfound splitter crack, or trekking down a well-traveled trail to one of the best crags in the country, the Red always shows me something new. I hope your experiences are as wonderful as mine.

22-BED HOSTEL
12 BEDS IN OPEN LOFT
2 MORE PRIVATE ROOMS:
6 BEDS IN ROOM · 4 BEDS IN ROOM

Group rates for 10 or more available
Hostel is open 24/7 year round.
Free WIFI with your stay

Come into our restaurant and start your day
with our famous "Hostel" breakfast.
Our menu has a variety of mouth-watering sandwiches,
burgers, entrees and freshly baked desserts.
We also provide catering services for
your special event or meeting.

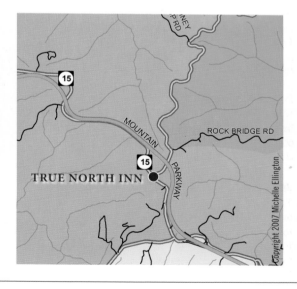

We provide rock-climbing
instruction for the gym climber
to transition to the outdoors. Our
AMGA certified single-pitch
instructors teach clinics for trad
and sport climbing disciplines.

True North Inn is conveniently located less than a mile from the Bert T. Combs Parkway.
Use exit 40, follow Hwy 715 West to the intersection of Hwys 715 and 15, which are also the
entrance of the Red River Gorge.

20 Sky Bridge Road, Pine Ridge, KY 41360
606-668-3745 • info@truenorthinn.com • www.truenorthinn.com

TRIP BETA

This section contains useful information for planning your trip and navigating the Red River Gorge and surrounding area.

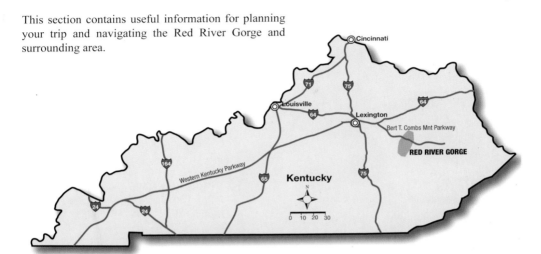

Getting to the Red River Gorge

The Red River Gorge is located in the state of Kentucky in central/eastern USA. The Red is in the eastern part of the state, about 60 miles southeast of Lexington. The closest airports are Lexington (one hour); Louisville, Kentucky, (two hours); and Cincinnati/Northern Kentucky airport (two hours). To reach the Red from Interstate 64, take exit 98 onto the Bert T. Combs Mountain Parkway. Drive 33 miles on the parkway, then take exit 33 at Slade. Turn right onto KY 11 and head south for 1.7 miles to reach Miguel's Pizza on the left, which is the starting point for direction to most climbing areas in this guide.

When to Visit

The best time to climb in the Red is the fall (September through November) when the humidity is relatively low and the daytime temperatures range from the high 70s to the mid 50s. Spring (March through May) is also a great season for climbing at the Red with temperatures similar to those in the fall, although the chance of rain is greater. It is possible to climb year-round in the Red, although the summer can be hot, humid, and buggy. Winter is normally relatively mild, with average highs in the 40s; unlike the western part of the country, however, the sun tends to remain behind the clouds. Snowfall is possible.

Journey's end: Miguel's Pizza.

DRIVING TIMES

Lexington, KY	1 hour
Louisville, KY	2 hours
Cincinnati, OH	2-2.5 hours
Knoxville, TN	3.5 hours
Indianapolis, IN	3.5 to 4 hours
New River Gorge, WV	4 hours
Asheville, NC	5 hours

Climbing at the Red can be exhausting. Our tips for camping and accommodation will help you find good places to crash.
Photo: Dawn Kish.

Where to Stay

Campgrounds

Many climbers camp at **Miguel's Pizza** (606-663-1975). Rates are currently $2 per night per person. Showers are available for $1.50. Climbers can camp year-round (the restaurant itself is open March 1 until Thanksgiving). It is not uncommon for the parking lot and camping area to reach capacity during the spring and fall, so try to get a spot early if you're coming on a weekend. See ad opposite.

If you want to escape the crowds, try **Lago Linda Hideaway** (606-464-2876). Nestled in the Southern Region of the Red River Gorge, near the Motherlode and Pendergrass-Murray Recreation Preserve, Lago Linda offers a tranquil retreat and quiet surroundings. All campsites are graveled, with electric hookups. Each site has its own water, picnic table, and fire ring. See page 270 for directions.

Land of the Arches Campground (606-668-7074) is another great option located near Muir Valley (see above).

Primitive camping with a permit is allowed almost anywhere in the Red on Forest Service land. Campsites must be at least 300 feet from roads and trails, and campers must have a permit. Permits can be purchased from the Shell station in Slade and cost between $3 and $5.

Hostels

True North Inn (606-668-3745). A great place for the individual passing through as well as group packages that may include breakfast. Located off Mountain Parkway exit 40. Make a right at stop sign. Hostel is on the right at three-way intersection of KY15 and 715, see previous page.

Cabin Rentals

Red River Outdoors (606-663-ROCK) see pages 7 and 301.

Torrent Falls (859-230-3567).

Lago Linda (606-464-2876) see page 270.

Miguels PIZZA *At The Red*

Campground

established 1984

$2 per person

Wireless & Computer Access
Heated Shower House & Laundry
Bedroom Rental and Indoor Kitchen
Restaurant Always Open

www.miguelspizza.com

1890 Natural Bridge Rd Slade, KY 40376 * 606-663-1975

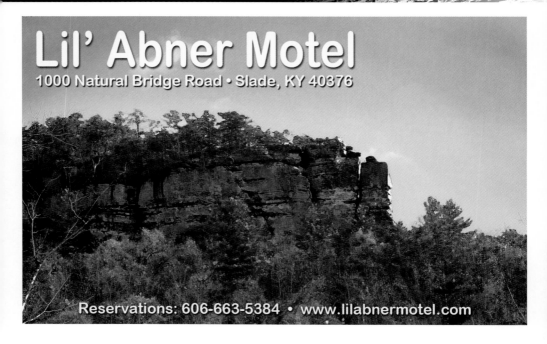

Lil' Abner Motel
1000 Natural Bridge Road • Slade, KY 40376

Reservations: 606-663-5384 • www.lilabnermotel.com

EMERGENCY INFO

The nearest hospital, Clark Regional Medical Center, is in Winchester, about a 40-minute drive from the Red.

Useful numbers:

Clark Regional Medical Center 859-744-5670
Don Fig (FS Search and Rescue) 606-663-2113
Kentucky State Police 606-784-4127
Powell County Dispatch 911
Wolfe County Dispatch 911

Motels

Lil Abner Motel (606-663-5384). Located about a half mile south on the left from the rest area on KY 11. www.lilabnermotel.com

Red River Inn (877-600-5586). Located about 3/4 miles south on the right from the rest area on KY 11.

Campton Inn (606-668-7072). Continue east on Mountain Parkway, past the Slade exit, to exit 42.

Abner's Motel (606-663-4379). Located in the small town of Stanton, about seven miles west on Mountain Parkway from the rest area.

Eats and Treats

Eating Out

Miguel's Pizza. Miguel makes great pizza and sandwiches, using homegrown ingredients. The price is impossible to beat and topping selections are unique – where else can you get black beans, pasta, and rice on your pizza? You can also grab a pint of Ben and Jerry's or choose from a wide selection of non-alcoholic drinks. See page 37.

Red River Outdoors. Closed by fire but reopening soon. If breakfast and good coffee are what you're after, check out Red River Outdoors, located on the right on KY 11 a few hundred feet south from the Mountain Parkway exit in Slade. Be sure to order their famous French toast.

True North Inn. Menu includes breakfast, lunch and dinner. From the hearty breakfast to a variety of entrees including vegetarian items. Located off Mountain Parkway exit 40. Make a right at stop sign. Hostel is on right at three-way intersection of KY15 and 715. See page 16.

Subway. Across from the Shell Station in Slade.

Stanton. The town of Stanton is seven miles west on Mountain Parkway and has several fast-food outlets including Dairy Queen, McDonalds, and Taco Bell.

There's no better time to visit the Red than fall. Arborist Jess Young. Photo John Borland.

USING THIS BOOK

This a comprehensive guide to the roped climbing, both traditional and sport, in the Red River Gorge. It is not a comprehensive bouldering guide, although we have listed classic boulder problems at established crags. Routes are rated for difficulty using the Yosemite Decimal System and for quality using a 5-star scale. The only convention that might tax a climber's brain is the use of color to differentiate routes:

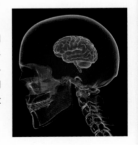

1 Blue denotes a sport climb. Blue routes can be led with a rack of quickdraws only.

2 Red denotes a traditional climb. It also denotes a mixed or aid climb. Red routes require the leader to carry and place natural protection devices.

3 Green denotes a boulder problem.

VETS

Stanton Veterinary Clinic
(606) 663-5866

Cundiff Jim L
(606) 464-2903

Minter Veterinary Services
(606) 464-1155

Groceries

The **Shell station** in Slade is pretty good about carrying supplies you might need during your visit. The nearest grocery store is **Kroger** in Stanton. If you're driving west on Mountain Parkway, turn right off the Stanton exit, drive a few blocks, turn left onto KY 11/15, and Kroger will be on the left. There is a **Super Wal-Mart** in Winchester. Head back toward Lexington on the Mountain Parkway. Join I-64 west, take exit 94, and head left on Bypass Road for about a mile and a half.

Climbing Gear

Miguel's sells a full range of climbing gear. For the widest selection of climbing gear, drive to: **Phillip Gall's** in Lexington 859-266-0469 (back cover); **J&H Lanmark** in Lexington 859-278-0730 (page 43); **The Benchmark Outfitters** in Cincinnati 513-791-9453 (back cover); and **Quest Outdoors** in Louisville 502-326-0424 (page 25).
True North Inn has harness and shoe rentals.

Internet Access

Red River Outdoors (606-663-ROCK). Located a few hundred feet on the right as you drive south on KY 11 from the rest area in Slade.
Miguel's Pizza. Wireless internet and one public computer.
Powell County Public Library in Stanton (606-663-4511). Located at 725 Breckenridge Street in the small town of Stanton about seven miles west on Mountain Parkway from the rest area.
Wolfe County Public Library (606 668-6571). Located on the east side of KY 15 about an eighth of a mile north of Campton.
True North Inn: Wireless internet and one public computer.

The mayor of Slade. Photo: Leslie E. Hensley.

Civilization

The nearest large shopping area is Hamburg Place, located just off I-75 at exit 108 in Lexington. Take Mountain Parkway west to I-64 west. Keep left when you reach the I-75 split to head south. After a couple of miles you'll reach the Man O' War exit (108). Turn right to get dumped directly into a wealth of places to drop money, including Barnes and Noble, Starbucks, Dicks Sporting Goods, Meijer, and Target, to name a few.

Rest Day Fun

Lexington has several movie theaters. Recommended is the **Kentucky Theatre** in downtown Lexington (859-231-6997). It shows some of the best "single sensation" or Indy-type films and serves beer!

Paintball is another fun option. See opposite.

The Lee County Recreation center, on the left side of Hwy 11, just south of the Motherlode turn off (498), has free pool tables, ping-pong, air hockey, cheap but pretty good pizza, and bowling for $5/hour.

For a taste of local life, check out the drive-in in Stanton. Just be careful not to get caught up in the ritualistic "circling of the cars" in town, unless you're into picking up local high-school chicks.

ALCOHOL

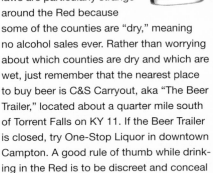

Beer and climbing go together like ... beer and climbing. However, don't get stuck Jonesing for a brew on Sunday, because alcohol isn't sold on Sunday in Kentucky. The laws are particularly strange around the Red because some of the counties are "dry," meaning no alcohol sales ever. Rather than worrying about which counties are dry and which are wet, just remember that the nearest place to buy beer is C&S Carryout, aka "The Beer Trailer," located about a quarter mile south of Torrent Falls on KY 11. If the Beer Trailer is closed, try One-Stop Liquor in downtown Campton. A good rule of thumb while drinking in the Red is to be discreet and conceal your beverage wherever you are.

NATURAL HISTORY

Flora/Fauna

Much of the Red River Gorge is forested in oak, poplar, silver maple, beech, hemlock, and numerous pines. Beneath the canopy you will see the beautiful spring bloomer, the redbud dogwood, sassafras, magnolia, mountain laurel, and rhododendron. Many plants carpet the forest floor, including dozens of species of ferns, mosses, and lichens, and wild flowers including columbine, iris, trillium, orchids, and the endangered white-haired goldenrod. Watch out for poison ivy, which is widespread, both on the ground and at the anchors of certain climbs, such as the rainy-day favorite, *South Side of the Sky* at Mt. Olive Crag.

You can encounter a diverse collection of wildlife in the Red River Gorge, including deer, bobcats, raccoons, skunks, chipmunks, flying squirrels, and bats. Many bird species can be seen, such as turkey vultures, hawks, ruffed grouse, turkeys, owls, woodpeckers, and many songbirds. Reptiles and amphibians common to the area include box turtles, fence lizards, skinks, copperheads, timber rattlesnakes, garter and green snakes, toads, spring peepers, and salamanders. Not to be taken lightly are the small but annoying insects of the Gorge. Climbers who brave the area in hot weather will become all too familiar with pesky mosquitoes, black flies, and deer flies. Wasps often build nests in pockets on rock faces, so use caution when climbing in the summer months.

Geology

The Red River Gorge has over 100 natural arches and one of the finest collections of pinnacles and cliffs east of the Rocky Mountains. Whether you're new to the area or have spent years exploring, the unique splendor of the area cannot go unnoticed.

The stone of the Red River Gorge was formed about 300 million years ago as a deposit at the edge of a shallow inland sea that covered much of the middle part of North America. Over millions of years, the Red River and its tributaries eroded layer upon layer of rock, exposing clifflines up to 200 feet tall made of tough Corbin Sandstone. The rusty red appearance of the sandstone comes from limonite, which acts as a cement, holding together the pebbly and sandy layers. Striking iron-oxide bands, created from the limonite, can be seen at many climbing

Otter. Photo Kelsey Gray.

areas, a good example is the *Table of Colors* wall. Millions of years of erosion and weathering have sculpted the sandstone cliffs, creating arches, cracks, and heavily pocketed faces. The solidity of the rock and abundance of features are what make the Red River Gorge a world-class climbing destination.

Archaeology

About 13,000 years ago, when glaciers still covered much of North America, the first people are believed to have inhabited the Red River Gorge. Small bands of Ice Age hunters followed herds of mastodons and wooly mammoths to Kentucky, and stayed, utilizing the abundant natural resources of the area. The rock shelters common to the Red made ideal habitats for these people. They hunted and harvested many items such as acorns, nuts, wild fruit, fungi, and various plants.

The dry, nitrate-rich soils found in the rock shelters and throughout the Red River Gorge provide an excellent environment for studying these prehistoric people because they help preserve plant materials and other normally perishable artifacts. Excavations of inhabited rock shelters have revealed seeds that indicate the people living in the area started domesticating and cultivating wild plants at least 3000 years ago.

The Red River Gorge has many recorded archaeological sites as well as many yet to be discovered. In 2003, the Clifty Wilderness and the Indian Creek area was designated a National Archaeological District and placed on the National Register of Historic Places. Please respect our archaeological heritage by not disturbing any sites you encounter.

CLIMBING HISTORY

Larry Day on the first ascent of *Insanity Ceiling* 5.11a at Tower Rock in 1979. Photo: Larry Day collection.

The history of rock climbing in the Red River Gorge dates back to the 1950s when the first line, *Caver's Route* at Tower Rock, is rumored to have been climbed. This route and others were established by local cavers, comfortable with the occasional chimney runout or even drilling a bolt here and there to get to the top of a pinnacle. Thus, while the piton was making it big in other parts of the country during the 1950s and early 1960s, it didn't have the impact on the initial development of climbing in the Red it had elsewhere.

The Gorge started getting more attention in the late 1960s and early 1970s. D. Britz and Ron Stokely made some of the earliest recorded ascents, in 1969, when they climbed historical classics such as *Chimney's Chimney* and *Tunnel Route* on Chimney Top Rock. Soon, a group including Larry Day, Frank Becker, Tom Seibert, and Ellen Seibert, started making regular visits. They came armed with Hexes, stoppers, tubular knotted slings, and Chouinard tube chocks. They found that Vietnam-War-style jungle boots, once the tread had worn off, made great climbing shoes, providing decent friction on the Kentucky sandstone. Fortunately, these climbers were heavily influenced by the clean-

climbing ethic proposed by Royal Robbins and Yvon Chouinard. This advocated climbing without the use of pitons and bolts, which were seen as "old school" by the younger generation. This is another reason the cracks of the Red River Gorge never suffered the abuse of pin scars.

The main focus of climbing during this era was making it to the top. If a line did not run continuously from the base to the summit, it was a waste of time. The determined group probably spent more days looking for acceptable lines than they did actually climbing, although they did manage to bag around 40 documented ascents between 1970 and 1975, with grades as hard as 5.9. Notable routes include the first ascent of Jewel Pinnacle via the still popular *Diamond in the Crack*, *G.I.* at Military Wall, *Arachnid* and the perfect hand crack of *Africa* at Tower Rock, *Frenchburg Overhangs* at Dunkan Rock, Buzzard's Roost North, and the first pocketed face route in the Red, *Face Farce* at Princess Arch.

1975 saw the publication of the first guidebook, *Red River Gorge Climber's Guide* by Frank Becker, which inspired more climbers to explore the area. During the late 1970s the number of first ascents more than doubled those of the previous five years. Over 80 lines were established, some of them within the 5.10 range. Much of this development was documented in the 1978 guidebook *Rawk! A Climber's Guide to the Red River Gorge*, by Ed Benjamin and Ed Pearsall. Larry Day, Tom Seibert, and Ellen Seibert remained at the forefront, and Day and Ed Pearsall teamed up to apply their honed skills to take on some of the more difficult and bold lines, including the possibly unrepeated *Tower of Power* at Tower Rock and *Last Day* at Chimney Top. The duo came close to the first free ascent of probably the most challenging and definitely the best and longest 5.10 line in the Red, *The Quest*, but slipped out of the final 25-foot offwidth section and never went back to complete the line. However, they did manage to reach the summit, which was important to them at the time. Anyone who has attempted *The Quest* will respect the efforts of these two men, who didn't have the security of the large camming devices available today. This period saw the first 5.11s in the Red, with Bill Strachan's strenuous offwidth *Here Comes Batman* at Staircase Wall in 1978, followed one year later by Day's *Insanity Ceiling* at Tower Rock (photo opposite). 1980 saw a third guidebook to the Red, by Ed Pearsall. It contained nearly 150 lines, established mainly during the previous 10 years.

The early 1980s mimicked the previous five years by doubling the number of routes, bringing the total to more than 300. A new generation of climbers stormed the Red with better gear, better shoes, bigger muscles, and wild tights. Two strong climbers from Cincinnati played cleanup, ticking off the proudest lines nobody had been able to do thus far. Nicknamed "the Beene Brothers," Tom Souders and Jeff Koenig bagged modern-day testpieces such as *The Return of Geoff Beene* at Skybridge Ridge (photo this page), *Pink Feat* at Military Wall, and the five-star classic *Inhibitor* at Skybridge Ridge. Souders also teamed up with Bob Hayes to do the first free ascent of *The Quest*.

Another important contributor who made an appearance in the early '80s was John Bronaugh, who with his partner Ron Snider, began what would become two decades of first ascents, including lines such as *The Battlement* at Fortress Wall and *Wishbone* at Window Wall. A strong and bold climber, Greg Smith, established several difficult and poorly protected testpieces, some of which, like *Whimpering Insanity* at Tower Rock and *Invisible Barrier* at Bee Branch Rock, fell within the 5.11 X range. One of his safer and more popular routes, the finger crack of *Synchronicity* (5.11a), stands out like a sore thumb on the heavily bolted 5.10 Wall of Roadside Crag. The most prolific contributor, however, was Martin Hackworth. Hackworth, with whatever partner he could find, managed to tick off about 70 lines between 1980 and 1985. His classics include the amazing finger crack *Finger Lickin' Good* at Hen's Nest and *Vector Trouble* at Long Wall. Much of this development was recorded in yet another guidebook, *Stones of Years,* by Martin Hackworth and Grant Stephens, published in 1984.

The pace of route development steadied from 1985 through 1990 as more climbers visited the area and the focus changed to repeating established climbs. Even so, new lines were established during the period. Souders added a few more difficult lines, such as *Fibrulator* (5.11b) at Indian Creek, and Bronaugh, Hackworth, Chuck Faulkner and Charles Tabor were still active. Although there were many people in the mix now, they had no idea of the madness that was about to consume their beloved sandstone. In the distance a faint sound could be heard – the sound of a power drill.

In 1990, with another edition of Hackworth's guide detailing close to 400 routes hot off the press, a young climber named Porter Jarrard stepped onto the scene. The Red already had a few rap-bolted face climbs, routes like *Captain One-Eye* at Purple Valley, but all of them had been established with hand drill. Armed with a power drill, Jarrard took things to a different level. The once unclimbable, pocketed, overhanging sandstone walls of the Gorge became prime real estate as he began rap bolting at a furious pace. By the end of 1990, 30 sport lines had been established. Jarrard bolted 20 of them and each became a classic: *Reliquary, Tissue Tiger, Stay the Hand, Wild Gift* ... the list goes on. Jarrard's *Table of Colors* in 1990, followed by *Revival* a year later, introduced 5.13 to the Red. He had an eye for a great line and the quality of his contributions quickly helped his tactics gain acceptance. It wasn't long before other climbers, including Jim Link, Jamie Baker, Neil Strickland, John Bronaugh, Jeff Moll, Chris Snyder, Stacy Temple,

Tom Souders on *The Return of Geoff Beene* (5.10d) at Western Sky Bridge Ridge, 1983. Photo: Jeff Koenig.

The turn of the century saw a surge in development in what would become the Pendergrass-Murray Recreational Preserve. Top: Neal Strickland on his route *Buddha Hole* (5.12a), the Solar Collector (2000). Bottom: Rob McFall on his route *Elephant Man* (5.13b), the Dark Side (2002). Photos: Rob McFall collection.

Mark Williams, and Charles Tabor were lugging Bosch or Hilti drills to the crag.

In 1993, John Bronaugh published *Red River Gorge Climbs*. The guide contained nearly 700 routes, over twice the number of lines published only three years earlier. It was clear that sport climbing was changing the face of rock climbing at the Red River Gorge, a fact made even clearer by the discovery in 1994 of the mother of all walls, The Motherlode. This crag solidified the grade of 5.13 and helped establish the Red as one of the best sport-climbing destinations in the country.

In 1995, with the sport-climbing craze gaining momentum, a quiet resurgence in traditional climbing was occurring. It became common to see climbers brushing cobwebs off old, abandoned trad lines. Kris Hampton and Ray Ellington started a campaign to tick the area's overlooked offwidths, previously dismissed as too wide, steep, or flaring, and with routes like *Country Lovin'* at Indian Creek Crag and *Hidden Dragon* at Pistol Ridge, brought the 5.12 grade to crack climbing at the Red. Around this time, the visiting finger-crack master Steve Petro sent the often-attempted *Nazi Bitch Crack* at Pebble Beach, renaming it *Welcome to Ol' Kentuck* and upping the ante for traditional lines to 5.13.

Bolting slowed down dramatically between 1995 and 1999 as Porter left the scene and many people found a new home: camped out under their 5.13 projects at the Motherlode. Others started exploring the cliffs lining the roads owned by the oil companies, opening up a few new areas in the Southern Region. In 1998, John Bronaugh released the second edition of *Red River Gorge Climbs*. The book was almost twice the size of the first edition and contained nearly 1000 routes. In 1999, child prodigy climber Dave Hume pushed the boundaries of possibility even further, bringing the unimaginable grade of 5.14 to the Gorge with his ascent of *Thanatopsis* at The Motherlode.

With the area quickly becoming known as one of the best sport-climbing destinations in the country, Miguel's Pizza began to run out of food on weekend nights as hundreds of climbers set up home in his backyard. It became common to stand in line for routes at Roadside Crag, Military Wall, and Left Flank. Climbing gyms opened up in surrounding cities, bringing even more weekend warriors to the area to test their skills on the real rock. It became close to impossible to find a camping spot at the once peaceful Roadside Crag camping area.

2000 marked a new explosion in route development. The oil fields in the southern region were still being explored and new rock was always being found. Remarkable walls such as the Dark Side and Gold Coast were discovered, providing a place other than the Motherlode for elite climbers to play, and the 5.14 grade was solidified by Bill Ramsey, Dave Hume, and Ben Cassel. John Bronaugh was still going strong, bolting just about anything he could rappel at the (currently closed) Oil Crack Crag, while Terry Kindred was across the way developing the Arena. The back roads of the oil company land became the new place to go. Although the land was privately owned, the oil company had the mining rights. Cars were getting stuck and parking became a major issue as oil workers often found climbers' cars in their way. With relationships turning sour between oil workers and climbers, access was saved when the RRGCC stepped up and purchased most of the property, creating the Pendergrass-Murray Recreational Preserve.

Several miles away, another private venture was being established. Landowners Rick and Liz Weber opened several hundred acres of land for route development, which they named Muir Valley. In a matter of only a couple years, between 2003 and 2005, Jared Hancock and his wife Karla, along with Tim Powers, J.J., Mike Susko, Barry Brolley, and others, developed nearly 200 bolted lines on the property. Muir Valley became an overnight hit for climbers and contributed significantly to decreasing the crowds at vintage cliffs such as Roadside Crag and Torrent Falls.

In 2007, the RRGCC joined forces with Petzl to bring the Petzl Rock Trip to the Red River Gorge. Nearly 35 professional climbers from all over the world made it to the backwoods of Kentucky to see what the Red had to offer. This proved to be a highly successful fund-raising event, and also put the Red on the map with the pros as having some of the best rock climbing in the world. Longstanding projects were quickly dispatched and local testpieces were flashed and onsighted with ease. It was an exciting time for locals to see legends such as Chris Sharma, Dave Graham, and Lynn Hill rave about the excellent climbing.

In 2005, the first edition of this guidebook was released, containing 1311 routes, over 300 more routes than John Bronaugh's guidebook six years earlier. Between 2005 and the present, bolting has

Rick Weber, owner of Muir Valley, on *One Armed Bandit* 5.9, one of many great moderate sport climbs established at the area in the last few years. Photo Rick Weber collection.

not slowed down at the Red. The second edition of the guidebook contained 300 more routes than only two years earlier. Here we are now with the third edition only a few years later and there are close to 200 more routes.

Contributing to the development are some newcomers as well as old timers. In 2006, Kipp Trummel, aka Pigsteak, moved from Illinois to Kentucky with drill in hand. His natural eye for a good line has delivered immediate classics in the 5.11-5.12 range, including *Amarillo Sunset, Samurai*, and *Iniquity*. To this day, Kipp continues seeking new areas and routes with no intentions of retiring his drill any time soon. Kenny Barker, known for bolting classic lines in the 5.13-5.14 range, such as *Lucifer* and *The Golden Ticket*, has moved away from the area, leaving an empty hole in consistent

route development within the 5.13 to 5.14 range. Although several new lines of that difficulty have been developed since his leaving, these have been by visiting climbers, at already established crags. Matt Tackett, who owns Red River Outdoors with his wife Amy, takes to the slabs with his Hilti on off days, giving climbers a chance to develop their fancy footwork and stealth technique. All, along with others such as Josh Thurston, Ron Bateman, Mark Ryan, Don McGlone, Andrew Wheatley, Russ Jackson, Dario Ventura, Jeff Neal, and Blake Bowling, continue devoting countless hours of their free time hanging in ascenders and bolting this Corbin sandstone for us to onsight, redpoint, hangdog, whine, whip, and curse on.

Private land purchases continue to be the way to go for securing climbing access at the Red. Following in the footsteps of the Pendergrass Murray Recreational Preserve purchase, Dr. Bob Matheny purchased Torrent Falls climbing area after the previous owner shut it down to climbing and put it up for sale. Also, Roadside Crag has been purchased by climbers Grant Stephens and John Haight, who intend to keep it open to public climbing. With land purchases comes large mortgages, though. In late 2005, the RRGCC was close to losing the Pendergrass Murray Recreational Preserve. Their annual mortgage payment of nearly $30,000.00 was due in June and they only had 10% of that in December. After learning of this, Michelle Ellington led fundraising efforts that raised $27,000.00 in a matter of months, helping the RRGCC to make their payment and retain the PMRP property. It was truly a display of the climbing community stepping up to the plate to save the climbing they love. The RRGCC continue leading the fundraising efforts to this day to prevent the threat of losing the PMRP from happening again.

The popularity of climbing at the Red is not slowing down. Parking areas must continually expand to accommodate vehicles from as far north as Quebec and as far south as Florida. It is not uncommon to hear numerous foreign languages being spoken at the crag on spring or fall weekends. Miguel continues to build on and improve his shop to better accommodate the needs of traveling climbers.

Terry Kindred. Photo Wes Allen.

However, despite the positives the Red has seen during the past several years, there have been some negatives. In 2006, the Red River climbing community experienced the tragic loss of the colorful Terry Kindred. Terry was well known for his methodic and calculated bolt placements. He approached each line like a surgeon, sometimes drilling new holes just to move a bolt a matter of inches and make a perfect clip. Terry is still missed by many, but the memory of him lives on in the wonderful routes he created. Another tragedy was the loss of Red River Outdoors cafe to a fire in 2007. No strangers to hard work, Matt and Amy Tackett have not slowed down and are now offering excellent cabin rentals and some of the best and most unique paintball courses in the South!

In 2008, another tragic loss occurred, when young climbers Ben Strohmeier and Laura Fletcher, both only 18, were killed in a climbing accident due to equipment failure at Emerald City. Ben and Laura were popular within the climbing community and their presence is sorely missed. Ben and Laura's deaths were tragic remembers of just how dangerous our sport can be. Please always be sure to check your equipment and especially any fixed anchors including webbing and fixed draws while climbing in the Red River Gorge.

Jonathan "J-Star" Siegrist flashing *The Legend* 5.13b at Military Wall. Siegrist visited the Red in the fall of 2009 and destroyed: ticking nearly every major testpiece, onsighting more than a dozen 5.13s, and flashing three 5.14s. No climber has had a more impressive trip to the Red.
Photo Keith Ladzinsky.

ACCESS

Please help preserve and secure access to climbing areas by joining the Access Fund and the Red River Gorge Climbers' Coalition.

The majority of cliffs in this guidebook are located on National Forest Service land or private land. Your behavior will help determine whether we retain the privilege to climb on these cliffs in the future. Please, please, please treat all climbing areas with the utmost sensitivity and respect. Obey signs, follow the rules specified by the Forest Service or landowner, and practice the responsible-climbing guidelines on the opposite page.

The following pages describe rules and things you should be aware of when climbing on Forest Service land (shaded green on the maps in this guidebook), or Forest Service land that has been designated part of the Clifty Wilderness (shaded yellow), where additional rules apply. **It is important that you read this section before climbing on any of the cliffs on Forest Service land.**

Closures/Fenced off Areas

Some cliffs have fenced-off areas. These protect archaeological sites or the endangered plant white-haired goldenrod. Please obey the closures and stay out of fenced-off areas.

The following is a list of closed routes at the time this guidebook went to press. Additional closures are possible. Stay out of any closed-off area, even if the area is not specifically listed as closed in this guide. The RRGCC posts current closure infomation on its website www.rrgcc.org.

Lower Small Wall	*Eggshell*
Hen's Nest	*The Edge*
	Close to the Edge
	Sultans of Stem
	Finger Lickin' Good
Dip Wall	*Suess Suess Sudio*
	Cindy Lou's Left Tube
	Fox In Locks
Military Wall	*Blade Runner*
	Hurricane Amy
	Revival
	Beenestalker
	Thirsting Skull
	Jac Mac
	Rad Boy Go
	Government Cheese
	Subatomic Fingerlock
	Right Turret
Tower Rock	*Crankenstein*
	Courtesy Cringe
	Jammin (bouder problem)
Funk Rock City	*Flashlight*
Gray's Wall	*(some bouldering problems)*

KEY FOREST SERVICE RULES

•In order to protect sensitive archaeological & biological resources, no camping or fire-building is allowed within 100 feet of clifflines or the back of rock shelters.

•No camping within 300 feet of any developed road or trail.

•Please stay out of fenced-off areas. These areas contain sensitive archaeological or biological resources.

•Forest Service authorization is required prior to any of the following cliff line developments:

Permanent installation of protection devices such as bolts, slings, camming devices, or chocks.

Construction of access trails.

Clearing of vegetation.

In Clifty Wilderness additional rules apply:

•Group size is limited to 10.

•No mechanical or motorized equipment or travel.

•No new rock-climbing routes with fixed anchors are allowed.

Jewell Rock	*(some bouldering problems)*
Long Wall	*(part of user trail)*
Woody's Wall	*(part of user trail)*
Western Sky Bridge Ridge	*Refraction*
	The Great Arch
	Guideline
	The Hook and The Pendulum
	Icarus

PRACTICE RESPONSIBLE CLIMBING,
SECURE CLIMBING FOR EVERYONE

The **Red River Gorge Climbers' Coalition** is a nonprofit corporation started in 1997 by local climbers to protect, promote, and ensure responsible climbing in the Red River Gorge area of Kentucky. The RRGCC believes that the world class climbing at the Red is a national treasure that deserves everyone's best efforts to help keep it open and available for all climbers to enjoy, experience, and appreciate. We have built a community-based organization to provide the public service of securing and preserving these unique climbing opportunities by becoming citizen trustees of climbing through direct ownership and climber participation.

We invite you to join us to help keep this important work going and to keep our vision alive for the next generation of climbers. Working together and with allies, and always promoting and practicing **responsible climbing**, all climbers can help ensure the future of climbing.

- **Learn and Follow the Rules** and speak with other climbers about following the rules. After safety the next most important goal in climbing is keeping it open for the next climber.

- **Park and Camp in Designated Areas** is one of the simplest ways to make a big difference to help keep climbing opportunities available for everyone.

- **Respect Private Property** and private landowners' requests. Climbing on private land is a privilege and every climber is a "climbing ambassador."

- **Use existing trails** to help protect the environment and sensitive resources. Stay on trails; short-cutting trails, especially on steep slopes, promotes damaging soil erosion.

- **Dispose of all Waste—including Human Waste—Properly** by burying or packing out; use plastic baggies to pack out soiled toilet paper, cigarette butts, and litter.

- **Practice "Leave No Trace"** Avoid damaging vegetation, displacing soil or disturbing rocks. The Red is home to 10,000 year-old archaeological sites and several sensitive and endangered species of plants and animals.

- **Get Involved—Volunteer and Join the RRGCC** and join the Access Fund. Or join a local climbing organization near you. If you need help to start a local climbing organization in your area contact us, or the Access Fund at www.accessfund.org.

RED RIVER GORGE CLIMBERS' COALITION

Protecting, Promoting, and Ensuring Responsible Climbing

PO Box 22156
Lexington KY 40522-2156

www.rrgcc.org

In addition to small, fenced-off areas, these cliffs have wider general restrictions on climbing:

Lower Sky Bridge Ridge is close to Sky Bridge Arch. No climbing is allowed within 300 feet of Sky Bridge Arch. The climb *Sky Bridge Layback* is on the arch and should not be climbed.

The **Spring Wall** & **Tunnel Wall** crags are close to Nada Tunnel. No climbing is allowed within 300 feet of Nada Tunnel.

No climbing is allowed within 300 feet of Chimney Top Overlook. Many of the climbs on **Chimney Top Crag** are within 300 feet of the overlook and should not be climbed.

Clifty Wilderness

The U.S. Congress designated Clifty Wilderness in 1985. The 13,000-acre Clifty Wilderness is bordered by Rock Bridge Road to the south and KY 715 to the west. The area is shaded yellow on the maps in this book. Managed according to the 1964 Wilderness Act, Clifty Wilderness is an area with no roads or buildings. No mechanical or motorized equipment or travel is allowed. The trails in the wilderness tend to be more rugged and less developed. The rugged nature of the area offers physical challenges as well as opportunities for quiet and solitude.

Key regulations to be aware of in Clifty Wilderness are:
• Group size is limited to 10.
• No mechanical or motorized equipment or travel is allowed (e.g. motorized drills or mountain bikes).
• No new rock-climbing routes with fixed anchors are allowed.

These are crags within the federally designated Clifty Wilderness:
Mariba Fork
Tower Rock
Lower, Middle, & Upper Small Wall
Moonshiner's Wall
Doorish Wall
Eagle Point Buttress
Wall of Denial
Woody's Wall
Funk Rock City
Wildcat Wall

White-haired goldenrod. Photo: US Forest Service.

White-haired goldenrod

The endangered white-haired goldenrod grows nowhere else in the world except near rock shelters and cliffs in the Red River Gorge. Please do not disturb this threatened plant.

Trail Issues

Most climbing areas do not have USFS-designated trails going to them. Please use official trails wherever possible and minimize your impacts when you travel off the official trails.

Limits of Acceptable Change (LAC)

The Daniel Boone National Forest started a public-involvement planning process for the Red River Gorge called Limits of Acceptable Change (LAC) in the summer of 2004. LAC involves finding ways to strike a balance between providing recreational use in an area like the Red River Gorge and protecting sensitive resources. The LAC process is open to everyone and public input is welcome. The LAC process involves concepts such as zoning, establishing acceptable standards of recreation impact, and defining what management actions are needed to allow the area to remain within specified standards. At the conclusion of the LAC process, there is a possibility of changes in the way rock climbing is managed in the Red River Gorge. The Forest Service hopes to complete the LAC process by the end of 2007.

Respect Rockshelters

Rockshelters provide excellent preservation for plant remains, animal bones, and other objects used by ancient Native Americans and early pioneers. The earliest signs of prehistoric agriculture have been documented from botanical remains found in rockshelters in eastern Kentucky. Rockshelters also provide habitat for unique plant and animal species like the white-haired goldenrod (found only in the Red River Gorge) and the Virginia big-eared bat.

Threats: Camping, climbing, rappelling, burning, and digging in rockshelters can impact or even destroy these special resources.

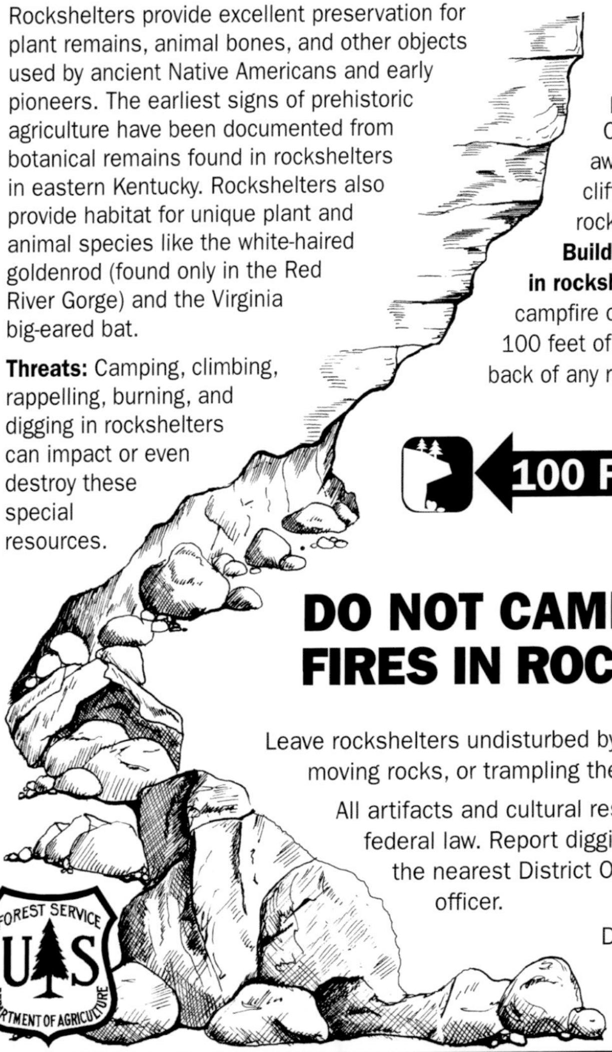

Camping in rockshelters is prohibited forestwide. Camp at least 100 feet away from the base of any cliff, or the back of any rockshelter. **Building a fire is prohibited in rockshelters.** Do not build a campfire or use a stove fire within 100 feet of the base of any cliff or the back of any rockshelter.

DO NOT CAMP OR BUILD FIRES IN ROCKSHELTERS

Leave rockshelters undisturbed by not digging in the soil, moving rocks, or trampling the ground.

All artifacts and cultural resources are protected by federal law. Report digging, looting or vandalism to the nearest District Office or law enforcement officer.

Daniel Boone National Forest
1700 Bypass Road
WInchester, KY 40391
859-745-3100

FOREST SERVICE
US
DEPARTMENT OF AGRICULTURE

Photo: Dawn Kish.

MIGUEL VENTURA

PROFILE: A climbing tradition

Climbers come to the Red to climb, camp, socialize, slackline, and to eat pizza in one of the most welcoming, climber-friendly places in the world, "Miguel's Pizza." Miguel Ventura is the owner and founder.

Born in Portugal, Miguel moved to Connecticut when he was seven. When Miguel was in his 30s, a friend offered him a chance to buy a share in some property in the beautiful green hills of Eastern Kentucky. Without a second thought, Miguel and his wife Susan – who was pregnant at the time – packed up the truck and headed straight out. The other shareholders had jobs that tied them to the city, but Miguel was able to move into an old building on the property and begin to fix it up.

After selling his house in Connecticut, Miguel opened an ice-cream shop, "The Rainbow Door" (until only a few years ago, the shop's sign was still visible). One day in 1985, Martin Hackworth and Tom Martin stopped by for ice cream. They asked Miguel if they could start selling climbing gear at his shop. Soon, climbers began to hang out at Miguel's and buy gear from Hackworth (the money from which helped put him through college), and Susan got the idea of selling pizzas. Miguel had always loved to cook, and, being a dedicated gardener, was soon serving unique and tasty pizzas to the small group of trad climbers who had become regulars at his shop.

In the early 1990s, after graduating college, Hackworth stopped selling gear and moved away. Nevertheless, climbers had found their hangout. Business really took off when Porter Jarrard moved to the Red and began establishing classic sport climbs, making the area hugely popular. "Porter brought in more climbers and basically made this place what it is today," says Miguel.

Those who have been to Miguel's on a crowded night can appreciate how hard he works. Ten- to 12-hour days are common. Throughout the years, Miguel has attracted dedicated workers to help him provide a consistently high-quality product. It's hard to get a complaint out of Miguel, always an incredibly friendly and giving man.

Off season, in winter, Miguel finds joy in woodcarving. You can see some of his beautiful work throughout the interior and exterior of the building. Winter also gives him a chance to spend more time with his parents, who live next door, as well as find peace in his passion for gardening.

When asked what he would purchase for his shop if he could have anything in the world, regardless of price, Miguel responded with two items. Although he's not one to take on technology without a great need, first was a dough-rolling machine that could help save his tiring elbows and help keep up with the growing demand for pizza and sandwiches. The other: a restoration of the 80-year-old historical building he currently occupies. ∎

WIRELESS

open 7am-10pm

FULL GEAR SHOP

photo by Mike Delian

RED RIVER GORGE, KY
MIGUELSPIZZA.COM
606-663-1975

RESTAURANT

serving since 1984

CLIMBERS CAMPGROUND

GRAY'S BRANCH

Lauren Lee on *The Legend* 5.13b, Military Wall, page 45. Photo Keith Ladzinsky.

Nada Tunnel. Photo: Elodie Saracco.

Character

Chances are you will be climbing in the Gray's Branch region during your visit to the Red, since two of the most popular sport crags, Military Wall and Left Flank, are located here. If you continue north past these crags, you'll see possibly the most impressive chunk of sandstone in the Red, Raven Rock.

Approach

Head north from Miguel's on KY 11 toward Mountain Parkway. Pass under Mountain Parkway, then turn left onto KY 15 near the Shell station. Continue west on KY 15 for about a mile until you reach KY 77 on your right. Turn right onto 77 and follow this road through Nada, winding past trailers, stray dogs, and the occasional church. After a couple of miles you'll reach the historic one-lane Nada Tunnel. The climbing areas in the Gray's Branch Region begin just before the Nada Tunnel and border 77 as it continues down through to the steel bridge crossing the Red River near Raven Rock.

Access

All Gray's Branch areas are on Forest Service land, so please respect signs and fences indicating closed routes or trails and read the guidelines for climbing on Forest Service land on page 32 of this book.

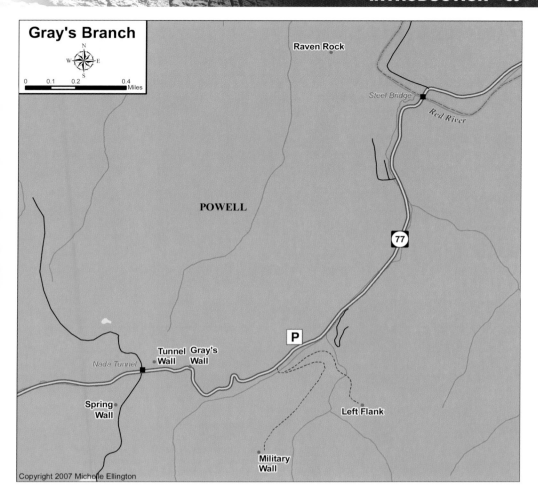

Gray's Branch

Raven Rock

Steel Bridge

Red River

POWELL

77

P

Tunnel Wall Gray's Wall

Nada Tunnel

Spring Wall

Left Flank

Military Wall

Copyright 2007 Michelle Ellington

CLIFF	SUN / SHADE	HIKE	RAIN	ROUTES	GRADE RANGE	CLASSIC ROUTES
SPRING WALL page 40	shade	15 mins		2	5.6- .7 .8 .9 .10 .11 .12 .13 .14	
TUNNEL WALL page 40	all day	5 mins		6	5.6- .7 .8 .9 .10 .11 .12 .13 .14	
GRAY'S WALL page 42	a.m.	5 mins		4	5.6- .7 .8 .9 .10 .11 .12 .13 .14	
MILITARY WALL page 44	a.m. p.m.	10 mins	rain OK	53	5.6- .7 .8 .9 .10 .11 .12 .13 .14	*Jungle Beat* 5.9+ *Fuzzy Undercling* 11b *Gung Ho* 12b *Nagypapa* 13d
LEFT FLANK page 52	all day	10 mins	rain OK	22	5.6- .7 .8 .9 .10 .11 .12 .13 .14	*Mercy, The Huff* 12b *Stunning The Hog* 12d *Table of Colors* 13b
RAVEN ROCK page 55	a.m.	20 mins		7	5.6- .7 .8 .9 .10 .11 .12 .13 .14	

TUNNEL WALL

all day | 5 mins | 6 routes
5.6- .7 .8 .9 .10 .11 .12 .13 .14

Character

Most of the routes at Tunnel Wall are close to the road. In fact, *Black Death* is directly over the road. The routes are all traditional and none of them is popular, although the severely overhanging hand crack of *Negative Energy* is definitely worth a short hike.

Approach

After you pass through the one-lane Nada Tunnel, park at the second pulloff on your right, just past a large overhang on your left. To reach the routes, follow the directions in the route descriptions.

Conditions

Most of the routes at Tunnel Wall face south, making for a warm area to climb during the winter. *Negative Energy* is usually dry during rain.

Access

The National Forest Service discourages rock climbing within 300 feet of the tunnel. *Black Death* falls within this range. Please respect the restriction and refrain from climbing the route.

Negative Energy

❶ No Doz 5.4 ★★

From the pulloff, walk back toward the tunnel. After you pass the large overhang directly over the road, hike up the hill to your right for about 125 feet to an obvious left-facing dihedral. To get down, downclimb a gully 25 feet left of the top of the route or rappel from a dead tree. **30 ft.** *FA Unknown.*

❷ Black Death 5.11b R 🚫

This route is included for historical completeness only. The Forest Service discourages climbing within 300 feet of the tunnel. *Black Death* falls within this boundary. Do not climb it. As you pass through Nada Tunnel, you will see a large overhang to your left. *Black Death* begins on the right side of this overhang. Climb a thin crack to reach a hand-sized crack. Climb it to the flake above, then traverse all the way out over the overhang to the left. Pull over the final lip and scramble to the top. To descend, rappel from a tree. **60 ft.** *FA Larry Day, Ed Pearsall, 1980.*

❸ Negative Energy 5.11d ★★★

To locate this route, walk to the right of the large overhang (*Black Death*) and head up the hill. Locate a 15-foot blocky dihedral leading to a ledge. Climb the dihedral, then walk to the left to locate this impressively steep crack in a pocketed wall. Rappel from a tree at the top. **40 ft.** *FA Grant Stephens, Martin Hackworth, 1984.*

❹ Sideshow 5.8 ★★

This obtuse dihedral is located about 150 feet right of the short dihedral you climb to reach *Negative Energy*. Climb the face near the dihedral, using natural gear for protection. To descend, head left to the short dihedral used to reach *Negative Energy*. **55 ft.** *FA John Bronaugh, Stacy Temple, 1991.*

❺ Big Top 5.8+ ★★★

This is the hand-sized dihedral 150 feet right of *Sideshow*. **50 ft.** *FA Unknown.*

❻ Exhibition 5.9- ★★

Walk right from *Sideshow* to locate this left-facing dihedral. It is fairly close to the road, so expect some gawking tourists. To descend, walk off the back side. **50 ft.** *FA Unknown.*

SPRING WALL

Although Spring Wall is fairly close to the road, an abundance of rhododendrons and the small number of routes make it questionable for a visit. Visit www.wolverinepublishing.com/downloads for a free download containing the information for this cliff.

Ray Rice on *Too Many Puppies* 5.12a, Left Flank, page 52. Photo Anne Skidmore.

GRAY'S WALL

a.m. ☁ ☀ 👤 5 mins

4 routes

5.6- .7 .8 .9 .10 .11 .12 .13 .14

Character

Gray's Wall is another esoteric wall in the Nada Tunnel area containing a few moderate trad routes and one seldomly climbed sport route.

Approach

To reach Gray's Wall, drive 0.6 miles from the tunnel. After passing a steep right hairpin bend, look for a pulloff on the right. From the pulloff, hike across the road and up the hill. Angle right to the far right side of the horseshoe-shaped wall to locate the first route.

On The Road

❶ On the Road 5.9- ★★

As you hike up the hill, look for a small pinnacle of rock. Just left of the pinnacle is a dihedral beginning on top of a slab. Climb the dihedral, then traverse left at the top. Rappel from a tree to descend. **100 ft.** *FA Martin Hackworth, Grant Stephens, 1984.*

❷ Hang Over 5.7

Walk left from the previous route to a gully. Scramble up the gully to locate a crack on the left side of a rockhouse. Climb the crack. **40 ft.** *FA Martin Hackworth, Garland Clark, 1981.*

❸ Never Again 5.9

From *Hang Over*, hike left for about 400 yards to locate another gully. Scramble up the gully to a ledge. Look for a crack in a corner and begin climbing. Eventually move right to a belay. Continue up the crack, which turns to a friction face at the top. *FA Steve Faulkner, Chuck Keller, 1988.*

❹ Coexistence 5.12b

From the parking area, walk back up the road, toward the tunnel, to the hairpin. Hike uphill, following a faint path, and find the next route on the rock to the right. **Caution:** The anchor for this route is currently only one bolt. **50 ft. 5 bolts.** *FA Jamie Baker, 1993.*

Coexistance

MILITARY WALL

 a.m. p.m. 10 mins OK in rain

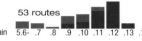 53 routes
5.6- .7 .8 .9 .10 .11 .12 .13 .14

Character

Military Wall has some of the best sport climbing in the South. Almost anyone who visits the Red is sure to spend at least one day getting a taste of the Red River pump on Military's "5.12 Wall." The wall boasts some of the earliest classic overhanging Porter Jarrard lines, including one of the Red's most popular 5.11 sport routes.

Approach

Drive 1.0 mile east past Nada Tunnel on KY 77 to the bottom of the hill and park at the large gravel parking lot on the left. This is the trailhead for Martin's Fork and is marked so by a Forest Service sign. Hike across the road and walk back toward the tunnel. You will see the trailhead for Military Wall and Left Flank on your left. Walk across the wooden bridge, then continue straight. The trail to Military Wall branches off to your right about 20 feet after crossing the bridge. Follow the trail uphill for about 10 minutes until you reach the wall.

Conditions

If you climb hard enough, you can have a great time on Military Wall's overhanging 5.12 Wall during a heavy rain. The sun exposure varies for different sections of the cliff. The routes at the far right side of the cliff get morning sun. Those on the left side, including the popular 5.9s *Sunshine* and *Moonbeam*, get afternoon sun.

Access

In 2001, the National Forest Service temporarily closed a portion of Military Wall for an archaeological dig to determine the historical significance of the area. The dig proved the area historically significant and the routes have remained closed ever since. The closure is marked by a wire fence barring access to routes 29 through 35. Please respect the closure and do not "poach" these routes.

The first four routes described is located about 100 yards left of where the trail reaches the cliff. Hike past the obvious amphitheatre containing routes 7-14 and around the corner. Continue on, past, some boulders, to locate two sport routes (routes 3 and 4) and the striking dihedral/roof system of Jungle Beat just to the left.

❶ Things That Go Bump in the Night 5.9 ★ ⬜
This crack system is located 50 feet left of *Jungle Beat*. Climb a chimney to a small ledge. Continue up the crack, then set a belay. Climb another chimney or a face to a friction finish. Rap from tree. Two ropes required.
175 ft. FA Larry Day, Tom Seibert, 1976.

❷ Jungle Beat 5.9+ ★★★★★ ⬜
Classic. This adventurous route ascends the intimidating dihedral and roof system left of the bolted routes 3 and 4. Take the chimney up to the beginning of the roof, then set a natural anchor for the belay. A #4 Camalot works great here. Climb the hand crack out the roof, then keep a lookout for a hanging belay. Continue up through a finger crack in a dihedral, then step off to a ledge on the right. Friction your way to the top. It is a good idea to break the route into three pitches to avoid rope drag. If you try it in one, you'll need a 70-meter rope. To descend, walk climber's left along the cliffline to locate a tree with slings. Rappel down to a ledge to locate another slung tree. From there, rappel to the ground.
180 ft. FA Larry Day, Tom Seibert, 1979.

❸ Another Doug Reed Route 5.11b ★★★★ ⬜
There are two sport routes just right of *Jungle Beat*. This is the left one. Scramble up to a ledge to begin. If you sneak right at just the right spot, you can make this route a lot easier than its original grade of 5.11b.
60 ft. 5 bolts. FA Doug Reed, Porter Jarrard, 1991.

❹ Forearm Follies 5.11d/5.12a ★★★★ ⬜
This is the righthand sport line up a heavily featured potpourri of rock. Climb either to the first set of anchors for a great 5.11d, or continue to the second set for a 5.12 pump. 60-meter rope required to lower.
100 ft. 13 bolts. FA Porter Jarrard, Tim Toula, 1990.

❺ Henry Kissinger's Glasses 5.10d ★★ ⬜
Just left of the main amphitheatre are two crack systems. This is the one on the left, beginning near a large tree. Take the crack to a ledge, then continue up the face, using bolts for protection. Belay on gear at the horizontal. Continue up past the overhang and two more bolts to anchors.
100 ft. 4 bolts. FA Jeff Moll, 1992. Equipper: Jeff Hughes

❻ Stacy's Farewell 5.5 ★ ⬜
This is the first crack you come to as you walk left and around the corner from the amphitheatre routes.
FA Unknown.

The Legend

Routes 7-14 climb the impressive swath of rock facing the approach trail.

⑦ Mental Health 5.11b ★★★
This is the dihedral left of the bolted lines in the amphitheatre. Climb up a narrowing chimney, then do some kung-fu to gain the face. Either continue up the face or stay in the crack. Descend from chain anchors.
80 ft. *FA Rich Purnell, Greg Purnell, 1999.*

⑧ Nagypapa 5.13d ★★★★★
This is the left-most bolted route on the overhanging wall. Sustained slopers to a crimpy crux. Can you say sick? Photo on previous spread.
80 ft. 6 bolts. *FA Dave Hume, 2002.*

⑨ The Legend 5.13b ★★★★★
This bouldery route starts 10 feet left of a short dihedral defining the start of *Mule*. Conquer the thin start, then surge up powerful slopers and underclings for the first few bolts. Stop at the first set of anchors if you have an appointment to get to or, better, continue up a much easier but fun finish to the original anchors near the top of the wall. A new chapter has begun for the character of this route. After consistently seeping for the past couple of years but finally drying out, two holds have broken off the initial bouldery section, making the start even more difficult, and the second bolt a very difficult clip. Photo page 38.
90 ft. 8 bolts. *FA Dave Hume, 1998.*

Jungle Beat

⑩ Mule 5.12c ★★★★
This long route begins just left and around the corner from the obvious 5.12 Wall, in a short dihedral. Climb the tricky dihedral to gain the face, then travel through a couple of cruxes to the anchors. This is a great route for those into a journey.
90 ft. 8 bolts. *FA Porter Jarrard, Tim Powers, 1991.*

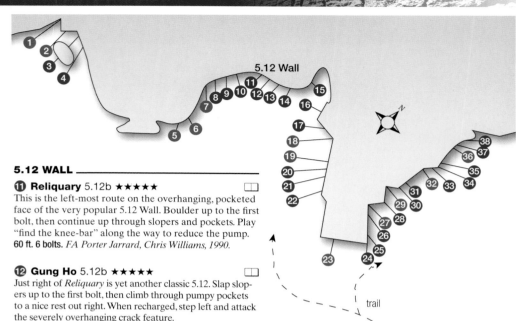

5.12 Wall

5.12 WALL

⓫ Reliquary 5.12b ★★★★★

This is the left-most route on the overhanging, pocketed face of the very popular 5.12 Wall. Boulder up to the first bolt, then continue up through slopers and pockets. Play "find the knee-bar" along the way to reduce the pump.
60 ft. 6 bolts. *FA Porter Jarrard, Chris Williams, 1990.*

⓬ Gung Ho 5.12b ★★★★★

Just right of *Reliquary* is yet another classic 5.12. Slap slopers up to the first bolt, then climb through pumpy pockets to a nice rest out right. When recharged, step left and attack the severely overhanging crack feature.
60 ft. 5 bolts. *FA Porter Jarrard, Mark Williams, 1990.*

⓭ Tissue Tiger 5.12b ★★★★★

Begin below attractive pockets on the right side of the wall. Get your feet off the ground, then continue through jugs and pockets to a good rest. Shake out, then move through a crux at the India-shaped feature.
60 ft. 5 bolts. *FA Porter Jarrard, Phil Olenick, 1990.*

⓮ Fuzzy Undercling 5.11b ★★★★

This classic is the first and easiest route on the wall. Begin directly left of the arete marking the right side of the 5.12 Wall. Boulder the tough start, then monkey up plates and jugs to the top. Don't miss the no-hands rest. The ground has eroded significantly during the past several years and the cheater stump is gone from the base, making the start very difficult for just about everyone.
60 ft. 5 bolts. *FA Porter Jarrard, Phil Olenick, 1990.*

⓯ Possum Lips 5.10d ★★★

Around the corner right of the 5.12 Wall is this tricky slab route.
40 ft. 5 bolts. *FA Tom Fyffe, Charles Tabor, 1992.*

⓰ Mercy Miss Percy 5.9 ★★

Find this and the next six routes on the south-west-facing wall up and left from where the approach trail splits. This one climbs a bolted green face on the far left, near a gully area.
50 ft. 4 bolts. *FA Jeff Hughes, 1992.*

⓱ Stay Left 5.10a ★★

Climb the bolted line just left of a nasty chimney. Stay left!
50 ft. 4 bolts. *FA Jeff Hughes, 1992.*

⓲ Top-Roper's Route 5.2

Toprope. At the left edge of a pleasant section of wall is this nasty chimney.
50 ft. *FA Unknown.*

⓳ Decay's Way 5.7 ★

This climb ascends the face and crack to the left of a trio of sport climbs. Rap from tree.
60 ft. *FA Larry Day, 1970.*

⓴ Moonbeam 5.9 ★★★

Just up and left from where the approach trail meets the crag is a nice wall with three bolted routes. This pocketed classic is the left-most line. A great introduction to the Red River forearm pump.
50 ft. 5 bolts. *FA Steve Cater, Porter Jarrard, 1991.*

㉑ Sunshine 5.9+ ★★★

The center bolted line. This route and its partner, *Moonbeam*, were two of the most popular beginner routes back when there were no other bolted moderates. Their popularity has faded with the introduction of dozens of higher quality moderates throughout the Red during the past several years.
50 ft. 5 bolts. *FA Porter Jarrard, Steve Cater, 1991.*

㉒ In the Light 5.10c ★★★

This is the right-most of the three bolted routes. Have fun clipping the anchors!
55 ft. 4 bolts. *Equipper: Terry Kindred. FA Brian Maslyar, 2002.*

5.12 Wall

Sunshine/Moonbeam

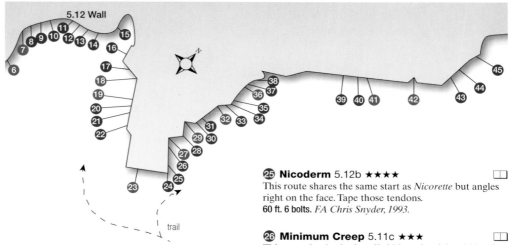

5.12 Wall

The remaining routes are found to the right of where the approach trail meets the cliff.

23 Sailing Shoes 5.9 R

Located on the buttress where the approach trail meets the cliff. Follow a crack that ends in the middle of the face. Continue to a rap tree.
60 ft. *FA Martin Hackworth, 1984.*

24 Nicorette 5.12a ★★★★

On the northeast face of the obvious buttress at the end of the approach trail, and around the corner to the right of the previous routes, is this beautiful arete. Pull up past some ledges to the business. Boulder through some pockets to a barn-door move at the arete. Continue up steep but easier ground to the anchors.
50 ft. 5 bolts. *FA Porter Jarrard, 1991.*

Nicorette

25 Nicoderm 5.12b ★★★★

This route shares the same start as *Nicorette* but angles right on the face. Tape those tendons.
60 ft. 6 bolts. *FA Chris Snyder, 1993.*

26 Minimum Creep 5.11c ★★★

This route begins in the offwidth to the right of *Nicoderm,* then veers left onto the face. Climb the crack for the first couple of bolts, then step left onto the face and fight the pump to the anchors.
60 ft. 5 bolts. *FA Chris Snyder, Brian McCray, 1993.*

27 Not Worth It 5.9 ★★★

Start in the obvious offwidth of *Minimum Creep* but stay in the crack to the top of the wall. Rap from tree.
50ft. *FA Unknown.*

28 Danita Dolores 5.10b ★★★

This route ascends the face a few feet to the right of the *Not Worth It* offwidth. Desperate start!
50 ft. 6 bolts. *FA Hugh Loeffler, Danita Whelan, 1991.*

The next seven routes (29-35) were closed for archaelogical reasons on 4/23/2001 by the National Forest Service. Please do not climb them.

29 Blade Runner 5.7 🚫

This is the hand crack in a shallow dihedral to the right of the bolted route *Danita Dolores.* Rap anchors.
80 ft. *FA Martin Hackworth, Harvey Johnson, 1982.*

30 Hurricane Amy 5.11c 🚫

This bolted route begins in the crack of *Blade Runner,* then angles to the right and up.
60 ft. 5 bolts. *FA Porter Jarrard, Mark Williams, 1991.*

31 Revival 5.13a 🚫

This route ascends the obvious, arching, pocketed face to the right of *Hurricane Amy.*
60 ft. 6 bolts. *FA Porter Jarrard, Steve Cater, 1991.*

32 Beenestalker 5.10d 🚫

This is the right-leaning dihedral to the right of *Revival.* Rap anchors.
80 ft. *FA Tom Souders, Jeff Koenig, 1983.*

Christina Austin checking her options on *All Things Considered* 5.11d (overleaf). Photo Dan Brayack

48 Super Slab 5.12c ★★★★★
This is the face a few feet right of *Pink Feat*. Plaster a left foot and leap to a high jug. Find the perfect mixture of power and balance to link the remainder of this masterpiece.
70 ft. 8 bolts. *FA Porter Jarrard, 1991.*

Climber: Zac Sands. Photo: Peter McDermott.

33 Thirsting Skull 5.12c ⊘
This is the pocketed face climb to the right of *Beenestalker*.
50 ft. 5 bolts. *FA Porter Jarrard, Mark Williams, 1990.*

34 Jac Mac 5.11d ⊘
This route ascends the overhanging line of huecos a few feet right of *Thirsting Skull*.
50 ft. 6 bolts. *FA Porter Jarrard, Mark Williams, 1990.*

35 Rad Boy Go 5.12a ⊘
This route starts on a 15-foot ledge. The first two bolts are shared with *Jac Mac*.
50 ft. 7 bolts. *FA Porter Jarrard, Mark Williams, 1990.*

36 Thought it was Bubbles 5.8 R ★
Incorrectly described in previous guidebooks, this line is to the left of *Government Cheese*.
80 ft. *FA Chuck Keller, Steve Faulkner, 1988.*

37 Government Cheese 5.11d ★★★
Begins directly in front of a boulder about 30 feet right of *Rad Boy Go*. Boulder to the first bolt, then climb through slopers and sidepulls to the anchors.
50 ft. 5 bolts. *FA Mark Williams, Matt Flach, 1991.*

38 Parting Gift 5.11b ★★★
Similar to but slightly easier than *Government Cheese*. Start a few feet right of *Government Cheese* on a small boulder and mantel onto a sloping ledge. Squeeze wide pinches up the overhanging face to hidden anchors above a bulge. Rappelling is recommended to avoid rope abrasion against the rock.
55 ft. 6 bolts. *FA Terry Kindred, 2006.*

39 Left Turret 5.11b ★★★
This route is located 50 feet right of *Government Cheese*. It begins in a left-facing dihedral to the left of a low rock house with a man-made stone wall. Ascend the faint dihedral to a roof. Pull over the roof, figure out a move, then continue up the face to anchors.
50 ft. 5 bolts. *FA Porter Jarrard, Shannon Langley, 1991.*

40 Right Turret 5.12a ⊘
Closed. Begins near the man made stone wall and to the right of *Left Turret*. Boulder up to the small roof then continue up easier face to the anchors.
50 ft. 5 bolts. *FA Porter Jarrard, Shannon Langley, 1991.*

41 Subatomic Fingerlock 5.10a ⊘
Closed This is the obvious short fingercrack to the right of the bolted route *Right Turret* and the man-made stone wall.
30 ft. *FA Unknown.*

42 Beene Material 5.10c ★★★★
This is the next crack to the right of *Subatomic Fingerlock*. Begins as a very acute dihedral. Take some large gear for the top. Rap from tree.
70 ft. *FA Tom Souders, Jeff Koenig, 1983.*

43 Nothing For Now 5.12a ★★
This is the bolted line to the right of *Beene Material* and a large rock house.
70 ft. 7 bolts. *FA Porter Jarrard, Shannon Langley, 1991.*

44 Bozo's Bogus Booty Biner 5.11c ★★★★
This is the bolted line directly to the right of *Nothing For Now*. Climb tricky moves through the initial crack section to reach a short roof. Step up onto the face and pump out on slopey holds to the anchors.
70 ft. 8 bolts. *FA Porter Jarrard, Matt Flach, 1990.*

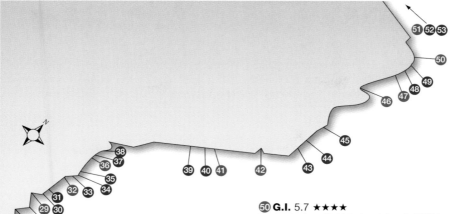

45 Special Impetus 5.12b ★★★
Just right of *BBBB* is a similar-looking line behind a large tree. Begin on a ledge, pull a bulge, then tackle a difficult boulder problem to gain the enjoyable pocketed face.
70 ft. 7 bolts. *FA Porter Jarrard, Matt Flach, 1990.*

46 Green Gully 5.3
50 feet right of *Special Impetus* is a green gully. Climb it, if you're into that sort of thing, or just use it as a descent for the following routes. You can rap from a tree.
100 ft. *FA Larry Day, 1970.*

47 Pink Feat 5.11d ★★★★
This route begins in the middle of the last face before the corner of the wall. Look for a U-shaped ledge about 10 feet up. Jump up to the ledge to start. Pull a tough mantel, then continue up the technical face to a large ledge before the crack. Take a breather, then crank through the finger crack to another ledge. Continue up through a sketchy dihedral to anchors.
120 ft. 1 bolt. *FA Jeff Koenig, Tom Souders, 1983.*

48 Super Slab 5.12c ★★★★★
See description and photo, previous page.

49 All Things Considered 5.11d ★★★★★
This route begins directly around the obtuse corner from *Super Slab*. Start either on the corner and traverse to the right, or climb the first few feet of *G.I.* and traverse left. Climb a blunt arete with hidden holds to anchors. A very unique route for the Red River Gorge. Photo on previous spread.
55 ft. 5 bolts. *Equipper: Terry Kindred. FA Bruce Adams, 2001.*

50 G.I. 5.7 ★★★★
Begins in the offwidth slot right of *All Things Considered.* Rap from bolted anchors; 60-meter rope required.
130 ft. *FA Tom Seibert, Martin Hackworth, 1974.*

51 Armed Forces 5.3 R
About 300 feet right of *G.I.* is a gully. Hike 200 feet past this gully to a long and wide dual crack system. Climb up to a ledge, then scramble to the top. Rap from a tree.
130 ft. *FA Jim Sharp, Ed Pearsall, 1979.*

52 Etrier 5.12b ★★★
Hike a long way past the previous routes – then keep hiking after you think you passed it. Eventually you'll come to a nice-looking overhanging wall with a low roof. Stick clip the first bolt and aid to the roof to start this slopey route.
50 ft. 5 bolts. *FA Porter Jarrard, Tim Powers, 1991.*

53 Daisychain 5.12c ★★
This route is located five feet right of *Etrier* and has a similiar "A0" start.
75 ft. 7 bolts. *FA Porter Jarrard, Jamie Baker, 1991.*

Super Slab

LEFT FLANK

all day | 10 mins | OK in rain | 22 routes
.8 .9 .10 .11 .12 .13 .14

Character

Left Flank, located just across the creek from Military Wall, is a popular destination, especially for those seeking their first 5.10a, *To Defy the Laws of Tradition*, or their first 5.13a, *Table of Colors*. Both routes are classics for their grade. The area also has numerous beginner routes, as well as one of the steepest 5.12s in the Red, *Stunning the Hog*.

Approach

Drive 1.0 mile east past Nada Tunnel on KY 77 to the bottom of the hill and park at the large gravel parking lot on the left. This is the trailhead for Martin's Fork and is marked so by a Forest Service sign. Cross the road and walk back toward the tunnel. You will see the trailhead for Military Wall and Left Flank on your left. Walk across a wooden bridge, then continue straight. The trail to Military Wall branches off to your right about 20 feet after crossing the bridge. Instead, continue ahead on the trail. Eventually you will cross a stream with some stepping stones. A few yards after the stepping stones, follow the trail uphill for a few minutes to reach the base of Left Flank. If you cross another bridge, you've walked too far.

Conditions

Left Flank receives excellent morning to mid-afternoon sun and offers good rainy-day and cold-weather climbing. The Table of Colors Wall is very well sheltered and sure to stay dry during the heaviest rain. The moderate routes tend to be less overhanging and sheltered. Don't count on them staying dry in a downpour.

Too Many Puppies

Mr. Bungle

❶ To Defy the Laws of Tradition 5.10a ★★★★
From the approach trail, go left about 100 feet, around a slabby buttress (containing routes 3-5), to a big, flat boulder below a large overhang. This is the left of two bolted lines, climbing a striking vertical face to an overhanging finish. **60 ft. 7 bolts.** *FA Porter Jarrard, Chris Snyder, 1992.*

❷ Too Many Puppies 5.12a ★★★★
This route begins on the large flat boulder and ascends a tricky arete. Begin with a bouldery start, then finesse your way up the arete to an interesting move just before the anchors. Photo page 41.
60 ft. 6 bolts. *FA Porter Jarrard, Chris Snyder, 1992.*

❸ Fast Food Christians 5.10a ★★
This is the left-most of three bolted routes on the slabby buttress left of the approach trail. Work out the opening sequence, then enjoy easier climbing to the anchors.
60 ft. 6 bolts. *FA Terry Kindred, 2003.*

❹ Face Up to That Crack 5.8- ★★★
Ten feet right of *Fast Food Christians* is a slab climb leading to a hand sized crack about 50 feet up. Tiptoe up the slab to the hand crack. Place a piece of gear if you like, or run it out to the anchors.
70 ft. 8 bolts. *FA Kevin Pogue, Elisa Weinman Pogue, 1992.*

❺ Mr. Bungle 5.8+ ★★
This line is the furthest right of the three lines on the slabby buttress. It begins about 25 feet right of *Face Up to That Crack*, on a flat boulder. Climb the slabby face just left of the obvious blunt arete.
60 ft. 6 bolts. *FA Jeff Moll, 1992.*

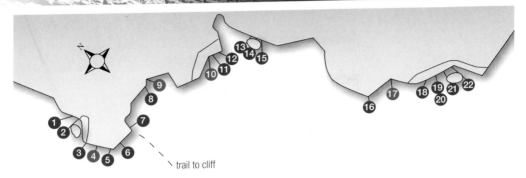

trail to cliff

⑥ Maypop 5.11a ★★★
This is the first route left of where the approach trail meets the cliff, located about 10 feet left of a low over-hang. Begin with a bouldery move, then balance your way to the anchors.
50 ft. 4 bolts. *FA Porter Jarrard, Matt Flach, 1991.*

The remaining routes are located right of where the ap-proach trail meets the cliff.

⑦ Brother Stair 5.9 ★★
When the approach trail meets the clifline, step right about 20 feet to an arete. Just around the corner and right of the arete is the beginning of *Brother Stair*.
40 ft. 4 bolts. *FA Porter Jarrard, 1992.*

⑧ Infectious 5.12b ★★★★
Bouldering on a rope is always fun. This route is located 75 feet right of *Brother Stair*, on a blunt arete marked by an obvious rail toward the top. Crank through pockets and slopers, then make a big move to the rail. Shake out, keep your cool, and you've got the route.
50 ft. 4 bolts. *FA Porter Jarrard, 1991.*

⑨ Birthday Party 5.9 R ★★
To the right of *Infectious* is a right-arching dihedral with a mossy slab to its right. This route ascends the slab, us-ing protection in an iron oxide pocket on the face.
75 ft. *FA John Lahr, Andy Shirk, 1996.*

Infectious

THE 10 BEST SPORT ROUTES 5.9 AND UNDER

The Red isn't just for elite sport climbers. Many easy sport routes have been established over the past few years, allow-ing novice leaders to get a feel for some of the best climb-ing in the country. Compiled from redriverclimbing.com, the following is a list of the 10 best sport lines under 5.10.

Stunning the Hog

⑩ Unsportsmanlike Conduct 5.11c ★★★
This route is located around the next buttress from
Birthday Party. Look for an obvious crack splitting an
overhanging face. Start on the boulder in front of the
route, then step into the crack and hang on for about 15
feet. Continue up through a pod and other funky stuff to
the finish ledge. Step right to belay from the anchors on
Stunning the Hog.
50 ft. *FA Tom Souders, Mark Schorle, 1992.*

⑪ Stunning the Hog 5.12d ★★★★★
Just right of the previous route is a severely overhanging
wall with two bolted routes beginning on a ledge. This is
the line on the left. Grab the starting holds, take a deep
breath, then race your way up the overhanging stone
past pockets, slopers, heel-hooks, pinches, a tricky clip,
and an accuracy move to a mailbox slot. This burly route
is a squeel.
45 ft. 5 bolts. *FA Porter Jarrard, 1991.*

⑫ Sex Farm 5.12b ★★★★
Starting from the same ledge and directly to the right of
Stunning the Hog is this left-angling route. Slap up the
blunt arete, then move out left toward the top. Continue
straight up, utilizing some crimps to reach the anchors.
50 ft. 5 bolts. *FA Porter Jarrard, 1991.*

⑬ Aquaduck Pocket 5.11b ★★★
Walk about 60 feet right from the previous routes until
you reach a flat spot on the trail directly in front of an
overhanging section of the wall. There are three bolted
lines on this wall. This route is the first one encountered,
on the left side of the wall. Begin on the ramp created
by a large boulder. Make the right pocket choices in the
overhanging section, then romp up larger holds to the
anchors.
50 ft. 5 bolts. *FA Porter Jarrard, Rob Turan, 1991.*

⑭ Relaxed Atmosphere 5.11c ★★★
This route is located directly right of *Aquaduck Pocket*.
Begin on the same ramp. Boulder out the overhang, make
a big move, then continue up the vertical face.
60 ft. 5 bolts. *FA Porter Jarrard, Jamie Baker, 1991.*

⑮ Third-World Lover 5.11c ★★★
This is the rightmost route on this wall, located about 10
feet right of *Relaxed Atmosphere*. Begin near the start
of *Relaxed Atmosphere*, then traverse right to clip the
first bolt.
60 ft. 5 bolts. *FA Porter Jarrard, Rob Turan, 1991.*

⑯ Hen-ry! 5.11b ★★★★
This route is located on a blunt arete 150 feet right of
the previous three routes. Tiptoe and stretch through
delicate moves to the anchors.
50 ft. 5 bolts. *FA Porter Jarrard, Shannon Langley, 1991.*

⑲ Table of Colors 5.13a ★★★★★ ☐
Just right of the direct start is the original version of *Table of Colors*. The first bolt is shared with the next route, *Mercy, the Huff.* Begin by standing on top of a large boulder. Pass the first bolt to reach a large shelf. Move left after the shelf, out to the second bolt, and power up good holds to hard moves on a blunt arete.
80 ft. 10 bolts. *FA Porter Jarrard, Mark Williams, 1990.*

Climber: Pauline Hsu. Photo: Dawn Kish.

⑰ Trad Boy Go 5.11a ★★ ☐
This route is located 30 feet right of *Hen-ry!* and ascends the thin crack beginning in a black, spherical alcove.
70 ft. *FA John Bronaugh, Tim Powers, 1993.*

⑱ Table of Colors Direct 5.13b ★★★★★ ☐
Walk about 75 feet right from *Hen-ry!* around a corner to reach a striking orange wall with large boulders at its base. The direct start for *Table Of Colors* begins on the left side of this wall on some small holds about 15 feet left of a thin seam. Power through the start, then crimp back right to join up with the original *Table of Colors*.
80 ft. 10 bolts. *FA Porter Jarrard, Mark Williams, 1993.*

⑲ Table of Colors 5.13a ★★★★★ ☐
See description above.

⑳ Mercy, the Huff 5.12b ★★★★★ ☐
This pumpy classic shares the first bolt of *Table of Colors*, then heads right. Continue up the remarkable face, with boulder problems separated by rests. Take your time, breathe, relax, focus – and don't fall at the top! Enjoy this ride.
80 ft. 9 bolts. *FA Porter Jarrard, Chris Snyder, 1991.*

The following two routes begin on top of the large boulder at the base of the wall.

㉑ The Dinosaur 5.12c ★★★★ ☐
This route begins about 20 feet right of *Mercy, the Huff.* Crimp on.
65 ft. 6 bolts. *FA Porter Jarrard, Tony Berlier, 1992.*

Mercy, The Huff

㉒ Wild, Yet Tasty 5.12a ★★★ ☐
Fifteen feet right of the previous route is a crack system. Walk to the right edge of the large boulder, then step out over the abyss to begin. A contender for the softest 5.12a at the Red. Nevertheless, a great line with a well-defined crux.
50 ft. 4 bolts. *FA Porter Jarrard, Jeff Moll, 1992.*

RAVEN ROCK

Home of one of the Red's longest routes, the 200-foot *Nevermore*. Visit www.wolverinepublishing.com/downloads for a free download containing the information for this cliff.

LOWER GORGE

Character

If you enjoy traditional climbing at beautiful, peaceful cliffs, the Lower Region is for you. It boasts 27 different walls and lots of excellent crack climbing, as well as the occasional great sport line. For the summit minded, there are plenty of spires, including Minas Ithil at Muscle Beach, the Arrowhead at Pebble Beach, and Major's Pinnacle at Backside Wall.

Approach

Head north from Miguel's on KY 11 toward Mountain Parkway. Pass under Mountain Parkway, then turn left onto KY 15 near the Shell station. Continue west on 15 for about a mile until you reach KY 77 on your right. Turn right onto 77 and follow this road as it winds through Nada Tunnel, past Military Wall, and crosses the steel bridge. Turn left onto 1067/FR 23 directly after the steel bridge and follow it to your destination.

Access

All areas are located on Forest Service land, so please respect signs and fences indicating closed routes or trails and read the guidelines for climbing on Forest Service land on page 32 of this book.

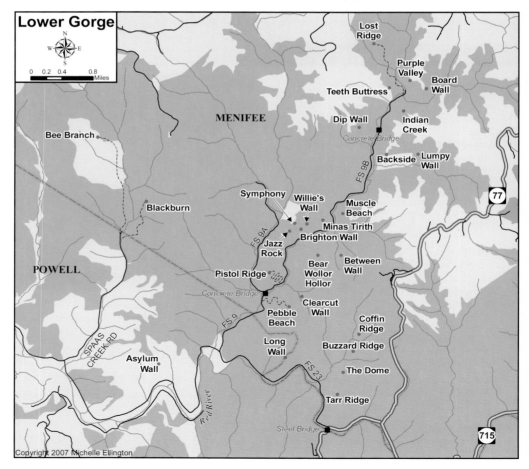

CLIFF	SUN / SHADE	HIKE	RAIN	ROUTES	GRADE RANGE	CLASSIC ROUTES
THE DOME page 65	shade	20 mins		8	5.6- .7 .8 .9 .10 .11 .12 .13 .14	
LONG WALL page 58	a.m. / p.m.	15 mins		42	5.6- .7 .8 .9 .10 .11 .12 .13 .14	Autumn 9- Rock Wars 10a B3 11b The Gift 12a
PEBBLE BEACH page 66	all day	15 mins		24	5.6- .7 .8 .9 .10 .11 .12 .13 .14	Welcome to Ole Kentuck 13a
PISTOL RIDGE page 70	all day / shade	15 mins		20	5.6- .7 .8 .9 .10 .11 .12 .13 .14	When Doves Cry V4 Hidden Dragon 12c
CLEARCUT WALL page 81	p.m.	15 mins		6	5.6- .7 .8 .9 .10 .11 .12 .13 .14	
MINAS TIRITH page 81		15 mins		3	5.6- .7 .8 .9 .10 .11 .12 .13 .14	
WILLIE'S WALL page 81	a.m.	15 mins		4	5.6- .7 .8 .9 .10 .11 .12 .13 .14	
BRIGHTON WALL page 81	a.m.	20 mins		3	5.6- .7 .8 .9 .10 .11 .12 .13 .14	
SYMPHONY WALL page 81	all day	20 mins		3	5.6- .7 .8 .9 .10 .11 .12 .13 .14	Boogered 11b
JAZZ ROCK page 81	all day / shade	20 mins		4	5.6- .7 .8 .9 .10 .11 .12 .13 .14	
BEAR WOLLOR HOLLOR page 81	shade	20 mins		5	5.6- .7 .8 .9 .10 .11 .12 .13 .14	
BETWEEN WALL page 81	all day	5 mins		5	5.6- .7 .8 .9 .10 .11 .12 .13 .14	
MUSCLE BEACH page 78	all day	15 mins		18	5.6- .7 .8 .9 .10 .11 .12 .13 .14	Rocket Man 8+
DIP WALL page 78	all day / shade	10 mins		19	5.6- .7 .8 .9 .10 .11 .12 .13 .14	
BACKSIDE WALL page 81	all day	25 mins		5	5.6- .7 .8 .9 .10 .11 .12 .13 .14	
LUMPY WALL page 81	a.m.	25 mins		7	5.6- .7 .8 .9 .10 .11 .12 .13 .14	
INDIAN CREEK page 82	a.m. / shade	15 mins		32	5.6- .7 .8 .9 .10 .11 .12 .13 .14	Crack Attack 9+ Country Lovin' 12b
PURPLE VALLEY page 88	all day / p.m.	10 mins		29	5.6- .7 .8 .9 .10 .11 .12 .13 .14	Into The Purple Valley 8 Burden of Dreams 11c
BOARD WALL page 81	p.m.	15 mins		7	5.6- .7 .8 .9 .10 .11 .12 .13 .14	
LOST RIDGE page 92	a.m. / shade	25 mins		7	5.6- .7 .8 .9 .10 .11 .12 .13 .14	Wide Pride 10c
ASYLUM WALL page 81		15 mins		4	5.6- .7 .8 .9 .10 .11 .12 .13 .14	
BLACKBURN ROCK page 81	p.m.	15 mins		3	5.6- .7 .8 .9 .10 .11 .12 .13 .14	
BEE BRANCH ROCK page 81	p.m.	30 mins		4	5.6- .7 .8 .9 .10 .11 .12 .13 .14	

LONG WALL

Photo: Elodie Sarraco.

Character

At over a mile in length, Long Wall lives up to its name. The wall contains an abundance of classic traditional lines, including two of the most popular crack climbs in the Red, *Autumn* and *Rock Wars*. Sport climbers shouldn't miss *The Gift*, one of the most beautiful and unique face climbs in the South.

Approach

To reach Long Wall, drive north on KY 77 two miles past Nada Tunnel (one mile past Military Wall), then turn left after crossing the steel bridge. Drive 1.3 miles down the gravel road (County Road 1067) until you see a small pulloff on your left overlooking the Red River. Park there and locate an old logging road just across from the parking pulloff. Follow the logging road for about 15 minutes up the steepening trail and past a band of limestone. The trail eventually meets the cliff in the vicinity of the first route, *Cruisemaster*.

Conditions

Due to the length of Long Wall, it is possible to find a sunny climb at any point during the day. Don't expect to find a large amount of rainy-day climbing, as most of the routes tend to be slabby or vertical. Two notable exceptions are *Rock Wars* and *Autumn*, which are almost guaranteed to be dry in the wettest weather – although you may have to stand in line to do them.

❶ Cruisemaster 5.11b ★★★

This route begins in the dihedral you see directly in front of you at the end of the approach trail. There is an overhanging hand crack above it. Climb the first pitch through a chimney, crawl across a ledge, and set a belay. The second pitch ascends the hand crack to an exposed hanging belay at a set of bolt anchors. From here, move out to the exposed face and begin climbing. Clip a bolt, then move up through small pockets. One of these pockets will take a small cam for protection. Will it hold a fall? You tell me. Pull a boulder problem to reach a good ledge. Don't look down. Fiddle in a nut if you can, then pull up into a shallow dihedral and cram in some more small gear. At this point you may be crying. I know I was. Continue up the beautifully exposed and wicked crack to the top. Rappel from a tree to descend.
120 ft. 1 bolt. *FA Tom Souders, Dave Veldhaus, 1986.*

❷ Cruise Control 5.9+ ★★★★

Fun. Just left of *Cruisemaster* is a crack system leading up the entire face. Climb this crack, making liberal use of good face holds along the way. You can rappel from a tree on the final ledge, or continue to the summit and walk off to the left.
90 ft. *FA Dave Veldhaus, 1986.*

❸ Suction Lipectomy 5.8 ★

This offwidth is located 75 feet left and around the corner from *Cruise Control*. Climb up easy ledges to get to the crack.
90 ft. *FA Philip Babiak, Dave Kanapell, 1988.*

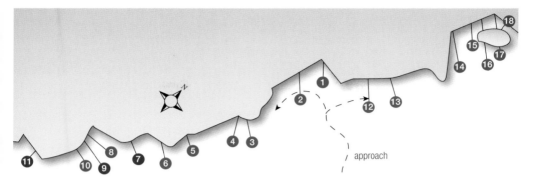

4 Ralph and Bob's 5.7 ★★

This route climbs the corner left of *Suction Lipectomy.*
You will see a set of cracks about five feet apart and
some small trees on the upper ledge. Climb the first
pitch to a ledge and belay. The second pitch ascends
the wide and dirty crack to the top. **Variation:** From the
belay, climb the 5.9 crack to the left.
90 ft. *FA Ralph Crawford, Bob Baker, 1977.*
Variation FA John Bronaugh, Tina Feezel, 1989.

5 Long Wall Chimney 5.7 ★★★

This large chimney is left of *Ralph and Bob's,* just past
a large overhang. Look for belay slings inside the hueco
just after the second offwidth section.
100 ft. *FA Unknown.*

6 Vector Trouble 5.10a ★★★★

Walk left from *Long Wall Chimney* and look for an
orange dihedral with a flaring crack at the top. Begin by
climbing the left of two cracks to the ledge about 25 feet
up. From there, continue up the thin dihedral to a final
roof. Chimney up through the slot or move out right to
some face holds. Rappel from the ledge, or continue up a
short second pitch to the summit.
100 ft. *FA Martin Hackworth, Grant Stephens, 1984.*

7 Boom! Boom! Out Go the Lights 5.10b ★★★

From the previous route, move left about 50 feet and
look for a bolted line beginning with a low overhang.
Crank through the overhang, then continue up the face
to some technical climbing up high.
70 ft. 8 bolts. *FA John Bronaugh, Stacy Temple, 1992.*

8 NEPA This 5.8- ★★

This route is located just right of the dihedral that marks
the beginning of *Stand and Deliver.* Scramble up to a
ledge to begin the route. Heave into a dirty offwidth and
continue to a second ledge. Move right, then continue to
the top.
90 ft. *FA John Bronaugh, Shannon Stuart-Smith, 1997.*

9 Stand and Deliver 5.11c ★★★

This is the dihedral just left of *NEPA.* Climb the dihedral, then step left out to the face. Reach up and left to a
small flake, then search hard for the remaining holds.
70 ft. 7 bolts. *FA Nick Cocciolone, Beth Cocciolone, 1992.*

10 Two Step 5.7 ★★★

This route is located a few feet left of *Stand and Deliver*
and begins in a wide hand crack just before a rockhouse.
Climb the crack to a chimney. Climb around the overhang on the left to a ledge. Continue up the overhanging
crack to a ledge beneath a chimney, which takes you to
the summit.
100 ft. *FA Bob Baker, Martin Hackworth, 1977.*

11 Whip It Out 5.11d ★★★

Walk about 30 feet left and around the corner from
the previous route to a bolted line with a small roof 20
feet up. Boulder through perfect finger pockets to the
overhang. Crank over it, then continue up the easier face
to the anchors.
40 ft. 5 bolts. *FA Nick Cocciolone, Beth Cocciolone, 1992.*

*The remaining routes are located right of where the
approach trail meets the wall.*

12 Xanthic Dance 5.9- ★

Veer to the right at the top of the approach trail and
look for a shallow dihedral with a small ledge about
15 feet up. Climb a thin crack to reach the ledge, then
continue to the top.
90 ft. *FA Martin Hackworth, 1984.*

13 Five Easy Pieces 5.9-

This route begins on top of a large boulder past a small
dihedral to the right of *Xanthic Dance.* Climb either
crack to a ledge, then follow a ramp to a corner to belay.
Continue up the corner to summit.
130 ft. *FA Martin Hackworth, Jeff Wurmser, 1977.*

14 Autumn 5.9- ★★★★★

This route and its partner *Rock Wars* are two of the most popular trad lines of their grade at the Red. Just looking at them, you will realize why. Walk right from the previous routes for about 200 feet, to a large open area of the cliff with a huge flat boulder at the base. *Autumn* ascends the hand crack in the flake on the left side of the face. Lower from bolt anchors.

80 ft. *FA Martin Hackworth, Tod Anderson, 1984.*

Climber: Yasmeen Fowler. Photo: Anne Skidmore.

Autumn / Rock Wars

14 Autumn 5.9- ★★★★★
See description opposite.

15 Hot September 5.9 ★★★
This angling flake begins at the base of *Rock Wars* and ends near the top of *Autumn*. It would add to the classics if it weren't so hollow and thin. Nevertheless, it makes for an exciting lead. Try not to fall.
100 ft. *FA Lou Gonano, John Long, 1985.*

16 Souders Crack 5.11d ★★★
Due to the hollowness of the flake, this route is usually toproped by first climbing *Rock Wars*. Begin on *Rock Wars* but continue straight up the flake to a bouldery finish.
80 ft. *FA Tom Souders, Jeff Koenig, 1986.*

17 Rock Wars 5.10a ★★★★★
Classic. *Rock Wars* looks like it was transported straight from the Utah Desert to the Red. Legend has it that Van Halen, after managing to get their tour bus through the Nada Tunnel, did a quick ascent of *Rock Wars* before a concert. It was also featured on the back cover of the second edition of John Bronaugh's *Red River Gorge Climbs* book. Climb the beautiful finger-sized flake on the right side of the face directly in front of the large boulder. Stop at the first set of anchors or continue up the tight-hands crack to the second set for an extra challenge (grade dependent on your hand size).
80 ft. *FA Grant Stephens, Anthony Snider, 1986.*

18 Now I'm Nothing V4 ★★★★
This highball boulder problem ascends the face of the large boulder directly in front of *Rock Wars*. Previously given an "X" rating in the pre-crashpad days.
20 ft. *FA Unknown.*

19 The Gift 5.12a ★★★★★
40 feet right of the *Rock Wars* alcove is another striking orange face with a single bolted line. Reach up through the remarkable face moves of the first few bolts to a bulge. Make an "in-your-face" clip, then power over the bulge and crank through long power moves to the anchors.
70 ft. 9 bolts. *FA Bill McCullough, Tim Powers, 1990.*

20 Mailbox 5.8 ★★
This route ascends the left-facing dihedral 50 feet right of *The Gift*. Begin by face climbing the slab, then move into the crack for the more challenging upper section.
70 ft. *FA John Bronaugh, Louis Petry, 1984.*

21 Yuk 5.9 ★★★★
This splitter offwidth/chimney is located just right of *Mailbox*. Lead it if you happen to own Big-Bros.
70 ft. *FA Jeff Koenig, Tom Souders, 1984.*

B3

The next five routes have a common start up the 5.10a initial section of Trinket Man *to the ledge.*

㉒ Trinket Man 5.11d ★★★

This route ascends the face left of the outside corner around the buttress and uphill from *Yuk.* The first section is used to access the following "ledge routes" and goes at 5.10a. To do all of *Trinket Man,* continue up the face past the ledge.
140 ft. 12 bolts. *FA John Bronaugh, Stacy Temple, 1992.*

㉓ Denial 5.12a ★★★

Climb the first part of *Trinket Man* to the large ledge to access this route. This is the bolted line 12 feet right of the arete. Power through the beginning, then continue up the easier face to the anchors.
60 ft. 12 bolts. *FA Nick Cocciolone, Beth Cocciolone, 1992.*

㉔ Fire and Finesse 5.11d ★★★

This is the bolted line just right of *Denial.* Tackle a bulge, then continue up the less overhanging face to the anchors.
60 ft. 6 bolts. *FA Nick Cocciolone, Beth Cocciolone, 1992.*

㉕ Slip It In 5.12a ★★★

Just right of the previous line is yet another bolted line. Boulder out the beginning moves, then continue up the face to anchors.
60 ft. 6 bolts. *FA Nick Cocciolone, Beth Cocciolone, 1992.*

㉖ Kazi and Mito 5.11a ★★★

This is the last of the ledge routes and the rightmost line of the four. As with the others, power through the bouldery start, then continue up through easier climbing to the finish.
60 ft. 6 bolts. *FA Nick Cocciolone, Beth Cocciolone, 1992.*

㉗ Game Boy 5.11c ★★★★

Fifty feet right of the ledge routes is a bolted line that ascends the entire 140-foot face. This may be the longest bolted line in the Red.
140 ft. 13 bolts. *FA Stacy Temple, John Bronaugh, 1992.*

㉘ Are the Pies Fresh? 5.12a ★★★★

This bolted line ascends the face 15 feet right of *Game Boy.* Make thought-provoking moves up the vertical face to anchors just before an overhang for a great 5.11c. Continue past the overhang to the second set of anchors if you can figure out "the move."
110 ft. 13 bolts. *FA Nick Cocciolone, Beth Cocciolone, 1992.*

㉙ Back Door to Paris 5.10c ★★★

This bolted line begins directly right of *Are the Pies Fresh?* and left of a large detached block.
70 ft. 7 bolts. *FA Nick Cocciolone, Beth Cocciolone, 1992*

㉚ B3 5.11b ★★★★★

See photo opposite.

30 B3 5.11b ★★★★★

Tom Souders and Jeff Koenig, also known as the Beene Brothers, named this route *B3* (or *BBB*) for *Beene Brother's Best*. Locate the obvious splitter hand crack that begins on top of the large detached block right of *Back Door to Paris*. Begin by climbing the first section of *Perforator*, then traverse left to reach the start of B3. Jam through perfect hands until the crack begins to fade, then make a move left to an obvious horizontal. Shake out for a while, then move back right and tackle a boulder problem to reach the "Thank God Ledge." Lie down in the coffin for a good rest, ask yourself why you're doing this, then creep out into the upper dihedral. Climb for about 20 feet through exposed and tricky leg-shaking moves to the anchors. Kiss them and lower to the ground.

120 ft. *FA Jeff Koenig, Tom Souders, 1984*

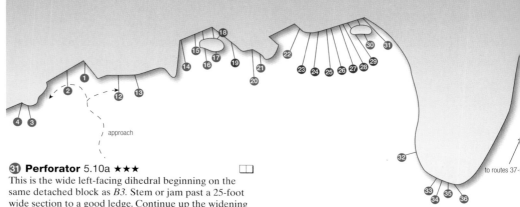

approach

to routes 37-

③① Perforator 5.10a ★★★
This is the wide left-facing dihedral beginning on the
same detached block as *B3*. Stem or jam past a 25-foot
wide section to a good ledge. Continue up the widening
hand crack to a small roof. Crank over the roof and pull
up into the muddy dihedral above. Climb through moss,
mud, and roots to belay from the anchors on *B3*.
120 ft. *FA Tom Souders, Jeff Koenig, 1984.*

③② Fear and Loathing In Nada 5.10b ★★★
This route is located 200 feet right of *Perforator*, past
a low and wet area. Look for a plated face containing
some cracks. Climb the face past some funky cracks to
a ledge and belay. Fist jam out the overhanging, slanting
crack that widens and turns to an awkward dihedral at
the top.
180 ft. *FA Grant Stephens, Martin Hackworth, 1984.*

To reach the next four routes, walk along the wall from
Fear and Loathing in Nada *for about 100 feet. Walk past*
an overhang and locate a dirty, steep gully that leads to a
ledge about 50 feet up. Carefully scramble up the gully to
reach this ledge. From the ledge, climb a short face (5.4
R) behind a big tree to a smaller ledge. Climb another
short face to a larger ledge with a bolted belay. This ledge
marks the start of the next four routes.

③③ Zen Master Dude 5.10a R ★★★
Zen Master Dude climbs straight up from the belay and
angles right.
40 ft. *FA Dave Chenault, 2000.*

③④ Accidentally Kelly Street 5.9+ R ★★★
From *Zen Master Dude*, traverse right along the ledge.
This route ascends the face just before the blunt prow.
Build a gear anchor for the belay, then ascend the face
using natural gear for protection. To descend, rappel
above *Big Country*. You can also walk off the wall to the
left and come out near *Whip It Out*.
45 ft. *FA Dave Chenault, Chris Chaney, Jason Burton,*
2001.

③⑤ Nautical Twilight 5.8 R ★★★
Traverse right from *Accidentally Kelly Street* a few feet
and just right of the blunt prow. Climb the face. The low
crux is well protected. Descend as described in *Accidentally Kelly Street.*
40 ft. *FA Mark Jackson, 1986.*

③⑥ Big Country 5.5 R ★★★
This route has been done naked, solo, naked and solo,
and just about any other way you can think of. There
may even still be an old barbecue grill on the ledge fro
some partying locals. From *Nautical Twilight*, traverse
right along the ledge, looking for the single bolt on the
face that marks *Big Country*. When you locate the rou
climb up above some trampled vegetation to clip the
bolt, then move left to a blunt arete. From there, head
straight for the summit.
45 ft. *FA Martin Hackworth, George Robinson, Grant
Stephens, 1984.*

③⑦ Rock Caddie 5.10a ★
From the previous routes, hike 100 yards to the right a
past a large rockhouse. This route is in the vicinity and
ascends a short slab near an arete.
50 ft. 5 bolts. *FA Nick Cocciolone, Beth Cocciolone, Eric
Szczukowski, Amy Szczukowski, 1992.*

③⑧ The Snatch 5.11d ★
Walk about 100 feet right from *Rock Caddie* to locate
this often-wet route that begins on a small ledge. Clim
the overhanging face, which eases toward the top.
45 ft. 5 bolts. *FA Nick Cocciolone, Beth Cocciolone, 1992*

③⑨ Feltch Me 5.9
This climb ascends the left-facing dihedral about 40 fe
right of *The Snatch.*
30 ft. *FA Nick Cocciolone, Beth Cocciolone, 1992.*

④⓪ Gladuator 5.12b ★★★
This powerful sport route begins about 15 feet right of
Feltch Me. Worth the hike? It was for me.
30 ft. 4 bolts. *FA Nick Cocciolone, Eric Szczukowski, Am
Szczukowski, 1992.*

41 Texas Tea 5.8+ ★★★

If you are just going to do this, or the next couple of routes, it is best to locate a direct approach from the road. Otherwise, hike about 250 yards right from the previous route to a large buttress. This route ascends a nice-looking black dihedral.

60 ft. *FA Dave Veldhaus, Jim Knapp, Paul Kopona, 1987.*

42 Block and Tackle 5.10d

Walk right from *Texas Tea* to locate this right-facing dihedral in suspect rock. Climb the dihedral to a ledge.

80 ft. *FA John Bronaugh, Scott Hammon, 1994.*

43 Sugar Daddy 5.9- R

Walk 300 feet right from *Block and Tackle* to another buttress. This route ascends a dihedral on this buttress. Climb the dihedral to a ledge then take a hand crack to the ending ledge.

90 ft. *FA John Bronaugh, Terry Ferg, 1995.*

The following cliffs have been removed from the print version of this guidebook. Visit www.wolverinepublishing.com/downloads for a free download of the information for them.

TARR RIDGE

A difficult approach will keep this crag from becoming popular.

THE DOME

The Dome is one of those obscure Lower Region crag that was popular for a brief time in its day but now only sees a few visits a year from dedicated backwoods traddies.

BUZZARD RIDGE

If you can find this area, it offers a couple of decent lines and potential for more first ascents.

COFFIN RIDGE

This remote crag has only one route and little potential for more.

PEBBLE BEACH

all day | 15 mins | 24 routes
5.6- .7 .8 .9 .10 .11 .12 .13 .14

Character

Pebble Beach has an interesting mix of good routes: sport lines, mixed lines, trad lines, and even aid lines. For the determined crack climber, the hardest crack in the Red, *Welcome to Ole Kentuck*, is worth an attempt or two. Sport climbers should borrow a rack of stoppers for the best 5.9 mixed route in the Red, *Central Scrutinizer*.

Approach

To reach Pebble Beach, drive north on KY 77 two miles past Nada Tunnel (one mile past Military Wall), then turn left after crossing the steel bridge onto County Road 1067. Drive 2.5 miles down County Road 1067 – you'll pass Long Wall on the way – and then turn right onto Forest Service Road 9, just past a barn on the left. The road turns to gravel at this point. Follow the gravel road for 1.1 miles, then park on the left, just before a single-lane bridge. You will see a National Forest Service kiosk at the pulloff. The trail is located directly across from the pulloff, near a retaining wall. Thanks to the RRGCC and its trail-building skills, the once dreaded steep uphill battle is now an enjoyable hike loaded with switchbacks. Follow the trail as it winds up the hill and ends just in front of the obvious pinnacle on which *The Arrowhead* is located.

Conditions

Although Pebble Beach is quite a long cliff, most of the routes are located in one area. Guide services have been known to set ropes on the routes at Pebble, which makes for quick congestion. If you see a large passenger van in the pulloff, you may want to find another crag for the day. Most of the routes receive lots of sunshine, making for some great winter climbing.

The Arrowhead

❶ **Broken Arrow** 5.9- ★★★
This route ascends the chimney on the left side of the pinnacle on which *The Arrowhead* is located. Enjoy the view from the top. Rappel from anchors.
50 ft. *FA Tracy Crabtree, Jeff Ashley, 1989.*

❷ **The Arrowhead** 5.7 ★★★
This route ascends the southwest face of the obvious pinnacle at the end of the approach trail. Clip a bolt to start, then continue up the face with small cams and stoppers for protection. Lower from anchors.
60 ft. 1 bolt. *FA Charles Tabor, Jeff Wilburn, 1987.*

❸ **Beachcomber** 5.4 ★★
This route ascends a crack system between the pinnacle on which *The Arrowhead* is located and a large overhang on the main wall. Climb the initial crack up to a ledge. Belay from here, then continue up through the chimney to the top. Rap from a tree or walk off to the right.
130 ft. *FA Geoff Manley, Charles Tabor, 1988.*

❹ **Halloween** A2 ★★★
To the right of *The Arrowhead* and *Beachcomber* is a huge rockhouse with a thin crack in the roof. Free climb up the vertical crack to gain the roof. Jump in your aiders and tackle the large roof, making use of many fixed pieces along the way.
70 ft. *FA Tracy Crabtree, Mike Norman, 1992.*

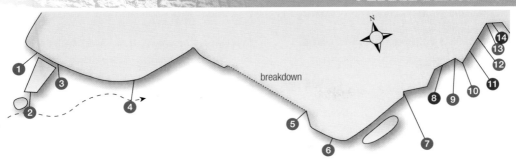

breakdown

⑤ Razorback 5.6 ★★

This route is the first crack encountered 200 feet right of *Halloween*, past a breakdown in the cliff.
40 ft. *FA Charles Tabor, Mark Strevels, 1987.*

⑥ Versatile Universe 5.10d R ★★★★

Walk right from the previous route to a point where the trail passes under a large detached flake leaning against the main wall. This route begins just left of the flake, in a hand crack. The crack fades toward the end and bolts become your source of protection. Enjoy the Horse-Pens-like finish! Apparently some bolts have been added next to natural protection placements so this route now meets the same set of standards set by Disney World for the Flying Dumbo ride.
65 ft. 3 bolts. *FA Tracy Crabtree, Mike Norman, 1990.*

⑦ Physical Attraction 5.10b ★★

Hike through the hallway created by the detached flake. Twenty-five feet past the flake is this offwidth and fist crack. Climb the dirty, moderate crack to a ledge near the top. Tackle the overhanging fist crack for the last 20 feet, then continue up through a 10-foot chimney to top out. Bring some large gear.
80 ft. *FA Jim Link, John Whisman, 1989.*

⑧ Scabies 5.9+ ★★★

Walk 40 feet right from *Physical Attraction* to locate this popular bolted flake. Find a good sequence up the thin flake, then make an exciting move out left to the anchors.
30 ft. 4 bolts. *FA, 1993.*

⑨ Zambezi Plunge 5.8 ★★★★

The first route climbed at Pebble Beach, this hand crack is located in a small dihedral 10 feet right of *Scabies*. Climb the crack to a ledge with a large boulder and tree. Continue through the offwidth to the anchors on *Ju-Ju*.
60 ft. *FA Jeff Wilburn, 1987.*

⑩ Ju-Ju 5.10b ★★★★

This route ascends the arete just right of *Zambezi Plunge*. A small cam (0.5-Camalot size) helps protect the lower section of the route.
60 ft. 5 bolts. *FA Charles Tabor, Frank Waters, 1989.*

Central Scrutinizer

⑪ Sundance 5.10c ★★★

To the right of *Ju-Ju* is an obvious short offwidth. This bolted line begins just right of the offwidth. Start by climbing the offwidth, then escape out onto the face for some tips and toes. Continue up the face with crimps and edges until you can move left to the finishing bolts on *Ju-Ju*. Lower from the bolted anchors.
60 ft. 5 bolts. *FA Tom Fyffe, Charles Tabor, 1989.*

⑫ Central Scrutinizer 5.9 ★★★★★

Classic. Look for a piton in the middle of the less-than-vertical face capped by a huge roof. Climb the face to the piton, then angle right to a bolt. Continue up the face, taking advantage of bomber stopper placements along the way. Lower from bolted anchors.
50 ft. 1 bolt. *FA Charles Tabor, Tom Fyffe, 1989.*

⑬ Environmental Impact 5.7 ★★★★

Great for the novice hand jammer! This route ascends the hand crack in the left-facing dihedral on the right side of the less-than-vertical face capped by a huge roof. Either climb the crack to the first set of anchors and lower, or continue up through the chimney above to the top of the cliff. Most people just do the first pitch. To descend from the top, walk off left or rappel with two ropes.
130 ft. *FA Charles Tabor, Jeff Wilburn, 1987.*

Climber: Mandy Byron. Photo: Frank Byron.

⑭ Straightedge 5.12a ★★★
This crimpfest ascends the vertical face just right of *Environmental Impact*. Originally a scary mixed route, but the first ascentionist later added more bolts.
50 ft. 6 bolts. *FA Hugh Loeffler, 1990.*

⑮ Reserved Seating 5.10b ★★★
This arete climb is located right of *Straightedge* and an obvious offwidth on the outside corner of a pinnacle.
50 ft. 6 bolts. *FA Mike Norman, Tracy Crabtree, 1991.*

⑯ High Noon 5.12a ★★★★
This is the mixed arete to the right of *Reserved Seating*. Take some gear for added protection. Sneak up the arete, then move right out onto the face near the top for a leg-shaking ending.
60 ft. 5 bolts. *FA Jamie Baker, Stacy Temple, 1989.*

⑰ Brontosaurus 5.10b ★★★★
Walk 50 feet right and around the corner from *High Noon*. Gawk at the impressively overhanging finger crack of *Welcome to Ole Kentuck*. *Brontosaurus* ascends the fun hand crack in the dihedral just to the left. Scramble up a chute of rock to a stance just beneath a small roof. Place a piece, then jump out into the crack and enjoy some of the best-feeling hand jams in the Red. Keep your focus for the thin section toward the top.
60 ft. *FA John Bronaugh, Charles Tabor, 1988.*

⑱ Welcome to Ole Kentuck 5.13a ★★★★★
Just to the right of *Brontosaurus* is this severely over-hanging splitter finger crack that begins on a ledge 25 feet up. Climb the first part of *Brontosaurus* and traverse right on the ledge to reach the crack. Climb through sequential fingerlocks seperated by the occasional flaring handjam. Use black magic or raw power to work through the final, more-overhanging crux section. When you can, reach back over into *Brontosaurus* for the final few feet. This route was a long-standing project named "Nazi Bitch Crack" until Steve Petro made quick work of it during a visit to the Red in 1995.
40 ft. *FA Steve Petro, 1995.*

⑲ The Seam 5.11c R ★★★
Directly beneath *Welcome to Ole Kentuck* is a short, thin seam. Make use of the seam and surrounding face holds to boulder to the ledge. Protection is good but scarce. Maybe just bring some crash pads and call it a highball? Lower from bolted anchors.
25 ft. *FA Mark Strevels, 1987.*

⑳ Small Change 5.8 ★★
This route ascends the short flake 15 feet right of *The Seam*. The gear is a bit tricy to place. Walk off the back side to descend.
25 ft. *FA Charles Tabor, 1989.*

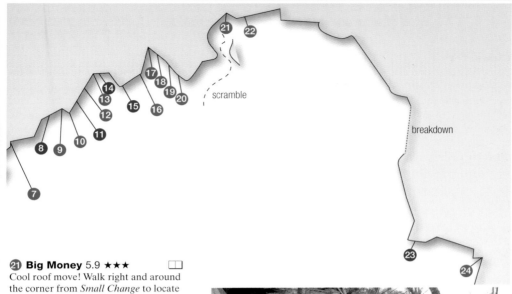

scramble

breakdown

21 Big Money 5.9 ★★★

Cool roof move! Walk right and around the corner from *Small Change* to locate a muddy gully. Scramble up the gully to reach this attractive dihedral with a roof about 25 feet up. It is also possible to reach the starting ledge by climbing *Small Change*. Climb up the dihedral, tackle the roof, then continue up past another roof to the top. Rappel from a tree to descend. **70 ft.** *FA Mark Strevels, 1987.*

22 Berlin Wall 5.8 R ★★

Walk 50 feet right from *Big Money*, staying on the same ledge, to locate a plated face just past an arete. Climb up the face on good holds, then traverse right to tackle the final bulges. Rappel from a tree to descend. Originally a toprope until led by John Bronaugh. **50 ft.** *FA John Bronaugh, 1988.*

23 Blood Money 5.9+ ★★

Hike back down through the gully from *Berlin Wall* and *Big Money* and head right for about 300 feet along the cliff. The cliff breaks down along the way, then picks back up where this route is located. Look for a bolted face near the first corner. Climb through pockets and a couple of roofs to the anchors. May be heady for novices. **50 ft. 5 bolts.** *FA Mark Strevels, Frank Waters, 1992.*

24 Punkin Head 5.9 R

This route ascends an A-shaped roof 150 feet right of *Blood Money*. Tackle the roof and end on a ledge. **60 ft.** *FA Mark Strevels, Charles Tabor, 1989.*

Reserved Seating

Welcome to Ole Kentuck

PISTOL RIDGE

 all day shade 15 mins

20 routes
5.6- .7 .8 .9 .10 .11 .12 .13 .14

Character

Pistol Ridge is a popular area for beginning climbers. Its many scrambles, gullies, and tunnels allow people to get a feel for climbing even before they get on a rope. Previous guidebooks described these scrambles and gullies. This guide, however, covers exclusively the fifth-class rock climbing, so I did not include that information. Aside from the beginner routes, the area now has a few offwidth testpieces. *When Doves Cry* is the offwidth version of *The Crack House* near Moab, Utah – 30 feet of upside-down, calf-cramping roof climbing only a few feet above the ground. After you've mastered the upside-down offwidth technique on *When Doves Cry*, walk around the corner and rope up for the twin routes *Crouching Tiger* and *Hidden Dragon*, offering offwidth roof climbing at its finest.

Approach

To reach Pistol Ridge, drive just across the bridge from the Pebble Beach parking area to a pulloff on the right. Cross to the opposite side of the road to find a trail with a steep start. Follow the long, winding trail through switchbacks until you reach the cliff. Walk left about 40 feet to reach the first route, *It's a Wonderful Life*, which ascends the obvious pinnacle in front of the main cliff.

Conditions

Most of the routes at Pistol Ridge remain in the shade and don't stay dry during heavy rain. An exception is *When Doves Cry*, a fun and sheltered boulder problem to play around on in wet weather.

It's a Wonderful Life

❶ It's a Wonderful Life 5.9+ ★★★
This route ascends the left arete on front of the main pinnacle described in the approach. Climb past four bolts to a large, flat ledge. Continue up the pinnacle to the anchors just before the top. It is possible to top out the pinnacle from the anchors. The lower bolts are often missing from this climb.
80 ft. 8 bolts. *FA Erik Farley, Mike Dunne, 1997.*

❷ The X Files 5.6 ★★★
Twenty feet right of the pinnacle is a crack system with an X-formation midway up. Climb up to the X, then continue to the top via a wide crack. Rappel from a tree to descend.
65 ft. *FA Erik Farley, Elke Breitbach, 1994.*

❸ The Misadventures of Nabisco County, Jr. 5.6
This wide and dirty crack is located 50 feet right of *The X Files*. Look for a leaning block at the base. Rappel from a tree to descend.
65 ft. *FA Erik Farley, 1994.*

❹ Trident 5.9 ★
Walk about 200 feet right from the previous route until you reach a large detached flake leaning against the main wall. Walk underneath the boulder and look for a set of three short cracks just as you exit the tunnel made by the flake. Climb any of the three cracks to a ledge to reach the main crack. Continue up the thin crack to the top. Rappel from a tree to descend.
50 ft. *FA John Bronaugh, 1995.*

To reach the next routes, walk left from It's a Wonderful Life *along a trail that winds down through the woods. After about five minutes the trail heads back up the hill and meets the cliff again.*

❺ People Gully 5.1
From the point where the trail meets back up with the cliff, hike to the right for about 150 feet. You'll pass a couple of dirty cracks on the way. Eventually you will reach a gully with a wide crack and a large tree growing from a ledge about 15 feet up. Climb up the wide crack past a couple of ledges to a short, dirty gully. Thrash up through the gully or climb the dirty face over some rhodos to reach the top. Down-climb to descend.
35 ft. *FA Erik Farley, Kirk Fatool, David Fatool, 1992.*

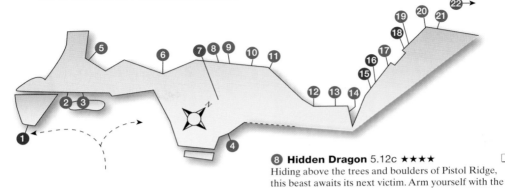

6 Land of the Glass Pinecones 5.6

From *People Gully*, walk left about 50 feet to locate a wide crack with a flake on the left face. Climb up the crack and then a short wall to your right at the top of the crack. Rappel from a tree to descend.
50 ft. *FA Erik Farley, Elke Fatool, 1992.*

The next three climbs are located on a second cliffline above the main wall. To reach them, scramble up through People Gully *to the top of the cliff.*

7 When Doves Cry V4 ★★★★★

From the top of *People Gully*, walk left a few feet, then straight ahead about 25 feet to a short cliffline on your left. Follow the cliffline for about 50 feet until you see a long cave split by a wide offwidth roof a few feet off the ground. Walk through the cave and start the offwidth where it is narrow enough for a fist jam. Climb all the way through until you can grab a jug four feet over the lip. Step off or continue to the top.

Variation I (Symbol Man) V6: Walk all the way back through the cave and sit-start the crack at its beginning. Reach up into a hand crack and undercling out it to the left. Reach out into a roof and finger lock out the lip until you can make a big move left to a handjam. Pull up into the chimney then climb down into the start of *When Doves Cry.*

Variation II (Purple Pain) V4: Start at the front of the cave on a good jug and climb all the way out the roof until you can stand up in the wide chimney at the end.
30 ft. *FA Kris Hampton, 2001*
Variation I and II: FA Ray Ellington, 2003

8 Hidden Dragon 5.12c ★★★★

Hiding above the trees and boulders of Pistol Ridge, this beast awaits its next victim. Arm yourself with the largest cams possible and attempt to slay the *Hidden Dragon*. From the top of *People Gully*, walk left a few feet, then turn left between two short clifflines. Walk down between the short cliffs about 25 feet until you see a ledge on your right beneath a 15-foot-high overhang. Scramble up to the ledge and you will be directly beneath an obvious crack splitting the roof. Begin by reaching up to a shelf, then advance into the hand crack. Climb out the hand crack until it widens at the lip. Go Vedauwoo style and kick your feet above your head. Shuffle your feet up until you can flip back over. Battle through armbars and chimney climbing to reach the final bulge at the top. Pull over the bulge and crawl to a good spot to pass out. Walk off to the right or rappel from the tree. Bring a couple of #5 or #4.5 Camalots.
50 ft. *FA Ray Ellington, 2001.*

9 Crouching Tiger 5.11b ★★★

Step a few feet left from *Hidden Dragon* to locate another wide crack splitting the roof. Reach up to a good hand jam, then kick your feet up high into the crack. Scoot out until you can flip around and gain a good stance beneath a bulge. Pull over the bulge and continue up through wide crack climbing to the top. Bring some #4.5 or #5 Camalots. Walk off right or rappel from a tree to descend.
50 ft. *FA Ray Ellington, 2001.*

Hidden Dragon

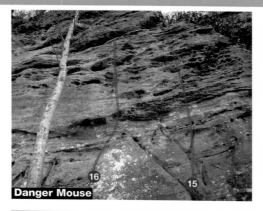

Danger Mouse — 16 — 15

Chem Studs — 18 — 17

The remaining routes are located back on the main wall.

⑩ **Armed** 5.10b ★★
Walk left about 50 feet and look for a large hueco about six feet off the ground. Climb up into the hueco and devise a way out of it and into a crack system. Follow this crack system to a ledge and rappel from anchors.
55 ft. *FA Erik Farley, Elke Breitbach, 1992.*

⑪ **Double Helix** 5.6 ★
Move left about 30 feet from *Armed* to a set of twin cracks near a corner. Climb the twin cracks to bolted anchors.
40 ft. *FA Erik Farley, Elke Breitbach, 1993.*

⑫ **A Fresh Start** 5.10c ★★★
About 30 feet right of *Ride 'em Cowboy* is a gully. Scramble up this gully to access a ledge. Walk left to spot a finger crack with a low overhang. Power past the overhang and continue up the finger crack to rappel anchors.
40 ft. *FA Justin Riddell, Todd Holtkamp, 2001.*

⑬ **Ride 'em Cowboy** 5.7 ★★★
This is the obvious left-facing flake 70 feet left of *Double Helix.*
40 ft. *FA Erik Farley, Elke Fatool, 1992.*

⑭ **Supergun** 5.9 ★★
Very short, but a great route to learn or practice hand jamming. Climb the dirty gully 20 feet left of *Ride 'em Cowboy* and look for a short splitter hand-and-fist crack on the right wall of the upper level.
20 ft. *FA Erik Farley, Elke Breitbach, 1993.*

⑮ **Please Don't Feed the Triceratops** 5.7 ★★
This bolted route is located just left of the gully leading up to *Supergun.*
35 ft. 4 bolts. *FA Erik Farley, 1993.*

⑯ **Danger Mouse** 5.8 ★★
Great beginner route. This is the bolted route just left of *Don't Feed the Triceratops.* Move left towards the top to the anchors. The 3rd bolt is currently missing. You can reach the anchors and toprope this route from *Please Don't Feed ...*
35 ft. 4 bolts. *FA Erik Farley, 1993.*

⑰ **The Refrigerator** 5.8- ★
About 30 feet left of *Danger Mouse* is an alcove with a large block in it. Climb either side of the block, then up into a cave. Exit the cave, then finish to a ledge via an offwidth, or traverse left out a roof to the anchors above *Chem Studs.*
40 ft. *FA Erik Farley, Mike Dunne, 1992.*

⑱ **Chem Studs** 5.10a ★★
This route climbs the bolted face left of *The Refrigerator.* Climb up to a roof, then move left to the anchors.
30 ft. 4 bolts. *FA Erik Farley, Dave Hill, 1993.*

⑲ **Way Of The Peaceful Warrior** 5.10a ★★★
Begin just a few feet left of *Chem Studs.* Boulder up to the arching overhang and traverse right over the top of *Chem Studs.* Continue up through the finishing offwidth of *The Refrigerator.*
55 ft. *FA Jerry Bargo, Steve Must, 1998.*

⑳ **Welcome to Bosnia** 5.7 ★
This route ascends the offwidth 80 feet left of *The Refrigerator.* Rappel from a tree to descend.
70 ft. *FA Erik Farley, 1993.*

㉑ **Bitchmobile** 5.8+ ★★★
Walk about 40 feet left from *Welcome to Bosnia* to locate this hand crack in an obtuse left-facing dihedral. Climb up the crack, then follow a dogleg right up a slab. Continue up the more vertical finish to a large ledge. Rappel from anchors.
65 ft. *FA Dave Hill, Erik Farley, 1991.*

㉒ **Dreams** V3 ★★★★
Head about a 100 yards past *Bitchmobile* to a large ampitheater. This is the obvious problem on the slightly overhanging face of the free-standing boulder.
FA Chris Chaney 2000.

DYNAMIC ROPES

Unsurpassed quality, durability and handling
Ask for them at your local outdoor specialty shop

www.petzl.com

MUSCLE BEACH

all day

15 mins   5.6- .7 .8 .9 .10 .11 .12 .13 .14

18 routes

[GPS: 37.8742N, 83.6538W, Minas Ithil 37.8756N, 83.6554W]

Character

If you want to learn how to climb pure, featureless cracks, Muscle Beach is the place. Known for its abundance of flaring fist cracks and offwidths, it has gained a reputation that lives up to its name. The crag has experienced a growth in popularity during the past decade since larger sized cams were introduced and became common pieces of gear on Red River trad climbers' racks.

Approach

From the intersection of Forest Service Road 9A with 9B, drive 1.5 miles on 9B and park in a large parking area on the right, near a concrete dam. Walk across the dam and immediately turn right onto an old dirt road. Follow the dirt road for a few hundred feet and look for a trail that ducks off to the left. Follow this trail uphill and eventually you will end up back on the dirt road. Follow this road until it levels out. Ignore the first road that branches off uphill to your right. Stay on the dirt road as it switches back up sharply to the right. Cross over a couple of dirt mounds in the road and look for a trail on the left. Head up this trail and bear right towards the top. You should meet the wall in the vicinity of the huge overhang near *Close Encounters With a Wench*.

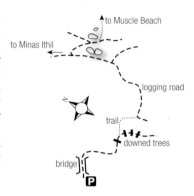

to Muscle Beach

to Minas Ithil

logging road

trail

downed trees

bridge

P

Conditions

Muscle Beach faces south and offers great winter climbing. It is possible to begin climbing near *When Gravity Fails* and work your way down the cliff, ending at *Close Encounters With a Wench* while staying in the sun all day. Most of the cracks at Muscle Beach turn to waterfalls during a heavy rain. *Rocket Man* is notorious for staying wet after a hard rain. Be sure to wear long sleeves and pants for most of the routes, and tape well. Socks are recommended if you're just learning how to climb wide and/or flaring cracks. When I was learning to climb offwidth, I even found it helpful to use iron-on patches on each side of my socks to protect my ankle bones. I looked like a scarecrow but it worked.

Close Encounters With a Wench

❶ **Minas Ithil** 5.2 R ★★

To locate this pinnacle, stay straight on the logging road before it angles sharply back right for the final stretch before the trail heads up through the woods to the main wall. Locate a groove to begin the route. Climb up the groove, then ride the blunt arete to the top. To descend, down-climb the route.
70 ft. *FA Unknown.*

❷ **Close Encounters With a Wench** 5.9+ ★★★★

As you near the end of the approach trail you should come to a huge roof above a house-sized boulder. Walk to the top of this boulder to reach the crack in the roof. Undercling, jam and armbar the crack to a ledge where you can bail out left to some rap anchors or continue 10 more feet to the top.
70 ft. *FA Martin Hackworth, Joe Pulliam, 1983.*

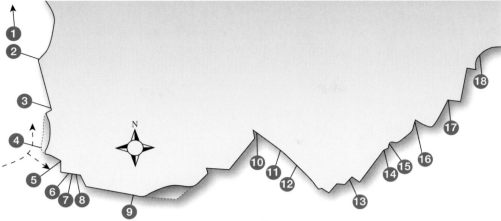

Muscle Shoals

❸ Casual Corner 5.6 ★★

Walk left and around the corner from *Close Encounters* to locate this wide left-facing dihedral. Rappel from a tree to descend.

45 ft. *FA Ron Snider, Martin Hackworth, 1982.*

❹ Carnivorous 5.8 ★★★

A great introduction to the routes at Muscle Beach, or for anyone wanting to learn the "art of the wide." Continue left from *Casual Corner* until the cliff rounds a corner and heads uphill. As you start to head uphill, look to the right for this short and wide crack just to the left of a large tree. Rappel from a tree to descend.

30 ft. *FA Ron Snider, Martin Hackworth, 1982.*

The remaining routes are located right of where the approach trail meets the cliff.

❺ Woman Trouble 5.7 ★

This wide dihedral is located 10 feet right of the large boulder beneath *Close Encounters*. To descend, rappel from the anchors above *Muscle Shoals*.

50 ft. *FA Martin Hackworth, 1983.*

❻ Muscle Shoals 5.8+ ★★★★

Throw your greatest bolt-clipping enemies at this one. Offwidth at its finest. Around the corner from *Woman Trouble* is a wide crack behind a boulder. Heel-toe your way up to a dog-leg crux, then dive back in for some ankle-thrashing fun to the ledge. Bring a couple of #4.5 or #5 Camalots if you want to stay safe. There are some horizontals inside the crack that take smaller cams, too.

40 ft. *FA Martin Hackworth, Ron Snider, 1982.*

❼ Coup de Graus 5.11b ★★

Directly right of *Muscle Shoals* is this bouldery finger crack. Climb to a ledge, then traverse left to the anchors above *Muscle Shoals*.

40 ft. *FA Dave Texter, 1999.*

❽ Cruising for a Bruising 5.8 R ★★

This route ascends the flake a few feet right of *Coup De Graus*.

90 ft. *FA Martin Hackworth, 1982.*

❾ Rock Rash 5.9+ ★★★★

This route starts in a low overhang directly behind a tree, before you come to a large rockhouse. Boulder the start and continue up the fist crack past a couple of bulges to the top. Remember to face left … or is it right? You figure it out.

80 ft. *FA Ron Snider, Bill Rieker, 1983.*

Rock Rash

Rocket Man

10

11

Surfing With Griz

13

⑫ Jaws 5.8+ ★★★

This route ascends the offwidth right of *Rocket Man*. Climb the offwidth and hand crack, with good help from a fat tree, up to a breather ledge. Take on the wide overhang and collapse on the next ledge. Belay from here. Climb up the remaining few feet to the top of the cliff. Rappel from a tree.

120 ft. *FA Martin Hackworth, Ron Snider, 1982.*

⑩ Last Wave 5.7 ★★

Walk beneath the large rockhouse and over some boulders. Head up the hill and follow the cliff for about 100 feet to a dihedral. Climb the dihedral to a ledge and belay. Continue through the chimney to the top.

110 ft. *FA Martin Hackworth, 1983.*

⑪ Rocket Man 5.8+ ★★★★★

One of the best fist cracks in the Red. To the right of *Last Wave* is an obvious wide crack splitting the face with a small bulge at 15 feet. Climb up to the bulge, then employ your technique and step up into the flaring and featureless fist crack. Reach deep for about 55 feet to gain a ledge with a small tree. Belay from the ledge. Bridge up the flaring chimney to a small roof. Duck and twist under the roof, then wrestle with the relentless finishing moves. Rappel from a tree to descend.

110 ft. *FA Martin Hackworth, Grant Stephens, 1983.*

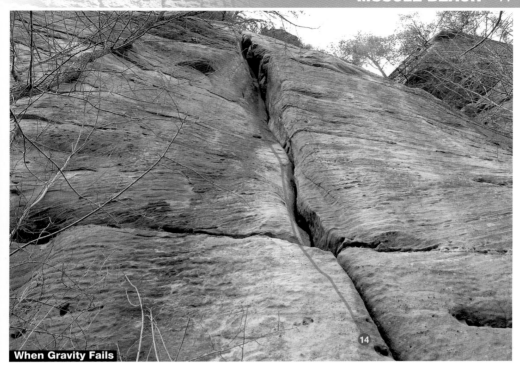

When Gravity Fails 14

13 Surfin With Grizz 5.6 ★★ ☐
Walk 80 feet right from *Jaws*, around the corner to a dihedral with a tree toward the top. Climb the chimney to the top. It is possible to place a 0.5 or 0.75 Camalot in the back of the beginning chimney. Otherwise, be prepared to run out the first 15 feet.
60 ft. *FA Martin Hackworth, George Robinson, 1982.*

14 When Gravity Fails 5.9- ★★★ ☐
Around the corner to the right of *Surfin With Grizz* is a left-angling hand crack to a flaring chimney. Climb the hand crack to the chimney. Jam or stem through the chimney and continue up the splitter to the top. Tape up, and beware of grabbing the dead tree. Rappel from a tree above the route.
80 ft. *FA Martin Hackworth, Ed Pearsall, 1982.*

15 Mama Told Me Not to Come 5.7 ★★★ ☐
If you're sick of offwidths, this will be a relief. Locate the dual crack system 30 feet right of *When Gravity Fails*. Climb the dihedral, the splitter, or both, up to a ledge. Walk over to the tree above *When Gravity Fails* to rappel.
85 ft. *FA Martin Hackworth, George Robinson, 1982.*

16 Lost Soul 5.9 ★★★ ☐
This route ascends the dihedral right of *Mama Told Me Not to Come* to some fixed slings.
50 ft. *FA Unknown.*

Grand Illusion 17

17 Grand Illusion 5.7 ★★ ☐
This route is located in the next dihedral right of *Lost Soul*. Climb the crack over a small overhang to fixed anchors just beneath a large ledge at the top.
60 ft. *FA John Bronaugh, Louis Petry, 1984.*

18 Bloody Fingers 5.8 ★★ ☐
Walk 100 feet right from *Grand Illusion* to locate a dihedral that begins above a short slab and some boulders. Climb the dihedral to a ledge with some slings.
60 ft. *FA Steve Faulkner, Dave Schoonerover, 1982.*

DIP WALL

all day | shade | 10 mins | 19 routes
5.6- .7 .8 .9 .10 .11 .12 .13 .14

Character

Dip Wall attracts a good bit of traffic. Although, like most crags in the Lower Gorge Region, Dip Wall has no sport routes, it does have two cracks *Green Eggs* and *Ham* that have become very popular for novice trad climbers. Also, don't miss the unique powerhouse route, *Winkin, Blinkin, and Nod*, a visionary line that follows a series of gashes, which provide handholds as well as great cam placements.

Approach

Drive down Forest Service Road 9B 2.9 miles to a concrete bridge that crosses Indian Creek. Park on the right before you cross the bridge, and hike across the road to a jeep trail. Follow the jeep trail until you reach a tributary. Cross the tributary twice and continue on the trail, keeping the tributary on your left. Eventually the trail cuts sharply uphill to the right. Continue on the trail, which eventually terminates at a horseshoe-shaped wall. Walk left past a huge amphitheatre housing two currently closed routes. Continue walking left to reach routes 1-7.

Those of us who have been climbing for many years in the Red remember attempting to find Dip Wall using John Bronaugh's first edition of *Red River Gorge Climbs,* only to end up completely lost after hours of searching. John later corrected his mistake for the second edition after he realized that the book read "left" where it should've read "right"! Now the approach is pretty tame and actually quite enjoyable.

Conditions

Dip Wall is horseshoe shaped. Fortunately for winter climbing, the east end of the wall, where routes 11-18 can be found, faces south. The western end of the wall receives more shade, providing cool conditions in the summer.

Access

On April 1, 2003, the National Forest Service closed off a section of Dip Wall for archaeological reasons. The closure affected two routes, *Seuss Seuss Sudio* and *Cindy Lou's Left Tube*. The closures are considered temporary, so these routes have been included in hopes that the section will someday reopen.

Sam I Am

❶ **Whoville** 5.6 ★★
Hike about 150 feet left from the end of the approach trail until you come to an open section with two obvious cracks. Climb the face and angle right to the crack.
35 ft. *FA Mark Schorle, Vicki Cullen, 1991.*

❷ **The Grinch** 5.4 ★
This route ascends the black dihedral just left of *Whoville* to a ledge.
35 ft. *FA Tim Stemerick, Mark Schorle, 1991.*

❸ **Sam I Am** 5.10d ★★★★
This route ascends the obvious left-facing dihedral 200 feet left of *The Grinch*. Stem and jam up to a hole, then layback to the anchors. Enjoy the runout! Rappel from bolted anchors.
60 ft. *FA Tom Souders, Jon Dinsmore, 1990.*

❹ **Logic and Proportion** 5.10a ★★★
Look for the plated face 40 feet left of *Sam I Am*. Eye out a line from the ground, then climb it using natural protection. Traverse right to rappel from the anchors on *Sam I Am*.
60 ft. *FA Tom Souders, Jon Dinsmore, 1991.*

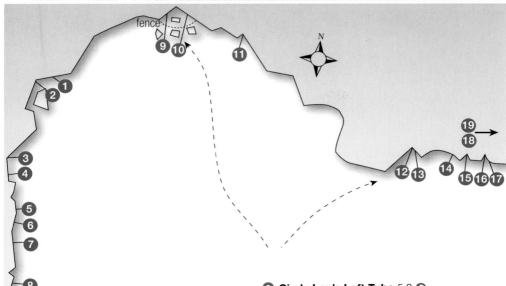

5 Hop on Pop 5.10c ★★★

Look for a large roof 70 feet up and split by a perfect hand crack about 75 feet left of *Logic and Proportion*. Begin in a chimney and climb up to a belay point just beneath the roof. Jam out the roof and belay at the lip to avoid rope drag. Continue up the offwidth, or dance around it to the top. Rappel from a tree to descend.
100 ft. *FA John Bronaugh, Ray Ellington, 2001.*

6 Griptospuridiam 5.11b ★★★★

This bouldery finger crack is located 25 feet left of *Hop on Pop*. Look for a finger crack splitting the face with a small bulge about 15 feet up. Climb up over the bulge, then enjoy moderate climbing to finish. Rappel from bolted anchors.
60 ft. *FA Tom Souders, Mark Schorle, 1991.*

7 Chickenhead 5.10a R ★★★
Better Than No Head

This crack and face route is 25 feet left of *Griptospuridiam*. Climb cracks, horizontals, chickenheads, and plates. Rappel from a tree to descend.
60 ft. *FA Bob Hayes, Dave Veldhaus, 1992.*

8 Winkin, Blinkin, and Nod 5.11d ★★★★

Walk around a corner 80 feet left of *Chickenhead Better Than No Head* almost to the left end of the wall. Look for a face with vertical gashes in it. Climb the face, angling left and placing pro in the three gashes: Winkin, Blinkin, and Nod. Gain a crack to the left and continue, with a big move, to the top. Lower from one bolt and slings.
35 ft. *FA Tom Souders, Jon Dinsmore, 1992.*

9 Cindy Lou's Left Tube 5.9 ⊘

Closed. Walk 150 feet right from the wet area at the end of the approach trail to two cracks angling away from each other. This route ascends the crumbling left-angling crack to some fixed gear.
40 ft. *FA Jon Dinsmore, Alex Cudkowicz, 1992.*

10 Seuss Seuss Sudio 5.3 ⊘

Closed. This route ascends the right-angling crack near a pocketed face right of *Cindy Lou's Left Tube*. Lower from fixed anchors.
40 ft. *FA Mark Schorle, Tim Stemerick, 1992.*

The remaining routes are located right of where the approach trail meets the cliff.

11 Purple Cleaning Company 5.8 ★

Climb the crack 100 feet right of *Seuss Seuss Sudio* to a ledge. Devise a belay anchor, then traverse right to rappel from a tree.
40 ft. *FA Pat Duffy, Lisa Souders, 1991.*

Griptospuridium

Green Eggs

⑫ Green Eggs 5.7 ★★★

Four-hundred feet right of *Purple Cleaning Company* are two cracks ascending a large detached flake. This route climbs the left side of the flake and thins down toward the top.
30 ft. *FA Roger Hausman, Mark Schorle, 1991.*

⑬ Ham 5.7 ★★★

Excellent first trad lead. This route climbs the flake directly right of *Green Eggs.*
30 ft. *FA Mark Schorle, Roger Hausman, 1991.*

⑭ Fox in Locks 5.9 ⦸

This route is closed. It ascended the crack 60 feet right of *Green Eggs* and *Ham.* Begin by climbing a thin crack up a ramp of sorts. Reach over an overhang to another ramp. Continue up the vertical crack to the anchors.
40 ft. *FA Mark Schorle, Alex Cudkowicz, 1992.*

⑮ Theodor Seuss Geisel 5.7 ★★

This is the next crack in the dihedral 30 feet right of *Fox in Locks.* Poor rock quality. Lower from fixed gear.
40 ft. *FA Unknown.*

⑯ The Lorax Tree 5.9+ ★★★★

This route begins as a splitter wide crack about 50 feet right of *Theodor Seuss Geisel,* near a corner and behind a tree. Climb the splitter hand/fist crack to a ledge. Continue up through the flaring offwidth in a dihedral to the top. Rappel from a tree to descend.
80 ft. *FA Kris Hampton, 2001.*

⑰ Star-Bellied Sneeches 5.8 ★★

This route ascends the hand crack in the dihedral 10 feet right of *The Lorax Tree.* Climb the crack to a ledge and traverse right to a rappel tree.
40 ft. *FA Alex Cudkowicz, Tim Stemerick, 1992.*

⑱ God Save the Queen 5.7 ★★

Walk around the first corner from *Star-Bellied Sneeches.* Start in the crack for one or two moves, then move onto the small arete with big holds on the left. Protect out of the crack, and climb to the big ledge. Rappel from a tree to descend.
40 ft. *FA Scott Hammon, Mark Strevels, 2000.*

⑲ One Fist, Two Fist, 5.8 ★★★ Red Fist, Blue Fist

Walk around two corners to the right of *Star-Bellied Sneeches* to locate this right-angling fist crack splitting a short slab. Rappel from a tree to descend.
40 ft. *FA Jason Burton, Steve Kaufmann 1999.*

Watch out for copperheads in the Red. Photo: Elodie Saracco.

20 UNTRODDEN CLASSICS

The Red can get crowded, especially at the popular sport crags. Here are some outstanding routes, both sport and traditional, that will get you away from barking dogs, screaming kids, and arguing couples. The lines either involve a long hike or are simply overlooked.

1. **Wide Pride** 5.10c, Lost Ridge ☐☐
2. **The Poacher** 5.11c, Lost Ridge ☐☐
3. **Diamond in the Crack** 5.6, Jewel Pinnacle ☐☐
4. **Long Live Trad** 5.10c, Jazz Rock ☐☐
5. **Electric Cowboy** 5.11b, Purple Valley ☐☐
6. **Mantel Route** 5.10c, Roadside Crag ☐☐
7. **Hemisfear** 5.11d, Roadside Crag ☐☐
8. **No Place Like Home** 5.11c, Emerald City ☐☐
9. **Yellow Brick Road** 5.11b, Emerald City ☐☐
10. **Game Boy** 5.11c, Long Wall ☐☐
11. **South Side of the Sky** 5.11a, Mt. Olive Rock ☐☐
12. **Dogleg** 5.12a, Bob Marley Crag ☐☐
13. **Soul Ram** 5.12b, Sky Bridge Ridge ☐☐
14. **Toxic Avenger** 5.10d, Wall of Denial ☐☐
15. **Central Scrutinizer** 5.9, Pebble Beach ☐☐
16. **Winkin, Blinkin, and Nod** 5.11d, Dip Wall ☐☐
17. **Rocket Man** 5.8+, Muscle Beach ☐☐
18. **Papa Love Jugs** 5.11d, The Far Side ☐☐
19. **Capital Punishment** 5.10b, Jailhouse Rock ☐☐
20. **Baptist Preacher** 5.6, Clearcut Wall ☐☐

The following cliffs have been removed from the print version of this guidebook. Visit www.wolverinepublishing.com/downloads for a free download of their information.

CLEARCUT WALL

MINAS TIRITH
This spire has one of the most popular sandstone tower climbs in the Red, *Minas Tirith* 5.9.

WILLIE'S WALL

BRIGHTON WALL

SYMPHONY WALL

JAZZ ROCK
Chek out *Long Live Trad* 5.10c. This splitter line on quality rock offers a little bit of everything.

BEAR WOLLOR HOLLOR

BETWEEN WALL

BACKSIDE WALL

LUMPY WALL

TEETH BUTTRESS

BOARD WALL

ASYLUM WALL

BLACKBURN ROCK
Features the beautiful and extremely difficult thin finger crack of *Stranger Than Paradise* 5.12c

BEE BRANCH ROCK

INDIAN CREEK

a.m.   shade   15 mins   32 routes   5.6- .7 .8 .9 .10 .11 .12 .13 .14

Character

Like its namesake in Utah, Indian Creek contains an abundance of quality cracks of all types and grades. During the late 1990s a number of difficult new lines were established, making the crag a crucible for hard crack climbing. *Country Lovin'* marked the beginning for a small group of climbers who began to incorporate exotic offwidth techniques to tackle the long-overlooked wide cracks at the Red. The line requires a good length of upside-down climbing to move out a roof too wide for anything but the feet. The technique was taken to the extreme in 2004 with the ascent of the largest offwidth roof climbed to date in the Red: *Better Red Than Dead.* This 20-foot exposed roof begins with a single fist jam, immediately widens to heel-toe width, then slowly increases to an upside-down chimney climb. Not everything at Indian Creek is desperate, and the cliff has something to offer every crack climber. Don't miss the comfortable hand jams of the perfect splitter, *Crack Attack.*

Approach

Drive down Forest Service Road 9B 2.9 miles to a concrete bridge that crosses Indian Creek. Continue 0.6 miles past the creek to a point where the road makes an obvious curve to the left. At this point you will see some wood pylons and a small trail, which becomes a drainage during heavy rain, leading to a campsite on your right. Park here and follow the trail straight back and past the campsite about 100 feet, to an old logging road that cuts up the hill to the left. Follow the logging road for 150 feet, then head up the hill to the right. Follow a faint path that angles to the right up the hill to reach a ridge. Continue along the trail, turning right at the top of the ridge, and follow it for about five minutes. Soon the small pinnacle at the end of Indian Creek Crag will become visible. TTo reach routes 1-19 (see map), walk left along the small pinnacle to a point where it meets the main wall. At this point it is possible to walk to the right and wrap around to the right side of the wall. This is where routes 20-32 are located.

Conditions

Indian Creek is a large, remote cliff. The distance between some of the routes, especially from route 25 to the final routes can involve lots of hiking and frustration. The wall faces just about every direction, so it is possible to climb in the shade or the sun. The right side of the wall receives excellent sun, while the left side tends to stay in the shade a bit longer. Many cracks can be mossy, but the established lines are mostly of great quality.

Dangling Angle

❶ It's Got It All 5.9 ★★
When the approach trail meets the island, head around to the left side of the main wall. Hike for about 400 feet until you see a set-back section of cliff with a car-sized hueco near the top. On the right side of this wall is a straight-in hand crack that terminates just before the hueco. Climb the crack to the hueco and rappel from fixed gear.
60 ft. *FA Chuck Keller, Steve Faulkner, 1988.*

❷ Dangling Angle 5.9+ ★★
This route follows the right-angling crack 60 feet left of the previous line and ends in the same hueco. Begin atop a platform and pull past some tough moves to get the first high piece of protection. Continue up the enjoyable hand crack to fixed gear in the hueco.
60 ft. *FA Steve Faulkner, Chuck Keller, 1988.*

Country Lovin'

③ Bring Out the Gent 5.9 ★

This is the wide crack in the main corner just left of *Dangling Angle*. Chimney to where it pinches down, then inch along until you can get back in and chimney to the top. Rappel from a tree to descend.
80 ft. *FA Matt Gentling, Bart Bledsoe, 2003.*

The next three lines can be accessed by tunneling through the crack at the base of Bring Out the Gent *to reach a tree covered ledge on the other side.*

④ Trunkline 5.8 ★

From the base of *Bring Out the Gent*, tunnel and squeeze through the crack to a tree-covered ledge on the other side. Move left to locate the next crack just behind a tree. Begin on the trunk, then stem off the tree to get established on the rock. Climb the wide hand crack to the top and rappel from a tree to descend.
60 ft. *FA Bart Bledsoe, Matt Gentling, 2003.*

⑤ Blissoming Into Manhood 5.9+ ★

Move right from *Trunkline* to the point where you squeezed through the chimney. Climb the offwidth up to a corner, through a small bulge, then chimney to the top. Rappel from a tree to descend.
60 ft. *FA Bart Bledsoe, 2003.*

⑥ Five Tree 5.7

The unattractive vegetated line to the right of route 5.
60 ft. *FA Unknown.*

⑦ Shit My Pants and Dance 5.10b ★

From *Bring Out the Gent*, walk left past two green cracks to a third crack, which is also a little green. Heave yourself off the ground and work up to a bulge, then fire up the corner and improvise a finish through the jungle. Rappel from a tree to descend.
60 ft. *FA Bart Bledsoe, Matt Gentling, 2002.*

⑧ Gumby In a Tree 5.9 ★★

From the previous group of routes, walk away from the wall and contour left past a green swath of rock. When the rock conditions improve, you will find this climb in a large corner. Offwidth to the top and rappel from a tree to descend.
70 ft. *FA Gehrig Austin, 1997.*

⑨ All In a Day's Work 5.10b ★★★

Immediately left of *Gumby In a Tree* is this route, which follows the wide crack in a shallow, acute dihedral. Stem, grunt, and slide to the top. Bring some large Camalots. Rappel from a tree to descend.
70 ft. *FA Ben Faber, Joseffa Meir and Eric Kampel, 1997.*

⑩ Number of the Beast 5.12c ★★★

From atop the large boulder just right of *Country Lovin'*, step across to a small ledge and begin this striking finger crack. Negotiate soft rock at the beginning, but reap the rewards after about 10 feet. At the crack's end, continue up a difficult face to the top. Rap from a tree.
50 ft. *FA Tony Frey, 2006.*

⑪ Country Lovin' 5.12b ★★★★

The wide crack just left of the previous route. Climb up through easy armbars to reach a spacious ledge just beneath a roof. Build an anchor and belay. Snag a bomber hand-fist stack in the roof the kick up over the lip. Climb upside down for a few feet, driving your legs as high as you can get them. Flip to a small crimp and crank through heinous gorilla armbaring to a large ledge and belay. Continue up through the chimney and crawl out of a hole to reach the top. Rap from a tree to descend.
90 ft. *FA Kris Hampton, Ray Ellington, 1999.*

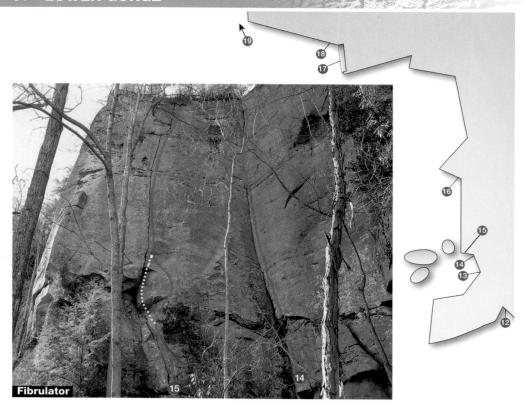

Fibrulator

⑫ Blood on the Nuts 5.8+ ★★

Head left from *Country Lovin'*, around the corner, and scramble up the gully to a small roof with a crack. Climb the crack to the roof, traverse left on the face, then continue up the corner and improvise a finish.

75 ft. *FA Chuck Keller, Jim Bailey, Steve Faulkner, Dave Foster, Dave Wilson, 1988.*

⑬ Over Easy 5.7

Walk left from the previous line and around a corner until you see a wall split by an obvious finger crack. To the right of the finger crack is a beautiful dihedral. Just right of the dihedral is an ugly crack with a low roof. Scramble up to the roof, traverse left, and continue to a ledge. To get down, squeeze through a chimney to the start of *Blood on the Nuts* then head down the gully to reach the trail.

40 ft. *FA Chuck Keller, Steve Faulkner, Jim Bailey, Dave Wilson, 1988.*

⑭ Jim's Dihedral 5.10a ★★★

Just left of *Over Easy* is a beautiful, long, intimidating dihedral. Claw through the dirty and wide start to reach the clean hand crack. Pump out for the remainder of the way and don't lose it at the awkward finish. Rappel from a tree to descend.

100 ft. *FA Jim Bailey and many others, 1988.*

⑮ Fibrulator 5.11b ★★★★

This classic line takes on the obvious finger crack splitting the face left of *Jim's Dihedral*. Step up to the roof, put in some gear, then work to the right and smear up to a ramp of sorts through a heart-stopping move, then step back into the crack. Continue up the pumpy hand-and-finger crack to a much-needed rest on a sandy alcove to the left just before the ending. Shake out as well as you can, then step back right into the crack for a powerful finish to the dirty ledge. Lower from bolts. Photos overleaf.

80 ft. *FA Tom Souders, Dave Veldhaus, 1988.*

Fibrulator Direct 5.11d ★★★★

Instead of moving right to get around the roof, negotiate a tough boulder problem to get through the roof. Bring a #00 sized Metolius cam or black Alien for the crux.

80 ft. *FA Ray Ellington, Kris Hampton, 1999.*

⑯ Drunked Up 5.11a ★★

Walk left and around the corner from *Fibrulator* to a wide dihedral with a small roof set back into the wall about 40 feet up. Climb hands and fists through dirty rock to a ledge beneath a small offwidth roof. Reach back over the roof, drive your knee into the lip, and press up into the wide crack. Continue up through the dirty but enjoyable offwidth to the top.

100 ft. *FA Ray Ellington, Bill Geimann, 1999.*

The remaining routes are located on the right side of the wall, which is accessed by walking through the passageway formed by the pinnacle and the main wall at the end of the approach trail.

⑰ Crack Attack 5.9+ ★★★★★

The route everyone comes here for. Walk about 250 left from the previous line to locate this perfect straight-in hand-sized splitter. Scramble up to a small platform beneath the wall to unpack and belay. Negotiate a muddy start to gain a ledge from which the real climbing starts. Pull past a low roof and launch into comfortable hand jams, which vary only slightly in size throughout the remaining 70 feet. Tackle the few feet of wide finish and lower from bolted anchors. No, you aren't in Utah!
80 ft. *FA Jim Bailey, Chuck Keller, Steve Faulkner, Dave Foster, Dave Wilson, 1988.*

⑱ Cave Cricket 5.10c ★★★

This is the crack on the opposite (left) side of the dihedral from *Crack Attack*. Scramble up and belay from the vegetated ledge. Starts as a nice hand crack and then shrinks to fingers for a few moves. End on a large ledge and rap from slings to descend.
45 ft. FA *Chris Esser, 2006.*

⑲ Made Me Sweat 5.8

Walk left of *Crack Attack* to the next corner. Seventy-five feet left of the corner is a rockhouse and ledge at 60 feet. Climb the cracks on the left to a V-shaped bulge. Negotiate the bulge on the right to reach the ledge. Lower from fixed gear.
60 ft. *FA Steve Faulkner, Chuck Keller, 1988.*

⑳ Indian Castle 5.6 ★

This route ascends the small island of rock at the end of the approach trail via a wide hand crack on the right side. To get down, locate a hole that comes out on the other side of the pinnacle.
70 ft. *FA Steve Faulkner, Chuck Keller, 1989.*

㉑ Slimy Creatures 5.7 ★★★

Walk right for 300 feet along the right side of the wall past the pinnacle to reach a right-facing dihedral. Climb one long, enjoyable pitch to reach the top of the wall. Rappel from a tree with double ropes.
120 ft. *FA Tim Schlachter, Chuck Keller, 1991.*

㉒ Gizmo 5.8 ★

This is the thin crack just to the right of *Slimy Creatures*. Climb the crack to a ledge, then work up and right through a slot and belay.
75 ft. *FA Steve Faulkner, Chuck Keller, 1988.*

㉓ G2 the Friction 5.8+ R ★

Walk right from *Gizmo* to a right-facing offwidth that begins just off the ground. Jump into the crack and follow it to its end. Wander right to a pine, then left to a flaring crack and the top. Runout in places.
90 ft. *FA Chuck Keller, Steve Faulkner, Tim Schlachter, 1991.*

Ryan Stocking taking big air on *Fibrulator* 5.11b, previous spread.
Photos: Dan Brayack: "That was such a scary sequence to shoot. I was like: 'Dude, get gear. Get gear! Get ...'"

24 Not Ice 5.12a ★★★

Walk right to the obvious large roof split by an offwidth. Beneath this roof and to the left is a short finger crack in black rock, with a small ledge halfway up. Step up to the crack and boulder to the small ledge. Continue up through a hand crack to a larger ledge.
60 ft. *FA Ray Ellington, 1999.*

25 Better Red Than Dead 5.12c ★★★★

This route climbs out the obvious enormous offwidth roof above *Not Ice*. Climb either *Not Ice* or the 5.8 crack directly beneath it (not listed) to get to the roof. Heel-toe and hand-fist stack out the roof until the crack widens to chimney size. Pull up into the chimney, then continue to the top. Rappel from a tree to descend.
150 ft. *FA Bart Bledsoe, 2003.*

26 Don't Come Easy 5.10b R ★

To the right of the previous lines is a low roof with two cracks. This route takes the left crack. Climb up to the roof, then traverse left. Pull over the lip to reach a thin seam, then stop at a ledge. Scramble right to a rappel tree.
65 ft. *FA Chuck Keller, Steve Faulkner, 1988.*

27 Another One Bites the Dust 5.9+ ★★

This is the crack just right of *Don't Come Easy*. Jam to a roof, work right through an offwidth, and crank over the lip. Belay on a ledge just below a rappel tree. Continue up a chimney, then take either the right or left crack to the top. Rappel from a tree.
130 ft. *FA Chuck Keller, Steve Faulkner, 1988.*

28 Curiosity 5.8 ★★★

Curiosity killed the cat ... and just about everyone's legs who has attempted to locate this route. Facing the Island, turn right and bushwack across the drainage to the next prominent buttress (500'). Hike up a breakdown between the main wall and the buttress to a hand crack on the right.
40 ft. *FA Chuck Keller, Steve Faulkner, 1991.*

29 Break the Edge 5.8+ ★

Several hundred feet right of *Curiosity* is a pair of short hand cracks. This is the one on the left. Jam to a ledge and rappel from a tree to get down.
40 ft. *FA Chuck Keller, Steve Faulkner, 1991.*

30 Don't Break the Edge 5.9 ★

Climb the hand crack just right of *Break the Edge* to the same ledge. Rappel from a tree.
40 ft. *FA Chuck Keller, Steve Faulkner, 1991.*

31 Orange Barrel 5.10b ★★★★

This excellent line is located around the corner from *Break the Edge*. Climb a finger crack and face to a small ledge with a fixed stopper and belay. Continue up the wide crack to the top. Rappel from a tree to descend.
100 ft. *FA Steve Faulkner, Chuck Keller, 1992.*

32 Lost Dihedral 5.10b ★★★

Just right of the previous line is this striking offwidth in a dihedral. Take it to the top. Bring some large gear. Rappel from a tree to descend.
110 ft. *FA Steve Faulkner, Chuck Keller, 1991.*

PURPLE VALLEY

all day

p.m.

10 mins

29 routes

5.6- .7 .8 .9 .10 .11 .12 .13 .14

Character

Purple Valley has a great mixture of moderate trad and sport routes with some beautiful topouts. The routes are well spaced, so even on a crowded day you can find seclusion. The classic 5.8 hand crack *Into the Purple Valley* offers exposed climbing on excellent rock and one of the most beautiful topouts in the Red. If you climb it in the spring, you will see why Purple Valley gets its name. *Burden of Dreams*, a fist-to-offwidth crack leading out of a 20-foot roof, is a classic that climbs too good to be true. If you've got enough juice left after *Burden of Dreams*, check out one of the best 5.11 sport lines in the Red, *Electric Cowboy*.

Approach

Drive down Forest Service Road 9B from its intersection with 9A for approximately four miles to reach a collapsed bridge. Park at the bridge and walk across the stream. Follow the road for about 150 feet and locate a trail on the right before a large boulder. Follow the trail through a short, muddy field, then head uphill to the wall. The approach trail meets the wall at the route *Coffee Talk*.

Conditions

Purple Valley is a good area for winter climbing. Routes 1-13 face south, receiving excellent sun; routes 14-18 receive afternoon sun only. Most of the lines are exposed, so the wall is not a rainy-day destination.

Coffee Talk

❶ Coffee Talk 5.10c ★★★

This is the first route encountered, on an arete where the approach trail reaches the wall. Overcome a tough start, then continue through a bulge and up the arete to anchors.
60 ft. 5 bolts. *FA Devin Pantess, Ray Pantess, 1991.*

❷ A Way of Life 5.10b ★★

Walk about 35 feet right from *Coffee Talk* to another bolted line behind a large tree. Begin on the right, then traverse left. Continue up past an old piton and three spinning bolts to the top. Walk off right to get down.
60 ft. 5 bolts. *FA Charles Tabor, Mark Williams, 1990.*

❸ Captain One Eye 5.10a ★★★

From *A Way of Life*, walk 50 feet right and up to a rounded arete with a large half-hueco near the bottom of its left side. Move right onto a slab, then head straight up the face to the top. Lower from bolted anchors.
70 ft. 5 bolts. *FA Mark Williams, Charles Tabor, 1990.*

❹ What About Bob? 5.10a R ★

Look for a 15-foot-high overhang with a large rock at its base, 50 feet right of *Captain One Eye*. Climb plates on the face left of the overhang to a ledge. Continue up shelves to a slot. Take the slot to the top. Rappel from a tree.
90 ft. *FA Bo Bohannon, Jamie Baker, 1989.*

❺ Candy Land 5.10b ★★★

Walk about 30 feet right from *What About Bob?* to locate this overhanging wide crack. Begin by climbing the left face of an arete, near a cave/overhang, to access a ledge where the crack begins. Sling a plate along the way for protection. Continue up the slightly flaring offwidth to another ledge, then take the chimney and face to the top. Rappel from a tree to descend.
100 ft. *FA Danny Rice, Paul Espinosa, 2003.*

Captain One Eye

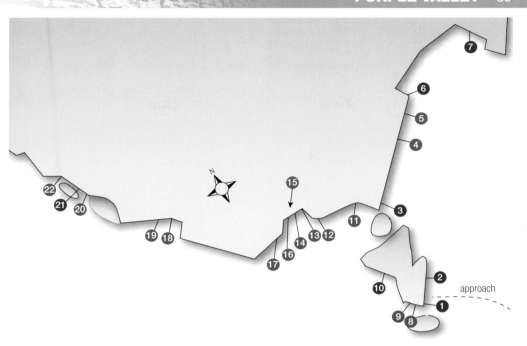

6 **Come in Your Lycra** 5.10b ★★★★ ☐

Walk right 20 feet and around the corner from *Candy Land* to an attractive, orange, east-facing face just left of a dihedral. Climb the face, staying right of the arete near the top.

45 ft. 4 bolts. *FA Gus Glitch, Alveno Ponns, 1990.*

7 **Hardman** 5.12c ★★★ ☐

Walk 75 feet right from the previous line to locate a string of bolts on a blank face. The bail biners on most of the bolts should give you an indication of the difficulty. 5.12c is an approximate rating.

50 ft. 7 bolts. *FA unknown.*

The remaining lines are located left of where the approach trail meets the cliff.

8 **Shish-kebab** 5.9 X ★★ ☐

This route is located just around the corner to the left of *Coffee Talk*. Climb an unprotected crux near the arete, then continue up with natural gear.

60 ft. *FA John Bronaugh, Jeff Ashley, 1994.*

9 **Pebbly Poo** 5.9 ★★★ ☐

Just left of the main arete is a face with one bolt. Climb the face, using natural gear and the bolt for protection.

60 ft. 1 bolt. *FA unknown.*

Come In Your Lycra

10 **Delusions of Grandeur** 5.11b ★★★★ ☐

Walk 25 feet left from *Pebbly Poo* and past a wide crack where two large boulders meet. Locate a bolted face with a boulder at its base. Climb to the top, using slab and big-move jug-throwing technique.

60 ft. 5 bolts. *FA Mark Williams, 1990.*

11 **Maybe, Maybe Not** 5.9 ★★ ☐

From *Captain One Eye,* on the main arete of the wall, move left 25 feet to the next crack. Climb the flake to a ledge, move out to the face for a few feet, then back to the crack and take it to the top. Rappel from a tree to descend.

70 ft. *FA Ralph James, Mitzi Henscheid, 1989.*

Til the Cows Come Home

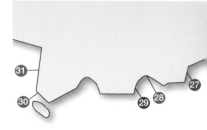

⑫ Till the Cows Come Home 5.12a ★★★
Rarely repeated. It's usually Elvis leg or lack of holds that thwarts most attempts at this line. Locate a blank face 40 feet left of *Maybe, Maybe Not* near a rounded corner. Make use of a pin, some bolts, and natural gear to climb this scary face. Believe it or not, this route was bolted on lead!
90 ft. 2 bolts. *FA Jim Link, 1990.*

⑬ Grunt 5.8- ★★
Walk 15 feet left from the previous line to the next dihedral. Climb the crack to a ledge then up through a hole.
80 ft. *FA Martin Hackworth, Bill Wade, 1986.*

⑭ Tour de Hooks 5.10d ★★★
Look for a high first bolt 10 feet left of *Grunt*. Climb to the bolt, then continue with natural gear and another bolt. Head right after the last bolt to a ledge. Finish on *Grunt* or *Hot Licks and Rhetoric*, or go left to a rappel station.
40 ft. *FA Jamie Baker, Jim Link, 1989.*

⑮ Hot Licks and Rhetoric 5.8 R ★★★★
Above and left of *Grunt* is a nice-looking orange dihedral. To reach the start, climb *Grunt* to a ledge, then move left. Make a scary step down and you'll be at the beginning of the dihedral. Climb the crack and face to the top, then head right to a belay tree. The crack is shallow in places, so don't expect solid gear the whole way. An alternate finish goes through the roof above the ledge with no protection.
95 ft. *FA Martin Hackworth, Tim Andriakos, 1986. Direct Finish: FA Tom Kwasny, 1992.*

⑯ Pleasant Surprise 5.11a ★★★
10 feet left of *Tour de Hooks* is a thin right-angling finger crack. Climb up to a low roof then pull over onto the face. Tread lightly to the ledge where *Hot Licks and Rhetoric* starts. Lower from chains.
50 ft. *FA Jim Link, 1988.*

⑰ Spinning Marty 5.9 ★
10 feet left of the previous line is a dirty hand crack that leads to the same ledge.
60 ft. *FA Chris Marchese, Russ Finch, 1987.*

⑱ Into the Purple Valley 5.8 ★★★★
Walk 150 left of *Spinning Marty,* around a corner and through some rhodos. Head back towards the wall and look for an obvious splitter with a small roof about 20 feet up. Scramble up the dirty start to the roof, step out over it, and climb the hand crack to the top. Lower from bolted anchors.
95 ft. *FA Martin Hackworth, Bill Wade, 1987.*

⑲ 5.11 Jimmy and Spike 5.10b ★★★
Go Craggin'
This route is located on the arete 15 feet left of *Into the Purple Valley.* Climb up to a horizontal slot and plug in some pro. Pull over the short roof and continue up to the fixed anchors.
40 ft. 3 bolts. *FA Martin Hackworth, Jimmy Guignard, 1989.*

⑳ Big Crack 5.6 ★★
Walk 40 feet left to a gully that leads to a ledge. Scramble up the gully and climb the crack just left of a dihedral.
40 ft. *FA unknown.*

㉑ The Love Shack 5.11c ★★★★
Great sandstone friction climbing. Smear up the face just left of *Big Crack*. The second and fourth hangers may be missing, but you can cinch the wires of stoppers over the heads of the studs.
30 ft. 4 bolts. *FA Tim Powers, 1991.*

㉒ Flaring Crack 5.7 ★★★
This short but enjoyable route ascends the left-facing crack just left of *The Love Shack.*
30 ft. *FA Unknown.*

Hot Licks and Rhetoric

Electric Cowboy   28

23 Off Width Your Head 5.7 ★★★
Locate a nice-looking hand crack that begins 15 feet off the ground, about 50 feet left of *Flaring Crack*. Climb up to the crack, continue to a ledge, and finish through an offwidth.
80 ft. *FA Jack Hume, Steve McFarland, 1994.*

24 Social Butterfly 5.10b ★★★
Walk 100 feet left around a corner to a flat area under a large overhang. This route ascends the short, slippery dihedral on the right to some anchors.
25 ft. *FA Steve McFarland, Tony Tramontin, 1994.*

25 Me-yommy V4 ★★★
Just left of *Social Butterfly* is a cave with a crack coming out of it. Start back in the cave from a good hand jam and continue out the crack, making liberal use of the left ledge for feet. Kick through at the end and whip around to some crimps on the face. Crank up to a good hand jam and stand up on the ledge. If you're bored, call out the left ledge for more of a challenge.
25 ft. *FA Kris Hampton, 1999.*
Variation: Ray Ellington 2004.

26 No Retreat 5.10b
Just left of *Me-yommy* is this crack system with a 12-foot-wide roof about 90 feet off the deck. Begin in the thin dihedral and climb to a belay ledge just beneath the roof. Tackle the roof and head for the top. Rappel from a tree to descend.
110 ft. *FA Jim Link, John Whisman, 1988.*

27 Anklebreaker V3 ★★★
Walk about 50 feet left of *No Retreat*, down a gully into a hallway of sorts. This problem climbs the obvious splitter finger crack directly in front of you to a ledge.
20 ft. *FA Scott Rennak, 1998.*

28 Burden of Dreams 5.11c ★★★★★
Keep walking left from *Anklebreaker* for about 100 feet. Look for a huge roof crack to the right of a bolted arete. Climb the left or right hand crack to reach a ledge beneath the roof. Belay here to avoid rope drag. Climb a few feet over easy shelves to reach the crack, form your fists, and step into the ring with the Mike Tyson of cracks. Fist jam out the roof and negotiate an offwidth section. Keep your cool for the final rounds and deliver the knockout mantel to the large ledge just over the lip. Fall over exhausted. Rappel from a tree to descend.
80 ft. *FA Martin Hackworth, Larry Day, 1987.*

29 Electric Cowboy 5.11b ★★★★
This route begins on the face 15 feet left of the start of *Burden of Dreams*. Climb the face, then make a commiting step left out to the exposed arete. Ride the arete, negotiating a tricky bulge at the end.
70 ft. 7 bolts. *FA John Bronaugh, Stacy Temple, 1992.*

30 Suckers at the Top 5.9
Walk along the wall 75 feet left of *Electric Cowboy*, staying on top of the ledge. Scramble up a short hill and walk through a passageway formed by a detached rock. As soon as you exit the passageway, there is a drilled pin about 10 feet up on the arete to your right. Climb to the pin, then step left out to a bolt. Continue up right to reach the top. Rappel from a tree to descend.
50 ft. 2 bolts. *FA Jim Link, John Whisman, 1990.*

31 The Bushman 5.8
This is the wide crack 25 feet left of *Suckers at the Top*. Rappel from a tree to descend.
50 ft. *FA Brian Temple, John Whisman, 1990.*

LOST RIDGE

a.m. / shade

25 mins   5.6- .7   .8   .9 .10 .11 .12 .13 .14

7 routes

Character

Lost Ridge is a large cliff in a remote setting. The wall contains a handful of climbable cracks, as well as a large number of moss-covered unclimbed cracks that would be amazing if they were clean. If you're an offwidth climber, you will salivate over *Wide Pride*, the 55 foot 4-5-inch crack splitting the featureless northeast face of Lost Ridge. This may be the purest offwidth line in the Red, requiring Leavittation techniques to reach the top.

Approach

Park in the same area as Purple Valley. The road is blocked by metal pylons, but continues on as a four-wheel-drive road. Hike past the pylons and over a mound of dirt. Continue in the same direction as the road, making use of a trail on your right to avoid crossing the stream. Cross the stream when you have to, about 300 feet from the parking area. Just before you are forced to cross again, look for a tributary known as Amos Creek on your left. Leave the road, cross Amos Creek, and walk north (to the right) up a steep ridge, through a limestone band, to a buttress. If you ended up in the right location, you will see an obvious crack splitting the wall, which is *Quality Crack*.

Alternate Approach for Wide Pride: Follow the approach above to Amos Creek, but don't head left up Amos Creek as you would for the approach to *Quality Crack*. Instead, cross the stream again and continue on the road/trail. Cross the stream two more times. About 500 feet after you cross the stream a fourth time, head off the trail to the left and cross the stream again. Wander up the hill near a drainage and past some boulders up a little higher. Eventually you'll see the cliff. You'll probably end up meeting the cliff about 600 feet left of *Wide Pride*. Hike to the right until you see the obvious wide splitter crack hidden behind a tree and a large flat boulder. Don't give up if you can't find it. The reward is an incredible climbing experience.

Conditions

Much of Lost Ridge faces north to northeast, so the wall does not receive much sun. Many high-quality cracks line the wall but due to the conditions, most of them are covered in moss to the point of being unclimbable. The lines listed are quite clean and well worth climbing. The approach can turn into a long bushwhack if you are not careful, but once you know the way it really isn't that bad.

Corner Cutter

❶ Quality Crack 5.10b ★★★

Follow the initial approach to reach the southeastern corner of the wall, where this line is located. The line is located directly behind a tree on an orange and grey section of the wall. Climb the wide crack to the top and rappel from a tree to descend.
70 ft. *FA Jim Link, Jamie Baker, 1992.*

❷ The Poacher 5.11c ★★★

This rarely climbed bolted route ascends the vertical face left of *Quality Crack*.
70 ft. 7 bolts. *FA Jamie Baker, Jim Link, 1992.*

❸ Tough Enough 5.10b ★★★

Walk left from *The Poacher* for about 15 minutes. Eventually you will spot this nice-looking hand crack. Ascend the hand crack with "reach-way-back" type jamming, then grunt up to the interesting finish. To get down, walk off left or rappel from a tree.
50 ft. *FA Ray Ellington, Michelle Artsay, 2003.*

The remaining lines are located right of Quality Crack. *It is recommended to follow the directions for the approach to* Wide Pride *to reach them.*

❹ Wide Pride 5.10c ★★★★★

See photo opposite.

④ Wide Pride 5.10c ★★★★★

Follow the directions listed in the approach for this line. Or, if you are hiking from *Quality Crack*, head right for about 15 minutes until you reach the line. The route ascends a 4-5-inch curving crack splitting the face behind a large flat boulder. Work your way up into the crack using a large ramp on the left for feet, then leave the comfort of the ledge behind as you dive into crack. Crawl your way to the finish using good handstacks and Leavittation technique. Abs of steel required. Rappel from a tree to descend. Bring several cams in the #4.5 to #5 Camalot size.

55 ft. *FA Ray Ellington, Michelle Artsay, 2003.*

⑤ Key Pebble 5.9 ★★

Hike about 300 feet right from *Wide Pride* and under a low over-hang. As you round the corner after the low overhang you will see a mossy face with a splitter crack, about 50 feet right of a dihedral. Climb the perfect hand crack, which cuts left through a short off-width section near the top. Rappel from a tree to descend.

65 ft. *FA Kris Hampton, Yasmeen Fowler, 2004.*

⑥ Corner Cutter 5.10d ★★★★

To the right of the *Key Pebble* is a nose-like feature hiding an acute dihedral. *Corner Cutter* follows this line up and through a large roof toward the top. Pull over a low roof to start, then continue up the sustained line to a roof. Traverse out the roof and move around the lip into a dirty and scary finish to the top. Rappel from a tree to descend.

55 ft. *FA Danny Rice, 2004.*

⑦ Boiler Room 5.10d ★★★★

From the previous line, hike right toward an orange wall on the other side of a large drainage. It is possible to follow the cliffline to reach this route, but it is easier to hike down to the drainage and back up the hill. The line ascends an acute dihedral with a low roof at the beginning. If you walk back into the cave at the beginning, you will hear gurgling water, which sounds like it is being boiled. Grab some holds and pull up into the crack. Continue up the sustained and pumpy dihedral, pulling past a couple of offwidth pods along the way. Keep it together for the final few feet of dirt climbing with not much protection, and bail left to a ledge before the top. Rappel from a tree to descend.

80 ft. *FA Ray Ellington, Michelle Artsay, 2003.*

Boiler Room

NORTHERN GORGE

Photo: Elodie Sarocco.

Character

If your rack has more cams than quickdraws, you will likely hit Fortress Wall at least once during your trip. The crag has many great climbs for both the novice and expert traditional climbers. Sport climbers should check out the classic pocket routes on the severely overhanging Phantasia Wall.

Approach

From Miguel's, head north on KY 11 toward Mountain Parkway. Pass under Mountain Parkway, then turn left onto KY 15 near the Shell station. Continue west on 15 for about a mile until you reach KY 77 on your right. Turn right onto 77 and follow this road as it winds through Nada Tunnel, past Military Wall, and crosses the steel bridge near the intersection with a 1067/FR 23. Bear right after the steel bridge, remaining on KY 77 until it intersects with KY 715. Bear left at this intersection and continue uphill to reach the first area listed, Fortress Wall.

Access

Most of the areas are located on Forest Service land, so please respect signs and fences indicating closed routes or trails, and read the guidelines for climbing on Forest Service land on page 32 of this book. Mariba Fork is located in the Clifty Wilderness area. Please pay special attention to additional Forest Service restrictions when climbing in Wilderness.

CLIFF	SUN / SHADE	HIKE	RAIN	ROUTES	GRADE RANGE									CLASSIC ROUTES
FORTRESS WALL page 96	a.m.	10 mins		34	5.6-	.7	.8	.9	.10	.11	.12	.13	.14	*Party Time* 7 *Where Lizards Dare* 9+ *Days of Rage* 12d
DUNKAN ROCK page 100	p.m.	10 mins		5	5.6-	.7	.8	.9	.10	.11	.12	.13	.14	*What's Left of The Beenling* 10c
PHANTASIA WALL page 103	a.m.	5 mins		17	5.6-	.7	.8	.9	.10	.11	.12	.13	.14	*Twinkie* 12a *Phantasia* 12d
SASSAFRAS ROCK page 105	a.m.	10 mins		2	5.6-	.7	.8	.9	.10	.11	.12	.13	.14	
MARIBA FORK page 106	all day	20 mins		10	5.6-	.7	.8	.9	.10	.11	.12	.13	.14	

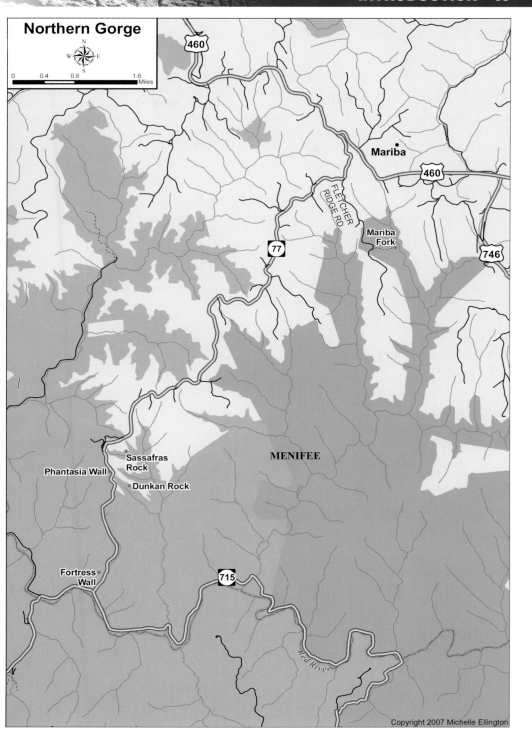

Northern Gorge

0   0.4   0.8   1.6
Miles

460

Mariba

460

FLETCHER RIDGE RD

77

Mariba Fork

746

MENIFEE

Sassafras Rock

Phantasia Wall

Dunkan Rock

Fortress Wall

715

Red River

FORTRESS WALL

a.m.   10 mins   34 routes   5.6- .7 .8 .9 .10 .11 .12 .13 .14

Character

Fortress Wall contains the largest number of pure traditional lines in the Red. The routes are great, the rock is clean, and the grades are solid. The intimidating and exposed corner of *Where Lizards Dare* offers incredible climbing on sun-hardened stone. Like many of the harder lines, it begins from the second tier splitting the middle of the wall. Most of the easier routes start from the ground and end at the second tier. *Bedtime for Bonzo* takes on two pitches of fun climbing and ends with a topout and a view of the Red that is hard to beat. *Days of Rage*, a recent addition to Fortress Wall and one of the most difficult cracks in the Red, will test every aspect of your crack-climbing abilities.

Approach

Turn right just over the steel bridge on KY 77. Stay on KY 77 until its intersection with KY 715. KY 715 heads right while KY 77 continues left and heads up the hill near a barn on the right. Stay on KY 77 for 0.3 miles until you reach the third pulloff on your right. Park in this pulloff and walk back down the road about 100 yards to locate the well-worn trail on your right.

Conditions

Most of the lines at Fortress Wall face southeast and get good sun until the afternoon hours. Many get some rain shelter due to the large roofs above the second tier. The large ledge above the lower wall may host several climbers and is covered by loose talus in some spots. Beware falling debris when walking along the base of the wall.

❶ Lost in Space 5.10b ★★★
This route ascends the left-facing dihedral 75 feet right of *Party Time*. Climb the dihedral to a ledge and belay. Continue over a roof and to the top. Rappel from a tree to descend.
150 ft. *FA Bob Molzon, Dick Shori, 1977.*

❷ Party Time 5.7 ★★★★
Fun multi-pitch climbing. As the approach trail nears the wall, look for the first trail that branches off to the right. Take this trail up to the wall and look for the first dihedral, about 60 feet right of an arete. Follow the crack to a bolted anchor on the first ledge and belay. Continue up the second higher quality pitch to a larger ledge a few feet from the top and belay. Rappel from bolted anchors. A single 70 meter rope will get you down.
140 ft. *FA Bob Molzon, 1977.*

❸ Brian's Farewell 5.9 ★
Follow the approach trail (do not take the right branch up to the previous routes) until it heads back uphill to the wall. Walk right and locate a section of orange rock with a finger crack splitting a short roof about 10 feet off the ground. Climb the crack to a horizontal then traverse left to the beginning of *The Rampart*.
35 ft. *FA John Lahr, Brian Bower, 1997.*

❹ The Rampart 5.8 R ★★
This route begins on a large block around the left corner of the main buttress near the end of the approach trail. Traverse right to reach the crack and climb it to a ledge. Move left to another crack and follow it to the end. Finish on a face to the top of the buttress.
130 ft. *FA Hugh Loeffler, 1985.*

❺ Route 49 5.8 ★
From *The Rampart*, head left and around the corner for about 60 feet to locate a large flake. Rappel from the anchors on *Horny Bitch*.
60 ft. *FA Bob Molzon, Dick Shori, 1977.*

❻ Horny Bitch 5.8- ★★★
Much better than it looks from the base. This route climbs the obvious dihedral about 20 feet left of *Route 49*. Begin by bouldering up to a ledge, where the route starts. Climb through interesting moves followed by good stances. You will reach a large ledge about 30 feet from the top with a wide crack on both sides. Climb the left side of the wide crack to a small ledge, then continue to the top. Belay from a tree.
140 ft. *FA Bob Molzon, Dick Shori, 1977.*

❼ Route 52 5.9
Head left from *Horny Bitch* for about 60 feet, past a left-facing dihedral, to the next crack. Climb the crack to a ledge and traverse left at the top to rappel anchors.
60 ft. *FA Bob Molzon, 1977.*

❽ Cussin' Crack 5.7 ★★
This route ascends a wide left-facing crack 20 feet left of *Route 52*. Rappel from the anchors on *Bombs Bursting* to descend.
65 ft. *FA Bob Molzon, Dick Shori, 1977.*

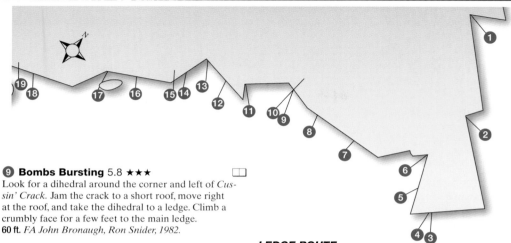

9 Bombs Bursting 5.8 ★★★ ☐☐
Look for a dihedral around the corner and left of *Cussin' Crack*. Jam the crack to a short roof, move right at the roof, and take the dihedral to a ledge. Climb a crumbly face for a few feet to the main ledge.
60 ft. *FA John Bronaugh, Ron Snider, 1982.*

LEDGE ROUTE
10 The Battlement 5.10c ★★★★ ☐☐
This route ascends the obvious roof on the upper ledge above *Bombs Bursting*. Climb just about any route on the main wall of Fortress to access it. Start in the thin crack and climb it to a ledge to reach the roof. From the ledge, reach out into the roof to place some gear. When ready, jump up into the roof and battle to the finish just over the lip. Rappel from a tree to descend.
50 ft. *FA John Bronaugh, Ron Snider, 1982.*

11 Route 48 5.5 ★★★ ☐☐
This route climbs the right-facing dihedral 30 feet left of *Bombs Bursting*.
60 ft. *FA Bob Molzon, Ray Rishel, 1977.*

12 Pigs in Space 5.10a X ★ ☐☐
This is the dirty face about 25 feet left of *Route 48* and 10 feet right of *American Crack*. Climb a short, dirty flake to a ledge. Climb right to thin edges and wallow to the top.
60 ft. *FA Unknown.*

13 American Crack 5.4 ★★★ ☐☐
If you didn't cut up early to reach any of the previous routes, you will be just left of this route at the end of the approach trail. Head right about 20 feet from the end of the trail (10 feet left from *Pigs in Space*) to locate this popular beginner's route. Climb a wide crack to a ledge about 15 feet up to reach a dihedral. Climb the dihedral with liberal use of surrounding face holds to a bulge near the top. Pull over the bulge to a ledge and lower from bolted anchors.
60 ft. *FA Bob Molzon, Dick Shori, 1977.*

14 American Wall 5.3 R ★★★ ☐☐
This route ascends the plated face just left of *American Crack*. Start by climbing the wide start of *American Crack*, then traverse left to a large horn. Continue up the face to a ledge and finish on a slab to the top.
70 ft. *FA Bob Molzon, Dick Shori, 1977.*

LEDGE ROUTE
15 Hollywood Boulevard 5.11a ★★★★ ☐☐
This route is located on the upper ledge above *American Wall*. Look for a right-facing dihedral that runs into a huge roof. Climb the dihedral to the roof, then undercling and crimp your way out to a belay on a ledge. The second pitch climbs out the overhang from the belay through some chossy rock to gigantic jugs and heel-hooks. Take this to the top and rappel from a tree for the descent.
90 ft. *FA Jack Dickey, Ron Snider, 1984.*

The Battlement

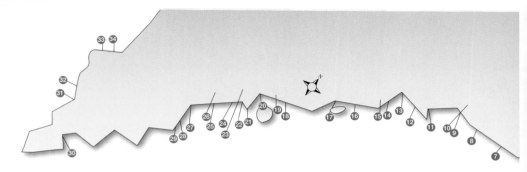

16 Calypso I 5.7 ★★★

Walk left from *American Wall* to the left side of the
rockhouse. Scramble up to a ledge 10 feet up and head
towards a flake. Take the flake to the ledge.
60 ft. *FA Bob Molzon, Dick Shori, 1977.*

17 Blue Runner 5.9- ★★★★

This route ascends the left-facing dihedral about 20 feet
left of *Calypso I* in front of a large boulder. Climb up to
the overhang about 20 feet up and move left and up to
gain the dihedral. Stem up through the dihedral, past an
obvious thin crux section, to a wide crack. Continue up
the wide crack to reach the ledge. Rappel from bolted
anchors. Bring a couple of #4 or #4.5 Camalots for the
wide section.
60 ft. *FA Ed Pearsall, Billy Bevins, 1979.*

18 The Wasp 5.10a R ★

Walk 70 feet left of *Blue Runner* around a corner to
where the trail squeezes around a huge flat-topped
boulder. Near the boulder you will see a dark face with
a short finger crack halfway up. Climb up to the finger
crack and continue to the top.
60 ft. *FA Tim Powers, 1990.*

LEDGE ROUTE
19 Thunder Chicken 5.11a ★★★★

This more recent addition to Fortress Wall is becoming
a classic. Locate a hand crack splitting a roof situated
on the upper ledge, about 30 feet right of *Where Lizards
Dare* and directly above *The Wasp*. Climb a short right-
facing dihedral to a ledge just before the roof. Place a
piece, then reach out into a good hand jam. Slowly creep
out into the roof, then reach deep for fist jams. Pull over
the lip and perch yourself on a small ledge. Become
the Thunder Chicken: look down at the other climbers
below and release a loud "*BRAWK!*" Continue up the
smooth hand crack and finish just before a large bush.
Be careful of loose talus on the ledge.
50 ft. *FA Aron Boyles, 2000.*

20 Calypso II 5.6 ★★★

Begin just left of *The Wasp* and directly in front of a
large flat-topped boulder. Climb up the right-facing
dihedral to anchors just before the large ledge.
60 ft. *FA Bob Molzon, Dick Shori, 1977.*

21 Lost 'n' Lichen It 5.10d R ★★★

Walk left a bit from *Calypso II* to an obvious arete before a dihedral. Climb the arete using natural protection.
60 ft. *FA Jamie Baker, 1989.*

22 Calypso III 5.5 ★★★

This route ascends the wide dihedral just left of *Lost 'n'
Lichen It.* Bring a couple of #4 or #5 Camalots for the top.
60 ft. *FA Bob Molzon, Dick Shori, 1977.*

LEDGE ROUTE
23 Where Lizards Dare 5.9+ ★★★★★

This classic, exposed line ascends the obvious orange dihedral, which starts on the upper ledge directly above *Calypso III* and about 30 feet left of *Thunder Chicken.* Climb
up an easy section to the dihedral. Reach around left
and step into the dihedral. Balance your way up the thin
fingercrack to a ledge with bolted anchors just before the
top. Photo opposite. The second pitch continues through
the thin seam in the roof to the top and goes at A2.
40 ft. *First Pitch FA Ed Pearsall, 1977.*
30 ft. *Second Pitch FA Greg Smith, 1984.*

24 Serpent 5.10b R ★★

This route ascends the face directly left of *Calypso III*,
making use of Tricam placements. Can be toproped from
the anchors on *Snake.*
60 ft. *FA Tony Bubb, John Cioci, 1994.*

25 Snake 5.8 ★★★★

Just left of *Serpent* there is a hand crack with a small
tree about five feet up. Chimney up to an awkward right-
leaning crack. Devise a way through this section to reach
a fun hand crack. Continue up the hand crack, then
make a big move out right to reach a large ledge. Lower
from anchors near the end of the crack.
60 ft. *FA Bob Molzon, Dick Shori, 1977.*

LEDGE ROUTE
26 Scratch Your Face 5.9+ ★★

This route climbs through a roof on the upper ledge
about 20 feet left of *Where Lizards Dare.* Rappel from
fixed gear.
40 ft. *FA Andy Shirk, Brad Shirk, 1997.*

Ben Faber, *Where Lizards Dare* 5.9+, Fortress Wall (opposite). Photo: Kris Hampton.

27 Bonzo's Revenge 5.4 ★

Locate a slightly overhanging dihedral 15 feet left of *Snake*. Climb the dihedral to a ledge and belay from a tree. Traverse left from the ledge to finish on the next route, *Fortress Grunges*.
70 ft. *FA George Robinson, Louis Petry, 1982.*

28 Fortress Grunges 5.4 ★★

It's a grunge, but combined with *Oozing Couth* you can reach the top for an enjoyable view. Climb the wide crack just left of *Bonzo's Revenge* to a large ledge. Rappel from a tree to descend.
70 ft. *FA Unknown.*

29 Oozing Couth 5.5 ★

This is the dihedral on the upper ledge above *Fortress Grunges*. Climb it to the top.
30 ft. *FA George Robinson, Louis Petry, 1982.*

30 The Turret 5.5 ★★★

Walk to the far left end of the wall to locate a large pinnacle. Climb up to a section between the main wall and the pinnacle near a tree. Continue up the face to the top of the pinnacle. Watch out for copperheads in the crack.
50 ft. *FA George Robinson, Martin Hackworth, 1983.*

31 Bedtime for Bonzo 5.6 ★★★★★

Walk around the left end of the wall past *The Turret* until the trail meets back up with the wall again. Spot the obvious left-facing dihedral directly in front of a small tree. Climb the ramp (5.4) to a large ledge and belay from bolts. Walk to the right and through a hallway to the base of the second pitch. Climb the right-facing dihedral to a hand ledge. Traverse across the hand ledge to a right-angling fist crack. Climb this to the top. Rappel from bolted anchors.
100 ft. *FA George Robinson, Martin Hackworth, 1983.*

32 Get Outta My Way 5.2 R

If you're in a hurry to get up to *Days of Rage* or *Afterburner*, take this line to jump ahead of the line for *Bedtime for Bonzo*. Start about 15 feet left of the first pitch of *Bedtime for Bonzo*. Climb up through dirt and stone to a large ledge.
40 ft. *FA Ray Ellington, Michelle Artsay, 2004.*

33 Days of Rage 5.12d ★★★★★

This difficult crack can be found by climbing the first pitch of *Bedtime for Bonzo*, then walking left around the corner. Follow the wall until you come to a roof about 15 feet up. Climb ledges to reach the roof. Power through the roof, then attack the overhanging fingers-to-fist crack. Rappel from a tree to descend.
50 ft. *FA Ray Ellington, 2004.*

34 Afterburner 5.11a ★★★

Just left of *Days of Rage* is a left-facing dihedral with a thin finger crack. Layback the finger crack to the top, using semi-challenging gear placements.
40 ft. *FA Jeff Koenig, Tom Souders, 1984.*

DUNKAN ROCK

p.m. 10 mins 5 routes

5.6- .7 .8 .9 .10 .11 .12 .13 .14

Character

Dunkan Rock only has five routes, but three of them are classics. *Frenchburg Overhangs* has introduced many novice trad climbers to horizontal roof climbing! Just around the corner are two of the best Beene cracks in the Red, *The Beeneling* and *What's Left of the Beeneling*.

Approach

Turn right just over the steel bridge on KY 77. Stay on KY 77 until its intersection with KY 715. KY 715 heads right while KY 77 continues left and heads up the hill near a barn on the right. Drive up KY 77 for one mile to a pulloff on the right, just past a sharp right turn. This is the same pulloff as Phantasia Wall. Walk back down the road a couple of minutes and try to locate a cliff off to your left. You should be able to see Dunkan Rock from the road. Before you reach another small pulloff, big enough for one car, head down a steep hill to your left and hike straight toward the cliff you spotted from the road. At the bottom of the hill is a creek. Cross the creek and head straight uphill. You should end up about 50 feet right of *Frenchburg Overhangs*. Head left until you see the obvious low roof marking the route.

Conditions

Frenchburg Overhangs faces southwest, so if you're looking for sun, hit it in the afternoon. The Beene cracks are on the north-facing side of the wall and make for a good escape from the summer heat. *What's Left of the Beeneling* can actually feel like an air conditioner in the summer due to its cave-like offwidth and chimney sections.

Frenchburg Overhangs

❶ Frenchburg Overhangs 5.8 ★★★★

When you reach the wall, hike left to a hand crack with a roof about 15 feet up. Climb the crack to a good shelf, scope some likely holds, then reach out and pull the overhang. Continue up the hand crack to a ledge. Take a breather, then move up the offwidth or stay to the right of it on the face holds to the top. Rappel, using two ropes or a single 70 meter rope, from a tree at the top. **130 ft.** *FA Tom Seibert, Larry Day, 1974.*

❷ Tom's Route 5.3

Walk right around the corner from *Frenchburg Overhangs* to a pair of cracks. This route ascends the crack on the left. Fight through rhodos to reach a ledge with a dead tree, then find a way down. **25 ft.** *FA Tom Seibert, 1974.*

❸ Joe's Route 5.3

This route climbs the crack about 30 feet right of *Tom's Route*. Don't expect anything better than *Tom's Route* except for the fact that it's longer. Rappel with two ropes from a tree above *Frenchburg Overhangs*. **90 ft.** *FA Martin Hackworth, Joe Weber, 1974.*

❹ What's Left of the Beeneling 5.10c ★★★★★

For the wide-crack connoisseur! Walk around the corner to the right about 200 feet from *Frenchburg Overhangs* to a pair of nice-looking cracks set back in a notch. This route ascends the wide crack to the left of an acute dihedral. Armbar or chickenwing your way up the initial offwidth to reach a narrowing chimney. Chimney up a good ways on large face holds as far as you can, then fight your way out an overhang into a wide fist crack. Fist or forearm jam up the wide crack to another overhang. Relax on good hand jams to the top. Rappel with two ropes from a tree above *Frenchburg Overhangs*. **80 ft.** *FA Jeff Koenig, Tom Souders, 1983.*

⑤ The Beeneling 5.10b ★★★★☐
This route ascends the acute dihedral to the right of *What's Left of the Beeneling*. Climb the right side of a boulder to access the ledge on which the route begins. Finger lock and stem the dihedral until it thins. Then either smudge to the top or step right to the arete to find a hidden hold. Rappel with two ropes from a tree above *Frenchburg Overhangs*.
80 ft. *FA Jeff Koenig, Tom Souders, 1983.*

THE BEENE CRACKS

Tom Souders and **Jeff Koenig** brought a new level to traditional climbing to the Red River Gorge in the early to mid 1980s. Both from Cincinnati, Ohio, these crack warriors started to take on lines that nobody else could accomplish. Jeff, with his graceful technique, and Tom, with his huge guns and amazing endurance, put up some of the best traditional lines in the Red, many of which remain testpieces to this day. These include *B3* (5.11b) at Long Wall and *Pink Feat* (5.11d R) at Military Wall. The two became known as the Beene Brothers due to Jeff, according to Tom, being "as thin as a beanpole." The nickname gave a theme to a series of classic climbs: the Beene Cracks. There are six cracks in the series, but unfortunately one of the best, *Beenestalker* at Military, is currently closed. If you want to send the others, they are:

Beene Material 5.10c, Military Wall ☐

What's Left of the Beeneling 5.10c, Dunkan Rock ☐

The Beeneling 5.10b, Dunkan Rock ☐

The Return of Geoff Beene 5.10d, Western Sky Bridge Ridge ☐

That's Enough of this Beene Shit 5.10d, Lower Small Wall ☐

3 **Twinkie** 5.12a ★★★★★

Walk around the corner about 150 feet to the right of *Creature Feature* and up a steep section to a flat area of rock. You will see two bolted routes ascending the steep face. This is the route on the left. Tech your way up the initial slab to reach the overhanging wall. Relax, meditate, count your draws, chalk your hands ... procrastinate. Eventually, summon the nerve to crawl out onto the overhanging wall and pump your way up one of the steepest 5.12s in the Red. 80 ft. 11 bolts. *FA Porter Jarrard, Chris Snyder, 1992.*

Collette McInerney. Photo Keith Ladzinsky.

PHANTASIA WALL

a.m. 5 mins

17 routes

5.6- .7 .8 .9 .10 .11 .12 .13 .14

Character
Phantasia Wall is right off the road and has a few good sport and trad lines. Its best-known route, *Creature Feature*, requires the climber to reach out over the lip of a roof, cut feet, and crank up on jugs to gain the plated face above. Pretty exciting terrain for 5.9! The wall also houses the incredibly popular *Twinkie*, a route that helped coin the phrase "overhanging jug haul" at the Red.

Approach
Turn right just over the steel bridge on KY 77. Stay on KY 77 until its intersection with KY 715. KY 715 heads right while KY 77 continues left and heads up the hill near a barn on the right. Drive up KY 77 for one mile to a pulloff on the right, just past a sharp right turn. Phantasia Wall will be visible directly to your left. Walk up the road about 50 feet to locate a trail to your left. Be careful crossing the road since vehicles coming down the hill may not see you right away. The trail meets the wall just right of *Creature Feature*. If you're headed to *Pogue Ethics* and the routes left of it, you may want to park before the main pulloff and hike up between two obvious drainages. This approach should dump you out near *Pogue Ethics*.

Conditions
Although I wouldn't call Phantasia Wall a rainy-day destination, it is possible to stay dry on the severely overhanging routes *Twinkie* and *Phantasia*. Expect early sun on most of the routes except *Twinkie* and *Phantasia*, which stay mainly in the shade. Many of the routes on the far left side of the wall tend to be a bit mossy and retain moisture after a good rain.

① Luck's Up 5.12b ★★
From the steep wall of *Twinkie*, walk about 200 feet right along a faint trail to a green, overhanging, plated wall near a corner with a horizontal band about 25 feet up. Pull big moves on sloping holds to reach the horizontal break. Step up onto the wall above and keep it together until the anchors.
65 ft. 6 bolts. *FA Porter Jarrard, Scott Lazar, 1992.*

② Phantasia 5.12d ★★★★
If *Twinkie* just didn't do it for you, then step a few feet right to take on *Phantasia*. Very similar to *Twinkie* but you won't find any fluff in the middle of this one.
85 ft. 10 bolts. *FA Porter Jarrard, Tim Toula, 1990.*

③ Twinkie 5.12a ★★★★★
See description opposite.

Twinkie

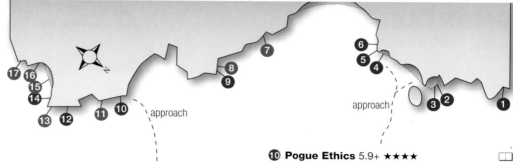

4 Creature Feature 5.9 ★★★★

This is the first route to your left at the end of the approach trail. Look for a plated face with a roof about 20 feet up. Climb up to the ledge beneath the roof, reach out over your head to find the magic holds, then pull the lip and continue on jugs to the anchors.
60 ft. 8 bolts. *FA Kevin Pogue, Elisa Weinman Pogue, 1991.*

5 Count Floyd Show 5.11b ★★★★

This route is located about 15 feet left and around the corner from *Creature Feature* (left of the approach trail), near an arete. Make your way up to the ledge, then pull up onto the wall and move right toward the arete. Continue straight up and past a faint flake to the anchors.
70 ft. 6 bolts. *FA Porter Jarrard, Mark Strevels, 1992.*

6 Creep Show 5.10d ★★★★

This classic line ascends a good part of the obvious rounded flake about 10 feet left of *Count Floyd Show*. Climb up to a ledge to begin, then reach up for some holds and crank through plates to reach the flake. Fight the barndoor to the anchors.
70 ft. 6 bolts. *FA Porter Jarrard, Jeff Moll, 1992.*

7 Le Petite Bazaar 5.5 ★★

From the previous lines, walk about 300 feet left, past an amphitheater, until you reach a short dihedral. Climb the dihedral, then figure out how to get down.
25 ft. *FA Dave Trowbridge, Jamie Elliot, 1992.*

8 Grand Bazaar 5.10a ★★

From *Le Petite Bazaar*, hike about 100 feet left to locate a wide and unappealing flake near an arete. Climb to a mossy topout and rappel from a tree to descend.
65 ft. *FA Dave Trowbridge, Scott Custor, 1992.*

9 Perverse Intentions 5.10a ★★

Just what were them perverts doing back there in them woods with that there power drill? Well, they weren't putting up a classic, that's for sure. If you're bored, clip up the face just left of *Grand Bazaar*.
40 ft. 5 bolts. *FA Tony Reynaldo, Richard Brashear, 1993.*

10 Pogue Ethics 5.9+ ★★★★

Either walk left of the previous climbs or take the alternate approach described in the directions to the wall. Look for a bolted line near an arete on a buttress with plated features. Work left around a bulge at the start, then wander up the long and enjoyable face to the anchors.
80 ft. 10 bolts. *FA Doug Hemken, Kevin Pogue, 1991.*

11 Bobsledding 5.7 ★★

Walk 50 feet left from *Pogue Ethics* to a crack with a low roof. Traverse out the roof, then grunt up and into the crack. Continue to a ledge and rappel from a tree.
60 ft. *FA Tom Seibert, Bob Hill, 1976.*

12 Lord of the Flies 5.8 ★★

From *Bobsledding*, walk about 75 feet left to a bolted face near a corner. Climb up the pocketed face to the anchors above a ledge.
40 ft. 5 bolts. *FA Kevin Pogue, Elisa Weinman Pogue, 1992.*

13 You Got Served 5.8 ★

Climb a hand crack to the left-leaning offwidth flake left of *Lord of the Flies*.
60 ft. *FA Scott Hammon, Scott Grass, 2004.*

14 Overlord 5.10b ★★★

Walk left and around the corner from the previous line to locate this fun and popular sport route. Make your way up the technical face on solid crimps to the anchors. There's crack just left of this which used to be listed, mistakenly, as *You Got Served*. The crack is dirty and not recommended.
50 ft. 5 bolts. *FA Terry Kindred, 2002.*

15 Attack of the Sand Shark 5.9- ★★★

Walk to the left of *Overlord*, around the corner to a dihedral with a roof at the top. Climb the left crack to a ledge, continue up the crack, and lower from anchors.
70 ft. *FA Jerry Bargo, Bridget Shoe, 1993.*

16 St. Alfonso's 5.7 ★★★

Walk 25 feet left from *Attack of the Sand Shark* to locate a nice-looking hand crack. Climb the crack to a ledge.
80 ft. *FA Eric Bostrum, Carol Beechy, 1976.*

17 Tomfoolery 5.5 ★★

Walk around the corner 40 feet left of the previous route to this layback crack.
25 ft. *FA Tom Seibert, 1976.*

Creep Show

SASSAFRAS ROCK

a.m.

10 mins   2 routes

5.6- .7 .8 .9 .10 .11 .12 .13 .14

Character
The main attraction of this small wall is a nice view from the top.

Approach
Park in the Phantasia parking area and head straight downhill to the right and back up to the crag.

1 Sassafras Tease 5.8 ★★★
This line faces the road and takes on a crack leading through rotten rock in the middle to an excellent topout. Rappel from a tree to descend.
90 ft. *FA Roger Pearson, David Gentry, 1986.*

2 Huevos Grande 5.10b ★
Walk right from the previous line, passing a dihedral, to another dihedral with a thin crack near a corner. Climb the thin dihedral up to a bulge. Crank over the bulge and continue up through the crack to a ledge. Head left to another dihedral and take it to the top. Rappel from a tree to descend.
90 ft. *FA John Bronaugh, Roger Pearson, 1986.*

MARIBA FORK

all day 20 mins | 10 routes

5.6- .7 .8 .9 .10 .11 .12 .13 .14

[Walkdown GPS 37.9002∞N, 83.5739∞W]

[Climbing area GPS 37.9004∞N, 83.5724∞W]

Character

Mariba Fork is quite a ways out from most of the other climbing at the Red River Gorge. Aside from being remote due to the long hike, the area is made even more remote due to the drive out of the Gorge required to reach it. The routes at this area are somewhat scattered, but are all on south-facing walls. The quality of the lines is decent enough to warrant a trip, but the beauty of the area makes it even more highly recommended. Mariba Fork has a magical feeling. While making the approach, you would swear that there is no rock in the vicinity. You then drop down through a hidden corridor opening up to a maze of tunnels and caves. The main wall is peppered with more large amphitheaters than any single wall in the Red. Although many of the lines are scattered, a couple of closely spaced good lines are *Laceration* and *Reach the Beach.*

Photo: John Borland.

Approach

Turn right just over the steel bridge on KY 77. Stay on KY 77 until its intersection with KY 715. KY 715 heads right while KY 77 continues left and heads up the hill near a barn on the right. Stay on KY 77 for about eight miles until you see Flecher Ridge road on your right. The road angles sharply back to the right. Turn right on this road and drive for about 1.3 miles. Look for Forest Service signs on your left. Shortly after you see the Forest Service signs on your left, look for a field directly after the wooded section ends. Park on the left and hike along the field, keeping the wooded section on your left. You will be following an old barbed-wire fence. After about 10 minutes the field will meet up with a wooded area. Continue on a trail through the woods, angling slightly left, until you reach the cliff's edge. Head left and look for an obvious dark and narrow corridor heading down to the base of the cliff. Continue down through the corridor and hike down to a creek. Cross the creek and head uphill to the base of the wall. You should come out of the rhodos somewhere near *Laceration.*

Conditions

Pay close attention to how you got to the climbing at Mariba Fork, because many people have gotten lost on the way out. My partner and I once left thinking I had found a shortcut only to end up being chased by dogs in the backyard of a family who were kind enough to drive us back to our vehicle. The drive back ended up taking 15 minutes. Add to that the fact that it was approaching dark, and we were very grateful that we found someone to help us. Don't expect to stay dry on any of the routes in this area. Although there are numerous amphitheaters, all of the routes are on the exposed vertical section of the cliff. The wall is south facing, though, so it makes for a great area to visit during the winter.

❶ Laceration 5.4 ★★★★

Look for a hand-sized crack splitting a slightly-less-than-vertical and jumbly face, directly beneath an overhanging orange headwall with two thin finger cracks. Climb the crack to bolted rappel anchors at the ledge.
50 ft. *FA John Bronaugh, Ron Snider, 1983.*

❷ Reach the Beach 5.9 ★★★★

Walk left from *Laceration* to locate a hand crack splitting the face about 15 feet up. Approach the crack by climbing a low overhang 20 feet right, then traverse left along a ledge to reach the crack. Climb the splitter crack to the ledge and belay from a single bolt. Rappel from the anchors above *Laceration*.
Variation 5.10a R: Climb straight up the wall beneath the crack on small pockets, with cams in horizontals for protection.
75 ft. *FA John Bronaugh, Ron Snider, 1983.*
Variation FA: Kris Hampton, Dave Texter, 1996.

❸ The Mayor 5.10a ★★

Walk a few feet left from *Reach the Beach* to a very short, overhanging dihedral. Climb the dihedral, then crank over a small roof to a single tied off fixed pin.
45 ft. *FA Ray Ellington, 1996.*

❹ Synergy 5.7 ★★★

Walk left from *The Mayor* for several hundred feet, past a very large amphitheater. Directly past the amphitheater is a nice-looking dihedral. Climb the dihedral to a ledge, then move right to a large tree and belay. Continue up a flake to a ledge near a crack splitting the roof and bail right to the top of the cliff.
Variation 5.10b: Climb through the splitter crack in the roof.
130 ft. *FA Whit Bronaugh, John Bronaugh, 1984.*

The remaining lines are located right of the first route, Laceration.

❺ Leo 5.5 R

Walk right from *Laceration* under a high roof to locate this right-facing dihedral. Climb the flake to the top.
80 ft. *FA John Bronaugh, Tina Feezel, 1987.*

❻ Rock Lobster 5.8 ★★

Walk right from *Leo* past a large amphitheater. Continue walking until you see a dihedral with a very thin seam. Look at the dihedral and wish it would take gear. Continue around the next corner to locate the next dihedral that does take gear. Climb the dihedral to a dirty finish. Rappel from a tree to descend.
75 ft. *FA Ron Snider, John Bronaugh, 1983.*

❼ Heartbreak of Psoriasis 5.4 ★★

Walk around the next corner right of *Rock Lobster* to locate this flake, just left of an offwidth. Climb to the top and rappel from a tree to descend.
60 ft. *FA John Bronaugh, Ron Snider, 1983.*

❽ The Gauntlet 5.10a ★★★

Walk right from *Heartbreak of Psoriasis*, past the offwidth, to a set of nice-looking twin cracks. Begin the route by chimneying up to the roof. Undercling through the roof, then pull around the lip to cleaner rock. Belay there to avoid rope drag. Continue up the left crack for a bit, then shift over to the right crack for a ride to the top.
80 ft. *FA Ron Snider, John Bronaugh, 1983.*

❾ One Thing Leads to Another 5.8 ★

Walk right from *The Gauntlet* to locate a right-leaning dihedral. If you reach another amphitheater, you've gone too far. Climb the dihedral to reach a plated orange face on the right. Continue up the face, then step back into the crack towards the top when the crack shifts left. Climb over a bulge, then continue to the top.
100 ft. *FA Whit Bronaugh, John Bronaugh, 1984.*

❿ Second Thoughts 5.8 ★

Walk right from *One Thing Leads to Another*, past a large amphitheater, to a dihedral before another amphitheater. Climb the dihedral to a large hueco, pull an overhang, then continue up the crack and face to a stance. Face climb using protection in pockets for about 15 feet. Move back into the dihedral and climb to the top.
70 ft. *FA John Bronaugh, Louis Petry, 1984.*

MIDDLE GORGE

Character

This region has mostly traditional crags, and some great ones at that. The deceivingly named Small Walls have many multi-pitch routes and some of the longest climbs in the Red. Hen's Nest is a good dry bet for wet-weather crack climbing.

Approach

The cliffs of the Middle Gorge Region border the Red River. Most are a short hike up the steep hill that borders KY 715 as it winds along the river. From Miguel's, head north on KY 11 toward Mountain Parkway. Pass under Mountain Parkway, then turn left onto KY 15 near the Shell station. Continue west on 15 for about a mile until you reach KY 77 on your right. Turn right onto 77 and follow this road through Nada Tunnel, past Military Wall, and across the steel bridge. Bear right after the steel bridge, remaining on KY 77 until it intersects with KY 715. Turn right onto 715 to reach the areas of the Middle Gorge region.

Access

Most of the areas are located on Forest Service land, so please respect signs and fences indicating closed routes or trails and read the guidelines for climbing on Forest Service land on page 32 of this book. Tower Rock and the Small Walls are located in the Clifty Wilderness area. Please pay special attention to additional Forest Service restrictions when climbing in wilderness.

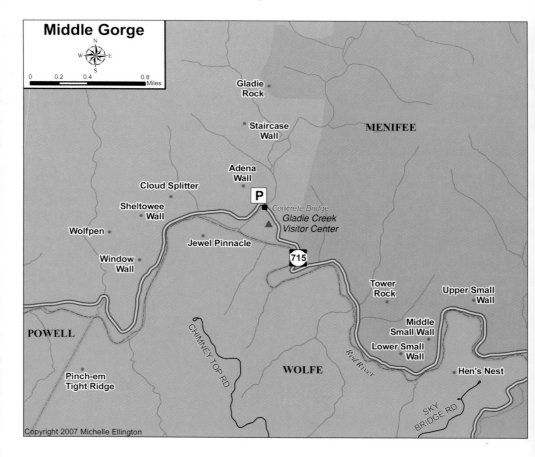

CLIFF	SUN / SHADE	HIKE	RAIN	ROUTES	GRADE RANGE		CLASSIC ROUTES
WOLFPEN page 112	a.m.	25 mins		5	5.6- .7 .8 .9 .10 .11 .12 .13 .14		
WINDOW WALL page 112	a.m.	10 mins		4	5.6- .7 .8 .9 .10 .11 .12 .13 .14		
PINCH EM TIGHT 112	shade	30 mins		5	5.6- .7 .8 .9 .10 .11 .12 .13 .14		
SHELTOWEE WALL page 112		15 mins		1	5.6- .7 .8 .9 .10 .11 .12 .13 .14		
ADENA WALL page 112	a.m.	10 mins		2	5.6- .7 .8 .9 .10 .11 .12 .13 .14		
STAIRCASE WALL page 112	all day	30 mins		6	5.6- .7 .8 .9 .10 .11 .12 .13 .14		
GLADIE ROCK page 112	all day	15 mins		1	5.6- .7 .8 .9 .10 .11 .12 .13 .14		
JEWEL PINNACLE page 112	a.m.	20 mins		4	5.6- .7 .8 .9 .10 .11 .12 .13 .14		*Diamond in the Crack* 5.6
TOWER ROCK page 114	all day / shade	10 mins		36	5.6- .7 .8 .9 .10 .11 .12 .13 .14		*Caver's Route* 5.3 R *Arachnid* 5.8
LOWER SMALL WALL page 119	all day	10 mins		22	5.6- .7 .8 .9 .10 .11 .12 .13 .14		*Dicey at Best* 5.8+
MIDDLE SMALL WALL page 122	a.m.	10 mins		12	5.6- .7 .8 .9 .10 .11 .12 .13 .14		*The Quest* 10c
UPPER SMALL WALL page 124	all day	15 mins		2	5.6- .7 .8 .9 .10 .11 .12 .13 .14		
HEN'S NEST page 126	all day	30 mins	rain OK	17	5.6- .7 .8 .9 .10 .11 .12 .13 .14		

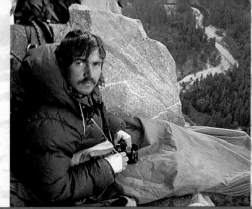

Photo: Larry Day Collection.

PROFILE: Old school

Larry Day was one of the first climbers to realize the staggering potential of the Red River Gorge. His first ascents date back to the early 1970s, and many remain classics to this day. Some of his best include *Jungle Beat* at Military Wall and *Insanity Ceiling* at Tower Rock. Attitudes towards ethics and goals have changed quite a bit since the 1970s. For Larry, the best lines all had one thing in common — they had to go to the top. Ol' "Layback Larry" now lives in Bozeman, Montana, but is still a regular contributor to www.redriverclimbing.com, where he offers recollections of early first ascents as if they happened only yesterday.

LARRY ON RATING A ROUTE

"Not only can you rate climbs without sending them, you can downrate climbs that you've never even been on! Gets done all the time. And if you are surprised to flail on a route that you thought you'd hike, then it's an automatic sandbag... way underrated. See, this rating business is easy."

LARRY ON ETHICS

"The one thing that I'd like to communicate is that preserving the particular and unique beauty of the Red River climbing experience was foremost in the minds of even those of us who were most desirous of bagging the best lines. We were so determined not to spoil the place we loved that we refused even the temptation of chalk. If we couldn't do a route without chalk, then it would just have to stand until we could.

We were not absolutely against bolting, but we would never have committed the grid bolting horrors that happened later."

LARRY ON JODIE FOSTER

"Jodie looks like her skin is on way too tight, kind of mummified looking if you ask me. Or maybe like she just got finished sucking on something real sour."

LARRY ON SANDBAGGING
(from www.kywilderness.com)

"So, as far as sandbagging in the Gorge goes, I plead not guilty. It's true we were using Seneca as a general standard. Most of us had never climbed in the Gunks, but we understood that the ratings there were pretty stiff. We weren't trying to be falsely modest either, but with a rating scale that only had four grades above 5.7 we figured we'd better not rate the stuff we were doing too highly. It wasn't until we started traveling West that we realized some of the Seneca grades were stiff to the point of being laughable. We used to sit around and speculate as to the reasons for this. I have a few good theories, but won't go into that now. So in general I'd say that the ratings of classic routes in the Gorge were pretty consistent with other Eastern routes of the same era (if not quite as wacky as some of the more obscure Seneca routes). So while I must confess that I do enjoy the sandbagger reputation, it really ain't so." ■

JEWEL PINNACLE

a.m. 20 mins   4 routes
5.6- .7 .8 .9 .10 .11 .12 .13 .14

Character
This pinnacle of rock can be seen by looking off to the right just before crossing the bridge near the Gladie Creek Visitor Center on KY 715. One of the most asthetic and moderate multi-pitch traditional lines in the Red, *Diamond in the Crack,* ascends this pinnacle, offering a great view and wonderful exposure.

Approach
Drive 3.1 miles down KY 715 from its intersection with KY 77 and park in a parking lot on the left just before a bridge. Cross the road and hike across a field to the river. Locate a low spot in the river and cross. Head straight up the hill to reach the pinnacle. You should end up directly beneath *Diamond in the Crack.*

Conditions
The approach is somewhat difficult, but only adds to the experience of climbing *Diamond in the Crack.* The river crossing can be pretty high during the winter and spring.

1 Seibert Route 5.8 ★
Walk around to the right side of the pinnacle and locate a left-leaning, fat, overhanging flake beginning on a ledge near the top.
60 ft. *FA Tom Seibert, Ellen Seibert, 1973.*

2 Diamond in the Crack 5.6 ★★★★★
This classic crack system is located on the north face of the pinnacle (facing the parking area). Climb a dirty crack to a ledge and belay. Take the clean dihedral to the top, passing a small roof on the way. Enjoy the wonderful top-out. To descend, turn around so the visitor center is to your back. Walk and scramble down to the left, then continue walking back until you see a steep trail to your left. Rappelling from the bolts is not recommended. Many people have had their rope stuck due to the distance the anchors are set back from the edge.
120 ft. *FA Larry Day, Tom Seibert, Bob Hill, Eric Bostrum, 1974.*

3 Kool Aid 5.11b ★★★★
This route ascends the beautiful splitter finger crack just left of the first pitch of *Diamond in the Crack.* Balance your way up the off-fingers crack then make a big move left to a ledge. Gain a heel hook and crank up into the finishing moves. Rappel from a tree.
80 ft. *FA Greg Smith, 1985.*

4 Copperhead 5.6 ★★★
This route ascends the wide crack around the corner left from *Kool Aid.*
70 ft. *FA Larry Day, Bob Compton, 1974.*

The following cliffs have been removed from the print version of this guidebook. Visit www.wolverinepublishing.com/downloads for a free download of the information for them.

WOLFPEN

WINDOW WALL

PINCH EM TIGHT RIDGE

SHELTOWEE WALL

ADENA WALL

STAIRCASE WALL

GLADIE ROCK

TOWER ROCK

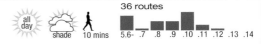

all day · shade · 10 mins · 36 routes · 5.6- .7 .8 .9 .10 .11 .12 .13 .14

Character

This traditional area contains numerous easy and moderate crack climbs and a large number of bold routes with little or no protection. Glance through the routes and you will notice the letters "R" and "X" more than at any other wall in the Red. Most of the lines go to the flat summit, offering a beautiful view of the area. With just a few pieces of gear, it is possible to follow many of the wandering lines at Tower Rock, providing the beginning leader with the full experience of a nice hike, a wonderful climb, and a beautiful top-out. Many of the routes are accessed by climbing the first pitch of another route, then traversing along a ledge. In addition, many lines join up with each other in order to finish at the summit. A few of the shorter "X-rated" routes may as well be referred to as boulder problems. Since the time of the first ascent, the advent of beefy crash pads has blurred the thin line between a short solo and a highball boulder problem. The routes in question remain with their original Yosemite Decimal System rating and referred to as X-rated traditional climbs. At 5.8 and 5.9, *Africa* and *Arachnid* are two of the most popular and intimidating crack climbs of their grade in the Red. *Arachnid*, first put up in 1974, was *the* route to bag back in the days before sticky rubber and #5 Camalots. To this day, it can still bring the Elvis leg out of even the most competent climbers. *Africa*, a tight hand crack splitting a featureless face, leaves most beginning crack climbers searching frantically for even the smallest handhold. If only for the historical nature of the route alone, every Red River trad climber must do *Caver's Route*. The line is easy, long, fun, and probably first climbed in the 1950s.

Approach

From the intersection of KY 77 with KY 715 near Fortress Wall, stay on 715 for 4.4 miles (one mile past the bridge over Gladie Creek) to a pulloff on your right. Walk back down the road in the direction you came for 150 feet to locate the trailhead for Tower Rock. There will be a small wooden Forest Service sign indicating the trailhead. Follow the trail as it winds uphill past some boulders. When the trail takes an obvious sharp right turn, locate a faint trail to the left that leads up to the first three listed routes. To reach the main pinnacle where the remaining lines are located, stay on the trail until it forks. The trail loops around the pinnacle, so take either fork. The initial routes listed are on the right side of the wall.

Conditions

Tower Rock is a pinnacle with routes on all sides, so it is possible to avoid or chase the sun all day. The quality of the rock is excellent, but some of the easier lines are very wandering and may have you climbing over rhodos and muddy cracks to reach the top. The vertical nature of the walls doesn't make for good rainy-day climbing, so avoid the area during wet weather. The top of Tower Rock is somewhat bare, so the opportunities for descent aren't abundant. However, there are many tree-covered ledges on the northwest side of the tower, from which it is possible to rappel with a single 60-meter rope. The ledges are 10 to 15 feet below the summit. Most people find a strong rhodo bush as rappel backup and bushwhack the short distance down to any of the ledges. There is also a good hemlock to rappel from in the middle of the east side of the tower about 50 feet south of *Arachnid*.

Access

Tower Rock has been subject to partial closures in the past, and this is currently the case. During the late 1980s, the area caught fire due to a careless camper and was closed to climbing to allow the vegetation to recover. A few years ago, a small boulder containing a few problems was closed off to protect sensitive archaeological/biological resources. Just this year, the first two routes listed below were also closed to protect sensitive archaeological/biological resources. Please respect the closures and do not climb the closed routes. There are plenty of other routes to climb and the closed lines aren't the best anyway.

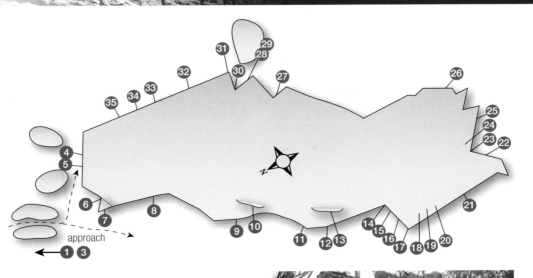

South of Zimbabwe

1 Crankenstein 5.10b ⊘
This route is closed. To locate this route, take the first trail mentioned in the approach directions. This trail branches off left of the main trail before it reaches Tower Rock. Take this trail to the end and walk a few feet left. Look for an obvious hand crack ending on a ledge. Begin by climbing the face until you can reach over to the crack for some protection. Continue to the ledge.
90 ft. *FA Jeff Koenig, Tom Souders, 1984.*

2 Courtesy Cringe 5.8+ ⊘
This route is closed. It ascends the arching crack just right of *Crankenstein*. Watch for loose blocks.
80 ft. *FA Kris Hampton, Tony Ulrich, 1997.*

3 The Cutting Board 5.11c ★
Walk 300 feet left of *Crankenstein* to locate this route. Look for an angling roof to a dihedral about 10 feet off the ground. Skate out the low roof and pull over the lip into the finger crack. Rappel from a tree to descend.
60 ft. *FA Jeff Koenig, Tom Souders, 1985.*

4 South of Zimbabwe 5.10d R ★★★
When you reach the north face of the pinnacle, take the right fork and walk left around a corner to locate a blank face with a single old bolt in the middle. Climb up to the bolt, then move left and up over small edges to a break just left of a triangular roof. Bring small cams and stoppers for additional protection. To descend, head to the right to reach the second set of rappel anchors mentioned in the introduction.
50 ft. 1 bolt. *FA Martin Hackworth, Grant Stephens, 1985.*

5 Heart of Darkness 5.10c ★★★
This route climbs the same face as *South of Zimbabwe*, but angles up and right after the bolt to horizontals. Get some protection and move up a flake and crank to the top. Bring small cams and stoppers for protection. Descend the same as the previous line.
Variation: 5.11b X ★★★
Begin on the arete to the right of the original start, climb up to a ledge, then crimp up to the horizontals for protection.
60 ft. *FA Grant Stephens, 1985.*

6 Delta Blow 5.10b X ★★
When Martin Hackworth first attempted this problem, a 20-pound flake broke off and he smacked the ground flat on his back! No bouldering pad, of course. This problem ascends a flake in a vague dihedral 20 feet right of the arete near *Heart of Darkness* and just left of a six-foot-high roof. Climb the flake, move right, and head for a ledge.
40 ft. *FA Martin Hackworth, 1985.*

Delta Blow

6 7

7 Anything You Want 5.9+ X ★★

Begin at the far corner of the six-foot-high roof mentioned in the previous route description. Reach up for some holds and continue up the face to a ledge.
40 ft. *FA Grant Stephens, 1985.*

8 Mighty Eidson 5.4 ★★★

Begin in the wide crack 30 feet right of *Delta Blow*. Climb a tough beginning to easier moves that lead to a ledge. Belay here, then scramble back to a ledge system. Head right along the ledge to join up with the last pitch of *Groundhog,* which takes a short slot to the top of the pinnacle. To descend, follow the directions in the introduction.
120 ft. *FA Bill Eidson, Nancy Eidson, 1974.*

9 The Grunges 5.2

This route ascends any of the three closely spaced and extremely dirty cracks 30 feet right of *Mighty Eidson* to a ledge. Continue to the top via last pitch of *Groundhog* if preferred.
25 ft. *FA Unknown.*

10 Green Grease 5.8+ ★★★

Climb the previous route to the ledge 25 feet up. Locate a nice-looking hand crack on the right face to a ledge. Rappel here or continue up the final pitch of *Groundhog* to reach the summit.
30 ft. *FA Ed Pearsall, Billy Bevins, 1980.*

11 Salad Days 5.6 ★★★

Walk 25 feet right of *The Grunges* to a corner to locate this crack. Climb to a ledge and rappel, or continue up the final pitch of *Groundhog* to reach the summit.
70 ft. *FA Doug Hemken, Jeff Hemken, 1979.*

12 Groundhog 5.6 ★★★

This route climbs the wide crack about 15 feet right of *Salad Days* to a ledge. Belay from the ledge. Climb up and left to another ledge and belay. Traverse left 100 feet along a ledge and summit via a short slot above *Mighty Eidson*.
120 ft. *FA Bob Heipler, Alan Guthrie, 1974.*

13 Horz 5.10c ★

Climb the first two pitches of *Groundhog* and look for a wide crack splitting a roof. Climb the short roof to a ledge, then head right to join up with *Caver's Route*.
30 ft. *FA Ed Pearsall, 1980.*

14 Curving Crack 5.8 ★★★★

Walk 40 feet right of *Groundhog* to the next dihedral. Climb the flake to a stance 30 feet up. Take a good rest, then tackle a bulge and dive into a crack. Continue to a ledge, then finish on *Caver's Route*.
80 ft. *FA Larry Day, Tom Seibert, 1978.*

15 Razor's Edge 5.9+ ★

This route ascends the crack directly right of *Curving Crack*. Finish on a face to a ledge.
50 ft. *FA Grant Stephens, 1984.*

16 Caver's Route 5.3 R ★★★★★

Locate a chimney system 20 feet right of *Razor's Edge*, near the southwest corner of the wall. Climb to a ledge about 25 feet up and belay. Chimney up to a bolt and continue to the large ledge. Belay from the ledge, then walk back up the gully behind you and squeeze through the rock to a chimney on the opposite side. Turn around and climb up the chimney to a ledge under an arch. Walk west under the arch and take the final chimney to the summit. To descend, follow the directions mentioned in the introduction.

Variation: Climb straight up through the chimney from the top of the second pitch and squeeze through a hole. Be careful not to get stuck in the extremely narrow portion of the chimney.
150 ft. *FA Unknown.*

17 Caver's Excitement 5.7 X ★★★

Walk to the right of *Caver's Route* to a face. Climb up the face with no protection to the first belay ledge of *Caver's Route*. Climb the section of rock to the right of the main chimney on the second pitch of *Caver's Route*. Continue to the top via the last pitch of *Caver's* or the variation.
150 ft. *FA Martin Hackworth, Henry Oxemann, 1973.*

18 Nose Traverse 5.6 R ★★★

From the first belay of *Caver's Route*, traverse right along a series of ledges across the south face of Tower Rock. End at anchors near a crack just right of an arete.
90 ft. *FA Tom Seibert, Ellen Seibert, 1975.*

19 Wimp Out 5.9 R ★★

Exposed and spooky. Climb 10 feet rightwards to a ledge from the second belay of *Caver's Route*. Traverse 20 feet to a vertical crack and climb it to an alcove beneath *Insanity Ceiling*. Move left to belay, then climb up to a small ledge left of the roof, traverse right to a tree, then to the top.
150 ft. *FA Larry Day, Ed Pearsall, 1979.*

20 Insanity Ceiling 5.11a ★★★★

This exposed route climbs the body-length roof above the first pitch of *Wimp Out*. You can get to the roof from the base of the last pitch of *Caver's Route*. From the belay tree, work down and right, then up to a stance below a thin crack in the roof. Reach out and over the lip to locate decent holds. Release your feet and crank up and over. Slap up through long reaches to sloping pockets to reach parallel thin cracks. Layback off the thin edges to reach a hand crack and fire to the summit.
45 ft. *FA Larry Day, Tom Seibert, 1979.*

21 Whimpering Insanity 5.11a R ★★★

Move right and around the corner from the beginning of *Caver's Excitement* to the middle of the south face of the pinnacle. Locate a single bolt in the middle of the face marking this insane line. Another way to locate the line is to look for the obvious vertical crack of *Wimp Out*, visible on the upper half of this section of the wall. Sight directly down from this crack and that is the line. Edge up past the zone of safe falling to clip the old high bolt. Move right, then crimp up to easier moves where you can place some poor stoppers. Move straight up to join up with *Wimp Out*.
75 ft. *FA Greg Smith, Martin Hackworth, 1985.*

22 Shower of Power 5.10a R ★★

Walk right from *Whimpering Insanity* and around the arete to a small west-facing section of the wall. This route ascends a small crack to the left of a dirty dihedral, over a small roof, then up the face. Link up with the next line by traversing right.
50 ft. *FA Greg Smith, Martin Hackworth, 1985.*

23 The Corner 5.9+

Climb the dirty and wide dihedral just right of *Shower of Power* to a ledge. From the ledge, head right and up to the top of the pinnacle.
110 ft. *FA Greg Smith, Paul Bennett, 1979.*

24 Tower of Power 5.10c R ★★★

This rarely climbed line doesn't get the attention it deserves. Just ask Larry Day what he thinks of this line and he'll lead into a vivid description of his first-ascent memories and shameless promotion of the line, which excites him just as much now as it did 16 years ago. Climb the first pitch of *The Corner* to reach this intimidating roof. Reach way out over the lip to locate a good hold and a great 1.5 Tricam placement in a vertical crack. Pull over the roof and run out the 5.10 face above to reach the top.
155 ft. *FA Larry Day, Ed Pearsall, 1979.*

25 No Brain, No Pain 5.10c X ★

This problem ascends the adjacent face right of the corner to a large ledge. Bring a crash pad and beware of the friable seam at mid-height.
25 ft. *FA Greg Smith, 1985.*

26 Tower Backside 5.3 ★★★

Walk right and around the corner from *Tower of Power* to locate a short, low-angle face leading to a large ledge. Climb the face to the base of a chimney, then continue up through the chimney to join up with the final pitches of *Caver's Route*.
120 ft. *FA Unknown.*

30 Arachnid 5.8 ★★★★★
Climb the obvious left-facing dihedral mentioned above to a large roof. Tip-toe traverse across the roof and place a large cam midway. At the end of the roof, get some pro in horizontals on the right face and pull up into a wide right-facing dihedral. Continue up the crack to a ledge with fixed anchors. **90 ft.** *FA Tom Seibert, Larry Day, 1974.*

27 Another Grunge 5.5
This low-quality line ascends the short crack 100 feet right from *Tower Backside* and 30 feet left of *Arachnid.* Climb to a ledge and rappel from a tree to descend. **45 ft.** *FA Unknown.*

28 Blow Me Down 5.12a R ★★★
Thirty feet right of the previous line is a flat area behind a large boulder. The obvious dihedral in this area is the next route, *Arachnid.* This line ascends the thin face just left of *Arachnid,* making use of three bolts and natural gear for protection. Climb up the thin face to the left edge of a roof where a crack begins and place some gear. Finish on *Shiver Me Timbers.* **30 ft. 2 bolts.** *FA Matt Flach, Tom Fyffe, 1989.*

29 Shiver Me Timbers 5.10c R ★★★
Begin by climbing the clean initial dihedral of *Arachnid,* then traverse left along a ledge beneath the left roof. Plug in some gear, then continue up the faint dihedral and arete to anchors. The second pitch continues up the face to the main ledge. **100 ft.** *FA Martin Hackworth, Keith Phelps, Todd McDonald, 1988.*

30 Arachnid 5.8 ★★★★
See photo above.

31 Anti-Gravity Acrobatics 5.10a X ★★
This death route takes on the arete just right of *Arachnid.* If you blow the cruxes, you will deck. **70 ft.** *FA Devin Pantess, Mark Johnson, Ray Pantess, 1991.*

32 Dog Days 5.8+ ★★★★
This sporty trad line ascends the crack 25 feet right of *Anti-gravity Acrobatics.* Climb the crack, then step right to the overhanging face when it fizzles. Crank through the overhanging face to a ledge and lower from fixed anchors. **75 ft.** *FA Rich Gottlieb, Gene Hancock, 1976.*

33 Bleak Future 5.10d X ★★★★
This route begins in a short, left-angling flake situated between *Dog Days* and *Africa.* Climb the flake, move right to some pockets, then head left to a ledge. Climb through some bulges to a right-facing dihedral under a roof. Move left around the roof, then back right over the roof on some pockets. Head up a blank section to the ledge. **80 ft.** *FA Tom Souders, 1989.*

34 Africa 5.9 ★★★★
Just right of *Bleak Future* is a clean hand crack splitting the featureless face. Spot the outline of Africa to the left of it. Jam up to a good ledge and reach over a small roof back into the crack. Take a big step over the roof and crank through tight hand jams to an alcove. Many people lower from here, but it is worth continuing past the second overhang and following a crack and dihedral to a ledge. Photo page 109. **80 ft.** *FA Tom Seibert, Rich Gottlieb, 1974.*

35 Madagascar 5.8- X ★
This route ascends the crack to the right of *Africa* to a narrow ledge, then traverses left to join *Africa.* **60 ft.** *FA Ed Pearsall, Martin Hackworth, 1982.*

LOWER SMALL WALL

all day
10 mins

22 routes

5.6- .7 .8 .9 .10 .11 .12 .13 .14

Character

Lower Small Wall is far from small. It hosts a number of long multi-pitch traditional lines as well as some great shorter classics, including the extremely popular and pumpy wide crack *Dicey at Best*. It sets the standard for the classic "5.8+" sandbagger grade in the Red. Beware! Another Lower Small Wall classic is *Good Tang*. At only 5.7 you'll find yourself shaking through a couple of tricky roofs and swearing you must be on the wrong route. If you're ever in need of a new cam, get on *Good Tang* – chances are you'll find a shiny new one abandoned by one of its victims.

Approach

From the intersection of KY 77 with KY 715 near Fortress Wall, stay on 715 for 5.0 miles (1.8 miles past the bridge over Gladie Creek) to a pulloff on your right. The pulloff is directly across from a wide, rectangular boulder on the left side of the road. Hike uphill just right of the boulder, following a faint trail. When the trail ends, head straight up to the wall. You will probably end up about 75 feet right of a fenced-off overhang near the first two routes listed here.

Conditions

Lower Small Wall faces south so expect lots of sunshine, especially on the more exposed multi-pitch lines. Although its not exactly a rainy-day crag, *Dicey at Best* is pretty well sheltered.

Access

The National Forest Service has recently closed a small section of Lower Small Wall for archaeological reasons. The only routes affected are *Eggshell* and *That's Enough of This Beene Shit*. Please respect the fenced-off area and do not climb the closed routes.

1 **That's Enough of This Beene Shit** 5.10d R ★★
It was on this line that Tom Souders and Jeff Koenig ended their "Beene" theme. From the end of the approach trail, walk left about 75 feet until you reach a thin right-facing dihedral just before a fenced-off overhang. Stem up the difficult line to a ledge, placing protection where you can get it. Improvise a descent.
50 ft. *FA Jeff Koenig, Tom Souders, 1985.*

2 **Eggshell** 5.8 R ⃠
Closed. Walk left a few feet from *That's Enough of This Beene Shit* to a large block under a low roof. Climb the crack on the right side of the block to an alcove.
55 ft. *FA Steve Mulholland, Max Reider, 1987.*

3 **Dancing Outlaw** 5.8 A2+ ★★★★
This long and difficult aid line begins 80 feet left of *Eggshell*, 20 feet left of a large tree set back about 30 feet from the cliff. Climb a short slab to gain a thin flake. Climb the flake to a ledge about 25 feet up, then continue up through a long, arching crack in white rock until it wanes. Pull a small roof and head for bolted anchors just beneath a large roof with a V-shaped slot. Aid through the slot and move right and up to the largest roof. Follow a thin seam out and right, then head for the summit. Watch out for wasps. Bring a standard aid rack up to 5".
150 ft. *FA Bart Bledsoe, 2004.*

4 **Delirium Tremors** 5.5
From *Dancing Outlaw*, move 40 feet left and climb the unpleasant crack in the dihedral. Rappel from a tree to descend.
90 ft. *FA Mike Getarius, Ken Bing, 1982.*

That's Enough of This Beene Shit

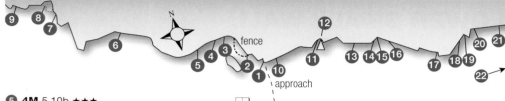

5 4M 5.10b ★★★

This route ascends the right-angling finger crack about 50 feet left of *Delirium Tremors*. Climb the crack and sloping face holds to a ledge with a tree. Rappel from the tree to descend.

45 ft. *FA Ed Pearsall, Tom Seibert, 1983.*

6 Invasion of the Love Queens 5.8+ ★★

This route ascends a hand crack beginning on a ledge 200 feet left of *4M*. Scramble up to the ledge to reach the crack. Take on a roof, then continue up to another ledge. Rappel from a tree to descend.

80 ft. *FA Martin Hackworth, Grant Stephens, 1984.*

7 Shattered 5.6 ★

Hike 250 feet left of *Invasion of the Love Queens* and around a couple of buttresses to a pair of dihedrals. Climb up to a 10-foot-high ledge, then climb the face between the two cracks to a ledge. Traverse left to a belay. To get down, traverse farther left to rappel from a tree.

70 ft. *FA Martin Hackworth, Grant Stephens, 1983.*

8 Der Kommissar 5.9 ★★★

This route is located about 20 feet left of *Shattered*. Chimney up to a low roof. Crank over the roof to reach a dihedral, then continue up the dihedral to a ledge. Walk left along the ledge to reach a rappel tree.

70 ft. *FA Grant Stephens, Martin Hackworth, 1983.*

9 The Green Wombat 5.8 ★

Walk 75 feet left of *Der Kommissar*, past a dihedral, to reach this route. Climb the crack up to a ledge with a belay tree. Continue up the crack through a boulder to another belay. Traverse right to find another crack, which will take you to the top. Rappel from a tree to descend.

100 ft. *FA Grant Stephens, Louis Petry, 1983.*

The remaining lines are located right of where the trail meets the wall.

Blue Biner

10 Poison Ivy 5.8+

From *That's Enough of this Beene Shit*, head about 300 feet right and past a large section of the wall with a rock ledge beneath it that you have to step up onto to follow the trail. If you reach the monolithic *Lost Dart* formation, you've hiked too far. Locate a finger crack hosting some poison ivy. Climb the crack to a ledge to the right and belay. Take on a dihedral to reach a roof, then traverse under the roof to reach another crack. Continue up this crack to another belay ledge. Rappel from here or continue up through a wide crack to reach the top. The FA party did not climb the final flaring pitch, so it may not have seen an ascent.

150 ft. *FA Ed Pearsall, Steve Alden, 1977.*

11 Lost Dart 5.2 R

Walk 100 feet right from *Poison Ivy* to a corridor formed by a large pinnacle of rock leaning against the cliff. Chimney up the left side of the pinnacle and through a narrow section to the other side. Continue up to the top of the formation.

50 ft. *FA Unknown.*

12 Lost Dart Crack 5.8 ★

Walk into the corridor formed by the pinnacle to locate a crack. Climb this crack to the anchors on *Lost Dart*.

50 ft. *FA John Bronaugh, Grant Stephens, 1983.*

13 Blue Biner 5.9 ★★★★

This pair of cracks is located 50 feet right and around the corner from *Lost Dart*. Climb a crack to reach a pair of cracks. Make use of both cracks to reach an overhang, then move left. Duck up onto a ledge and belay. Continue up the crack through an overhang and head for the top. Lower from fixed anchors. A single 60-meter rope will get you down.

150 ft. *FA Ed Pearsall, Jay Collins, 1979.*

14 Caterpillar Crack 5.6 ★★

Walk 45 feet right from *Blue Biner* to a right-facing dihedral. Climb the crack to a ledge and belay. Move right along the ledge to *Double Caves Crack* and follow that line to the top.

150 ft. *FA Ron Heinsman, Julie Heinsman, 1994.*

15 Double Caves Crack 5.3 ★★★

Climb the wide crack a few feet right of *Caterpillar Crack* to a ledge, and move through an opening to a rockhouse. Chimney up the crack to a belay ledge and continue to the top via *Pogue's Path*.

150 ft. *FA Bill Hurley, Jim Hanners, 1975.*

16 Pogue's Path 5.1 ★

Begin a few feet right of *Double Caves Crack*. Climb a short crack to a ledge, then move right along the ledge and up a left-angling hand crack. Jam the crack, then continue up to a large ledge on the right. Move left along the ledge to locate another short crack. Climb this to the top.
150 ft. *FA Kevin Pogue, 1970's.*

17 The Spider Squat 5.7 ★★★

This route ascends the left-facing dihedral 100 feet right of *Pogue's Path*. Climb the dihedral to a ledge under an overhang. Move left and traverse the face around the corner to reach a tree. Climb the right side of a roof through an overhanging dihedral to reach a belay ledge. Continue up a short section of face climbing to reach the top.
150 ft. *FA Ed Pearsall, Jay Collins, 1979.*

18 DAB Chimney 5.2

Walk 25 feet right and around the corner from *The Spider Squat* to a short chimney. Climb the chimney to a large ledge. Scramble off right.
30 ft. *FA Unknown.*

19 Dicey at Best 5.8+ ★★★★★

This classic line takes on the beautiful, clean, wide dihedral beginning on the ledge above *DAB Chimney*. Scramble up to the ledge from the right to begin. Arm-bar and knee-jam your way up the crack to a ledge and belay. Continue up the crack to a roof and traverse right along a ledge to reach a rappel tree. Most people only do the first pitch, which by itself makes for a classic line.
150 ft. *FA Dante Leonardi, Ken Staufer, 1979.*

20 Stinger 5.10b R ★

This route ascends the crack system 15 feet right of *Dicey at Best*. Climb chossy rock up to and over a bulge and belay on the ledge. Take on a roof and continue up a flaring hand crack to the top. The second pitch was only top-roped and goes at 5.11.
150 ft. *FA John Bronaugh, Roger Pearson, 1987.*

21 Stratocaster 5.8 R ★

This route is located 75 feet right of *Stinger*, past a dihedral and behind a tree. Climb through a couple of overhangs and belay. Follow a crack to the top of a flake, then move over a bulge and into an alcove. Traverse right 50 feet along an unprotected ledge, then up a short face to the top.
150 ft. *FA John Bronaugh, Louis Petry, 1981.*

22 Good Tang 5.7 ★★★★

Walk about 250 feet right of *Stratocaster*, passing a small stream along the way. Look for an acute dihedral with a couple of obvious overhangs. From the ground, the route does not look like it could be only 5.7. Climb up to the overhangs and gain a large belay ledge on the right. Tackle the first overhang and bail out left or continue up through the second overhang to a large ledge. The third pitch climbs the chimney to the top.
150 ft. *FA Larry Day, Frank Becker, 1974*

Michelle Ellington *Dicey at Best* (5.8+), Lower Small Wall
Photo: Ben Cassel; www.casselphotography.com

MIDDLE SMALL WALL a.m. 🚶

12 routes

10 mins   5.6- .7 .8 .9 .10 .11 .12 .13 .14

Character

As with the other small walls, this one isn't so small. One of the Red's longest and most exposed traditional lines, *The Quest*, is found at this wall. If you are a solid 5.10 crack climber, you should definitely try the route. Finding yourself perched at a natural hanging belay, with the ground almost 200 feet beneath you, is a rare experience at the Red. Wide-crack climbers will find that Middle Small has a lot to offer. Take on *Handjob, Marmalade, Layback Crack,* or the upper pitch of *The Quest* and your abs will be sore for weeks! Bring big cams if you hit this wall.

Approach

From the intersection of KY 77 with KY 715 near Fortress Wall, stay on 715 for 5.7 miles (2.5 miles past the bridge over Gladie Creek) to a pulloff on your right. The pulloff will be just past another pull off that has been known to swallow cars that don't have 4WD – just look for deep tire tracks and drive a little further. Hike back down the road toward the muddy pulloff and locate a faint trail on the right, just right of a ravine that begins with a steep muddy section right off the road. Follow the trail straight uphill for about 10 minutes and you should meet the wall about 200 feet right of *The Quest*. To locate *The Quest*, look for a large roof with a crack splitting it about 150 feet up. *The Quest* is about 50 feet left of that roof.

Conditions

Due to their northeast-facing nature, a few routes at Middle Small Wall can be a bit mossy at times. These include *The Quest* and *Basecamp,* so try to avoid them in damp or humid conditions or you'll risk a bad experience, and hunt me down for recommending them. Routes 5-9 get more sun and stay in better condition. They're also shorter, so it's possible to knock a few of them out in a day. Plan on at least a half day to climb *The Quest* or *Basecamp*. The routes are long and difficult.

The Quest

❶ The Quest 5.10c ★★★★★

From where the approach trail meets the wall, head left about 150-200 feet, passing through some boulders. Locate a section of the wall about 40 feet behind a large tree with two cracks 20 feet apart. Start in the right crack and pull over a small roof. Climb through thin and technical cracks to a ledge with some loose rock directly beneath a roof. Power through the roof and continue through fists to a nice belay ledge on the right.

Climb up to another roof and traverse right to gain a hand crack in a slightly overhanging dihedral. Climb this, then set a hanging belay directly beneath a large roof. Beware setting gear in what looks like a solid crack in the roof, but upon closer inspection may eventually be a large loose block.

Now, try to talk your partner into leading. Traverse out another large roof, then dive up into a squeeze chimney when you feel like you can fit. Be sure to look down at this point to add to your leg shake. Kick and scream while you lose your feet for a few seconds trying to swim up into the chimney, then relax once you get them bridged again. If your offwidth technique isn't up to par, begin to lose skin as you struggle through what may be the most difficult 20 feet of your life. Grab a huge ledge, place a piece for your partner so he doesn't pendulum if he falls, then crawl across a ledge for 15 feet to a tree that you just may kiss at this point.

To descend, walk left to locate a large tree with webbing and rappel with two ropes. Bring some #3.5-#4 sized Camalots for the final pitch.

220 ft. *FA Tom Souders, Bob Hayes, 1984.*

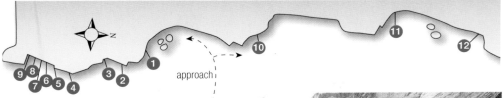

② Which Way is Up 5.10d R ★★

Walk left from *The Quest* about 100 feet, around the corner, to locate a crack system near a small pond. Climb
the crack through some roofs to a vertical face with
sketchy gear. Continue up to a large ledge and rap from
a tree to descend.
85 ft. *FA Greg Smith, 1984.*

③ Basecamp 5.11b ★★★★

Walk 40 feet left of *Which Way is Up*, to a dihedral with
a roof about 20 feet up. Climb to the roof, crank out to
a hand jam at the lip, then pull up into the dihedral. Follow the dihedral to a belay beneath a large roof. Move
back right and climb to the roof for some pro. Pull over
the roof and turn the lip to gain a belay ledge. Continue
up the face, using natural protection to reach the top of
the wall. Rappel with two ropes.
180 ft. *FA Jeff Koenig, Tom Souders, 1984.*

Basecamp

④ Hidey Ho 5.10a R ★★★

Walk about 30 feet left from *Basecamp* to locate a
chimney about 10 feet left of a fat flake. Climb the short
chimney to reach a belay ledge beneath a 25-foot roof.
Work your way out the roof to gain the crack again, then
continue up the crack to another belay. Head left on a
short face (R-rated) to a crack that takes you back right
to a belay ledge. Continue up through a short slot to
reach the top.
175 ft. *FA John Bronaugh, Roger Pearson, 1986.*

Hidey Ho

⑤ Investigator 5.7 ★★★

This short left-facing dihedral is located 50 feet left
of the previous line and marks the start of a wall with
a horizontal break 40 feet up. Rappel from a tree to
descend.
40 ft. *FA Unknown*

⑥ Lactic Acid 5.9 ★★★

Climb the finger crack on the face left of *Investigator*.
Finger lock and face climb up the crack, then shift left
just before the end to reach a ledge. Rappel from a small
tree to descend.
40 ft. *FA Greg Smith, Chris Bennett, 1983.*

⑦ Handjob 5.9+ ★★★★

This obvious splitter begins about 15 feet left of *Lactic
Acid.* Climb through fists to an offwidth section just
before a small roof. Maneuver through the wide section,
then pull around the roof. Dive deep for good jams the
second half of the way. Rappel from bolted anchors.
80 ft. *FA Ed LeCroix, Tom Seibert, 1980.*

Hand Job

Devine Climb

The next three routes are located right of The Quest.

⓿ Devine Climb 5.8+ ★★

This route is 125 feet right of *The Quest*, past a couple of small streams and around a corner. Look for a hand crack splitting the face, that becomes a dihedral about 40 feet up. The crack is about 30 feet right of a left-facing dihedral. The right face of the route becomes bright orange halfway up and there is a large oblong hueco on each side of the crack halfway up. Climb the crack to a small roof. Pull around the roof and continue up the crack to a low-angle and poorly protected section just before a large ledge. Rappel from here or take a second pitch, which begins to the right and follows a dihedral to the top. Rappel from a tree to descend.
165 ft. *FA Tom Seibert, Larry Day, 1976.*

⓫ Spiderweb Tearoom 5.8 ★★

Walk about five minutes right from *Devine Climb* to locate a right-facing flake with an orange face above. If you reach two very large boulders, you've walked too far. Climb the flake to a ledge and belay. Pull a small overhang, then move left on small holds to a ledge. Rappel with two ropes from a tree at the top of the cliff.
150 ft. *FA Larry Day, Tom Seibert, 1976.*

⓬ Mickey Mantle 5.6

Walk 250 feet right of *Spiderweb Tearoom*, past the large boulders, to a left-facing dihedral near a small stream. Scramble up to a ledge, then climb a crack system to the left of a slab. End on a ledge and rap from a tree to descend.
30 ft. *FA Tom Seibert, Ellen Seibert, 1981.*

❽ Marmalade 5.9 ★★★★
See description opposite

❾ Layback Crack 5.9 ★★★
Another one for the big cams. Be sure to place your cams really deep so your partner doesn't cheat by getting to layback the whole way. This is the obvious right-facing dihedral just left of *Marmalade*. Scramble up to a ledge to start. Pull over a low roof, then make use of fists and armbars to the top.
60 ft. *FA Larry Day, Tom Seibert, 1976.*

UPPER SMALL WALL

 all day   15 mins   2 routes   5.6- .7 .8 .9 .10 .11 .12 .13 .14

Character

This wall offers the least of the three Small Walls. The approach is somewhat difficult, due to the dense vegetation and recent fallen trees, and the lines are low quality.

Approach

Drive about 0.3 miles past the pulloff for Middle Small Wall to a pulloff on the left. Hike across the road and up the hill to the wall. Walk left along the base of the wall until you reach a south facing slabby wall with a dihedral on the left side.

❶ Cliff Hanger 5.6 X ★★
This line ascends the purplish south facing section of the wall to a large ledge 25 feet up. Continue up the face between two water streaks then head up a steep ramp on the right to the top of the wall. Don't expect to find too much in the way of protection. Rappel from a tree to descend.
Variation 5.8 X: Climb straight up the face.
150 ft. *FA Ed Pearsall, Larry Harmon, 1977. Variation FA: John Bronaugh, Tina Feezel, 1988.*

❷ Bumblebee Junction 5.5
The line ascends the rotten dihedral left and around the corner from *Cliff Hanger*. Lower from fixed gear or continue through more torture to the top.
150 ft. *FA Tom Seibert, Ellen Seibert, Eric Bostrum, mid 1970s.*

⑧ Marmalade 5.9 ★★★★

Break out the big cams for this one. It climbs the next wide crack splitting the face just before a right-facing dihedral. Chicken-wing and armbar the crack, pulling through a tough section or two along the way. Descend by traversing left along a ledge and rappel from the tree above *Layback Crack*.

60 ft. *FA Tom Seibert, Ed Pearsall, 1980.*

HEN'S NEST

all day
15 or 30 mins OK in rain

17 routes

5.6- .7 .8 .9 .10 .11 .12 .13 .14

Character

The brilliant orange wall of Hen's Nest hosts a few excellent traditional lines, including the striking finger crack, *Finger Lickin' Good*. However, in 2006 the Forest Service fenced off the best lines here. Hen's Nest still has a number of short moderate lines open, making it a great venue for novice leaders. Hopefully the "temporary" closure here won't mirror the "temporary" closure of routes at Military Wall.

Approach

From the intersection of KY 77 with KY 715 near Fortress Wall, stay on 715 for 7.1 miles until you reach a one-lane concrete bridge. Cross the bridge and park in a pulloff on your left. Walk across the road and head straight down to the river. Follow a muddy path near the river bank downstream for about 0.5 miles. About five minutes after you cross a large ravine and just before a large boulder on the near side of the river, start heading uphill (left) toward Hen's Nest. You should be able to spot the orange wall at this point. If you reach a point where you see a very large boulder across the river a few minutes after the river bends sharply to the right then you hiked too far.

An alternate and easier approach, if you're willing to wade the river, is to drive 6.5 miles from the intersection of KY 77 with KY 715 and park in a pulloff on your right, near a popular camping spot. This is the location of the large boulder marking the point indicating you hiked too far if you took the previous approach. Hike down the trail to the river, wade across, and head straight uphill. This way will save you about 15 minutes. Either way, you should meet up with the wall around *Masters of the Universe*.

Conditions

Hen's Nest is a great place to climb in the rain. The height of the wall and the roofs near the top shelter the lower section of wall pretty well. It's also a wonderful cold-weather crag with a sunny southeastern aspect.

Access

The National Forest Service asks that you limit climbing at Hen's Nest from April 1 through November 1 to allow vegetation to recover.

Masters of the Universe

❶ **Lip Appeal** 5.10b

If you hike between the river and a lower limestone band during the approach to the crag, look for two cracks in a large roof. Remember, this is limestone you're looking for. If you find something that looks climbable in the limestone band, you've probably found this route. Traverse into a hand crack in the roof, turn the lip, and face climb to a tree.
45 ft. *FA Chuck Keller, Steve Faulkner, 1988.*

❷ **Masters of the Universe** 5.9+ ★★

If you ended up in the right spot at the end of your hike, you should be somewhere close to this route. Look for a left-facing dihedral with a low roof. Jam over the roof and climb to a belay ledge. Pull another roof into a dihedral and continue to a large ledge.
100 ft. *FA Martin Hackworth, Grant Stephens, 1984.*

❸ **Fingers in a Light Socket** 5.11c ★★

Toprope. This powerful line ascends a thin seam and face about 30 feet right of *Masters of the Universe* and directly left of *Astro Flex*.
50 ft. *FA Jamie Baker, 1988.*

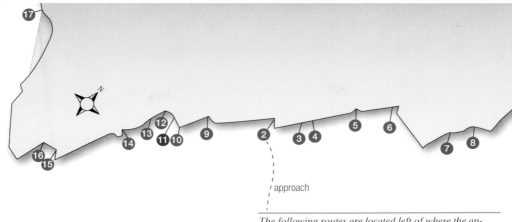

approach

The following routes are located left of where the approach trail meets the wall.

9 Atomic Cafe 5.10c ★★

Just left of where the trail meets the wall, spot a crispy-looking left-facing dihedral. Manage to get started, then scrape your back up the stiff dihedral while hoping that your footholds don't break and you don't fall during the first 15 feet. Maybe bring a crash pad?
60 ft. *FA Jeff Koenig, 1984.*

4 Astro Flex 5.10a ★★★★

Walk about 35 feet right of *Masters of the Universe* and look for a crack that starts wide and flaring, with a finger crack in the back. Creep up the finger crack and reach for a good hand jam. Make a couple of long, sporty moves to reach the ledge. Lower from fixed gear.
40 ft. *FA Grant Stephens, Martin Hackworth, 1984.*

5 Planet Waves 5.9 ★★★

Walk about 15 feet right to the next crack system, just before a wide chimney. Climb to a ledge, then head right to a good rappel tree.
60 ft. *FA Martin Hackworth, Grant Stephens, 1984.*

6 Mindy 5.5 ★

Just right of *Planet Waves* is an obvious long and dirty chimney system. Climb it to the top and rappel from a tree to descend.
150 ft. *FA Bob Compton, Chuck Kifer, 1972.*

7 Starship Trooper 5.10a ★★★

If only it were longer. Walk around the corner from *Mindy* to locate this nice-looking short, splitter hand crack with two cracks at the base. Climb the right off-width to the overhang, pull the overhang and belay from the ledge. Take a #4 Camalot or two for the first 15 feet or so. Crawl off the ledge to your left.
40 ft. *FA Martin Hackworth, Grant Stephens, 1984.*

8 Gold Digger 5.9+

Walk 20 feet right of *Starship Trooper* to the next crack. Climb the short crack to a ledge and belay. Climb another short crack to an overhang and belay again to avoid rope drag. Pull the overhang and continue up the crack to another overhang and belay. Pull the bulge and belay yet again. Continue up the chimney to the top. Walk off left or rappel.
130 ft. *FA Larry Day, Ed Pearsall, 1979.*

Astro Flex

Starship Trooper

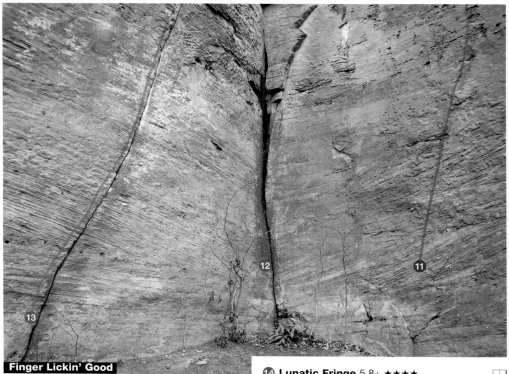

Finger Lickin' Good

The Forest Service has closed the following routes (10-13) for archaeological reason. Please do not climb them.

⑩ The Edge 5.11b ⊘
Toprope. This powerful line ascends the arete left of *Atomic Cafe*.
50 ft. *FA Bill McCullough, 1985.*

⑪ Close to the Edge 5.10a R ⊘
This route ascends the low-angle face just left of *The Edge*. You can place natural protection in the pockets between the first and second bolts.
50 ft. 3 bolts. *FA Martin Hackworth, Grant Stephens, 1984.*

⑫ Sultans of Stem 5.9+ ⊘
Move left from the previous line to the next dihedral.
70 ft. *FA Martin Hackworth, Grant Stephens, 1984.*

⑬ Finger Lickin' Good 5.10c R ⊘
The beautiful right-angling finger crack just left of *Sultans of Stem* was a classic before its closure.
50 ft. *FA Martin Hackworth, Grant Stephens, 1984.*

⑭ Lunatic Fringe 5.8+ ★★★★
The obvious splitter hand crack about 35 feet left of *Finger Lickin' Good*. Climb through great fist and hand jams to a small roof. Pull the roof, then follow the crack until it turns to face climbing. Tiptoe up the face, making sure to not think about where your last piece of gear is. Pull to the ledge, then head right to the belay anchors. Due to the placement of the belay anchors way out right, your follower gets to experience a little excitement as well. Lower from bolted anchors.
75 ft. *FA Grant Stephens, Martin Hackworth, 1984.*

⑮ Right Crack 5.8 ★★★
Head about 50 feet left and around the corner from the previous lines to locate two short cracks. This route takes the right crack. Jam over a low roof to start, then enjoy the rest of the short trip to the top. Rappel from slings around a flake.
40 ft. *FA Grant Stephens, Martin Hackworth, 1985.*

⑯ Wrong Crack 5.8 ★★★
This route follows the wider crack just left of *Right Crack* to the same set of slings.
40 ft. *FA Martin Hackworth, Grant Stephens, 1985.*

⑰ Mr. Freeze 5.11a ★★
Walk left along the cliff line from the previous lines, about 100 feet and around an obvious corner, to an amphitheater. This route takes on the overhanging thin crack past a couple of fixed pieces to a ledge. Continue up the easier crack to the top. Rappel from a tree to descend.
70 ft. *FA Tom Souders, Dave Veldhaus, 1987.*

John with his son, Alex Yeakley, in Colorado. Tragically, Alex died in a car accident shortly after John in December 2004.

JOHN BRONAUGH

PROFILE: King of the Red River Gorge

I remember purchasing the first edition of *Red River Gorge Climbs* by John Bronaugh. My friends and I would read that guidebook like a novel, remembering route descriptions and quoting them with each route we climbed. We became walking guidebooks, John's witty words burned into our brains as if we were members of a cult.

"This offwidth and fist crack extravaganza has become a nightmare for most climbers who attempted it." —*Burden of Dreams*

"There's no need biting off more than you can chew— take a huge rack." —*Jaws*

"Finagle features to a finicky, funky, fickle, flakey flake. Crack climb cranky crevice, craftily cruising clear of crud to creaky clips." —*Fox in Locks*

John's descriptions either struck fear or brought a smile to the faces of the thousands of people who purchased one of his guidebooks. Probably the best description I've heard come from him occurred as he stared up at an 80-foot crack with 20 feet of poorly protected choss leading to an overhanging offwidth slot and severely exposed changing corners roof at the top. He looked at me and said, "This is one of those routes that makes me feel like I've gotta take a dump." Anyone who has felt that level of intimidation from a route will understand.

Aside from climbing, John was extremely educated, with three degrees to his name: one in Wildlife Biology from Colorado State, a music degree from a school in Hollywood, California, and a law degree from the University of Kentucky. Yet despite all of John's ventures away from home, he always ended up back in his beloved Red River Gorge,

bushwhacking through the rhododendrons and looking for that next unclimbed chunk of Corbin sandstone.

Once focused on just getting to the top of a cliff with natural gear, as most old schoolers where, John changed his ways and rap bolted with the best of them. His love of exploring and passion for adventure brought hundreds of first ascents to the Red, both bolted and traditional, during his almost 30 years of climbing there. At different points in his life he tried to set athletic climbing goals, as most of us do, but he always became sidetracked by his need to explore new areas.

As well as being a guidebook author, a route developer, a climber, and a musician, John was also a devoted father, a loving husband, and successful attorney. His law expertise proved invaluable when his voluntary counseling helped the RRGCC purchase the Pendergrass Murray Recreational Preserve in 2004.

John valued his more than 500 climbing partners, each of whom he could vividly recollect. He was their island in the storm as he cajoled them into jumping onto the sharp end for one of his frightful trad leads. His calming demeanor, witty humor, and sincere appreciation for his partners made a lasting impression on everyone he climbed with. John gained his inspiration from a climbing legend, the late Bob Kamps, whom he later befriended during a visit to the Red. He probably never knew it but many people looked up to and were inspired by John, just as he was by Bob. John Bronaugh was a legend and a hero to many. John suffered a fatal heart attack in the backwoods doing what he loved best on August 21, 2004. His legend will live in the Red River Gorge forever. ∎

UPPER GORGE

Character

The Upper Gorge has only a handful of walls and only two of them are frequently visited. Wall of Denial has some high quality crack climbs, including the very popular 5.9 corner, *Strick-9*. Eagle Point Buttress features the adventurous multi-pitch 5.7, *Foxfire*, as well as the severely exposed *Blister in the Sun*. The climbing in the Upper Gorge is predominantly traditional, with only a few bolted lines.

Approach

The cliffs are located alongside a gorgeous trail that follows the Red River upstream from 715. From Miguel's head north on KY 11 toward Mountain Parkway. Pass under Mountain Parkway then turn left onto 15 near the Shell station. Continue west on KY 15 for about a mile until you reach 77 on your right. Turn right onto 77 and follow it through Nada Tunnel, past Military Wall, and over the steel bridge. Bear right after the steel bridge, remaining on KY 77 until it intersects with KY 715. Turn right onto KY 715 and follow the road alongside the Red River to the parking area on the left just before the one-lane bridge that crosses the river.

Access

All of the areas in the Middle Gorge Region are located on Forest Service land and in the Clifty Wilderness area. Please respect signs and fences indicating closed routes or trails and read the guidelines for climbing on Forest Service land on page 32 of this book, paying special attention to additional Forest Service restrictions when climbing in wilderness.

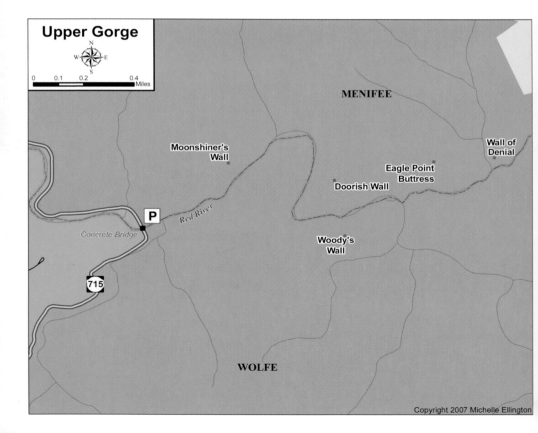

Wes Allen trying the low roof of *Drug Pusher* 5.12a, Wall of Denial, page 138. Photo by Amy Tackett.

CLIFF	SUN / SHADE	HIKE	RAIN	ROUTES	GRADE RANGE		CLASSIC ROUTES
MOONSHINER'S WALL page 133		5 mins		6	5.6- .7 .8 .9 .10 .11 .12 .13 .14		*Oberon* 5.10c
DOORISH WALL page 133	shade	15 mins		10	5.6- .7 .8 .9 .10 .11 .12 .13 .14		
EAGLE POINT page 132	all day	20 mins		18	5.6- .7 .8 .9 .10 .11 .12 .13 .14		*Blister in the Sun* 5.9
WALL OF DENIAL page 136	all day	30 mins		24	5.6- .7 .8 .9 .10 .11 .12 .13 .14		*Strick 9* 5.9
WOODY'S WALL page 133	shade	15 mins		14	5.6- .7 .8 .9 .10 .11 .12 .13 .14		

EAGLE POINT BUTTRESS

18 routes

all day | 20 mins | 5.6- .7 .8 .9 .10 .11 .12 .13 .14

Character

Eagle Point Buttress is best known for the multi-pitch route, *Foxfire*. At only 5.7 it allows the adventurous beginning leader to take on a long and exposed multi-pitch line offering excellent climbing and a gorgeous summit. Precede that with the long approach alongside the beautiful Red River, throw in a limestone cave and a sandstone arch, and you have a wonderful day of climbing. Less popular but of higher quality is the amazing *Blister in the Sun*. This naturally protected line ascends a long and highly exposed 85-foot line that begins in the middle of the wall and takes you to the summit.

Approach

From the intersection of KY 77 with KY 15 near Fortress Wall, stay on KY 715 for 7.1 miles until you reach a one lane concrete bridge. Park on the left just before crossing the bridge. Hike down to the river and follow the trail along the river past some garbage, modern man petroglyphs (aka graffiti), firepits, hungover campers, and a couple of limestone caves. After about a half mile you will cross a tributary and come to a large, flat campsite. Veer left and away from the main trail at this point and follow an old logging road that heads uphill toward the cliff. To locate the first route, *Cranky*, head left where the trail splits near the base of the wall. Then walk right about 50 feet to locate the first unattractive crack.

Conditions

The exposure and south facing orientation of this wall can make it an extremely hot location to climb. Don't expect to stay too dry on a rainy day. Beware of the occasional hungover camper or drunk rappeller. If solitude is your thing, then avoid this area on holiday weekends as it is a very popular camping area.

❶ Cranky 5.8
This route ascends a dirty, green moss-covered crack through a jungle to a ledge. After seeing it, you probably won't want to climb it. Rappel from a tree to descend.
70 ft. *FA Alex Cudkowicz, Tracy Best, 1990.*

❷ Southern Comfort 5.8 ★
Walk 40 feet left from *Cranky* to locate a perfect hand-sized crack with a small roof at the beginning. Climb the crack to a ledge and rappel from a tree to descend.
70 ft. *FA Alex Cudkowicz, Tracy Best, 1990.*

❸ Foxfire 5.7 R ★★★
Walk 60 feet left from *Southern Comfort* and locate a wide crack behind a tree just around the corner of the main buttress. Use your offwidth skills or thrash up the initial wide section to a ledge and belay.
 Walk back right to the margin of the ledge and take off leading on the easy face while locating the occasional opportunity for gear placement. Belay from a large ledge, then crawl around the corner on a large ledge with no gear. Climb a left-leaning corner, then traverse left across a slab to a ledge with a tree. Belay from here, then continue up the best pitch that takes on the final attractive crack up and around a small roof then climb a short face to the ledge. Belay from here to avoid rope drag, then traverse left to locate a break that will take you to the summit. To descend, walk off to the left, or rappel the route with two ropes.
200 ft. *FA Larry Day, Martin Hackworth, Bob Baker, 1974.*

❹ Day Dreaming 5.9+ ★★★★
50 feet left and around the corner from *Foxfire* is this black dihedral. Battle up the crack to fixed gear and lower.
80 ft. *FA Larry Day, Ed Pearsall, 1979.*

❺ Twin Cracks 5.9+ ★★★
This line takes on the twin cracks 10 feet left of *Day Dreaming*. Begin in the right crack, then step left and pump to the ledge. Lower from fixed gear.
70 ft. *FA Ed Pearsall, 1980.*

❻ Pussy Whipped 5.10a ★
Toprope. Move 35 feet left to locate this toprope that climbs a thin, right-angling crack up to a changing corners dihedral.
50 ft. *FA Alex Cudkowicz, Tracy Best, 1990.*

❼ The Integral 5.7 R
Climb the disgusting mud slot just left of *Pussy Whipped* to a ledge. Move right along the ledge and climb up to another ledge. Traverse right along this ledge and spot another crack. Climb this crack to yet another ledge, then move right to join the upper half of *Foxfire*. Descend as for *Foxfire*.
Variation: Climb the main corner above the second pitch (5.8).
200 ft. *FA Martin Hackworth, Bob Baker, 1976.*
Variation FA: Grant Stephens, Martin Hackworth, 1983.

walk up to
ledge routes

approach

⑧ **Southern Hospitality** 5.7

50 feet left of the previous line is a flake with a low roof behind a tree. Traverse the flake over a mossy slab, then pull over the flake to a thin crack surrounded by a plated face. Climb the crack and face past a couple of small trees to a ledge. Rappel from a tree to descend. **70 ft.** *FA Alex Cudkowicz, Tracy Best, 1990.*

⑨ **Crude Boys** 5.7

100 feet left of *Southern Hospitality* is a wide dirty dihedral. Climb it to a ledge and rappel from a tree. **70 ft.** *FA Alex Cudkowicz, Tracy Best, 1990.*

⑩ **The Hangover Problem** 5.8 ★★★

Walk 125 feet left from *Crude Boys* to locate a nice-looking pair of cracks in a blocky dihedral with yellow and black rock. This route ascends the right crack taking on a small flaring roof near the top. Lower from fixed gear. **70 ft.** *FA Jerry Bargo, Alex Cudkowicz, 1989.*

The following cliffs have been removed from the print version of this guidebook. Visit www.wolverinepublishing.com/downloads for a free download of the information for them.

MOONSHINER'S WALL

This small wall hosts *Oberon*, an amazing hand crack in an overhanging dihedral.

DOORISH WALL

This wall doesn't contain many great lines but it is a good place to scramble up and set topropes.

WOODY'S WALL

This wall overlooks a large section of the Red river but the quality of the rock and the amount of decent climbing is not impressive.

Day Dreaming

If My Number's Up

11 If My Number's Up 5.9 ★★★
This route follows the left crack of the pair to the same anchors.
70 ft. *FA Jerry Bargo, Alex Cudkowicz, 1989.*

12 Crackaluffagus V2 ★★
Walk about 100 feet left from *Hangover Problem* to a low overhang. Spot this roof crack on the left side of the overhang. Start back as far as you can and climb out the roof with good fistjams. Turn the lip and stand up. Shout "I did it" and jump down.
15 ft. *FA Ray Ellington, 2003.*

Hike left around the wall and locate a break on the right that leads to the top of the cliff. As you near the top of the cliff, look for a pocketed wall to the right, leading to a ledge in the middle of the cliff. Traverse right along this ledge and head around the corner to the south face of the wall. Continue to an open area containing the remaining routes.

13 Blister in the Sun 5.9 ★★★★★
This line ascends the fat flake on the rightmost edge of the ledge up to a stance beneath a bulge. Pull over the bulge and continue to a ledge beneath an overhang. Get some gear in and pull over the overhang onto the enjoyable face leading you to the summit. Walk off left to descend.
85 ft. *FA Jerry Bargo, Alex Cudkowicz, Keith Curtis, 1989.*

14 Scary 5.9 ★★★
Toprope. The face between the previous line and the next line.
85 ft. *FA Alex Cudkowicz, Braden Hale, 1989.*

15 Scared As a Virgin 5.8+ R ★★★
Move left from *Scary* a few feet to an orange flake with a low roof. Climb to the roof for a piece of gear, then head left up the face to a slot. Continue left on the face, then move right to a dihedral. Continue up the face to the summit. Walk off left to descend.
85 ft. *FA Jerry Bargo, Alex Cudkowicz, 1989.*

16 Tinker's Toy 5.8- ★★
Toprope. The face 10 feet left of the previous line.
85 ft. *FA Tina and John Bronaugh, 1997.*

17 Quantum Mechanics 5.9 ★★★★
25 feet left of *Tinker's Toy* is a line containing a bolt about 20 feet up. Climb the face making use of the bolt and natural gear placements for protection. Walk off left to descend.
85 ft. *FA Alex Cudkowicz, Braden Hale, 1990.*

18 Cooler Than Kissing 5.10a ★★★
Toprope. The face left of *Quantum Mechanics*.
85 ft. *FA Jerry Bargo, Alex Cudkowicz, 1989.*

WALL OF DENIAL

all day · 30 mins · 24 routes
5.6- .7 .8 .9 .10 .11 .12 .13 .14

Character

Wall Of Denial is remote yet popular. The approach ranks as one of the longest in the Red but is mostly flat on a good trail through beautiful surroundings. The climbs are mainly traditional with a smattering of decent sport routes. *Strick 9* is a classic 5.9 dihedral complete with a small roof to pull for the finish. It has marked the leap into the 5.9 grade for many people. *Funhouse*, a classic 5.7, climbs through one long pitch of varied climbing with a soundtrack of the gushing Red River as background.

Approach

From the intersection of KY 77 with KY 715 near Fortress Wall, stay on KY 715 for 7.1 miles until you reach a one-lane concrete bridge. Park on the left just before crossing the bridge. Hike down to the river and follow a trail along the river past some garbage, modern-man petroglyphs (aka graffiti), firepits, hungover campers, and a couple of limestone caves. After about a half mile you will cross a tributary and come to a large, flat campsite. Do not veer left from the main trail at this point or you will head uphill to Eagle Point Buttress. Stay on the main trail and cross two more tributaries. Just past the second tributary, look for a smaller trail which ducks off to the left and goes uphill to Wall of Denial.

Conditions

Wall Of Denial faces south so expect excellent winter climbing. The area isn't a great rainy day retreat but *Strick 9* is often dry. As mentioned before, the approach is one of the longest but also one of the prettiest. Enjoy.

➊ Cold Shot 5.11a ★★
As the approach trail meets the wall, you will see a line of bolts on the main arete to your left. Follow the arete past a couple of cruxes and to a ledge.
100 ft. 7 bolts. *FA Stacy Temple, John Bronaugh, 1992.*

➋ Hair of the Dog 5.9+ ★★★
Walk 40 feet right from the arete to locate a wide crack left of a dihedral. Climb the crack to a ledge with a tree and belay. Continue up the round boulder split by an attractive hand crack to the summit. Take some large cams for the belay. Rappel from the tree above *11:11* to descend.
100 ft. *FA Steve Must, Bhavani Pathak, 1990.*

➌ Testosterone Testpiece 5.9 ★
This route ascends the offwidth a few feet right of *Hair of the Dog*. Rappel from the ledge with a tree or traverse left to the second pitch of *Hair of the Dog*.
45 ft. *FA Alex Cudkowicz, Braden Hale, 1990.*

➍ Apehouse 5.8 ★
This route ascends an obtuse dihedral 25 feet right of *Testosterone Testpiece*.
50 ft. *FA Mark Schorle, Tracy Best, 1990.*

➎ Double Trouble 5.10d ★★★
Walk around the corner 30 feet right from *Apehouse* to locate a pair of cracks with a small roof about 15 feet up. Climb the right crack until it fades away, then continue up thin face to a ledge. Climb easier face to bolt anchors.
60 ft. *FA Hugh Loeffler, Neal Strickland, 1990.*

➏ Gorge Factor 10 5.9 R ★★
This route ascends the dihedral capped by a large roof 75 feet right of *Double Trouble*. Climb the crack to a ledge and belay. Continue up the crack to a roof, then traverse right out the face under the roof to a ledge. Climb a dirty crack to the summit. Rappel from a tree to descend.
130 ft. *FA Hugh Loeffler, Neal Strickland, 1990.*

Cold Shot

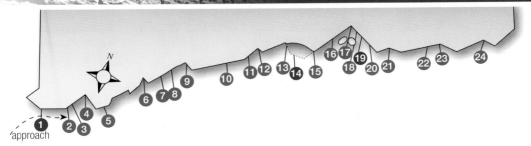

approach

---

7 Anne's Crack 5.10a ★★

This route ascends the hand crack 50 feet right of *Gorge Factor 10* to a ledge. The start is a bit mossy but the quality quickly improves. Bring some large cams for the belay. Rappel from a tree to descend.

35 ft. *FA Steve Must, Hugh Loeffler, 1990.*

8 F.O. Nazi Art Police 5.10b R ★

This route ascends the thin crack 20 feet right of *Anne's Crack*.

35 ft. *FA Hugh Loeffler, Steve Must, 1990.*

9 Pink Panties Pulldown 5.7 ★★★

This route ascends the offwidth in a dihedral about 25 feet right from the previous route. Rappel from a tree to descend.

40 ft. *FA Alex Cudkowicz, Braden Hale, 1990.*

10 11:11 5.11b ★★★

Look for a thin crack to the right of *Pink Panties Pulldown* with a small roof about 15 feet up. Climb the face to the right of the dihedral and move left to gain the crack. Continue up the crack to a small ledge, try to get a rest and move up the overhanging face to a large ledge with a tree and belay.

60 ft. *FA Kris Hampton, 2001.*

11 Bongo 5.6 ★★★

Great first trad lead. Locate a hand crack in the middle of a face about 30 feet right of *11:11*. Climb the crack with liberal use of face holds, play the bongo, and continue to the ledge. Lower from bolt anchors.

50 ft. *FA Debbie Sarabia, Dick Montione, 1990.*

12 Red River Renaissance 5.9 ★★★

Move about 20 feet right from *Bongo* to locate this route. It ascends a short dihedral to a ledge. To descend, lower from fixed anchors.

45 ft. *FA Hugh Loeffler, Neal Strickland, 1990.*

13 New Red River 5.9 ★★★

From *Red River Renaissance*, walk 40 feet right to a curving dihedral. Climb the dihedral to a set of bolted anchors.

60 ft. *FA Neal Strickland, Hugh Loeffler, 1990.*

14 Campfire Crank 5.12a ★★★

This bolted route is located on the left side of a low overhang about 20 feet right of *New Red River*. Reach the first holds with cheater stones or aid and boulder up and over the bulge to gain the thin face. Continue up the face to a small ledge with bolted anchors.

45 ft. 6 bolts. *FA (toprope) Hugh Loeffler, Neal Strickland, 1990. First lead unknown.*

15 Icy Fresh 5.11b ★

Toprope. Walk under the low overhang right from *Campfire Crank* and around the corner to locate this route. Step up into a dihedral and traverse left along a roof. Move around the roof and up into a thin finger-crack. Continue up the finger crack until it fades.

50 ft. *FA Hugh Loeffler, Neal Strickland, Paul Woodrum, 1980.*

16 Sisyphean Labor 5.10a ★★★

To the right of the large overhang and a horizontal under the roof is a finger crack leading to an obtuse dihedral. Power through the start, then continue up the narrow dihedral to a dirty ledge.

70 ft. *FA Ray Ellington, Bill Geimann, 2000.*

17 Strick 9 5.9 ★★★★★

Classic corner. From *Sisyhpean Labor*, head right and around the corner to the next dihedral. Stem and jam the crack to a short roof. Step right under the roof, get a good piece, and reach up into a positive layback. Scurry for the ledge and lower from bolted anchors.

50 ft. *FA Neal Strickland, Anne Lucas, 1990.*

Sisyphean Labor

Strick 9

Funhouse

18 **Buckeye Testpiece** 5.6 R ★★

This route ascends the well-featured but poorly protected face 10 feet right of *Strick 9* to the same large ledge. It is possible to spare your underwear and toprope this from the anchors on *Strick 9*.
50 ft. *FA Hugh Loeffler, 1990.*

19 **Toxic Avenger** 5.10d ★★★★

Great runout slab climbing. Move right from Buckeye Testpiece to locate a line of bolts. Tiptoe up the face past some scary clips to a roof. Plug a cam, or don't, then move left and mantel to the large ledge on which the previous routes end. Photo page 135.
50 ft. 4 bolts. *FA Neal Strickland, Hugh Loeffler, 1991.*

20 **Chemical Imbalance** 5.11b ★★★

Originally an all-gear route, the first ascentionist was peer pressured into making this line a little safer. Climb the slab to the right of *Toxic Avenger*, past 3 bolts, then continue to the ledge using small- to medium-sized cams.
50 ft. 3 bolts. *FA Hugh Loeffler, 1990.*

21 **Must Dihedral** 5.8

Walk around the corner from the previous routes to locate this short dihedral. Climb it to a ledge.
35 ft. *FA Steve Must, Bhavani Pathak, 1990.*

22 **Drug Pusher** 5.12a ★★★

Walk right from *Must Dihedral* to locate a crack with an 8-foot roof about 15 feet off the deck. Climb up to a horizontal and place some gear. Reach out, release, and crank over the lip into an offwidth slot. Continue up the finger crack to fixed gear anchors. Photo page 131.
60 ft. *FA Ray Ellington, 1996.*

23 **Blue Balls** 5.9 ★

This route is located 20 feet right of *Drug Pusher*. Climb the chimney to a nice dihedral and past a couple of roofs to a ledge.
60 ft. *FA Mark Schorle, Neal Strickland, 1990.*

24 **Funhouse** 5.7 ★★★★

Pure fun! Walk 75 feet right from *Blue Balls* to locate this dihedral. Stem up the sandy beginning, then enjoy great climbing to the ledge. Rappel from bolt anchors.
85 ft. *FA Mark Schorle, Tracy Best, 1990.*

LIVEWIRE QUICKDRAW

BUILT FOR THE
SEND

Sam Elias, *Ne Pas Toucher a Ma
Bite* (5.13c), Kalymnos, Greece
📷 BOONE SPEED

BlackDiamondEquipment.com

SEARCH 🔍 LIVEWIRE

EASTERN GORGE

Character

The two most popular areas in the Eastern Region, Funk Rock City and Sky Bridge Ridge, have lots of amazing technical climbing, both sport and trad, on vertical to slightly overhanging, solid sandstone. Some of the Red's most difficult trad climbs are found in this region.

Approach

Sky Bridge Ridge, Funk Rock City, and Camp Store Crag are located off KY 715. Most of the other areas in this region are located off Chimney Top Road, which overlooks the Red River. From Miguel's, head north on KY 11 toward Mountain Parkway. Pass under Mountain Parkway, then turn left onto KY 15 near the Shell station. Continue west on 15 for about a mile until you reach KY 77 on your right. Turn right onto 77 and follow the road through Nada Tunnel, past Military Wall, and over the steel bridge. Bear right after the steel bridge, remaining on KY 77 until it intersects with KY 715. Turn right onto 715 and follow the road alongside the Red River until you reach the one-lane bridge crossing the river near the pulloff for Wall of Denial. After crossing the bridge, you are near the crags located in this area. Continue south along 715 for a few miles as it twists out of the gorge to locate the gravel Chimney Top Road on the right.

Access

All of the areas are located on Forest Service land, so please respect signs and fences indicating closed routes or trails and read the guidelines for climbing on Forest Service land on page 32 of this book. Wildcat Wall and Funk Rock City are located in the Clifty Wilderness area. Please pay special attention to additional Forest Service restrictions when climbing in wilderness.

CLIFF	SUN / SHADE	HIKE	RAIN	ROUTES	GRADE RANGE	CLASSIC ROUTES
LOWER SKY BRIDGE page 140	all day	5 mins		8	5.6- .7 .8 .9 .10 .11 .12 .13 .14	Jack the Ripper 11c Mr Get It On Jones 12c
EASTERN SKY BRIDGE page 145	all day	5 mins		30	5.6- .7 .8 .9 .10 .11 .12 .13 .14	Inhibitor 11a King Me 11b The Learning Curve 12a Soul Ram 12b
WESTERN SKY BRIDGE page 150	a.m.	10 mins		11	5.6- .7 .8 .9 .10 .11 .12 .13 .14	The Return of Geoff Beene 10d
FUNK ROCK CITY page 152	all day	20 mins		32	5.6- .7 .8 .9 .10 .11 .12 .13 .14	Orange Juice 12c Snotrocket 12+ Appalachian Spring 13a
CAMP STORE CRAG page 158	a.m.	5 mins	rain OK	2	5.6- .7 .8 .9 .10 .11 .12 .13 .14	
BUZZARD'S ROOST page 158	shade	10 mins		3	5.6- .7 .8 .9 .10 .11 .12 .13 .14	
WILDCAT WALL page 158	a.m.	30 mins		5	5.6- .7 .8 .9 .10 .11 .12 .13 .14	
ROUGH TRAIL page 158		10 mins		1	5.6- .7 .8 .9 .10 .11 .12 .13 .14	
HALF MOON page 160	shade	5 mins		14	5.6- .7 .8 .9 .10 .11 .12 .13 .14	
PRINCESS ARCH page 162	shade	10 mins		8	5.6- .7 .8 .9 .10 .11 .12 .13 .14	
CHIMNEY TOP page 163	shade	15 mins		11	5.6- .7 .8 .9 .10 .11 .12 .13 .14	

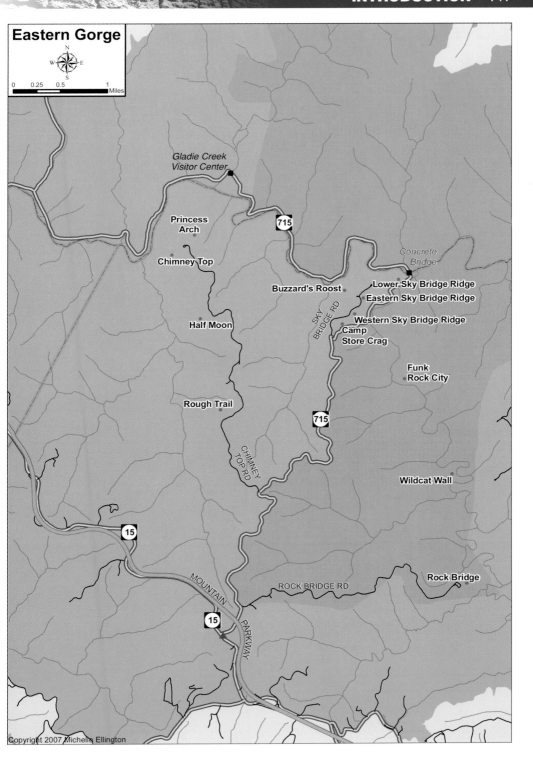

Eastern Gorge

N
W · E
S

0   0.25   0.5   1
Miles

Gladie Creek Visitor Center ■

715

Princess Arch

Chimney Top

Concrete Bridge ■

Buzzard's Roost

Lower Sky Bridge Ridge

Eastern Sky Bridge Ridge

Western Sky Bridge Ridge

SKY BRIDGE RD

Camp Store Crag

Half Moon

Funk Rock City

Rough Trail

715

CHIMNEY TOP RD

Wildcat Wall

15

MOUNTAIN

ROCK BRIDGE RD

Rock Bridge

15

PARKWAY

Copyright 2007 Michelle Ellington

LOWER SKY BRIDGE RIDGE

  8 routes

5 mins   5.6- .7   .8   .9 .10 .11 .12 .13 .14

all day

Character

The bolts disappear at Lower Sky Bridge Ridge. A handful of individuals, determined to bag some first ascents, established most of the routes relatively recently. The area contains only a handful of traditional routes but includes some of the toughest. There are quite a few dihedrals in the Red, but not many like *Jack the Ripper*. This stemming nightmare will leave your calves cramped for days. Don't miss taking a shot at the dynamic and powerful finger crack *Mr. Get It On Jones*, a testpiece for the Red River Gorge crack climber.

Approach

From the intersection of KY 77 with KY 715 near Fortress Wall, stay on KY 715 for 7.1 miles until you reach a one-lane concrete bridge. Cross the bridge and park in a pulloff on your left. Walk across the road then go straight up the ridge near the bridge. Follow the ridge for about five minutes until you meet the wall. You should end up directly in front of a corner where *The Specimen* is located.

Conditions

The lines at Lower Sky Bridge Ridge face southeast and receive great sunlight. The routes right of *The Specimen* can be a bit green, however, they are still pretty clean. Watch out for falling debris from tourists on the trail above.

Pangaea

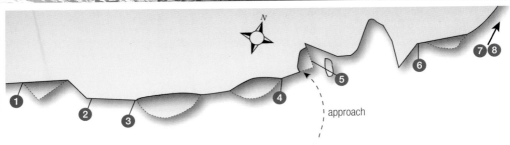

approach

1 Strokin' the Nut 5.9+ ★★

Walk left from *Mr. Get It On Jones* to locate a wide, right-facing crack that has a ledge about 30 feet up. Climb the crack to the ledge, then continue up through the left angling hand crack over a bulge to the top. Rappel from a tree to descend.
120 ft. *FA Tim Powers, 1994.*

2 Mr. Get It On Jones 5.12c ★★★★★

Ghetto Fabulous. Walk left from *Jack the Ripper* about 30 feet to locate this overhanging crack in black rock. Begin by pulling up to a ledge about 10 feet off the ground. Fingerlock out the roof and launch to a jug. Continue up the off-fingers crack to a good handjam. Take a breather, then crank through painful fingerlocks to a ledge.
50 ft. *FA Ray Ellington, 2001.*

3 Jack the Ripper 5.11c ★★★★★

A bit of Randy Leavitt's stemming mastery would help you on this one. This route ascends a left-facing dihedral 120 feet left of *As Luck Would Have It*. Look for a small tree midway up and a striking, featureless section towards the top.
60 ft. *FA Jack Dickey, 1985.*

4 As Luck Would Have It 5.9+ ★★★

Walk left from *The Specimen* about 25 feet to locate a short finger crack in a right-facing dihedral with a low overhang. Boulder up into the dihedral and climb to the ledge.
35 ft. *FA Kris Hampton, 1999.*

5 The Specimen 5.10c ★★★

This route is located at the end of the approach trail, a few feet left of a 3-foot boulder with a sharp edge on top of it. It begins as an overhanging and flaring offwidth with an obvious mail slot on the right face at about 4 feet. Armbar through the offwidth to gain a short fist crack that leads to a ledge. Set a belay, then continue up the easier crack to the top near the handrails of the Sky Bridge tourist trail.
100 ft. *FA Kris Hampton, Ray Ellington, 1998.*

The remaining routes are located right of The Specimen.

6 The Whistle Driller 5.9 ★★★★

Walk right from *The Specimen* about 100 feet and look for a hand crack that leads to a chimney of sorts about 30 feet up. Climb up to the chimney where it turns to a finger crack. Continue up the finger crack to finish.
75 ft. *FA Kris Hampton, 1999.*

Jack the Ripper

7 Pangaea 5.11a ★

Walk along the wall to the right of The *Whistle Driller* about 250 feet until you reach a huge amphitheater with a large boulder at the bottom and a gigantic roof split by an offwidth about 80 feet up. To the left of the amphitheater is this dihedral which leads out a hand crack in the roof to another dihedral above. Climb the dihedral, then undercling and jam out the roof. Pull over the lip and into another dihedral. Turn sideways and head scum up the dihedral until the crack opens up again. Get some gear in and race for the ledge.
70 ft. *FA Ray Ellington, Kris Hampton, 1999.*

8 Choss Factor 9 A2 ★★★

30 feet right of *Pangaea* is a thin seam in a dihedral. Aid up the seam to belay just below a large offwidth roof. Carefully aid around a loose block to reach the roof. Continue out the exposed roof, turn the lip, and finish above.
130 ft. *FA Bart Bledsoe, 2004.*
The lower dihedral has been freed and named **Twelve Step Program** 5.12a. *FA Loren Wood, Jordan Wood, 2005.*

Katie Erickson sending *Dave the Dude* 5.11d, Eastern Sky Bridge Ridge, page 148. Photo: Dan Bravack

EASTERN SKY BRIDGE RIDGE

all day

5 mins

30 routes

5.6- .7 .8 .9 .10 .11 .12 .13 .14

Character

This wall has it all: classic trad, classic sport, a great boulder problem, and a great aid line. The approach takes five minutes and the wall is in the sun. The only downside is that the routes get wet in the rain. Most of the sport lines are pretty unique for the Red in that they are vertical, technical, and have well-spaced bolts. There are a great bunch of routes here for the solid 5.11 climber including *Inhibitor, Dave the Dude, Commencement, Corpus Delicti, King Me, Martin Rides Again, Super Dario*, and *Sick Puppies*. Send all of these and you'll be ready to climb 5.12 elsewhere in the Red.

Approach

From the intersection of KY 77 with KY 715 near Fortress Wall, stay on KY 715 for 7.1 miles until you reach a one-lane concrete bridge. Cross the bridge and drive another 0.7 miles to a large pulloff on your left. If you end up at a pulloff with a blocked dirt road, then you drove about a mile too far and are at the Funk Rock City parking area. Park your car and walk back down the road in the direction you approached for about 300 feet and look for the trail to your left. Follow the trail straight up the hill to the wall.

An alternate approach from the Rest Area in Slade is to jump back on Mountain Parkway and head east to the next exit (Exit 40). Turn right off the exit on KY 15 and drive 0.7 miles through the town of Pineville. Turn right onto KY715 and drive 6.5 miles along the road. Be sure to stay on the road when it takes a hairpin turn to the right or you will end up at the Sky Bridge parking area for the tourist trail. After the sharp turn to the right and then left, the road will head sharply downhill. Look for a pulloff on your right about .1 mile past the larger pulloff for Funk Rock City.

Conditions

Eastern Sky Bridge Ridge is a great wall, especially in the winter. However, as mentioned earlier, the vertical cliff doesn't provide much protection from the rain. Even on humid days, the routes tend to "sweat" a little bit. Expect crowds since the short approach and great climbing here is no secret.

❶ No Return 5.9+ ★★★★

At the end of the approach trail you will see this wide crack in black rock. Climb the hand and fist crack to a ledge, then continue up through a dihedral being careful not to pass the ledge with the anchors. Belay on the ledge to the right from bolt anchors on *Commencement*. **100 ft.** *FA Ed Pearsall, Tom Seibert, 1979.*

❷ Commencement 5.11a ★★★

This bolted line is located about 15 feet right of *No Return*. Climb up through pockets to a blank section, then head straight up or make things hard on yourself by heading out right. Enjoy the rest of this long pitch on larger holds to the anchors. **90 ft. 10 bolts.** *FA Rob Turan, 1991.*

❸ Corpus Delicti 5.11d ★★★

This is the bolted route 20 feet right of *Commencement*. Climb through large jugs to gain the blank face. Leave the comfort of huge footholds and begin the crimpfest. Make a tough final move, then clip the anchors. If you're lucky, there will be chalk on the holds. **70 ft. 7 bolts.** *FA Porter Jarrard, Jeff Moll, 1991.*

❹ Ex Post Facto 5.10b ★

This route ascends the crack system 15 feet right of *Corpus Delicti* to the anchors on that route. **70 ft.** *FA John Bronaugh, Ron Snider, 1984.*

No Return

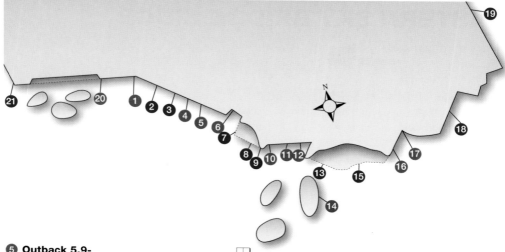

5 Outback 5.9-

This route ascends a wide crack system about 20 feet right of *Ex Post Facto*. Climb the slot to a hand crack over a bulge. Pull a roof and climb the face to the right to a ledge. **90 ft.** *FA Tom Seibert, 1980.*

6 The Underling 5.9 ★★★★

See description opposite.

7 What's Right 5.12a ★★★
With the Underling?

This bolted line ascends the face next to the arete near *The Underling*. Begin by climbing the face beneath the rockhouse, then move right out onto the other face after the third bolt. Continue up the face to a sit-down rest, then continue up the thin face with a slight runout at the anchors. **75 ft. 8 bolts.** *FA Porter Jarrard, Mark Strevels, 1992.*

8 Out on a Limb 5.12c ★★★

Re-equipped in 2004, it is now possible to enjoy this line without the fear of a bed frame hanger holding your fall. Move right from the previous line to the next two bolted lines, which share a start. Reach up to a high jug beneath a roof, then crank over the lip to gain the face. After the first couple of bolts, head out left to fall your way up the rest of the route. This route doesn't get many ascents. That may say something about its difficulty. Hmmmm… old-school Porter face climb. Look out! **70 ft. 9 bolts.** *FA Porter Jarrard, Jamie Baker, 1990.*

9 King Me 5.11b ★★★★★

Classic 5.12. Wait a minute… it's only 5.11! But I saw it on the cover of *How To Climb 5.12* by Eric Horst? You mean to tell me I didn't climb a 5.12!? Same start as the previous line but don't move out left. Pull through pockets and sidepulls to an underling crux near the top. Continue up the final slab to the anchors. **90 ft. 10 bolts.** *FA Porter Jarrard, Tim Toula, 1990.*

10 Right On, Solid, and Far Out 5.8 A2 ★★★

This aid line ascends the obvious right-facing dihedral around the corner from *King Me*. Aid the seam to an arete, then head for the anchors on *King Me*. Beware of horrendous rope drag on the upper, poorly protected traverse to the anchors on *King Me*. **90 ft.** *FA Eric Kamper, Jason Bach, 1996.*

11 The Learning Curve 5.12a ★★★★

Right of *Right On, Solid, and Far Out* is a short, thin finger crack leading to an obtuse dihedral with some cold shuts. Climb the finger crack, step in the dihedral, then hand-shuffle, slap, and crimp your way to the anchors. **35 ft.** *FA Nick Reuff, 1999.*

12 Inhibitor 5.11a ★★★★★

Are we in Yosemite? To the right of *The Learning Curve* is this massive left-facing dihedral. Pump up the thin-hands crack until you reach a point of not knowing what to do next just before the chimney. Place a #4 Camalot, then fight your way into the chimney. Catch your breath, try not to get rock rash on your nose, ignore the questions from below, and don't piss yourself. You're almost half way there. Swim up the overhanging chimney that begs to spit you out, then place a #5 above your head when you can. Slowly creep out of your safe zone and go for a good hand jam in the constriction above. Battle through a fist and forearm crack to another good hand jam, then pace yourself to the top. Don't plan any strenuous activities for the next day. Lower from bolted anchors. **90 ft.** *FA Tom Souders, Jeff Koenig, 1983.*

13 Nolo Contendere 5.12a ★★★

Rarely done, but kind of cool for the first two bolts. This route begins just around the corner from *Inhibitor*. Boulder up a slopey rail, then make a throw to a jug. Move left into a large hueco, then back right out onto the crimpy face. Crimp for a few bolts, then pull on jugs to the anchors. **90 ft. 9 bolts.** *FA Porter Jarrard, John Mallery, 1993.*

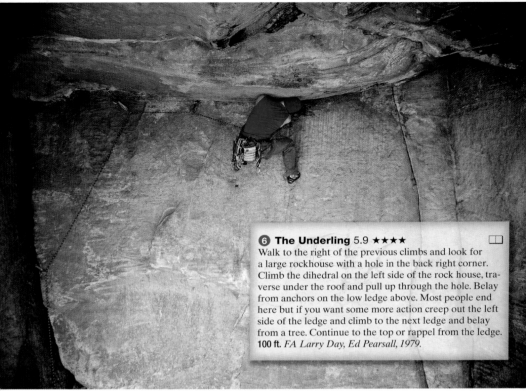

❻ The Underling 5.9 ★★★★
Walk to the right of the previous climbs and look for
a large rockhouse with a hole in the back right corner.
Climb the dihedral on the left side of the rock house, traverse under the roof and pull up through the hole. Belay
from anchors on the low ledge above. Most people end
here but if you want some more action creep out the left
side of the ledge and climb to the next ledge and belay
from a tree. Continue to the top or rappel from the ledge.
100 ft. *FA Larry Day, Ed Pearsall, 1979.*

Kris "Odub" Hampton on the *Underling*. Photo: Anne Skidmore.

⑭ The Pearl V5 ★★★★★
Just behind *Nolo Contendre* is one of the few truly great
boulder problems in the Red. Sit start on a rail, then
traverse right to a tough gaston. Crank it high, then slap
for the lip. Mantel your way up the sloping finish and
walk off right.

⑮ The Route Goes Where!? 5.11d
The bolted line to the right of *Nolo Contendere*.
50 ft. 7 bolts. *FA Unknown, 1993.*

⑯ The Big Bang 5.10c ★★
Toprope. Walk 40 feet right of *Nolo Contendere* past a
stream and around a corner to a dihedral with a left-
angling finger crack at the top. Climb a vertical finger
crack 10 feet left of this dihedral to some anchors.
50 ft. *FA Martin Hackworth, 1984.*

⑰ Doppler Effect 5.10b ★★★★
Walk right from *The Big Bang* and look up. When your
jaw drops, you've found *Doppler Effect*. Climb the
left-facing dihedral to the roof. Milk the weird hand jam
until you're ready to go, then undercling and finger lock
out the beautiful roof. Lower from bolted anchors.
50 ft. *FA Tom Souders, Jeff Koenig, 1983.*

Doppler Effect   17

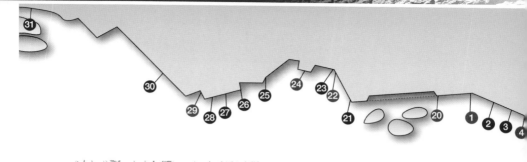

18

Dave the Dude

18 Dave the Dude 5.11d ★★★★

50 feet right of *Doppler Effect* is this bolted seam. Begin by climbing a finger crack, then move right onto a crimpy face. Crimp until the face turns blank, then move left to a flake for some eye-opening moves. Continue up the flake to the anchors. Photo page 144.
70 ft. 7 bolts. *FA Porter Jarrard, Dave Jacobson, 1992.*

19 Drop the Anchor 5.8+ ★★

Although moderately graded, this route tends to scare beginners. Walk right from *Dave the Dude* to a point about 50 feet right of an obvious corner. Move up through huecos, then pull over a small roof to clip the anchors.
60 ft. 5 bolts. *FA Tracy Crabtree, Neal Strickland, 1993.*

The following routes are located left of where the approach trail meets the wall.

20 Shelter From the Storm 5.11d ★★★

This striking line was originally an aid route climbed by John Bronaugh and Jim Link and named *Heavy Weather.* Directly left of the end of the approach trail is an obvious, thin dihedral beginning about 30 feet up. Climb up the initial dihedral, then pull a tough move when the dihedral changes corners. Stem your way to fixed anchors.
80 ft. *FA Kellyn Gorder, 1998.*

21 Soul Ram 5.12b ★★★★★

Be prepared, it's a tough one. Move left from *Shelter From the Storm* over some large boulders to a blunt arete. Begin on a ledge a few feet off the ground. Clip the first bolt, then move left around the arete onto the extreme face. Crimp and high step for 90 feet while trying to keep your sanity. Take advantage of a couple of handjams along the way.
100 ft. 9 bolts. *FA Porter Jarrard, Rob Turan, 1991.*

22 Good Times 5.8+ ★★★★

This route ascends the pair of cracks located 25 feet left of *Soul Ram.* Climb the cracks to a wide slot and chimney up until you can move out right to the face. Follow the second crack, then move left to some anchors.
100 ft. *FA Ed Pearsall, Tom Seibert, 1979.*

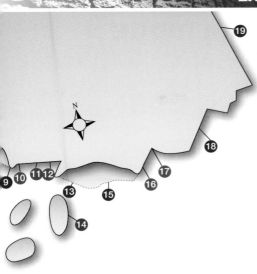

Good Times

Super Dario

23 The Rifleman 5.12b ★★★
This bolted route begins just left of *Good Times*. Begin by climbing a layback flake then follow the bolts left onto the face. Continue up the crimpy and sequential face to a good rest on a ledge just beneath the final two bolts, then fire when ready. You're in luck if the last draw is already hanging for you.
75 ft. 8 bolts. *FA Jamie Baker, Jim Link, 1990.*

24 Old Friends 5.8 R ★
Climb up to a ledge left of *The Rifleman* using either of two cracks. Climb a face, then move right into a hole. Jam the crack to a rappel tree using horizontals for pro.
70 ft. *FA John Bronaugh, 1984.*

25 Martin Rides Again 5.11d ★★★★
This is the bolted line near an arete 30 feet left of *The Rifleman.* Reach your way up a slab to the slightly overhanging face. Clip a bolt, then move left for a few powerful moves. When you can't see any more bolts, move right to the arete and continue to the anchors.
70 ft. 7 bolts. *FA Doug Reed, Porter Jarrard, 1991.*

26 Super Dario 5.11a ★★★★
This bolted route begins near a dihedral to the left of *Martin Rides Again.* Climb up to a ledge, then make a couple of crack moves to reach sinker holds on the face. After a few bolts, jump out left onto an obvious black streak that provides fun climbing to the anchors.
70 ft. 7 bolts. *FA Doug Reed, Porter Jarrard, 1991.*

27 Grunge Face 5.12a ★
This poorly bolted line ascends the face 15 feet left of *Super Dario.* Bolted on lead. Maybe it should be stripped on rappel?
70 ft. 7 bolts. *FA Steve Grossman, 1996.*

28 Jack in the Pulpit 5.10d ★★★
This bolted line ascends the face a few feet left of *Grunge Face* near an arete. Step left near the top to go for the anchors.
70 ft. 7 bolts. *FA Doug Reed, Porter Jarrard, 1991.*

29 Fungus Fantasy 5.5
Ascends the chimney around the corner and left of *Jack in the Pulpit.*
120 ft. *FA Charles Tabor, Geoff Manley, 1987.*

30 Physical Graffiti 5.11d ★★★
This line ascends the face left and around the corner from *Jack In the Pulpit.* Consider yourself fortunate if you catch it dry.
60 ft. 6 bolts. *FA Doug Reed, Porter Jarrard, 1991.*

31 Sick Puppies 5.11c ★★★★
Walk about 150 feet left of *Physical Graffiti* until you come to a jumble of boulders. Look for this bolted line on the overhanging wall in front of a large flat boulder. Climb the short but pumpy face to anchors.
50 ft. 4 bolts. *FA Neal Strickland, Hugh Loeffler, 1994*

WESTERN SKY BRIDGE RIDGE

a.m. · 10 mins · 11 routes · 5.6- .7 .8 .9 .10 .11 .12 .13 .14

Character

Another extension of the vast Sky Bridge Ridge climbing area, the western end of Sky Bridge Ridge has a different atmosphere from the eastern end, offering mostly traditional lines and receiving less sun and traffic.

Approach

Although it is possible to approach this area by hiking left for several hundred feet from *Sick Puppies*, a quicker and more direct approach is as follows: From the Eastern Sky Bridge Ridge parking area, walk across the road to locate a faint trail. Hike up the trail, which passes a popular campsite. Eventually you will end up near the overhang where the first few routes are located.

Access

The Forest Service recently fenced off and closed several routes at this crag to protect sensitive resources. Please do not climb the closed routes.

Into The Void

❶ Fleshy Headed Mutant 5.9+ ★★

Walk 250 feet left of *Sick Puppies* (if you took the approach for Eastern Sky Bridge Ridge) past an amphitheater to locate this offwidth in a fat flake. If you took the direct approach to Western Sky Bridge Ridge, this route can be found 175 feet right of the huge amphitheater beneath which you probably ended. Climb the flake to a large roof and belay from a bolted anchor. Move left beneath the roof and climb to another anchor to finish. Rappel from fixed gear.
80 ft. *FA Jack Hume, Michael Harned, 1994.*

❷ Take Off, Eh 5.7 ★

20 feet left of *Fleshy Headed Mutant* is a short dihedral. Climb the hand crack making liberal use of positive holds on the right face.
30 ft. *FA Jack Hume, Ellen Hume, 1993.*

❸ Refraction A2 ⊘

This route is closed. Walk left from *Take Off, Eh* to a huge amphitheater with an arching crack in its ceiling. Look for a crack on the overhanging right side of the wall that will more than likely be seeping. Aid the crack past a small alcove to bolted anchors above.
60 ft. *FA John Bronaugh, Ron Snider, 1984.*

❹ The Great Arch 5.10d ⊘

This route is closed. It ascended the large arching crack in back of the amphitheater, begining on the left, climbing to the apex and traversing right back down to the ground.
120 ft. *FA Tom Souders, 1993.*

❺ Void Direct 5.11b ★★★

Walk left from *The Great Arch* until you reach a right-facing dihedral capped by an impressive roof and chimney system. This old-school sport line ascends the face about 30 feet right of the dihedral. To figure out where to start, look for an old drilled pin about 10 feet off the deck. Pull past an overhang, then wander up the technical face, placing gear in the occasional horizontal slot or clipping the occasional bolt. If you really want to experience the route in its original form, put on striped tights, a pink headband, and play some Def Leppard on your boom box while you're climbing.
50 ft. 2 bolts. *FA Ron Snider, Tom Souders, 1988.*

❻ Into the Void 5.10c ★★★

Climb the dihedral just left of *Void Direct* to the ledge and belay from the anchors of that route. Then move up the face and into the deep, dark chimney. Undercling your way to the right and crank around a large chockstone. Continue up to belay at fixed gear near the end of the roof.
110 ft. *FA Tom Souders, Martin Hackworth, 1985.*

❼ Upstream Swimmer 5.9 ★★★

Walk 150 feet left of *Into the Void* until you see the obvious finger crack of *The Return of Geoff Beene* splitting the face in front of you. *Upstream Swimmer* ascends the offwidth in the dihedral to the right of the finger crack. Climb a wide chimney to gain a ledge about 20 feet up. Dive into the offwidth and do armbar and chickenwing strokes to the anchors. Bring a few Camalots sized between #4.5 and #5.
60 ft. *FA Kris Hampton, 1997.*

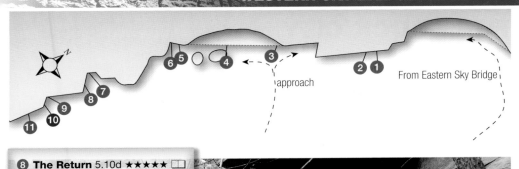

⑧ The Return 5.10d ★★★★★ ☐
of Geoff Beene
One of the best finger cracks the Red has to offer. This route ascends the obvious finger crack splitting the face left of *Upstream Swimmer*. Pull past the funky start, then layback or fingerlock past some good stances to a rest before the final 15 feet. Climb the thin crack past a couple of painful locks, then make a big reach out left and power to the ledge. If you get your partner to hang long draws, you're gonna miss the fun part.
60 ft. *FA Jeff Koenig, Tom Souders, 1983.*

⑨ Guideline 5.9 R ⊘
Closed. Head left and around the corner from the previous lines to a right-facing dihedral just left of what looks like a splitter hand crack. Make your way up the dihedral passing a few bolts along the way. Lower from bolted anchors.
60 ft. 3 bolts. *FA Eric Anderson, 1991.*

⑩ The Hook and the Pendulum 5.10b ⊘
Closed. This is the bolted line to the left of *Guideline*.
40 ft. 5 bolts. *FA Tony Reynaldo, Richard Brashear, 1983.*

⑪ Icarus 5.9 ⊘
Closed. Walk left from the previous route around a corner to a crack that begins about 10 feet off the ground. Stand on a boulder and jump out to grab a horn, then continue up the crack.
70 ft. *FA Ron Snider, Bill Rieker, 1982.*

The Hook and The Pendulum

FUNK ROCK CITY

all day | 20 mins | 32 routes
5.6- .7 .8 .9 .10 .11 .12 .13 .14

Character

Funk Rock City hosts a number of excellent vertical face climbs. Its bright-orange faces offer climbing that is more technical than most sport crags in the Red. *Orange Juice*, ascending a striking line of holds up a beautiful orange- and brown-streaked wall, is the classic face route at Funk Rock City—if not the whole Red River Gorge. Funk Rock City also has excellent trad lines like *Headstone Surfer*, a long, beautiful, curving bright-orange dihedral.

Approach

From the intersection of KY 77 with KY 715 near Fortress Wall, stay on KY 715 for 7.1 miles until you reach a one-lane concrete bridge. Cross the bridge and drive another 0.8 miles to a large pulloff on your left with a dirt road, which is blocked with large mounds of dirt to keep vehicles from travelling down it. The pulloff is located about 0.1 miles past the parking for Sky Bridge Ridge. Park here and walk the road 0.6 miles to a crossing over Swift Camp Creek. The crossing may or may not have some stepping stones. Wade the creek and walk upstream along an old road for 200 feet to locate an approach trail on your left that winds uphill to the wall.

   An alternate approach from the Rest Area in Slade is to jump back on Mountain Parkway and head east to the next exit (exit 40). Turn right off the exit on KY 15 and drive 0.7 miles through the town of Pineville. Turn right onto 715 and drive 5.5 miles along the road. Be sure to stay on the road when it takes a hairpin turn to the right or you will end up at the Sky Bridge parking area for the tourist trail. After the sharp turn to the right and then left, the road will head sharply downhill. Look for a large pulloff on your right before the road levels out.

Conditions

Although the approach to Funk Rock City is time consuming, it is relatively flat. The approach follows an old road alongside the Swift Camp Creek as it winds north to the Red River. It was once possible to drive the road for a ways and even camp alongside the Swift Camp Creek, but the entrance was gated off in 2003. The gunshots from bored campers surely won't be missed. It definitely makes for a more peaceful approach. Funk Rock City faces south so expect great winter climbing. Its exposed walls soak up the heat so you may want to avoid this area in the summer.

GLUE-IN BOLTS

In 2010, a group of people are taking on the task of re-bolting Funk Rock City. You can expect to find glue-ins here. Please be respectful of the area and the difficulty of maintaining these routes, as they are a part of the Clifty Wilderness and no power tools are allowed.

When you come across glue-ins, be aware that they are bomber. To keep them that way, please do not lower or bail directly from one, which causes premature wear.

Treat a glue-in like a regular hanger and use a bail biner!

❶ Scary Monsters 5.10b R ★★
and Super Freaks
From where the approach trail meets the wall, walk right around the corner to this route in an orange dihedral. Climb to a stance beneath a bulge, then move right to exit. 80 ft. *FA Lynn Watson, Hugh Loeffler, 1992.*

❷ Gyana Mudra 5.13a ★★★
This route will definitely go free soon. Walk right from the previous route to an obvious fingercrack splitting the face and doglegging left in the middle. Boulder the inital section to a good rest just before the dogleg. Crimp along the edge of the left-angling crack, passing the occasional decent finger lock. Make a couple of big moves to reach the anchors. The climbing is harder than it appears from the ground. Bring some small stoppers for the dogleg section. 40 ft. *FA Andrew Gearing, 2006.*

❸ Frugal Chariot 5.12a ★★★
Continue right along the wall from *Scary Monsters* around a buttress to an orange- and black-spotted wall with a thin seam running up it. This line is the furthest left on the wall. 85 ft. 8 bolts. *FA Hugh Loeffler, 1992.*

4 Smokin' Joe 5.11b ★★★
This route ascends the line of bolts just left of the thin seam mentioned above and 5 feet right of *Frugal Chariot*. Climb up a short dihedral to reach the top of a boulder and the first bolt. Reach up onto the face and continue up through technical climbing to a small over-hang. Crank the bulge and continue to the anchors.
80 ft. 8 bolts. *FA Tim Cornette, 1996.*

5 Joe Camel 5.8 ★★
Move 10 feet right from *Smokin' Joe* to a hand crack in a short black dihedral. Climb up about 40 feet to fixed gear and lower. An extension, **Emphysema 5.11a**, pulls the bulge left of the anchors on *Joe Camel* then follows the crack to the top. Rappel from a tree to descend.
40 ft. *FA Hugh Loeffler, Dave Lutes, 1993.*
Extension. *FA Danny Rice 2004.*

6 The Infidel 5.11d ★★★★★
This bolted line begins 40 feet right of *Joe Camel* in a concave face. Start on a small ledge a few feet up. Climb the technical face making use of edges and small pockets. Switch to slopers and jugs when the wall gets steeper and save some gas for the exciting moves before the anchors.
70 ft. 6 bolts. *FA Porter Jarrard, Jake Slaney, 1992.*

7 Just Another Trad Route 5.9 ★
This route ascends the dihedral a few feet right of *The Infidel*. Improvise an anchor to belay from, then rappel from the anchors on *Go Easy Billy Clyde!*
70 ft. *FA Cliff Cooper, Tim Powers, 1992.*

8 Go Easy Billy Clyde! 5.12a ★★★★
This bolted line begins 15 feet right of *Just Another Trad Route* above a boulder. Ten years ago, climbers used a cam placement to reach the first bolt but now you can just use one of those fancy stick clip things. Enjoy fun climbing for the first half, then take advantage of a good rest for the more technical second half.
75 ft. 8 bolts. *FA Tim Powers, 1992.*

9 Goodstone 5.10d ★★★
Walk 50 feet right from *Go Easy Billy Clyde!* to a pair of cracks about 20 feet apart. Begin by climbing the left crack until you can step out to a small ledge on the left face. Continue up the striking thin finger crack until it fades. Continue up a protectable face to pick the crack back up toward the top. Rappel from the anchors on *Cruising Lane*.
80 ft. *FA Hugh Loeffler, Dave Lutes, 1992.*

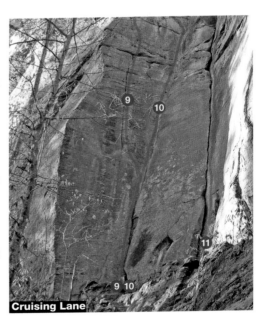
Frugal Chariot

Cruising Lane

10 Cruising Lane 5.10a ★★★★
A popular first 5.10 lead. This is the crack that you begin climbing to access *Goodstone*. Instead of stepping left onto the face, continue up the dihedral and past a thin layback section. Continue through easier climbing to bolted anchors.
80 ft. *FA Lynn Watson, Hugh Loeffler, 1992.*

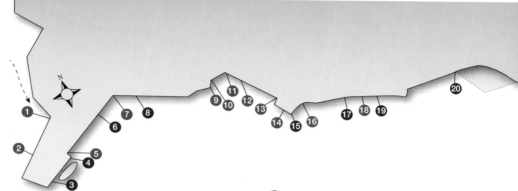

11 Rite of Passage 5.9+ ★★★

This is the left-facing dihedral directly right from *Cruising Lane*. Climb slammer hands to a small ledge with a funky dihedral. Continue up the funky *B3*-like dihedral to bolted anchors.
75 ft. *FA Neal Strickland, Dave Lutes, 1992.*

12 Local Color 5.10b

Toprope. This route ascends the face 40 feet right of *Rite of Passage*. Climb *Rite of Passage* to reach the ledge, then walk right to reach fixed anchors above the face.
65 ft. *FA Neal Strickland, Dave Lutes, 1992.*

13 Veldhaus Route 5.8+ ★

25 feet right of *Local Color* is a wide left-facing dihedral. Climb the wide crack to a ledge and rappel from a tree to descend.
90 ft. *FA Dave Veldhaus, Anne Hayes, 1991.*

14 Eye of the Needle 5.11b ★★★★

Walk around the corner from *Veldhaus Route* to locate this bolted arete just left of a wide dihedral. Climb the right side of the arete using the occasional reach-around for good face holds. Try to spot the eye of the needle.
85 ft. 10 bolts. *FA Tim Powers, Neal Strickland, 1992.*

15 Sparky Goes Crack Climbing 5.6 ★★★

This route ascends the wide crack just right of *Eye of the Needle*. To descend, rappel from anchors on *Manic Impression*. Bring large cams for protection.
90 ft. *FA Tim Powers, Cindy Porter, 1992.*

16 Manic Impression 5.10a ★★★★

Classic slab climbing that keeps your attention the whole way. This is the first bolted line encountered on the face right of *Sparky Goes Crack Climbing*. Tiptoe up to the first bolt, then continue up the face to a bulge near the top. Pull the bulge and run to the anchors.
90 ft. 7 bolts. *FA Dave Lutes, Neal Strickland, 1992.*

17 Trad Wagon 5.9 ★

This is the crack to the right of *Manic Impression*. Climb the crack and face to some anchors.
90 ft. *FA Dave Lutes, Neal Strickland, 1995.*

18 Funkadelic 5.10b ★★★★

This is the bolted line to the right of *Trad Wagon*. Bring a small cam if you want to protect the runout between the fifth and sixth bolt. The climbing isn't too bad at that point, though, so most people don't bother with it.
90 ft. 6 bolts. *FA Dave Lutes, Neal Strickland, 1992.*

Sparky Goes Crack Climbing

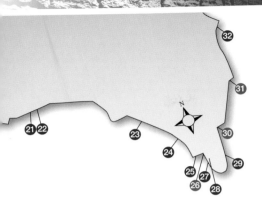

Flashlight

Orange Juice

⑲ Flashlight 5.12c ⊘
This route was recently closed. Please do not climb it.
Move about 50 feet right from *Funkadelic* to another
steep section of the wall. Locate a line of bolts just left
of a large overhang. Climb up to a five-foot high ledge to
begin. Step up onto the arete, then move left through the
slightly overhanging pocketed face to a vertical finish.
Keep it together during the runout from the last bolt to
the anchors.
70 ft. 7 bolts. *FA Porter Jarrard, 1992.*

⑳ Appalachian Spring 5.13a ★★★★★
Hike about 60 feet right from *Flashlight* to a slightly
overhanging orange- and black-streaked wall. Locate
the first line on the left and scramble up to a ledge to
begin. Move up the striking line making long reaches
to sparse holds. A positive ape index will definitely help
you on this one.
80 ft. 8 bolts. *FA Hugh Loeffler, 1995.*

㉑ Seppuku 5.12d ★★★★
Begin by climbing the initial moves of *Appalachian
Spring*, then follow the line of bolts that heads right. Make
your way up the technical face along the edge of the obvious orange-and-black streak. There is often a wet section
near the 4th bolt but it doesn't affect the climbing.
75 ft. 8 bolts. *FA Bill Ramsey, 1998.*

㉒ There Goes the Neighborhood 5.11c ★★★★
From the previous line, walk about 250 feet right to
locate the next bolted line on a vertical face with horizontal bands toward the bottom. Climb to a ledge about
five feet off the ground to gain the face. Tech your way
to the third bolt on small edges and pockets, then enjoy
larger holds to the anchors.
95 ft. 8 bolts. *FA Neal Strickland, 1992.*

㉓ Orange Juice 5.12c ★★★★★
Classic. Head right 40 feet from *There Goes the Neigbor-
hood* to locate this beautiful line on an orange- and
brown-streaked wall. Grab the first holds and crank up
through the obvious line of holds to a stopper crux toward the top. Boulder the crux and don't let your guard
down until you reach the anchors. Photo page 159.
95 ft. 10 bolts. *FA Hugh Loeffler, 1995.*

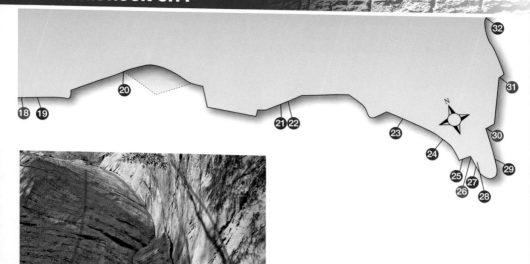

Headstone Surfer

25   26   27

Snotrocket   31

27 L'Ile au Ciel 5.11c ★★★

This aesthetic line ascends the exposed face above *Hard-core Jollies*. Either climb *Hardcore Jollies* or the first half of *Prime Directive* to reach the ledge from which it starts. **50 ft. 7 bolts.** *FA Hugh Loeffler, Dave Lutes, 1992.*

28 Prime Directive 5.11b ★★★★

Despite its moderate grade, this intense line thwarts most on-sight attempts. Walk around the corner and right from *Hardcore Jollies*. As you head up a short hill, this route will be to your left near an arete. Begin by climbing near the arete, then move left onto the face. Continue up to a roof, eye out the next bolt, then make a decision about how you're going to get to it. **95 ft. 11 bolts.** *FA Dave Lutes, Neal Strickland, 1992.*

29 Up Swift Creek Without a Paddle 5.9 ★★★

This sustained line, located in a dihedral just right of *Prime Directive*, doesn't get the attention it deserves. Layback or jam the black crack to anchors just beneath a roof. **60 ft.** *FA Neal Strickland, Hugh Loeffler, 1992.*

30 Snotrocket 5.12+ R ★★★★★

Walk right from *Up Swift Creek* to locate this stunning, thin dihedral, which was only recently freed. Requires technical foot scumming, stemming, laybacking, and other weirdness. Take a good assortment of small gear and very large balls. It's the "Book of Hate" of the South. **100 ft.** *FA Hugh Loeffler, 1996, as the aid route* Armageddon. *FFA Matt Massey, 2005.*

31 Glory Be 5.12a ★★★★

You can find this route hiding about 50 feet right from *Armageddon*. Creep up a slab, then continue up the pocketed face to the anchors. **80 ft. 8 bolts.** *FA Tim Cornette, Neal Strickland, 1993.*

24 Red Hot Chili Pepper 5.10d R ★★★

Walk 30 feet right of *Orange Juice* to a striking left-facing dihedral with a large boulder at its base. This route ascends the face left of the dihedral. A couple of small cams can be used to protect horizontal bands in the lower section, but most people tend to just run it out between bolts. Lower from bolted anchors. **90 ft. 6 bolts.** *FA Neal Strickland, Tracy Crabtree, 1992.*

25 Headstone Surfer 5.10a ★★★★

See description opposite.

26 Hardcore Jollies 5.12a ★★★

Just to the right of *Headstone Surfer* is this short and bouldery route. Power through the first couple of bolts, then edge to the anchors. **45 ft. 5 bolts.** *FA Dave Lutes, Hugh Loeffler, 1992.*

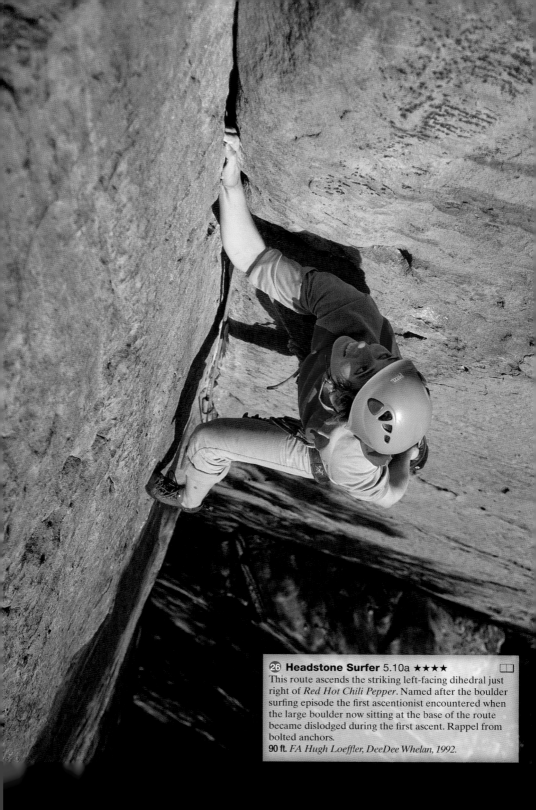

㉖ Headstone Surfer 5.10a ★★★★

This route ascends the striking left-facing dihedral just right of *Red Hot Chili Pepper*. Named after the boulder surfing episode the first ascentionist encountered when the large boulder now sitting at the base of the route became dislodged during the first ascent. Rappel from bolted anchors.

90 ft. *FA Hugh Loeffler, DeeDee Whelan, 1992.*

CAMP STORE CRAG

a.m. | 5 mins | OK in rain | 2 routes
5.6- .7 .8 .9 .10 .11 .12 .13 .14

Character
With its short approach and proximity to Sky Bridge Ridge and Funk Rock City, this wall offers a great supplement to climbing at those two areas. Although it has only two roped routes, both are high quality.

Approach
From the intersection of KY 77 with KY 715 near Fortress Wall, stay on KY 715 for 7.1 miles until you reach a one-lane concrete bridge. Cross the bridge and drive another 0.8 miles to a short muddy road on your right just past the parking for Funk Rock City. Hike up the dirt road for about 150 feet to a flat open area, then bushwhack uphill to your left for a few minutes to reach the cliff. You should end up directly beneath both routes.

Conditions
The lines are slightly overhanging and well sheltered from the rain.

1 Store 5.10c ★★★★
This is the route on the right and is located near an arete. Climb pockets and crimps to the arete, then pull an overhang. Continue up the face right of the arete to the anchors.
70 ft. 7 bolts. *FA Porter Jarrard, Leslie Thorn, 1991.*

2 Camp 5.11d ★★★★
This is the bolted line 15 feet left of *Store*. Begin to the right of a rock shelter. Power through the beginning moves and pull past a small overhang. Continue up the more overhanging face to the anchors.
70 ft. 7 bolts. *FA Porter Jarrard, Leslie Thorn, 1991.*

3 Crag V4 ★★★
Walk about 50 feet left of *Camp* to locate this low off-width roof boulder problem. Start back as far as you can and hunker your feet up into the roof to start. Under-cling out and turn the lip. Climb up a few feet and jump off when you feel satisfied.
FA Ray Ellington, 2003.

The following cliffs have been removed from the print version of this guidebook. Visit www.wolverinepublishing.com/downloads for a free download of the information for them.

BUZZARD'S ROOST
This buttress offers a couple of decent moderate traditional lines.

WILDCAT WALL
The main attraction of this remote wall is a pretty hike on a well-maintained trail.

ROUGH TRAIL
This wall offers a single short but fun crack.

Matt Fanning gets his *Orange Juice* 5.12c, Funk Rock City, page 155. Photo: Dan Brayack.

HALF MOON

14 routes
shade   5 mins   5.6- .7 .8 .9 .10 .11 .12 .13 .14

Character

Half Moon is a gorgeous cliff from a distance, but upon closer inspection the initials carved in the rock and the trash are a turnoff. The area is popular for tourists and party campers so don't expect a peaceful and serene climbing experience. Half Moon is a historically significant climbing area with routes that date as far back as 1969.

Approach

From the parking area for Sky Bridge Ridge or Funk Rock City, continue south on KY 715 for about 1.4 miles until you reach an intersection with Sky Bridge Drive. Do not turn right onto this road. Instead, take a sharp left turn and remain on KY 715 for 2.7 miles until you see a gravel road to the right named Chimney Top Road. Turn right on this road and follow for 3.3 miles to a pulloff on the right. Locate an un-marked trail across the road that leads past a number of popular campsites and hungover campers. Follow the trail for about five minutes until you reach a point where the sandstone hump of Half Moon becomes visible. At this point, locate a faint trail on the left that winds down to the base.

Graffiti on the top of Half Moon.

❶ Fallout 5.10a ★★★

As you scramble down the trail to the base of *Half Moon*, this line is located on the right just after you pass a small arch. Look for a nice short, overhanging dihedral that leads to double cracks halfway up. Walk off right.
45 ft. *FA Larry Day, 1976.*

❷ Ellen's Descent 4th Class ★

Hike down to the base then all the way around to the west face to locate this steep gully which leads to the top of Half Moon.
70 ft. *FA Ellen Seibert, 1973.*

③ Initiation 5.3 ★
Somewhere on the west end of the rock is this short crack.
25 ft. *FA Martin Hackworth, Tom Seibert, 1973.*

④ Eclipse 5.9 ★
Toprope. Walk left from the previous routes to the north side of the cliff. This line ascends a left-facing overhanging dihedral behind a large boulder.
90 ft. *FA John Bronaugh, Dirk Wiley, 1982.*

⑤ Honeymoon 5.10a ★★
Move left from *Eclipse*, past an obvious dihedral, to locate this crack system which begins a few feet right of an arete. Climb to a small roof, then move left to the arete. Place protection in horizontals and continue up the face to a ledge on the right. Traverse left to meet up with the second pitch of *Full Moon*.
80 ft. *FA John Bronaugh, Tina Feezel, 1991.*

⑥ Waning Moon 5.9+ ★
A variation of the second pitch of *Full Moon*, this route surmounts the overhang 10 feet right of the original line.
30 ft. *FA Martin Hackworth, 1981.*

⑦ Full Moon 5.7 ★★★★
The classic line at Half Moon. Move left and around the corner from *Honeymoon* to a rectangular buttress. Begin by climbing a wide crack on the right side of the buttress to a ledge. Belay from the ledge and climb to another ledge. Belay again, then continue up the remaining chimney to the top.
 Variation 1 5.4: Climb a flake and ramp to the right on the last pitch.
 Variation 2 5.8: Climb a hand crack on the left wall of the chimney on the last pitch.
100 ft. *FA Tom Seibert, Ellen Seibert, Frank Becker, Larry Day, 1973.*

⑧ Meteor Fall 5.9- R ★
Climb the hand crack 15 feet left of *Full Moon*, then traverse right to the first belay of *Full Moon*.
40 ft. *FA Rich Gottlieb, Gene Hancock, 1976.*

⑨ Meteor Maker 5.10a ★★★
Move left a few feet from *Meteor Fall* to this line that begins near an arete. Climb up and left around the arete, then face climb to a ledge. Pull over a bulge, taking note of the historical but scary bolt, to a stance just beneath an overhang. Grab sack and pull over the overhang to a ledge. From the ledge, move left and continue to the summit being careful not to fall.
120 ft. *FA Larry Day, 1983.*

Fallout

⑩ Rockhouse 5.4
From *Meteor Maker*, move left to the next arete. Climb to a ledge, then scramble up a gully on the left side of the buttress.
75 ft. *FA Unknown.*

⑪ Ron's Garden 5.6
Climb *Rockhouse* to the ledge, then take on the wide crack to the right.
50 ft. *FA Ron Stokely, D. Britz, Bob Stokes, 1969.*

⑫ Scared Shitless 5.6 R ★
Climb the first pitch of *Rockhouse*, then scramble to the next crack to the left. Jam the crack until it ends, then move right across the face to a sloping ledge. Walk left up a ramp to reach the top.
60 ft. *FA Ed Pearsall, 1978.*

⑬ It Ain't Over Yet 5.8+ ★★
Walk left from the previous crack to the next crack. Climb a thin crack to a wide hand crack that leads to the top.
60 ft. *FA Ed Pearsall, Kevin Pogue, 1980.*

⑭ Bob's Moon 5.10b ★★
Move left from *It Ain't Over Yet* to locate another crack with a low roof. Crank over the roof to a fist crack that leads to the top.
50 ft. *FA Ed Pearsall, 1978.*

PRINCESS ARCH

shade 10 mins

8 routes

5.6- .7 .8 .9 .10 .11 .12 .13 .14

Character
This area has an easy approach along a good trail and several worthwhile cracks of easy to moderate difficulty. The ease of setting up a toprope makes it a good beginners area.

Approach
From the parking area for Sky Bridge Ridge or Funk Rock City, continue south on KY 715 for about 1.4 miles until you reach an intersection with Sky Bridge Drive. Do not turn right onto this road. Instead, take a sharp left turn and remain on KY 715 for 2.7 miles until you see a gravel road to the right named Chimney Top Road. Turn right on this road and follow for about 3 miles to the end. Park and locate the trailhead on the right side of the loop which leads to Princess Arch. Follow the trail for about 0.5 miles over a small arch to a buttress on the end of the ridge. Rappel down from any tree in the area to reach the base of the climbs. Alternatively, to avoid rappelling, head left down a steep hill along a faint trail from the small arch. Then head right, skirting around the base of some small walls to reach the routes.

Conditions
The climbs are north-facing and can become a little more difficult on humid days.

Ripp-Off

① Beginner's Nightmare 5.1 ★
More of a scramble than a route, this line climbs an easy right-angling ramp on the front of the buttress right of Adrenaline and finishes up a short squeeze chimney.
60 ft. *FA Cliff Bond, Tom Seibert, Ellen Seibert, 1973.*

② Adrenaline 5.10d ★★★
Walk about 40 feet left from *Beginner's Nightmare* to an attractive curving crack that splits a bulge. Climb slippery holds on a slabby section left of the crack. Reach out to the crack near the lip of a bulge and pull over onto the slab. Lower from there or continue to the top.
60 ft. *FA Ed Pearsall, 1980.*

③ Ripp-Off 5.6 ★★
Walk left and around the corner from *Adrenaline* to an attractive orange left-facing dihedral. Pull the tough start, then climb up to and around an overhang near the top.
45 ft. *FA Tom Seibert, Ellen Seibert, Bob Hill, Gene Hancock, 1975.*

④ Face Farce 5.8 R ★
This line climbs pockets on the slabby face just left of *Ripp-Off*.
45 ft. *FA Tim Powers, 1987.*

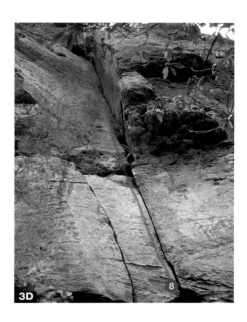

⑤ Golden Fleece 5.6 ★★　　　　⬜
The crack left of *Face Farce*.
50 ft. *FA Gene Hancock, Bob Hill, Tom Seibert, Ellen Seibert, with a top-rope, 1975.*

⑥ Finger Filet 5.8 ★　　　　⬜
Ascends a thin flake 30 feet left of the previous line.
50 ft. *FA Brent Lewis, Mark Lewis, with a top-rope, 1981.*

⑦ What a Maroon 5.10a ★★　　　⬜
Move left from Finger Filet to the next obvious crack splitting the face. Hand jam and finger lock the crack past a couple of wide sections to the top.
50 ft. *FA Martin Hackworth, Tim Andriakos, with a top-rope, 1989.*

⑧ 3D 5.9 ★★★　　　　⬜
Walk left about 100 feet to a left-facing dihedral with a rotten orange roof on the right side of the crack halfway up. Climb up a crack splitting the face to a small ledge. From the ledge, move up into a dihedral and continue to a large ledge. Traverse right to a rappel tree to descend.
75 ft. *FA Ed Pearsall, 1980.*

CHIMNEY TOP

shade　15 mins

8 routes

5.6- .7 .8 .9 .10 .11 .12 .13 .14

Character

Chimney Top, like Half Moon, has suffered the abuse of thousands of careless campers and tourists. The formation can be seen in its beauty when viewed from KY 715 near the parking area for Sheltowee Wall. However, upon closer inspection expect to find the area littered with trash and full of tourists. Climbing dates back to the late 60s, making the climbs on Chimney Top historically significant. Most of the good lines on the south side are now closed to climbing. There are still several worthwhile lines on the north side although the quality of the rock is generally not as good.

Approach

From the parking area for Sky Bridge Ridge or Funk Rock City, continue south on KY 715 for about 1.4 miles until you reach an intersection with Sky Bridge Drive. Do not turn right onto this road. Instead, take a sharp left turn and remain on KY 715 for 2.7 miles until you see a gravel road to the right named Chimney Top Road. Turn right on this road and follow for 3.6 miles to the end of the road. On the right side of the loop at the end of the road is the trailhead for Chimney Top. Follow the trail for a few minutes until you see a bail-out trail on the right just before a wooden fence. Follow this trail down, as it winds through a series of ledges, to the base of the wall. From the base, bushwhack toward the end of Chimney Top in the direction you were walking. After several hundred feet you should be able to spot *Hamburger* and *Last Day*.

Access

The National Forest Service prohibits climbing or rappelling from Chimney Top overlook. Maybe they are worried that you'll be injured by a carelessly tossed Budweiser bottle. This closure affects *Chimney's Chimney, The Prow,* and *Tunnel Route*.

❶ Hamburger 5.10b ★ ☐☐
Locate the first hand crack along the approach, which is just left of a wide crack system. Climb the crack until it fades then traverse right to join *Last Day*.
60 ft. *FA Jack Posten, 1979.*

❷ Last Day 5.10c R ★★ ☐☐
This line ascends the wide crack system just right of *Hamburger*. Look for a seven-foot-high pointed boulder near the base. Climb to an overhang and through an offwidth crux to a belay on a ledge. Continue left to a large tree for another belay. From the belay, climb a left-angling crack to a narrow ledge, then traverse right (5.8 R section) and climb up to another ledge. Move left to a tree and dart for the top.
160 ft. *FA Larry Day, Ed Pearsall, 1979.*

❸ Check Canopy 5.7 ★★ ☐☐
From *Last Day*, hike right to a small pinnacle near the main wall. Start on the pinnacle and climb a right-facing dihedral which changes corners and ends on a ledge. Belay from the ledge, then continue up a left-angling crack, which leads to a bit of face climbing to reach the top.
100 ft. *FA John Bronaugh, Martin Hackworth, 1982.*

❹ Dirty Crack 5.7 ☐☐
Move right from *Check Canopy* to the next dirty crack. Climb it to the top.
100 ft. *FA Tom Seibert, 1970.*

❺ Zig-Zag 5.6 ☐☐
From *Dirty Crack* walk right to the final crack before the main chimney that gives Chimney Top its name. Climb the crack, then move right along a ledge to a belay. Continue up the crack to a small overhang, crawl left, then face climb to a small ledge and another belay. Traverse right to a set of twin cracks that leads to a roof. Dodge the roof by traversing left to a flared crack that ends in an alcove near the top. From the alcove, climb a few more feet to reach the top. Now you know why it's called *Zig-Zag*.
130 ft. *FA Ed Pearsall, 1977.*

❻ Chimney Direct 5.7 ★ ☐☐
Move right and around the corner from *Zig-Zag* to an offwidth. Climb the offwidth to a ledge and belay. From the ledge, climb a short dihedral to another ledge and traverse left to an alcove to meet up with the final pitch of *Tunnel Route*. Follow the crack to the top.
  Variation 5.7 R: From the second pitch, climb the crack on the face left of the dihedral.
130 ft. *FA Bob Stokes, D. Britz, John Hubbard, 1969. Variation FA: Bob Compton, Bud Compton, early 1970s.*

❼ Chimney's Chimney 5.2 X ⊘
This route is closed. (Forest Service prohibits climbing or rappelling anywhere along the overlook.) Walk around the end of the buttress to the south-facing side of Chimney Top, which faces Half Moon. Chimney up anywhere in the first and obvious crack to the top.
100 ft. *FA D. Britz, Bob Stokes, 1969.*

❽ The Prow 5.10c R ⊘
Closed. Climb the first pitch of *Chimney's Chimney* then traverse left along a ledge to a fixed pin and belay. Continue up and left along chossy rock to a ledge with a fixed anchor and belay. Head right to locate a hand crack that leads to the top.
100 ft. *FA Larry Day, Martin Hackworth, 1985.*

❾ Tunnel Route 5.5 ⊘
Closed. Before its closure, this route was one of the best long and exposed easy routes in the Red. Move right from *Chimney's Chimney* to the next crack system. Begin by scrambling up a gully to a ledge 20 feet up. Pull over an overhang to reach another ledge and belay.
  Scramble through a tunnel in the rock to the north face then traverse 15 feet to reach an exposed belay in an alcove. Pull over a small roof, then continue up the slab to the top.
Variaton 1 5.4 R: Climb the face left of the first pitch.
Variation 2 5.5 R: Instead of crawling through the tunnel, chimney to the top.
150 ft. *FA D. Britz, Ron Stokely, 1969.*

❿ True Grit 5.9 ★★★ ☐☐
Move right from *Tunnel Route* to the next gully that leads to a large ledge. Climb an overhanging wall to the right of a crack and step left to a ledge. Continue up a dihedral and pull an overhang. Traverse right along the ledge to reach the top.
60 ft. *FA Greg Smith, Chris Bennet, 1983.*

⓫ Shipwrecked 5.8 ★★ ☐☐
Walk right a ways from *True Grit* to locate a pillar that forms an arch with the main wall. Climb the crack near the inside of the arch, then pull over a roof and jam to the top.
55 ft. *FA Chuck Keller, Steve Faulkner, 1988.*

Photo: Rudaw Janowic

PROFILE: The visionary

Porter Jarrard is well known for the incredible number of classic sport climbs he established at the Red in the early 1990s. Born in North Carolina, Porter found his love for overhanging face climbing in 1985 when he began climbing at the traditional area of Moore's Wall, North Carolina. He put up his first new routes there with his partner and mentor, Tim Fisher, using a hand drill and "traditional" bolting-on-lead ethics. Porter quickly sought out other climbing areas, including the New River Gorge in West Virginia and the extremely overhanging walls of Little River Canyon in Alabama. In 1987, after purchasing his first cordless Hilti, Porter teamed up with Doug Reed and established *Freeky Stylee* at the Endless Wall, one of the first bolted lines at the New River Gorge. In 1990, with the second release of Martin Hackworth's guide to the Red hot off the press, and the weather at the New getting cold, Porter and his Hilti made their way to the overhanging sandstone walls of the Red River Gorge.

Porter quickly made a home in an abandoned house on Miguel's property, aka "The Love Shack," which has since been torn down, and camping at the end of Tunnel Ridge Road. Living the dedicated climber lifestyle, he and a friend had a deal where Porter would purchase the beer and cigarettes while his friend would use his food stamps to buy the food. With those necessities secured, Porter started bolting like a man possessed. During the week he would call from the Junior Williamson Rest Area

payphone, begging friends from surrounding cities to climb with him that weekend. Finding a partner in the Red back then was much more difficult than it is today. As bait, he began establishing easy lines such as *Sunshine* and *Moonbeam*. He says he bolted the 5.9 *Brother Stair* at Left Flank so people would have a reason to come belay him on his project, *Table of Colors*.

Porter took a break from climbing beginning in 1993 to obtain a degree in geography. With the discovery of The Motherlode in 1997, he returned to climbing and developed a few more lines including *Hoofmaker* and *Fourty Ounces of Justice*. Porter has since become a little burned out on climbing at the Red due to having climbed there so frequently for so many years but does manage to get out a few times a year. His favorite climbing areas are Pilot Knob, NC, The New, and of course, Moore's Wall, NC. His favorite lines at the Red are *Bare Metal Teen*, *Soul Ram*, *Stunning the Hog*, *Reliquary*, and *King Me*.

Oh yeah, what's up with those infamous "Porter Hangers"? In the late 1980s during a two-day period, Porter crafted 200 of them at his dad's shop using 1/8" angle iron. Despite popular belief, Porter claims they are extremely strong and have been tested in Black Diamond's lab at 5000 lbs. "Plus," he says, "they make a hell of a foothold, especially on *Soul Ram*!" ∎

TUNNEL RIDGE ROAD

Character

This small region offers some great remote trad climbing at Jailhouse Rock. Most of the other areas are within a short distance of one another and, although lacking in quantity, can be combined to make a full day of climbing. The majority are heavily used by tourists and campers, so expect well-maintained trails, along with regular tourist questions.

Approach

Tunnel Ridge Road branches north off of KY 15 and passes directly atop Nada Tunnel, giving the road its name. From Miguel's, drive north on KY 11 toward the rest area. When you reach the stop sign near the Shell Station, turn right onto KY 15 and follow it for a few miles until you see Tunnel Ridge Road to your left. Cross over the highway and follow the gravel road back to the pulloffs for the climbing areas.

Access

All of the areas in this region except Jailhouse Rock are located on Forest Service land. Jailhouse Rock is located on Army Corps of Engineers land, which is maintained by the Forest Service. Please respect signs and fences indicating closed routes or trails and read the guidelines for climbing on Forest Service land on page 32 of this book.

CLIFF	SUN / SHADE	HIKE	RAIN	ROUTES	GRADE RANGE	CLASSIC ROUTES
D. BOONE HUT CRAG page 169	shade	15 mins		7	5.6- .7 .8 .9 .10 .11 .12 .13 .14	
HAYSTACK ROCK page 169	p.m.	30 mins		3	5.6- .7 .8 .9 .10 .11 .12 .13 .14	
AUXIER RIDGE page 169	p.m.	30 mins		3	5.6- .7 .8 .9 .10 .11 .12 .13 .14	
COURTHOUSE ROCK page 169		35 mins		4	5.6- .7 .8 .9 .10 .11 .12 .13 .14	
STAR GAP ARCH page 169	all day	20 mins		3	5.6- .7 .8 .9 .10 .11 .12 .13 .14	
JAILHOUSE ROCK page 168	a.m.	45 mins		7	5.6- .7 .8 .9 .10 .11 .12 .13 .14	
DOUBLE ARCH page 169		60 mins		2	5.6- .7 .8 .9 .10 .11 .12 .13 .14	

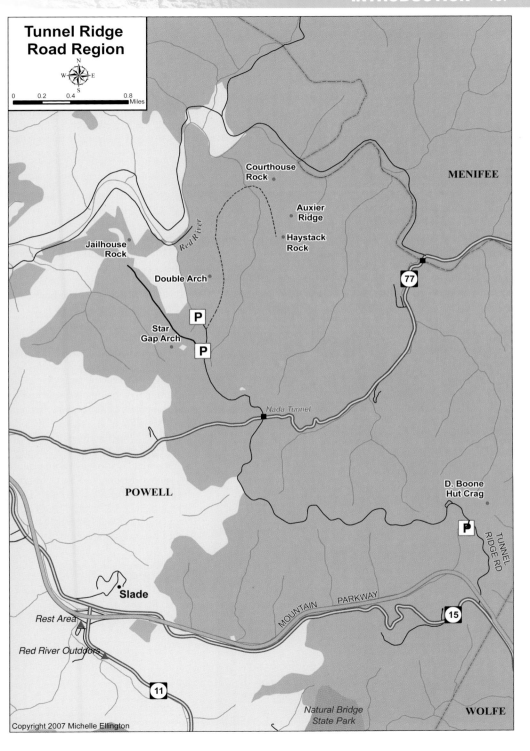

Tunnel Ridge
Road Region

N
W   E
S

0   0.2   0.4   0.8
Miles

Courthouse
Rock

MENIFEE

Auxier
Ridge

Red River

Haystack
Rock

Jailhouse
Rock

Double Arch

77

P

Star
Gap Arch

P

Nada Tunnel

D. Boone
Hut Crag

POWELL

P

TUNNEL RIDGE RD

Slade

MOUNTAIN   PARKWAY

Rest Area

15

Red River Outdoors

11

Natural Bridge
State Park

WOLFE

Copyright 2007 Michelle Ellington

JAILHOUSE ROCK

a.m. | 45 mins | 7 routes
5.6- .7 .8 .9 .10 .11 .12 .13 .14

Character

This remote crag has become even more remote since the closure of the last couple miles of Tunnel Ridge Road. The closure added over a mile onto the already long approach. The area offers only a handful of crack climbs but a few of them make it worth the trip if you're feeling up for a gorgeous and secluded hike. Not to be missed is *Capital Punishment,* a perfect pumpy finger and hand crack splitting the main buttress of the wall. Opportunity exists for additional lines for those willing to bushwhack through the rhodo thicket covering much of the base.

Approach

From the Shell gas station in Slade, turn left out of the parking lot onto Route 15 and drive 3.4 miles until you see a sign for Tunnel Ridge Road. Turn left onto Tunnel Ridge Road and follow it for a few miles until it ends at a large parking area for Auxier Ridge. Park and walk back up the road about 100 feet to a gate blocking the old road. Walk past the gate and follow the gravel road for about half a mile until the third road on your left (a few hundred feet past the road leading to Star Gap Arch). Follow the trail back for about half a mile past a couple of old camping areas and continue to the right along the ridge for another half mile, past a couple of rocky sections. When you see the obvious orange buttress of Jailhouse Rock ahead and to the right, hike for another five minutes or so and look for a faint trail down to the wall on your right. Hike down the steep trail and head left (right if you're facing the wall) to the majority of the routes.

Tracy Borland and friend. Photo Kelsey Gray.

Conditions

The approach to Jailhouse is long and many people have gotten lost attempting to locate the area. Pay close attention to looking off ahead and to the right to locate the obvious buttress that is visible after about a half mile of hiking along the ridge. It is best to visit this crag in the late fall through early spring to allow for more visibility along the trail. The northeast-facing nature of the wall makes for some greenish rock on some of the routes so avoid climbing in high humidity when the moss becomes slick.

1 Petty Theft 5.10d ★★★

After descending from the ridge to the base of the cliff, walk left and look for this thin double finger crack. Begin climbing a thin dihedral just right of a short offwidth using small nuts for protection. Tackle the overhanging wall and save some juice for the last tough move to the ledge. Rappel from a small but strong rhodo to descend. **30 ft.** *FA Ray Ellington, 1997.*

2 Hung Jury 5.8 ★★★

Walk right from *Petty Theft* to a left-facing dihedral about 50 feet left of the main arete of the buttress. Layback and jam the crack to the top of the cliff. Rappel from a tree or walk off left to descend. **20 ft.** *FA John Bronaugh, Louis Petry, 1985.*

3 Mole Vision 5.8 ★

Move right from *Hung Jury* and locate a flake system just before the main arete of Jailhouse Rock. Climb the flake system to a corner, then move through a slot to join up with the second half of *Hung Jury*. Rappel from a tree or walk off left to descend. **120 ft.** *FA Whit Bronaugh, John Bronaugh, 1985.*

4 Capital Punishment 5.10b ★★★

This beautiful splitter crack is located a few feet right of the obvious main arete. Balance up through shallow handjams on the initial green section to reach a small roof midway up. Pull over the lip and crank through a tough pumpy sequence with help from the arete near the top. Lower from anchors. **50 ft.** *FA Ron Snider, John Bronaugh, 1984.*

5 Suspended Sentence 5.6 ★★

Locate a left-facing dihedral about 25 feet right of *Capital Punishment*. Climb the dihedral to a ledge and belay from a tree. Continue up a dihedral to the top of the cliff and rappel from a tree or walk off left to descend. **120 ft.** *FA Ron Snider, John Bronaugh, 1984.*

6 Hard Labor 5.10a ★★★★

Walk about 150 feet right of the main arete to a handcrack with a wide section near the bottom. Pull past the difficult overhang to good jams over the lip. Climb to a ledge and belay. Continue up through a squeeze chimney, then move out of the chimney to take the exposed hand crack to the top. Rappel from a tree or walk off left to descend. **120 ft.** *FA John Bronaugh, George Robinson, 1984.*

7 At Death's Door 5.10b ★★★

This tough offwidth problem is located on the opposite side of where the trail brought you down to the base of the cliff. From where the trail cuts down to the wall, instead of taking a left, turn right and hike for 250 yards to another buttress. You will cross a large ravine along the way. 100 feet around the buttress, locate an overhanging handcrack with a low roof. Climb up to the low roof, get horizontal, and reach around the lip to a good jam. Continue up the crack to fixed anchors just beneath another overhang. **60 ft.** *FA Terry Acomb, Steve Must, 1988.*

The following cliffs have been removed from the print version of this guidebook. Visit www.wolverinepublishing.com/downloads for a free download of the information for them.

D. BOONE HUT CRAG

This cliff has only a few routes of low to moderate quality.

HAYSTACK ROCK

This rock has only a few routes but combined with the nearby Auxier Ridge and Courthouse Rock can give you a full day of climbing.

AUXIER RIDGE

Best known for the beautiful line *Excalibur*.

COURTHOUSE ROCK

Some historic lines exist at this eare, including one that follows the remains of an old bolt ladder.

STAR GAP ARCH

This area has three sandstone pinnacles, all of which can be summited.

DOUBLE ARCH

Double Arch is an amazing sight, but you probably won't want to haul your gear all the way back there to climb the two easy routes it offers.

NATURAL BRIDGE

Character
This area contains the extremely popular sport-climbing destinations Roadside Crag, Torrent Falls, and Lady Slipper. These cliffs also have some good traditional climbing. The overhanging walls of Roadside Crag and Torrent Falls provide good shelter on rainy days. Adding to the greatness of this area, most of the walls are only a short hike off of KY 11.

Approach
Head left out of Miguel's parking lot and drive south on KY 11 for a few miles. Most of the areas are accessed from pulloffs or parking areas alongside KY 11.

Access
Torrent Falls, Beer Trailer Crag, and Roadside Crag are located on private property, so please respect the wishes of the landowner, which may include parking restrictions, donation boxes, leash laws, etc. The remaining areas are located on Forest Service land, so please respect signs and fences indicating closed routes or trails and read the guidelines for climbing on Forest Service land on page 32 of this book.

CLIFF	SUN / SHADE	HIKE	RAIN	ROUTES	GRADE RANGE	CLASSIC ROUTES
SEE ROCKS page 170		10 mins		3	5.6- .7 .8 .9 .10 .11 .12 .13 .14	
FRICTION SLAB page 170	a.m. / shade	1 min		2	5.6- .7 .8 .9 .10 .11 .12 .13 .14	
EMERALD CITY page 174	all day	10 mins		18	5.6- .7 .8 .9 .10 .11 .12 .13 .14	*Diamond in the Rough* 10c *No Place Like Home* 11c
GLOBAL VILLAGE page 178	all day	15 mins		19	5.6- .7 .8 .9 .10 .11 .12 .13 .14	
ROADSIDE CRAG page 182	all day / shade	5 mins	rain OK	49	5.6- .7 .8 .9 .10 .11 .12 .13 .14	*Roadside Attraction* 7 *Mantel Route* 10c *Return of Chris Snyder* 11d *Hemisfear* 11d *Wild Gift* 12c
THE ZOO page 190	a.m.	10 mins	rain OK	14	5.6- .7 .8 .9 .10 .11 .12 .13 .14	*Hippocrite* 12a
TORRENT FALLS page 192	all day / shade / a.m.	5 mins	rain OK	47	5.6- .7 .8 .9 .10 .11 .12 .13 .14	*Windy Corner* 11b *Centerfire* 11c *Seek The Truth* 11d *Bare Metal Teen* 12a *Steelworker* 12c *Racer X* 12d
BEER TRAILER CRAG page 202	a.m.	5 mins		11	5.6- .7 .8 .9 .10 .11 .12 .13 .14	*Morning Wood* 12a *Hang Over* 12c *Falls City* 13b

The following cliffs have been removed from the print version of this guidebook. Visit www.wolverinepublishing.com/downloads for a free download of the information for them.

SEE ROCKS
The easiest approach to these towers involves crossing private land.

FRICTION SLAB
The backside of this roadside boulder contains one of the Red's best boulder problems, *Bulldog* v8.

Kelsey Gray on *Oz 5.11c* Lady Slipper, Emerald City, page 174. Photo John Borland. www.morffed.com

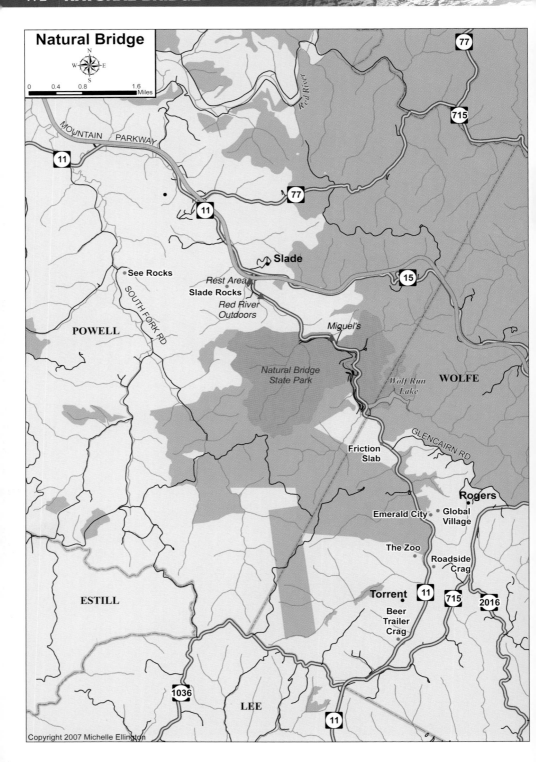

Natural Bridge

N W E S

0   0.4   0.8   1.6
Miles

MOUNTAIN PARKWAY

Red River

77

715

11

11

77

Slade

See Rocks

Rest Area
Slade Rocks
Red River
Outdoors

15

POWELL

SOUTH FORK RD

Miguel's

Natural Bridge
State Park

Wolf Run
Lake

WOLFE

GLENCAIRN RD

Friction
Slab

Rogers

Emerald City   Global
Village

The Zoo
Roadside
Crag

ESTILL

Torrent   11
715   2016

Beer
Trailer
Crag

1036

LEE

11

Photo: Wes Allen.

BOB MATHENY

PROFILE: Saving climbing access

You may have heard the name "Dr. Bob." More than likely, the words "saving climbing access" were mentioned in the same sentence. Although this humble man would never admit to such a thing, it is true. Dr. Bob Matheny has been a significant contributor to saving climbing access on the Pendergrass Murray Recreational Preserve (PMRP) as well as Torrent Falls in the Red River Gorge.

How has he done it? A heart of gold and cold hard cash. When the Red River Gorge Climber's Coalition (RRGCC) was trying to purchase the PMRP, Dr. Bob provided the entire 10% down payment, plus significant portions of the first year's mortgage on the property. A few years later, when the owner of Torrent Falls shut the area down to climbers and put the property up for sale, Dr. Bob stepped in and bought it, thus preserving access to this outstanding cliff for climbers. You may never get a chance to meet Dr. Bob since he works a demanding job as an emergency room physician, frequently pulling 10-12 hour graveyard shifts for several days in a row, and also contributes a significant portion of his leftover spare time to the RRGCC as a board member. This doesn't leave him as much time for climbing these days as he would like, but hopefully one day he will have the time he deserves to appreciate the land he helped secure.

Dr. Bob Matheny, 49, has had a passion for the outdoors since he was a kid. When he was 15 years old he spent five and a half weeks alone on the Appalachian Trail, hiking as far as Virginia. Supporting his love of the outdoors, his parents bought him a bus ticket to the Tetons in Wyoming for the summer. After that, he arrived back home in Kentucky and put together a rack from an old REI catalog. Armed with his shiny new gear, young Dr. Bob got his feet wet on the cliffs of the Cumberland Falls area near the Kentucky and Tennessee border. In 1987, after completing medical school at Tulane University in New Orleans, he decided on Lexington for his residency. During this time he made a few trips down to the Red, mostly to take on the man-eating offwidths at Muscle Beach. A few years later, after spending time out West, he decided to make Lexington his permanent home. Initially oblivious to the sport-climbing boom that had taken place while he was away, he partnered with Terry Kindred, who would slowly convert him to the ways of the stick-clip-carrying Red River sport climber.

Dr. Bob has a true passion for climbing, but also a deep appreciation for nature. When asked about his immediate plans for Torrent Falls, he said the area was "loved to death" and needs some time to heal. He asks that no single climber feel entitled, and to remember that climbing access is a community effort that involves all of us who climb here. If you ever happen to run into Dr. Bob Matheny, buy him a Guiness and tell him thanks for saving climbing access in the Red River Gorge. ∎

LADY SLIPPER ✦ EMERALD CITY

all day

10 mins

18 routes

5.6- .7 .8 .9 .10 .11 .12 .13 .14

ledge

approach

Character

Due to its length, Lady Slipper is broken up into two sections: Emerald City and Global Village. Emerald City offers excellent sport routes, featuring vertical face climbing on solid, exposed rock, as well as some great traditional lines. The ledge routes (1-5) all begin on a 30-foot-high ledge, providing the added benefit of exposure, and are a bit more run out than the average Red River Gorge sport line. Being vertical, these routes rarely attract lines of people; nonetheless, they are not to be missed. Save them for cold-weather days because the sun bakes this wall. Whatever you do, don't leave without climbing *No Place Like Home* – with well-spaced bolts, technical moves, and lots of exposure, it has to be the most classic arete in the Red.

Approach

From Miguel's, drive 3.2 miles south on KY 11 and park in a muddy pulloff on the right, just across from mile-marker 4. Head across the road to a trail, follow it straight uphill, and continue until it forks near a large boulder. Follow the left fork around the boulder and up the hill. The trail meets the wall directly beneath the 30-foot ledge upon which routes 1-5 begin.

Conditions

Emerald City is exposed, faces south, and bakes in the sun. Due to the lack of overhanging rock it is not a place to visit on rainy days. The approach is short and moderately steep. If there are lots of cars in the parking area, don't be put off. The parking is shared with Global Village, which is where most people end up.

---

❶ Lollipop Kids 5.11b ★★★
At the end of the approach trail is a 30-foot-high ledge with a gully approach. Scramble up the gully to access this and the next four routes. This is the right-most line that starts on the ledge. Crank through a bouldery start, then continue up the vertical face.
70 ft. 6 bolts. *FA Jamie Baker, 1992.*

❷ Oz 5.11c ★★★
This is the next route to the left of *Lollipop Kids* and starts on the same ledge. Often wet. Photo page 171.
70 ft. 6 bolts. *FA Jamie Baker, Rob Butsch, 1991.*

❸ Diamond in the Rough 5.10c ★★★★
Classic face climbing. Step left from *Oz* a few feet to the next bolted line. Climb straight up past nice finger ledges and well-spaced bolts to the anchors.
80 ft. 7 bolts. *FA Jamie Baker, Rob Turan, 1991.*

❹ Ruby Slippers 5.10d ★★★★
Left of the previous route is a large hueco about six feet up. This route climbs up the right side of the hueco, then continues up the vertical face to the anchors.
70 ft. 6 bolts. *FA Rob Turan, Jamie Baker, 1991.*

❺ Flying Monkeys 5.11c ★★★
If your bouldering skills are up to par, expect success. This route climbs out of the hueco mentioned in the previous route. Crank over the lip of the large hueco and locate hidden holds on the vertical face for the remainder of the route.
70 ft. 5 bolts. *FA Tim Powers, Jamie Baker, 1991.*

❻ Spiny Norman 5.9+ ★
Just left of the ledge with the aforementioned routes is a hand crack splitting the wall. Scramble to the top of a boulder to gain the crack. Climb the crack, then move right at an overhang. Pull over the overhang into the flaring crack and take it to the top. Rappel from a tree to descend.
120 ft. *FA Ron Snider, Bill Rieker, 1984.*

❼ Friable 5.9 R ★★★
This route ascends the obvious arching crack visible from the road. From *Spiny Norman*, head left about 225 feet to locate two cracks about 15 feet apart. Begin by climbing the crack on the right, and take it to an overhang. Move left over chossy rock (5.6 R) to a belay near a corner. Continue up a crack and battle past an overhang. Belay when the crack forks to avoid rope drag, then continue up the arching right crack to the top. Rappel from the anchors on *Whiteout*.
120 ft. *FA Ed Pearsall, Tom Seibert, 1980.*

The Ledge Routes 1-5

8 Whiteout 5.8 ★★★★

This multi-pitch line offers a fantastic view and great climbing. Head 100 feet left of *Friable* to a point just before the main corner of the wall. Climb up easy ground via a left-facing flake or a short line of bolts (5.7) and belay. Continue up the hand crack in a dihedral for the bulk of the route, then move left onto the face when the crack ends.

100 ft. *FA John Bronaugh, Ron Snider, 1984.*

9 The Man Behind the Curtain 5.11a ★★★★

Reach this impressive dihedral by climbing *Whiteout*, but finish to the tree ledge out right instead of the anchors out left. From the big tree on the ledge, rap halfway down the wall to a small ledge. Crawl around the arete and end up at a small belay stance below this extremely steep, featureless, acute dihedral.

40 ft. *FA Kris Hampton, 2006.*

10 No Place Like Home 5.11c ★★★★★

Classic. This route ascends the obvious arete visible from the road, to the left of *Whiteout*. Begin by climbing *Whiteout*, then move to an alcove beneath an overhang. Step up and shake your way up the arete, making some difficult clips along the way. Convince your partner to hang the draws for you!

100 ft. 9 bolts. *FA Jim Link, Jamie Baker, 1992.*

11 Sharp 5.9 ★★★

Walk left and around the corner from *No Place Like Home* to locate a hand crack. Lower from anchors at the top of the crack.

45 ft. *FA Jamie Baker, Chris Linderman, 1989.*

12 Father's Day 5.5 ★

This route ascends the next dihedral left of *Sharp*. Climb the dihedral to a flake and belay. Continue up the flake to the top of the wall.

100 ft. *FA Pete Huggybone, 2003.*

13 Pumped Puppies 5.10b R

From *Father's Day*, head left to locate a thin crack in an overhanging face. Climb the face to a ledge, then move right to a rotten section of rock. Pull the lip with no protection.

50 ft. *FA Jamie Baker, Rik Downs, 1989.*

The remaining routes are located right of where the approach trail meets the wall.

14 Scarecrow 5.10c ★★★

From the end of the approach trail (beneath *Diamond in the Rough*), head right about 400 feet to locate a section of rock containing a fat flake and two other cracks, which meet at a roof about 30 feet up. Climb the left crack to the roof, then move left to a corner. Arrange some gear near the corner, then move left to a finger crack and climb it to a belay ledge. Continue up easier ground to a ledge with a tree, then ascend a short face to the summit. Rappel from a tree to descend.

140 ft. *FA John Bronaugh, Stacy Temple, 1993.*

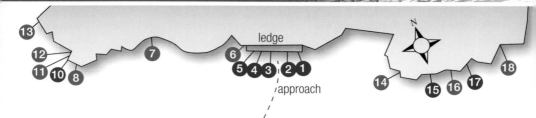

The Shining

⓯ Yellow Brick Road 5.11b ★★★★

Walk around the corner 100 feet from *Scarecrow* to a thin, detached boulder about 15 feet high. To the right of the boulder you will see a nice-looking line on lichen-streaked rock. Climb the slab, with long reaches and thought-provoking moves. Move right when you get stumped, then make a difficult move back left to gain better holds. Climb large ledges to the anchors.
50 ft. 5 bolts. *FA Neal Strickland, Tim Powers, 1992.*

⓰ The Shining 5.8+ ★★★★

Walk 50 feet right from *Yellow Brick Road* to locate this obvious, short finger crack in black rock. Tackle the awkward start, then lock your way up the granite-like finger crack to the anchors.
30 ft. *FA Brent Lewis, Ron Snider, 1983.*

⓱ The Bulge 5.12a ★★

From *The Shining*, walk right about 75 feet to locate a line of bolts near a section of rock with a 35-foot-tall flake. Crimp through a boulder problem and continue to the anchors.
45 ft. 5 bolts. *FA Nick Cocciolone, Eric Szczukowski, 1992.*

⓲ T N T 5.10b ★★★

This route is located in a short dihedral 50 feet right of *The Bulge*. Stem and lock up the interesting dihedral to a ledge. Lower from fixed webbing on the ledge or continue up the dirty crack to the top.
80 ft. *FA Tim Powers, Tony Rooker, 1987.*

Yellow Brick Road

LADY SLIPPER ✦ GLOBAL VILLAGE

all day | 15 mins | 19 routes
5.6- .7 .8 .9 .10 .11 .12 .13 .14

Character

Although the approach is twice as long as Emerald City, Global Village is the more popular section of Lady Slipper. It offers a mix of great trad and sport routes. Long, exposed, and only 5.6, *Eureka* is an incredible first sport lead if you can catch it in an "unchopped" state. (The route was first chopped by traditional-climbing activist "The Wolfman" in 2000. Since then, threats and rumors have surrounded the state of the bolts. *Eureka* also makes an excellent traditional lead for those willing to shun the bolts.) For the neophyte crack climber, *Father and Son* is a excellent first lead. It takes bomber gear and climbs a mostly juggy face with only a few crack moves.

Approach

Follow the same approach as for Global Village, but take the right fork instead of the left when the trail branches near the large boulder. Follow the trail for about 10 minutes, crossing over two ravines. After crossing the second ravine, the trail heads uphill to the right. Follow the trail uphill to an outcropping, where it forks. To reach routes 1-6, ignore the fork and continue up the hill and over a sloping rock. For the remainder of the routes, bear right where the trail forks and continue another 100 feet.

Conditions

You'll have a little more luck in the rain at Global Village than you will at Emerald City. *Deep Six, Wreaking Havoc,* and *The Frayed Ends of Sanity* are steep enough to be sheltered from light rain. However, this is still not a destination rainy-day crag. Global Village gets lots of sun.

❶ Eureka 5.6 ★★★★
This route is located near the obvious main arete on the wall as you near the end of the approach trail. Walk left from the main arete about 100 feet to locate a plated face just left of an overhanging dihedral. Negotiate the tricky start, then continue up the face on positive holds. 85 ft. 8 bolts. *FA Unknown.*

❷ Howard Roark 5.9+ ★★
Ascends the obvious, wide, overhanging dihedral just right of *Eureka.* Rappel from a tree to descend. 100 ft. *FA Alexis Scott, 2001.*

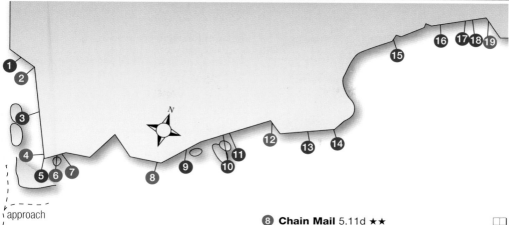

approach

③ The Wheel of Time 5.13b ★★★★

This line ascends the vertical to overhanging face about 30 feet right of *Howard Roarke*. The route has recently had its "Porter hangers" replaced with modern day hardware so expect this route to become more popular than it has been in the past.
80 ft. 10 bolts. *FA Dave Hume, 1996.*

④ Father and Son 5.7 ★★★

John and Alex, father and son, spent many wonderful moments together. I'm sure this first ascent was one of their finest. This popular first trad lead climbs the left-facing dihedral about 30 feet right of *The Wheel of Time*. Climb the flake, making liberal use of face holds on the left wall. Pull a couple of crack moves at the top to reach a ledge with bolted anchors.
40 ft. *FA John Bronaugh, Alex Yeakley, Dario Ventura, Miguel Ventura, 1993.*

⑤ Kentucky Pinstripe 5.10a ★★★

Just right and around the corner from *Father and Son* is a line of bolts ascending an arete behind a tree. Climb up to a tricky little roof and balance your way over the lip. Continue up the slabby face to a good ledge. Rest your feet, then take on the remainder to the anchors.
80 ft. 9 bolts. *FA Unknown.*

⑥ Vision 5.7 ★★★★

This line ascends the hand crack just to the right of *Kentucky Pinstripe*. Begin on top of a five-foot-high boulder and climb the splitter hand crack to a ledge with a tree. Continue up the fat flake past many good stances to the top.
80 ft. *FA Scott Hammon, James Neukam, 1999.*

⑦ Jake Flake 5.8 ★★★

Ascends the next thin flake to the right of *Vision*. Take the seam to a flake and continue on face holds to the top.
80 ft. *FA Scott Hammon, 1999.*

⑧ Chain Mail 5.11d ★★

Walk right about 75 feet from the main arete of the wall to locate a bolted face, which begins in some sandy rock. Climb past some short cracks, placing protection in them if desired. Continue up through the line of bolts to chain anchors.
100 ft. 6 bolts. *FA Porter Jarrard, 1992.*

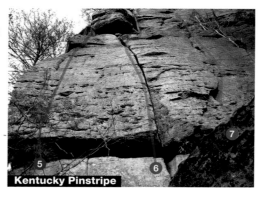

Father and Son

Kentucky Pinstripe

Disappearer

⑨ Deep Six 5.12b ★★★★

Move 20 feet right from *Chain Mail* to another line of bolts on an overhanging face. Battle up the bouldery face, with long moves separated by decent rests.
110 ft. 11 bolts. *FA Porter Jarrard, Frank Waters, 1992.*

⑩ Wreaking Havoc 5.11d ★★★

From *Deep Six*, walk 30 feet right to locate this route. It shares its start with the following route. Boulder the beginning to gain an overhanging face above.
80 ft. 8 bolts. *FA Jeff Moll, Porter Jarrard, 1992.*

⑪ The Frayed Ends of Sanity 5.12a ★★★

Begin by climbing the initial moves of *Wreaking Havoc*, then move right.
80 ft. 9 bolts. *FA Porter Jarrard, Jake Slaney, 1992.*

⑫ Pain is a Spice 5.7 ★

This route ascends the thin finger crack in a dihedral to the right of *The Frayed Ends of Sanity*. Improvise a descent.
35 ft. *FA Ethan Cumbler, Jane Kim, 1996.*

Casual Viewing

⑬ Disappearer 5.11c ★★★★

Move right and around the corner a few feet from the previous line to a vertical wall with many horizontal breaks. This is the first line encountered. Climb up through easy ground for about 20 feet to reach a blank section of the wall. Locate the few holds it has to offer and figure out how to use them to reach the jug above. Continue through easier climbing to reach the anchors.
70 ft. 7 bolts. *FA Porter Jarrard, Jeff Moll, 1992.*

⑭ Loosen Up 5.10b ★★★

This bolted line ascends a slightly overhanging face 20 feet right from *Disappearer* and just before the wall turns a corner. Climb the face, making use of positive holds to reach a short roof. Step up and over the roof, then balance to the anchors.
50 ft. 6 bolts. *FA Porter Jarrard, Jeff Moll, 1992.*

⑮ Seeker 5.12b ★★

Traverse the trail to the right and uphill from *Loosen Up* to an upper cliff band. Walk left past a slabby section of the wall containing a few bolted lines to a wide crack near a boulder. Ascend the blunt arete, then step onto the face to reach a ledge with anchors.
50 ft. 7 bolts. *FA Porter Jarrard, Jeff Moll, 1992.*

⑯ Circa Man 5.10d ★★★

From *Seeker*, move back right to the slabby wall. This is the first route from the left corner and has a small roof. Climb up the face, making use of well-spaced bolts for protection. Be careful clipping the fifth bolt or you may take a very long fall.
60 ft. 5 bolts. *FA Unknown, 1994.*

⑰ Out for Justice 5.11b ★★★★

This line begins about 25 feet right of *Circa Man*. A short, overhanging start leads to a horizontal break. Pull up and over the break and continue up the slabbier face to the anchors.
65 ft. 8 bolts. *FA Porter Jarrard, Frank Waters, 1992.*

⑱ Down by Law 5.11d ★★

A few feet right from *Out for Justice* is a line of "Porter hangers" with a short roof about 10 feet up. Climb up to and over the roof to reach the slabby face above. Continue up through more short roofs to reach the anchors. Beware of a dead tree that may still be covering the final two bolts.
65 ft. 8 bolts. *FA Porter Jarrard, Frank Waters, 1992.*

⑲ Casual Viewing 5.7 ★★★★

Great line. Just right of *Down by Law* is this popular and sustained flake. Climb up to a pod, get some gear, then creep out and up into the flake. Stem and layback to the top. Lower from bolted anchors.
70 ft. *FA Porter Jarrard, Jeff Moll, 1992.*

Yasmeen Fowler, *Andromeda Strain* 5.9+, Roadside Crag, next page.
Photo: Ben Cassel.

ROADSIDE CRAG

   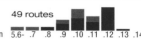

all day | shade | 5 mins | OK in rain | 49 routes
5.6- .7 .8 .9 .10 .11 .12 .13 .14

Character

It doesn't get much better than this. Five-minute approach, amazing routes of all but the very hardest grades, and a big overhang to keep everything dry. Roadside Crag has it all. Being privately owned Roadside has seen a considerable amount of route development during the past few years. This development includes a slew of great new beginner routes now populating the slab on the far right side of the cliff. The 5.10 Wall at Roadside cannot be surpassed. The routes serve as a great warm-up for the 5.12 wall just around the corner, and a great introduction to the world-class pocket pulling at the Red. *Ro Shampo*, the route whose grade has been discussed on the Internet as much as the presidential election, still manages to spit off the occasional 5.12 climber. Don't underestimate it!

Approach

From Miguel's Pizza, drive about 3.8 miles south on KY 11 to a large parking area on the right. Park, and cross the road, and find the trailhead about 200 feet south of the parking area. Follow the trail uphill for about 300 feet. As the trail meets the wall, you will see the obvious dihedral of *Roadside Attraction* directly in front of you. **During the past few years a number of vehicles have been broken into at the Roadside parking area. It is highly recommended that you remove valuable items from your car before climbing at the area.**

Conditions

Fortunately for some great winter climbing, most of the routes at Roadside are located on the south-facing section of the horseshoe-shaped wall. It is also possible to escape the heat during the summer by climbing the less traveled mixed and traditional lines on the north end of the wall. To thwart the rain, check out the sheltered routes 13 through 37. This is not secret though – expect to share these routes with just about everyone else who wants to climb that day.

Access

Roadside Crag is privately owned. The wooded area behind the parking lot used to be one of the most popular camping areas in the Red for climbers. However, "No Camping" signs were put in place in 2003 so please don't camp in the area.

Andromeda Strain ❶

❶ Andromeda Strain 5.9+ ★★★★

Where the approach trail meets the cliff, walk left about 300 feet, rounding a corner, to a broad wall bounded on its left side by an incredible dihedral. You can't miss it. The climbing is as good as it looks. To begin, climb up the short slab to the base of the crack. Jam to the top, passing a couple of short roofs along the way. This route is often slimy and damp on humid days. Catch it on a good day and you'll never forget it. Photo previous page. **90 ft.** *FA Ron Snider, John Bronaugh, 1984.*

❷ Wicked Games 5.12d ★★★★

This wickedly difficult line follows a line of bolts just right of *Andromeda Strain*. Notice the plethora of bail biners abandoned like wounded soldiers on a battlefield. Try not to join the crowd. **85 ft. 9 bolts.** *FA Jamie Baker, Rob Butsch, 1992.*

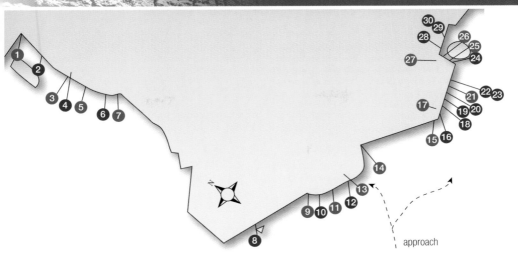

approach

3 Mantel Route 5.10c ★★★★★
Look for a line of bolts left of a conspicuous gray-and-orange section of wall with a large hueco 50 feet up, and about 60 feet right of the *Andromeda* dihedral. Climb up through some "nose to the wall" mantel moves, clipping bolts and placing gear in horizontals for protection.
60 ft. 3 bolts. *FA Ron Snider, Matt Flach, 1989.*

4 Headwall 5.12b ★★
A continuation of *Mantel Route.* From the anchors on *Mantel Route*, head straight up for about 10 feet, make a toss, then thrash through dirt to a big tree.
30 ft. 5 bolts. *FA Matt Flach, Ron Snider, 1990.*

5 Home is Where the Heart Is 5.12a ★★★★
...Or is it "Home is Where the Hueco Is"? Start directly beneath a hueco about 50 feet up an impressive gray-and-orange wall. Climb straight up to the hueco, past one bolt. Bring some small cams and stoppers for placements in small cracks along the way.
40 ft. 1 bolt. *FA Mark Williams, 1989.*

6 Hemisfear 5.11d ★★★★
This short but excellent line ascends the line of bolts right of *Home is Where the Heart Is*, sharing that route's anchors. Begin on a boulder and climb up the vertical face, crimping on wicked eyebrow-like gashes. Gravitate left to the hueco for a spicy ending.
40 ft. 3 bolts. *FA Matt Flach, Charles Tabor, 1989.*

7 Hard Left 5.10a ★★★
This route begins in an obvious left-angling crack that fades out in the middle of the wall. Climb up a short slab to the base of the crack to begin. When the crack ends, traverse left and down to the large hueco and anchors shared with routes 5 and 6.
70 ft. 3 bolts. *FA Charles Tabor, Mike Torbett, 1990.*

8 Science Friction 5.12c ★★★★
About 100 feet left of the split in the approach trail, find a 10-foot-tall pyramid-shaped boulder. This bolted line begins from the top of the boulder and climbs up through a blocky arete and a low roof at the top.
70 ft. 7 bolts. *FA Eric Greulich, 2005.*

9 Five-Finger Discount 5.8 ★★★★
Fat Finger Nightmare. Just left of the obvious dihedral of Roadside Attraction is a cluster of climbs. This one is the farthest left, and ascends a flake with a finger crack. Traverse right at the top on a ledge to anchors beneath *Runnin' Down a Dream.*
50 ft. *FA Tod Anderson, Martin Hackworth, 1984.*

10 Fadda 5.10a ★★★
Locate a line of bolts just right of *Five-Finger.* Climb through pockets, crimps, and underclings to a delicate "blank" section at the top. Step left to the anchors.
50 ft. 5 bolts. *FA Chris Chaney, Brian Rogers, 2002.*

Hemisfear

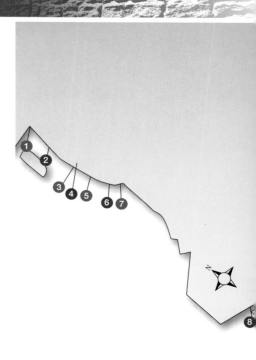

⓫ Motha 5.6 ★★★

Between the bolted lines of *Fadda* and *Jump For Joy* is a pocketed face with some horizontal bands. Climb the face, making use of pockets for protection. Lower from a set of anchors just below the ledge, or continue up to the ledge and rap from the anchors beneath *Runnin' Down a Dream*. Bring hand-sized cams for the horizontals: they are larger than they appear from the ground.
50 ft. *FA Grant Stephens, 1986.*

⓬ Jump for Joy 5.9+ ★★

Too short? Just jump to reach the first holds. Walk left from *Roadside Attraction* to a line of bolts above a boulder. Start on top of the boulder and climb the face to bolted anchors.
50 ft. 4 bolts. *FA Tracy Crabtree, Jeff Ashley, 1993.*

⓭ Runnin' Down a Dream 5.10a R ★★★

...Or is it "Run It Out and Scream!" Climb either *Jump For Joy, Motha,* or *Five-Finger Discount* to the ledge on which they end. Move right along the ledge to locate a single bolt on the wall above. Climb the line, making use of this bolt and some horizontals for gear. Head right for an alcove, then traverse left and over a bulge to the top. Keep your head. Rappel from anchors.
75 ft. 1 bolt. *FA Jim Link, John Whisman, 1989.*

⓮ Roadside Attraction 5.7 ★★★★★

This is the most classic line of its grade in the Red. Locate the obvious dihedral at the end of the approach trail when it reaches the wall. Scramble up to a ledge to begin. Climb the low-angle hand crack to a ledge with a tree. Continue up the hand crack past a couple of wide sections to another ledge and some anchors. If you want to summit, belay from this ledge, then continue up to the top.
140 ft. *FA Greg Smith, Ron Snider, 1984.*

5.10 WALL

The following routes are located right of where the approach trail meets the wall.

⓯ Milkin' the Chicken 5.11d ★

From the end of the approach trail, make a right instead of heading up to *Roadside Attraction*. The trail will wind down through some trees and head back up to the section of cliff referred to as the 5.10 Wall. This route ascends the arete on the left side of the wall, making use of a couple of bolts and a slung chickenhead for protection.
50 ft. 3 bolts. *FA Mark Williams, 1990.*

⓰ A.W.O.L. 5.10a ★★★

This is the obvious, heavily chalked, bolted line just right of the arete. Start at a low overhang and move up through pockets and bulges to a blank section. Circumvent this with a long move and a crimp, then pull past a small roof to reach the anchors.
50 ft. 5 bolts. *FA Mark Williams, Porter Jarrard, 1990.*

⓱ Battle of the Bulge 5.10a R ★

Freak out your sport-climbing buddies and keep climbing above the anchors on *A.W.O.L.* via this crack system to the top of the wall. This route also included *A.W.O.L.*, before *A.W.O.L.* was bolted.
80 ft. *FA Matt Flach, Ron Snider, 1989.*

⓲ Dragonslayer 5.10d ★★★

Just right of *A.W.O.L.* is another popular line. Climb up and past deep mono pockets, then fight the pump to the anchors.
50 ft. 5 bolts. *FA Mark Williams, Charles Tabor, 1990.*

⓳ Crazyfingers 5.10c ★★★★

Move right from *Dragonslayer* to the next line of chalk. Crank through a sidepull crux at the bottom, then pace yourself the rest of the way to the anchors.
50 ft. 5 bolts. *FA Rob Turan, Mark Williams, 1990.*

⓴ Pulling Pockets 5.10d ★★★★

This is the next bolted route on the wall just to the right of *Crazyfingers*. This route was originally a mixed route, but was retro-bolted for that amusement-park-like feeling. Nevertheless, it is an excellent route and can now be enjoyed by those without cams. Many variations exist from the last bolt to the anchors – including a hands-off dyno.
50 ft. *FA Greg Smith, Tom Souders, 1987.*

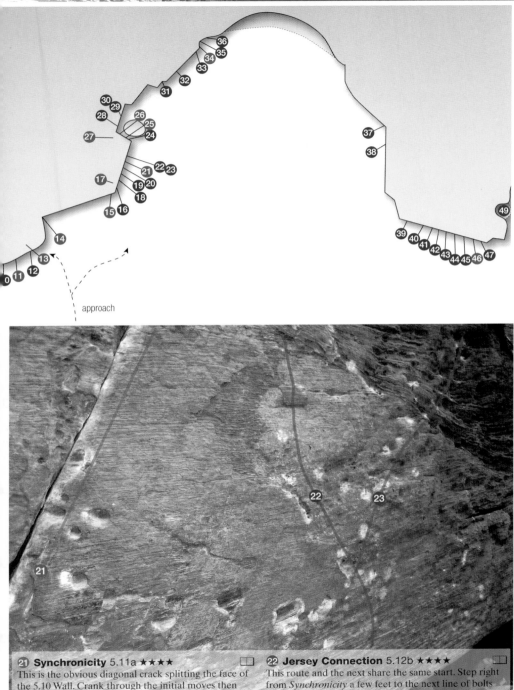

21 Synchronicity 5.11a ★★★★

This is the obvious diagonal crack splitting the face of the 5.10 Wall. Crank through the initial moves then enjoy long reaches past good rests to the anchors. Protects great with stoppers.

50 ft. *FA Greg Smith, Tom Souders, 1984.*

22 Jersey Connection 5.12b ★★★★

This route and the next share the same start. Step right from *Synchronicity* a few feet to the next line of bolts (the first bolt may be missing). Crimp up the edge of a flake and pockets to a decent rest out right. When ready, move back left to a hideous crimp rail. Launch for a good hold, then relax on large jugs to the finish.

50 ft. 5 bolts. *FA Matt Flach, Rob Turan, 1990.*

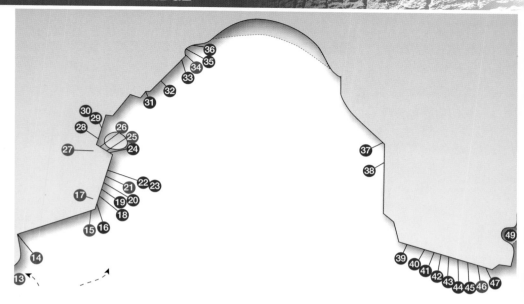

㉓ **Stay the Hand** 5.12a ★★★★

Start as for *Jersey Connection* but don't angle left. Instead, make a difficult move to reach a set of pockets, then angle right, pull another big move, then escape right to the juggy face. A more difficult **direct start** ascends the three bolts beneath the anchors (**5.12c**). 50 ft. 5 bolts. *FA Porter Jarrard, Mark Schussler, 1990. Direct Start: Tim Steele.*

㉔ **Valor Over Discretion** 5.8 ★★

Like *Pulling Pockets*, this route, originally a trad line, recently fell to the power drill. Start by standing on the large boulder to the right of the 5.10 Wall. Climb the face a few feet right of the arete. Move left around the arete at a roof and continue up to a ledge. 50 ft. 4 bolts. *FA Roger Pearson, John Bronaugh, 1987.*

㉕ **Psycho Killer** 5.10c R ★

This route begins just right of *Valor Over Discretion*, on a large boulder. Climb up the face to a roof. Crank over the roof and continue up to the ledge. 50 ft. *FA Greg Smith, 1984.*

㉖ **Harder Than Your Husband** 5.11b ★★★

A few feet right of *Psycho Killer* is a roof with a finger crack. Traverse across the shelf, then make a long reach to a good hand jam at the lip. Power up to a fingerlock, then continue up the short dihedral to bolted anchors. 40 ft. *FA Greg Smith, 1984.*

㉗ **Holly Golightly** 5.10b ★★

Located on the ledge above *Harder Than Your Husband* and *Valor Over Discretion*. Climb the face to an overhanging crack. Continue up the crack to anchors. 40 ft. *FA Scott Hammon, Frank Waters, 2003.*

5.12 WALL

㉘ **Scissors** 5.11d ★★★

Right of *Harder Than Your Husband* is a well-sheltered, overhanging, plated wall. This is the first line on the left side of the wall and has a very high first bolt. Stick clip the bolt and jump up to a jug. Move left, then power up to a good pocket. Continue up the plated face past long moves and good heel-hooks. 50 ft. 4 bolts. *FA Porter Jarrard, Steve Cater, 1991.*

㉙ **Ro Shampo** 5.12a ★★★★★

Is it 11d? Or is it 12a? I've even heard it called 11b! You make the decision. Either way, it's a classic so who really cares? Start in a sand pit about 25 feet right of *Scissors*. Step up onto a boulder to grab the first holds. Climb straight up over plated jugs, then kick out left. Crank the crux, then continue hauling on the steep plated jugs. If you pitch trying to clip the anchors, you will join the majority. 60 ft. 6 bolts. *FA Jamie Baker, Jim Link, 1992.*

㉚ **Tic-Tac-Toe** 5.12b ★★★★

This often-overlooked line shares the start with *Ro Shampo*, but moves right after the first bolt. Move up the steep face through good horizontals separated by long reaches. Gain the occasional hand jam rest to prepare yourself for the boulder problem at the last bolt. 60 ft. 4 bolts. *FA Brian McCray, 1993.*

㉛ **The Adventure** 5.11d ★★

Locate a line of bolts near the second dihedral right of *Tic-Tac-Toe*. Climb up through a variety of movements to the anchors high above. Be careful not to knock loose rock onto the passing climbers below. 100 ft. 11 bolts. *FA Eric Anderson, Brian McCray, 1993.*

Ro Shampo

㉜ Strevels Gets In Shape 5.12b ★★★

This bouldery line is located near an arete to the right of the previous line. Climb up an arching feature, then make an accuracy move to a wide pocket. Don't relax yet. Continue up the steep face to the first set of anchors. Take a good rest, then begin to make your way up to the overhanging wall above. Continue up the overhanging wall past long crosses and high steps to the second set of anchors.
90 ft. 12 bolts. *FA Porter Jarrard, Eric Anderson, 1990.*

㉝ Wild Gift 5.12c ★★★★★

Classic power endurance. Move right from *Strevels* about 20 feet to a steep, angling line just left of an arete. Jump up to the first hold, then angle right to begin the business. Crank through tough moves and difficult clips to a sick undercling move at the top. Most people stick clip the second bolt to avoid having to stray off route to reach it. Photo page 201.
45 ft. 5 bolts. *FA Porter Jarrard, Mark Schussler, 1990.*

㉞ Camel Toe Jockey 5.9 ★

This dihedral is located just around the corner from *Wild Gift*. Inch your way up the dihedral, trying not to succumb to the tempting bolts of *Way Up Yonder*.
40 ft. *FA Unknown.*

㉟ Way Up Yonder 5.12a ★★★★

The line of bolts just right of *Camel Toe Jockey*. Climb through sloping pockets up an overhanging wall to the

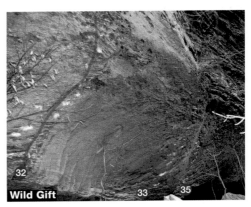

Wild Gift

first set of anchors. Continue up through the massive overhanging wall to the second set of anchors "way up yonder." Or you can stop at the first set of anchors for **Up Yonder,** a good **5.11b**.
95 ft. 13 bolts. *FA Porter Jarrard, 1993.*

㊱ Sand 5.11d

Start by clipping the first bolt of *Way Up Yonder*, then angle right through an overhang. Not too popular for reasons made obvious by its name.
45 ft. 5 bolts. *FA Porter Jarrard, Hassan Saab, 1993.*

The Return of Chris Snyder

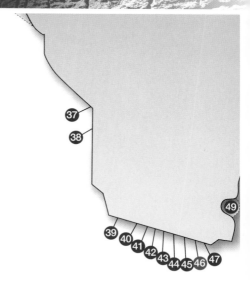

③⑦ The Return of Chris Snyder 5.11d ★★★★★ □□
Steep jug hauling at its best. Walk 250 feet right from
Sand, past a wet amphitheater and around a corner, to
a couple of bolted lines ascending a massive, pocketed
face. Begin by climbing a flake up to a short roof. Crank
over the roof to gain the overhanging face. Marathon
climb for about 65 more feet, past a couple of no-hands
rests, to the anchors 95 feet up.
95 ft. 11 bolts. *FA Porter Jarrard, Mike Norman, 1992.*

③⑧ Pine 5.12a ★★★★ □□
Similar to *The Return of Chris Snyder* but a bit more technical,
with fewer rests. Begins a few feet right of the previous route.
95 ft. 10 bolts. *FA Porter Jarrard, Jeff Moll, 1992.*

③⑨ Just Duet 5.10d ★★★ □□
Walk around the corner and right from *Pine* about 150
feet to a slabby wall peppered with bolts. This is the first
line encountered and begins on a five-foot-high ledge
with a high first bolt. Climb the inital slab to a bulge
with a good stance. Power over the bulge and continue
through delicate moves to the anchors.
70 ft. 9 bolts. *FA John Bronaugh, 2002.*

④⓪ Kampsight 5.9+ ★★★★ □□
Named after a Bob Kamps sighting just after this route
was bolted. He even managed to bag the second ascent!
This route ascends the low-angle face 10 feet right of *Just
Duet* and just left of a crack. Begin on a three-foot-high
sloping ledge. Enjoyable and thought-provoking climbing topped off with a great view from the anchors.
80 ft. 8 bolts. *FA Tina Bronaugh, John Bronaugh, 1992.*

④① Trouble Clef 5.9 ★★★ □□
This is the next bolted line 10 feet right of *Kampsight*. Begins on a three-foot-high sloping ledge just right of a crack.
80 ft. 9 bolts. *FA John Bronaugh, 2002.*

④② Altered Scale 5.9+ ★★ □□
Begin on a three-foot-high sloping ledge, 10 feet right of
Trouble Clef, and pull through a tough sequence to reach
the first bolt. Climb through easier moves to reach a thin
section toward the middle of the route. Relax again until
the final bulge before the anchors.
80 ft. 7 bolts. *FA John Bronaugh, 2002.*

④③ All Cows Eat Grass 5.8 ★★★ □□
This is the next bolted line 20 feet right of *Altered Scale*.
Begin just left of a crack with some bushes. Climb fun
moves to an exciting finish.
80 ft. 9 bolts. *FA John Bronaugh, 2002.*

④④ Ledger Line 5.7 ★★★ □□
Step right from the previous line to locate this route.
Climb a thin start to reach the first bolt, then move up
on large ledges to the vertical face. Sink a hand jam or
two along the way while continuing up on smaller ledges
to the anchors in a roof.
80 ft. 7 bolts. *FA Ryan Adams, 2002.*

④⑤ C Sharp or B Flat 5.7 ★★★ □□
Move right from *Ledger Line* to locate this classic beginner's route.
60 ft. 6 bolts. *FA Tina Bronaugh, Jennifer Rannells, 1993.*

④⑥ Gumby Land 5.3 ★ □□
Just right of *C Sharp or B Flat* is this thick flake. Climb
the flake and face to the anchors on *C Sharp or B Flat*.
Probably the only route in the guide first climbed top-
down.
60 ft. *FA Tim Powers, solo downclimb, 1994.*

④⑦ You Can Tune a Piano, 5.10b ★★★ □□
but You Can't Tuna Fish
This route begins just right of *C Sharp or B Flat*. Climb
15 feet of slab to reach a high first bolt. Climb up
through a series of crimps and underclings to reach a
short technical crux. Solve the crux, then continue up the
fun face to the anchors. This route was stripped by the
bolter soon after it was bolted so the hangers could be
used for another route. The route was rebolted in 2004
by John Bronaugh.
60 ft. 7 bolts. *FA Mike Woodhouse, 1997.*

Trouble Clef

48 I Didn't Know This 5.7 R ★★★
Was the End
This route was named by Scott Brown in memory of the first ascentionist, Mason Allen. Mason passed away just days after he and Scott climbed this route together. Begin 15 feet right of the previous bolted line. Scramble to a ledge to gain a finger crack, then dive into an offwidth section. Follow the offwidth to a crumbly ledge to gain a hand crack. Run the unprotected slab to the barbed wire fence at the top of the cliff or sneak left to a tree for a belay.
150 ft. *FA Mason Allen, Scott Brown, 2006.*

49 Chunnel 5.13a ★★★
Walk right from the main wall to locate this route which climbs out of the notorious "pee cave". Please don't pee in this cave though since it now hosts what has turned out to be a pretty decent roof climb. Boulder out the roof and turn the lip to be greeted by a somewhat blank face and the true crux.
50 ft. 7 bolts. *FA Lee Smith, 2010. Equipper Greg Martin.*

So you wanna climb 5.12?

Sport climbing is all about the numbers, right? Maybe not, but if you're trying to make the transition from 5.11 mortal to 5.12 rock god(dess), you need to find some classic easier routes of the grade. Here's a list, compiled from redriver-climbing.com, of the most popular 5.12a's in the Red.

1. **Ro Shampo** Roadside
2. **Kick Me in the Jimmie** Motherlode
3. **Buddha Hole** Solar Collector
4. **Bare Metal Teen** Torrent Falls
5. **Hippocrite** The Zoo
6. **Check Your Grip** Drive-By Crag
7. **Too Many Puppies** Left Flank
8. **Chainsaw Massacre** Motherlode
9. **Hardcore Jollies** Funk Rock City
10. **Wild, Yet Tasty** Left Flank

THE ZOO

a.m.   10 mins   OK in rain

15 routes

5.6- .7 .8 .9 .10 .11 .12 .13 .14

Character

The Zoo is a small crag that offers decent moderate sport lines. Not as popular as nearby Roadside and Torrent Falls, it is a good place to get away from the crowds. If anything, make a trip to the Zoo to climb *Hippocrite*. It's a short and powerful line that ascends a steep face via long moves between huecos. Its newer neighbor, *Scar Tissue*, also offers steep climbing but on more fragile rock.

Approach

Park in the same parking lot as Roadside but do not cross the road. Instead, hike back through the woods on the south side of the parking area toward the creek. Hike upstream a short way and cross the creek at a tree-trunk bridge. Follow a trail steeply uphill for about 10 minutes to the wall. You will arrive near a low arch. Hike left around the arch to reach the side of the wall containing the routes.

Chimp

Conditions

The numerous amphitheaters of this southeast-facing, horseshoe-shaped wall keep it reasonably cool in the summer. The price to pay is that the rock is slightly green and of poor quality on a few of the routes. It's still worth a visit though, especially since it's usually less crowed than Roadside and Torrent Falls and the approach isn't too bad. Unfortunately, the driest routes in heavy rain are the ones of lower quality, although the others will be OK in a light rain.

❹ Chimp 5.10b ★★★
This route begins about 20 feet left of *Jailbird*. Begin on easy holds, then move over the lip of a small roof into the thin zone. Edge for a bit, then continue over some bulges to reach the anchors.
60 ft. 5 bolts. *FA John Bronaugh, Tina Bronaugh, 1992.*

❺ Edgehog 5.11a ★★★
Move 60 feet left from the previous lines to another bolted line just before a large overhang. Edge up a thin slab, then pull a bulge to reach more forgiving holds.
60 ft. 6 bolts. *FA John Bronaugh, Alex Yeakley, 1998.*

❻ Skin the Cat 5.11a ★★★
Hike past an amphitheater to a ledge with a boulder. This route starts on the boulder and begins with a low roof. Pull over the low roof, then angle right past hand jams and bulges to a finishing groove.
80 ft. 10 bolts. *FA John Bronaugh, Alex Yeakley, 1999.*

❼ One Brick Shy 5.10c ★★★
Begin on the same boulder as the previous line. Pull the roof and climb up left of a crack to a ledge. Move up and over some bulges to a vertical face. Pull on pockets to the anchors.
80 ft. 8 bolts. *FA John Bronaugh, Stacy Temple, 1992.*

❽ Geezers Go Sport 5.11b ★★★★
This pumpy route is the next bolted line, 25 feet left of *One Brick Shy*. Bring a medium-sized cam for optional pro at the first ledge.
80 ft. 9 bolts. *FA John Bronaugh, Stacy Temple, 1992.*

❶ Put Me in the Zoo 5.9+ ★★★
Walk left from the small arch and around the corner to a dirt ramp that heads up to the right. Follow the dirt ramp to a ledge. This route is the bolted line on the right that heads up a vertical face.
70 ft. 7 bolts. *FA John Bronaugh, Tina Bronaugh, 1998.*

❷ Armadillo 5.10d ★★★
This is the bolted line directly left of *Put Me in the Zoo*. Begin just right of a tiny rockhouse.
70 ft. 6 bolts. *FA John Bronaugh, Tina Bronaugh, 1998.*

❸ Jailbird 5.10d ★★★
Walk about 30 feet left from the dirt ramp leading to the previous lines until you see a low-angle slab with a roof at the top. Begin on an easy slab, then gain a ledge and crimp up to better holds. Pull a small overhang, then follow larger holds to the anchors.
90 ft. 10 bolts. *FA John Bronaugh, Ryan Adams, 2003.*

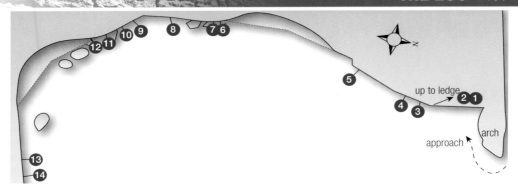

Monkey in the Middle 5.11a ★★★★

Move another 25 feet left from the previous line to the next bolted route. Crank through the steep beginning section on pockets to a slightly overhanging headwall. 80 ft. 8 bolts. *FA Stacy Temple, John Bronaugh, 1992.*

Cannonball 5.11b ★★★

Walk 20 feet left from *Monkey in the Middle* to a point just before another amphitheater. Start on a boulder and climb through a short overhanging section to the second bolt. Continue up the pocketed face on rock of not the greatest quality (aka choss) to the anchors. 80 ft. 8 bolts. *FA Stacy Temple, John Bronaugh, 1992.*

On Beyond Zebra! 5.11c ★★

This route begins to the left of *Cannonball* and on top of a large boulder near the end of an amphitheater. 80 ft. 9 bolts. *FA John Bronaugh, Stacy Temple, 1993.*

Lynx Jinx 5.11c ★★★

This route ascends the steep face a few feet left of *On Beyond Zebra!*. Climb through a low overhang and continue up the face through some bulges. Ditto on the choss factor. 50 ft. 7 bolts. *FA Jim Link, John Bronaugh, 1995.*

Scar Tissue 5.12a ★★★★

Although a little green at the start, this route serves as a great companion to *Hippocrite*. Steep and powerful. Walk left about 200 feet from *Lynx Jinx*, past an amphitheater to a steep, pocketed section of the wall. This route begins on the left side of a low overhang. Climb through a very steep section to reach the hard moves on the not-so-steep section above. Crank through the final moves to reach the anchors. 45 ft. 5 bolts. *FA Phil Nemes, 2002.*

Hippocrite 5.12a ★★★★★

A short, classic route with incredibly cool moves. Crank up the obvious line of big huecos just left of *Scar Tissue*. 45 ft. 4 bolts. *FA Eric Lowe, 1998.*

Aviary 5.12b ★

Left of *Hippocrite* is an arete with a high first bolt. Begin on a large boulder and power up to a ledge at the second bolt. Get a shake, then make reachy moves on sandy holds to gain a roof. Traverse left to clip a stray bolt, then gun through more awkwardness to meet a good shake on an epoxied flake. Continue on thinning and disappearing holds to the anchors, which are way right from the last bolt. Use a 70-meter rope if you want to get down without any issues. Equipped by Mark Strevels. 20 ft. 12 bolts. *FA Doug Curth, 2007.*

Monkey in the Middle

Hippocrite

TORRENT FALLS

all day | a.m. | shade | 5 mins | OK in rain | 48 routes
5.6- .7 .8 .9 .10 .11 .12 .13 .14

Character

Torrent Falls is a privately owned crag that offers some of the best sport climbing in the Red. Ownership of the property changed hands a few years ago when Dr. Bob Matheny purchased it in 2007. Torrent is open to climbing, but only after registering on the website. See the Access section below for details, or visit the website. The routes here are, for the most part, grouped into their own grade on different sections of the cliff. For example, you will find a 5.10 Wall, a 5.11 Wall, and a 5.12 Wall. The 5.12 wall hosts some of the longest and pumpiest 5.12s around, including the five-star classic *Steelworker* and the hardest 5.12a in the Red, *Bare Metal Teen*. The area even includes a five-star 5.11 overhanging hand crack, *Windy Corner*. It all sounds too good to be true, but this place really does exist.

Approach

From Miguel's, drive south on KY 11 for 5.3 miles until you see the sign for Torrent Falls Bed and Breakfast on your right. Turn right and park in designated parking areas, paying close attention to any signs the owner may have posted concerning parking. To reach routes 19-28, hike straight back from the parking area and cross a small creek. Head up a hill, which leads to the base of the 5.10 Wall. To reach the rest of the routes, walk up the gravel road to a set of stairs on the right. Follow the stairs to the base of the 5.11 Wall.

Conditions

Due to its horseshoe-shaped layout, Torrent Falls offers climbing suitable to most any conditions. The 5.11 and 5.12 walls face south, so expect excellent sun exposure on those walls. For shade, check out the 5.10 Wall, and for early morning sun, head to the routes on the east side of the wall. Most of the lines remain dry during a light rain, but the walls do seep during periods of heavy rain.

Access

To climb at Torrent, you must register on the website www.torrentfallsclimbing.com. The number of spaces for vehicles and registered climbing are limited. Each registrant is valid for one vehicle only, and each group is asked to limit its size to no more than three climbers. All individuals must sign a waiver before entering the property; individuals not signing a waiver will be considered to be trespassing. The area does occasionally close for weddings, RRGCC meetings, and other events, so plan ahead. Please throw some cash into the donation box just before heading up the stairs.

Wadcutter

❶ Cordelia 5.8 ★★

At the top of the stairs used for the approach, walk to the wall directly in front of you and locate this route on a slabby section of the wall to the right of the taller 5.11 Wall. Balance up the well-bolted slab to the anchors.
50 ft. 9 bolts. *FA Unknown, 2002.*

❷ Hmmm 5.2 ★

50 feet left of *Cordelia* is a short, thin dihedral. Climb it to the ledge, then move right to rappel from the anchors on *Cordelia*.
50 ft. *FA Joe Finney, 1992.*

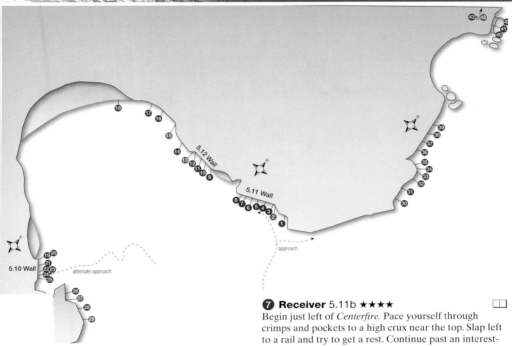

3 Dream of a Bee 5.8 ★★

This route ascends the face just left of the previous line.
45 ft. 6 bolts. *FA Unknown, 2002.*

4 Wadcutter 5.9+ ★★★

Left of the previous lines is a more vertical line, which becomes slightly overhanging and heavily pocketed towards the top. Climb up and left to dodge an overhang. Move back right and head up the pumpy face to the anchors.
50 ft. 5 bolts. *FA Porter Jarrard, Jeff Moll, 1993.*

5.11 WALL ───────────────

5 Bandolier 5.11a ★★★★

A great introduction to pumpy Red River Gorge sandstone for the visiting 5.11 climber. This line ascends the face just left of *Wadcutter*. Climb the slightly overhanging face past a couple of cruxes to a no-hands rest out left if desired. Pump out on the final overhanging flake to the chains.
70 ft. 7 bolts. *FA Porter Jarrard, Jeff Moll, 1993.*

6 Centerfire 5.11c ★★★★

This is the bolted line 10 feet left of *Bandolier*. Boulder through a starting section to a stance, take a breather, then continue up the sustained pumpy face to the anchors.
75 ft. 8 bolts. *FA Porter Jarrard, Jeff Moll, 1993.*

7 Receiver 5.11b ★★★★

Begin just left of *Centerfire*. Pace yourself through crimps and pockets to a high crux near the top. Slap left to a rail and try to get a rest. Continue past an interesting finish to the anchors.
65 ft. 8 bolts. *FA Porter Jarrard, Jeff Moll, 1993.*

8 Recoil 5.11d ★★★★

This route begins five feet left of *Receiver*. Climb a small dihedral to an overhanging face. Crank big moves on good holds and enjoy a nice run to the anchors.
55 ft. 5 bolts. *FA Porter Jarrard, Jeff Moll, 1993.*

Centerfire

⑩ Steelworker 5.12c ★★★★★

Classic. One of the best lines of its grade in the Red. This route begins just left of *Racer X* in a low overhanging section. Pull the low overhang, then race up a steep section on good holds, passing a couple of bouldery cruxes. **80 ft. 8 bolts.** *FA Porter Jarrard, Jeff Moll, 1993.*

5.12 Wall

5.12 WALL

9 Racer X 5.12d ★★★★

This route begins 100 feet left and around the corner from *Recoil*, on what is known as the 5.12 Wall. *Racer X* is the first route on the right side of the wall. Begin by climbing through a low steep section near the left side of an overhang 20 feet above the ground. Continue up the face on small edges to a big move towards the top, then shift right to the anchors.
80 ft. 8 bolts. *FA Porter Jarrard, Jeff Moll, 1993.*

10 Steelworker 5.12c ★★★★★

See route description on photo.

11 Bare Metal Teen 5.12a ★★★★★

Historically rated 5.12a, this is one of the cruelest jokes the Red has to offer. Move a few feet left of *Steelworker* to the next bolted line. Climb up to a horizontal. Then, with the pump clock ticking, sprint up the sustained and overhanging face, taking full advantage of each jug you locate.
80 ft. 8 bolts. *FA Porter Jarrard, Jeff Moll, 1993.*

12 Big Money Grip 5.12b ★★★★

After *Bare Metal Teen*, this one may seem easy. It begins by climbing the dihedral on the left side of the 5.12 Wall to a high first bolt. Continue up through pockets and crimps to a slabby section, then fire to the anchors.
70 ft. 7 bolts. *FA Porter Jarrard, Jeff Moll, 1993.*

13 Burcham's Folly 5.8 ★★★

Ascends the left-leaning crack just to the left of *Big Money Grip*.
100 ft. *FA John Burcham, 1993.*

14 Torrential 5.12c ★

Move left 50 feet from the previous line to a bolted line that moves through a series of overhangs low down and more toward the top. Look for a fixed extended draw. This might be where you bail, due to choss or wet rock.
70 ft. 10 bolts. *FA Bruce Adams, Dave Scott, 2000.*

15 Neither 5.11a ★★

About 20 feet left of *Torrential* is this left-facing dihedral. Climb through 25 feet of questionable rock to the clean dihedral above, where the rock improves. Layback and stem the dihedral and lower from chain anchors.
60 ft. *FA Unknown.*

16 Into the Mystic 5.12c ★★★

Move 40 feet left from *Neither* to locate an intimidating line with fixed chain draws. Climb a pocketed face to a section of black, blobby rock and a severely overhanging finish.
85 ft. 11 bolts. *FA Greg Martin, 2000.*

17 Paranoia 5.13b ★★★

This difficult and rarely repeated line begins 40 feet left of *Into the Mystic*, near a black boulder. Climb the steep, thin face and pull tough moves past a roof. Hang on for another big move and gun for the anchors.
90 ft. 12 bolts. *FA Dave Hume, 1996.*

18 Hydro Shock 5.12c

This uncompleted project is located left of *Burcham's Folly*. Climb the face and lower from the last bolt.
70 ft. 9 bolts. *FA Unknown.*

Paranoia

5.10 WALL

⑲ It's Alive 5.10d ★★★

Walk way left from *Paranoia* past a huge amphitheater to a wall with some bolted lines. This is the first line encountered and shares a start with *Reanimator*. Begin with or without some cheater stones to grab the first jugs under the low roof. Pull the roof, traverse left to a stance, and then move right to follow the line of bolts to some anchors. **55 ft. 7 bolts.** *FA Terry Kindred, 2001.*

5.10 Wall

⑳ Reanimator 5.10b ★★★

This route has the same start as *It's Alive*, but instead of angling right move straight up the face on pockets and crimps. **70 ft. 8 bolts.** *FA Terry Kindred, 2001.*

㉑ About Five Ten 5.11b ★★

Reachy-start route left of *Reanimator*. If you're about five ten you shouldn't have any issues. **70 ft. 8 bolts.** *FA Blake Bowling, 2008.*

㉒ Rest Assured 5.10a ★★★

This is the bolted line left of *About Five Ten*. **60 ft. 7 bolts.** *FA Terry Kindred, 2001.*

㉓ Family Values 5.10d ★★★

This shares the start of *Rest Assured* and continues up the left bolt line. Climb the face using slopers and pinches to an obvious crux, then hang on to reach the anchors. **80 ft. 9 bolts.** *FA Terry Kindred, 2001.*

㉔ Last Resort 5.10c ★★

Move left from *Family Values* to the next bolted line. Originally the dirtiest line on the wall, this route seems to be cleaning up nicely. Don't expect a bolt every time you want one though. The crux is somewhat height dependent. **80ft. 6 bolts.** *FA Terry Kindred, 2005.*

㉕ Tourist Trap 5.9 ★★★

This route climbs the arete left of *Last Resort*. After a funky start, move left to reach the second bolt. Head right for the arete and fun climbing to a mantel before the anchors. **80 ft. 9 bolts.** *FA Terry Kindred, 2003.*

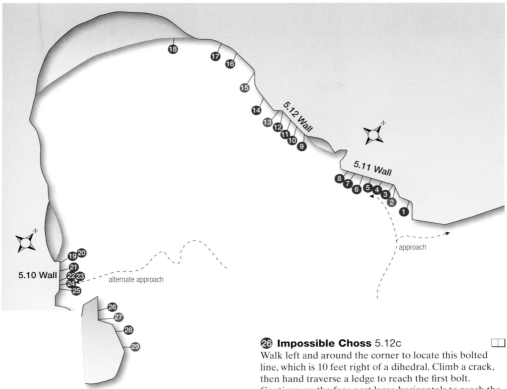

Windy Corner

26 Impossible Choss 5.12c

Walk left and around the corner to locate this bolted line, which is 10 feet right of a dihedral. Climb a crack, then hand traverse a ledge to reach the first bolt. Continue up the face past large horizontals to reach the overhanging headwall. Pull a small roof at the top to clip the anchors.
60 ft. 6 bolts. *FA Unknown.*

27 Smoke Screen 5.9 ★

Climbs the dihedral just left of *Impossible Choss*. Be careful on the unprotected mud slide towards the top. Rappel from a tree or walk off left to descend.
90 ft. *FA Dave Veldhaus, 1984.*

28 Sam's Line 5.13b

Move left from the previous line to a blank wall with a thin seam just right of an overhanging hand crack. Figure out how to get your feet off the ground, then continue up more difficult terrain to the anchors.
70 ft. 8 bolts. *FA Unknown.*

29 Windy Corner 5.11b ★★★★★

This classic overhanging hand crack is located around the corner and left from *Smoke Screen*. Climb the dihedral to a roof about 15 feet up. Pull the roof and pump through long reaches to decent jams. Follow the crack as it switches off right and take on a couple of fist jams to reach belay anchors at the ledge. Most people lower from here, for a classic and well-protected line.
  The second pitch continues up a thin seam leading to a long runout on unprotected face to the top. Rappel from a tree or walk off right to descend.
100 ft. *FA Tom Souders, 1983.*

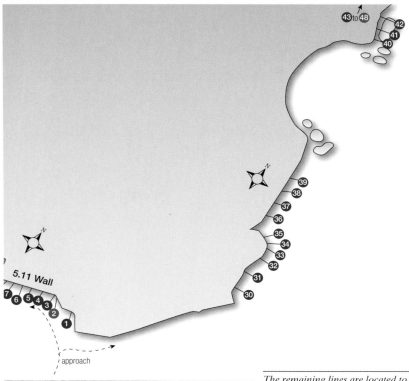

5.11 Wall

approach

Sex Show

The remaining lines are located to the right of the top of the wooden stairs used during the approach.

③⓪ Us and Them 5.12a ★★★★

From the top of the stairs, hike 300 feet right to a ledge atop a flat boulder. This is the left-most bolted line that starts from the ledge. Climb through solid rock and flowing moves to meet up with a smack down crux that may thwart anyone not familiar with the fine art of sloping on *dah slopah*.

70 ft. 7 bolts. *FA Greg Martin, 2002.*

③① Del Boy 5.11b ★★★

This route is just right of *Us and Them* and is marked by a small roof about 15 feet up. Climb the steep face to the roof, pull the roof, then wander through interesting moves to another roof. Sidestep the roof and finish on a steep face.

75 ft. 6 bolts. *FA Jeff Moll, Porter Jarrard, 1993.*

③② Pocket Pussy 5.10d ★★★

This is the left-angling bolted line 20 feet right of *Del Boy*. Climb the steep face, then step out left to a small ledge. Continue up more-vertical terrain to the anchors.

50 ft. 6 bolts. *FA Unknown.*

③③ Sex Show 5.11c ★★★★

This route ascends the face just left of the arete to the right of *Pocket Pussy*. Climb the arete, then follow the bolts left onto the face. Continue up through some bouldery moves to a long reach at the top.

50 ft. 5 bolts. *FA Jeff Moll, Porter Jarrard, 1993.*

Seek the Truth

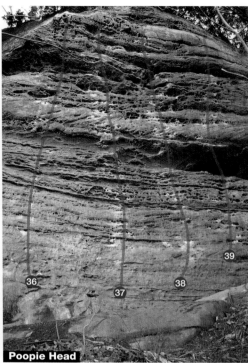

Poopie Head

34 Seek The Truth 5.11d ★★★★★

This mega-steep line climbs the severely overhanging face just right of *Sex Show*. Begin on the arete, then move right to take on the steepness using big moves and heel-hooks and passing a well-defined crux just before the anchors.
50 ft. 4 bolts. *FA Jeff Moll, Porter Jarrard, 1993.*

35 Sport for Brains 5.11d ★★★

Step about 10 feet right from *Seek the Truth* to another extremely steep route. Relatively easy climbing on a vertical face gains the high first bolt, then continue through the steepness to a decent rest on a small ledge. Climb a few more feet to clip the anchors.
60 ft. 6 bolts. *FA Steve Grossman, 1996.*

36 Ode to Poopie Head 5.11b ★★

Walk to the right of *Sport for Brains*, past a wide crack, to the first route on a short wall. Climb through small pockets and footholds to reach better holds. Continue up the pumpy face to a roof, mantel the lip, and clip the anchors.
40 ft. 4 bolts. *FA Steve Grossman, 1996.*

37 Poopie Head 5.10c ★★★

This is the next line just right of *Ode to Poopie Head*.
40 ft. 4 bolts. *FA Neal Strickland, Chris Snyder, 1995.*

38 Stool Sample 5.10c ★★★

This is the next bolted line right of *Poopie Head*.
40 ft. 4 bolts. *FA Tony Reynaldo, 1996.*

39 Rectal Exorcism 5.11a ★★

This route begins on a short slab to an overhang just right of *Stool Sample*.
45 ft. 5 bolts. *FA Tony Reynaldo, 1996.*

40 G'sUs 5.11c ★★

Walk to the right of *Rectal Exorcism*, past a waterfall and up a steep sandy section of the trail littered with loose boulders. At the top of the steep hill, near a large boulder, are a few bolted lines. This is the left-most line.
80 ft. 7 bolts. *FA Greg Martin, Gregg Purnell, 2003.*

41 Onaconaronni 5.11d ★★★

Move 10 feet right from *G'sUs* to the next line. Climb through the overhang near the bottom and move up a vertical rib for a few bolts. Continue on larger holds to the top.
65 ft. 8 bolts. *FA Greg Purnell, 2001.*

42 Hoosier Buddies 5.11d ★★★

The bolted line 20 feet right of *Onaconaronnyi*.
65 ft. 7 bolts. *FA Greg Martin, Greg Purnell, Tim Powers, 2001.*

43 Hired Guns 5.7

Walk right about 20 feet and head up a short, steep hill to reach the next group of very short "kid routes." These were put in place by the request of the landowner for Boy Scout Troops. Begin with a ladder step made of rebar.

20 ft. 5 bolts. *FA Tim Powers, Jared Hancock, Mike Susko, 2002.*

44 Physically Strong, Mentally Awake, and Morally Straight 5.5

This is the slabby, blunt arete with big easy ledges 20 feet right of the previous route.

30 ft. 4 bolts. *FA Jared Hancock, Mike Susko, Tim Powers, 2002.*

45 Livin' in the UK 5.11c ★★★

Walk downhill and around the corner 50 feet right of the previous lines to the next group of routes. This line begins 20 feet right of an arete and climbs to a horizontal ledge 25 feet up. From the ledge, move over a small roof and continue up the pocketed face to the anchors.

65 ft. 5 bolts. *FA Jeff Moll, 1992.*

46 Mad Porter's Disease 5.12d ★★★★

Move 35 feet right from the previous line to a blank-looking section of wall. Climb up to a flat triangular roof at mid-height and crank a series of difficult moves around the lip. Continue past a stopper crux to a much easier finish.

70 ft. 6 bolts. *FA Jeff Moll, 1992.*

47 My How Things Have Change 5.11d ★★★★

Thirty feet right of *Mad Porter's Disease* is another great line on a vague arete. Climb thin holds to fun moves up high.

60 ft. 6 bolts. *FA Jeff Moll, 1992.*

48 Retroflex 5.9 ★★★

This route ascends a crack 20 feet right of the previous sport lines. An easy start gains a rest, then continue up a dihedral to chain anchors.

75 ft. *FA John Bronaugh, Ron Snider, Brent Lewis, George Robinson, 1984.*

Michelle Ellington, *Wild Gift* 5.12c, Roadside Crag, page 187. Photo: Dan Brayack.

BEER TRAILER CRAG   11 routes

5 mins   5.6- .7   .8   .9   .10 .11 .12 .13 .14

Show your appreciation and buy a six-pack after climbing! Photo: Elodie Saracco.

Character

If you like beer, powerful climbing, and short approaches, then this is your crag. Since the last edition of this guide the number of lines here has jumped from 3 to 11! The right side of the wall gets great sun and also stays dry in a downpour.

Approach

Park in the gravel lot, walk around to the right of the beer trailer, and head uphill to the left for routes 1-6 and uphill to the right for routes 7-11.

Access

The landowners are OK with people climbing on their property, but ask that you do not block business parking. If you see more than a couple of climber cars (look for climbing stickers, out of state license plates, or any evidence of road-trip grunge inside of the car), then head to another crag. If it's Sunday the beer trailer is closed so you're OK.

❶ Falls City 5.13b ★★★★

This is the furthest route left on the left side of the Beer Trailer crag. Punch through a series of difficult boulder problems through the first half of the line, then ease up to the chains.
50 ft. 5 bolts. *Equipped by John Cioci. FA Frank Byron, 2009.*

❷ Beer Trailer Project 1 5.13? ★★★

Just right of *Falls City* is another tough line marked by a small flake in the lower half of the route. Currently a **closed project**. Grade and quality are estimates. *Equipped by Frank Byron.*
50 ft. 5 bolts.

❸ Evening Wood 5.12a ★★★

This route was partially completed when the first lines were established at this crag. Recently it was finished and stands as a decent addition to the wall. Begin on *Morning Wood* and break left at the third bolt.
50 ft. 5 bolts. *FA John Cioci, Frank Byron, 2009.*

❹ Morning Wood 5.12a ★★★★

This route may give you just that! Boulder up through sequential pocket moves to an overhanging and more featured face above. After the third bolt, continue angling right to the next bolt.
40 ft. 4 bolts. *FA Chris Snyder, 1996.*

⑤ Sluts are Cool 5.12a ★★★

Move right to the next line beginning 10 feet left of a green dihedral. Crank through a tough start, then continue up the sustained steep face to the anchors.
40 ft. 4 bolts. *FA Todd Burlier, 1996.*

⑥ Beer Trailer 5.12b ★★★

Move right and around two corners from the previous lines to locate this line, which ascends an ivy-choked blank face.
40 ft. 4 bolts. *FA Unknown*

⑦ Beer Trailer Project 2 ★★

This and the remaining routes can be found on the wall opposite the previous routes. When approaching from the beer trailer, take the trail up and right to reach the wall instead of going left as for the previous lines. This is an **open project** and is located about 50 feet left of where the trail meets the cliff. It follows a left-leaning flake up to a blank section of vertical rock.
60 ft. 7 bolts. *Equipped by Dario Ventura.*

Project

⑧ Better Than Homemade 5.12d ★★★

This is the next route right of the open project and the first from the left on the main wall where the trail meets the cliff. Begin with a tough move right off the mud castle and crimp up to a decent ledge. From the ledge, choose your path through the crux based on your ape index to reach another decent ledge. Crawl up on more sloping pockets to the next bolt, then pinch increasingly better holds to the chains.
55 ft. 7 bolts. *FA Adam Taylor, 2009. Equipped by Dario Ventura.*

⑨ Hang Over 5.12c ★★★★

Right of *Better Than Homemade*. Start with a jug, then bust through a tough start and gun for the ledge. Scum out of the ledge on small crimps and slap hard at chalk spots to reach the next bolt. A few more moves gets you a reward ledge and easier climbing to the chains.
55 ft. 7 bolts. *FA Dario Ventura, 2009.*

⑩ High Life 5.12b ★★★

Next route right of *Hang Over*. Begin on a ledge and pull through long moves on good edges to a lie-down rest in a horizontal. When rested, crawl out of your coffin and take on a crimpy groove to another comfy shake before the final haul to the chains.
55 ft. 5 bolts. *FA John Roark, 2009.*

⑪ Liquid Courage 5.12b ★★★

Begin with the first bolt of *High Life* but continue straight up through decent edges to reach the main coffin horizontal. If you're desperate, crawl in. Continue up through some groove crimping to reach a final jug, from which you can contemplate how you'll reach the distant chalk spot near the chains. Photo page 199.
50 ft. 4 bolts. *FA Shadow Ayala, 2009.*

Hangover

MUIR VALLEY

Muir Valley owners Rick and Liz Weber.

Introduction

Muir Valley Nature Preserve, LLC (MVNP) is a nature preserve and rock-climbing arena owned and maintained by Rick and Liz Weber. The Valley is approximately 400 acres in size and walled in by seven miles of majestic sandstone. Waterfalls cascading off the cliffs abound, as do caves and stone-bottomed creeks. Mountain laurel, rhododendron, and many other species of wildflowers and plants grace the valley floor and hillsides.

Although privately owned, MVNP may be freely enjoyed by all – hikers, climbers, and folks just sauntering through taking in the spectacular beauty of the valley.

Visitors are asked to respect the privacy of MVNP neighbors by driving slowly in and out on the graveled access road. The MVNP parking lot can accommodate about 50 cars. If you arrive and find the lot full, please do not park on adjoining property or grassed and landscaped areas around the parking lot. Please park efficiently so that the lot can hold the maximum number of cars. This is especially important on weekends when attendance can be heavy.

No admission fees are charged, so MVNP falls under the provisions of Kentucky's Recreational Use Laws. Visitors may climb, hike, and enjoy the natural beauty as guests, but at their own risk. Rock climbers are required to fill out a legal release form prior to climbing, which can be done on line at www.muirvalley.com. This Muir Valley website also includes a set of rules and guidelines that *all* visitors *must* agree to follow. Some of the more important rules are listed here:

- **1.** No admission fees are charged to any visitor including professional rock guides and their clients. There are no affiliations between the MVNP owners and any guide service. All professional guide services must meet MVNP requirements and receive written permission from MVNP owners in order to guide in Muir Valley.
- **2.** Visitors must be experienced and competent rock climbers or be in the company of those who are.
- **3.** Hanger brackets have been bolted to the walls of many of the climbing routes in Muir Valley by various individuals. Although hanger brackets and the bolts that attach them to the rock and peripheral hardware, such as chains, quicklinks, rings, and cable, have been chosen and placed with care, *NO* warranties of safeness of this hardware have been given by these individuals, nor by MVNP owners. Hanger brackets have been known to pull loose from the rock. And, rock in which anchor brackets have been affixed has been known to fail. If you climb in Muir Valley and rely on any piece of hardware affixed to any rock surface for your personal safety and/or the safety of others with you, you do so at your own risk and with the full knowledge that this hardware may fail catastrophically and without warning.
- **4.** Effective January 1, 2008, dogs are no longer permitted in Muir Valley.
- **5.** Other important rules are listed on the MVNP kiosk in the main parking lot and also on the www.muirvalley.com website. Visitors who are not willing to accept full responsibility their presence in Muir Valley should not enter the property.

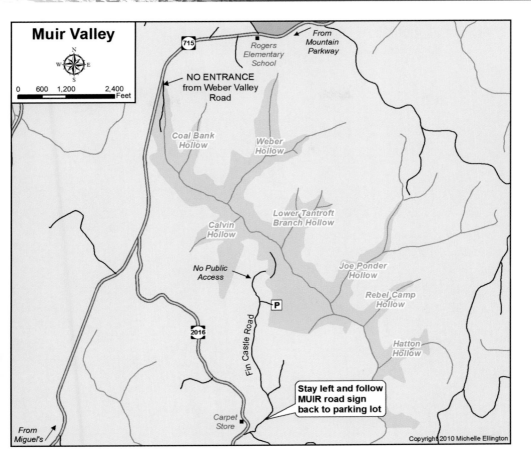

Muir Valley

0   600   1,200   2,400
Feet

715

Rogers Elementary School

From Mountain Parkway

NO ENTRANCE from Weber Valley Road

Coal Bank Hollow

Weber Hollow

Lower Tantroft Branch Hollow

Calvin Hollow

No Public Access

Joe Ponder Hollow

Rebel Camp Hollow

P

2016

Fin Castle Road

Hatton Hollow

Stay left and follow MUIR road sign back to parking lot

Carpet Store

From Miguel's

Copyright 2010 Michelle Ellington

Approach

To reach Muir Valley from Miguel's Pizza, drive south on KY 11 for 6.3 miles and turn left onto KY 715. Follow KY 715 for 2.7 miles and turn right onto road 2016. Drive 1.4 miles until you see an old carpet store on your right. Just after the carpet store, when the road curves downhill, take the first gravel road on the left. After about 100 feet, turn left. Follow the gravel road for 0.7 miles, bearing left at each fork, until you see a road on the right heading down to a large parking area near a garage. This is the only parking area for Muir Valley. There are two main trails leading to the climbing areas. The first trail leads to Coalbank Hollow, Weber Hollow, Main Valley North and Central, and Lower Tantroft Hollow. It is reached by walking back toward where you drove in and walking down the dirt road to the right until you see the trail on the left. The second trail leads to Joe Ponder Hollow and Rebel Camp Hollow and is at the far end of the parking area past the garage.

The Webers do not personally accept donations. Although no admission fee is charged, those who wish to contribute time or money toward building and maintaining visitor infrastructure can contact the volunteer organization, **Friends of Muir Valley**. It can be emailed at: Friends.of.MuirValley@gmail.com or through their website: www.friendsofmuirvalley.org.

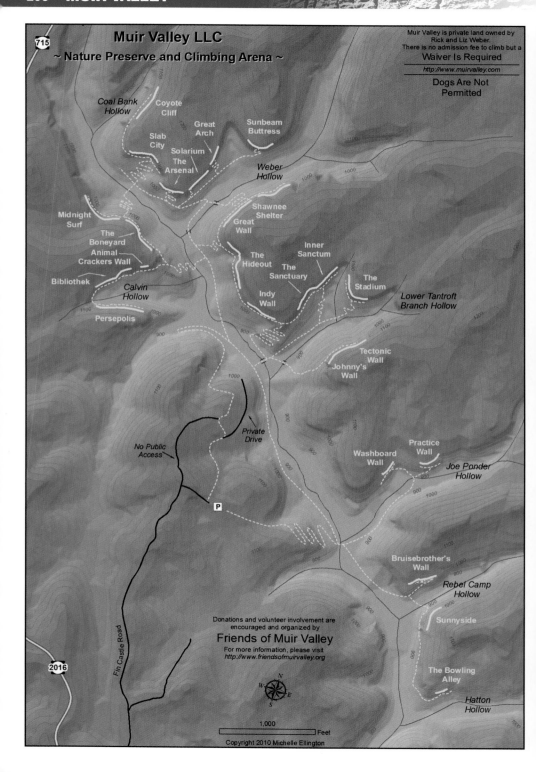

Muir Valley LLC
~ Nature Preserve and Climbing Arena ~

Muir Valley is private land owned by
Rick and Liz Weber.
There is no admission fee to climb but a
Waiver Is Required

http://www.muirvalley.com

Dogs Are Not
Permitted

Coal Bank
Hollow

Coyote
Cliff

Great
Arch

Sunbeam
Buttress

Slab
City

Solarium

The
Arsenal

Weber
Hollow

Shawnee
Shelter

Midnight
Surf

Great
Wall

The
Boneyard

Inner
Sanctum

Animal
Crackers Wall

The
Hideout

The
Sanctuary

The
Stadium

Bibliothek

Calvin
Hollow

Indy
Wall

Lower Tantroft
Branch Hollow

Persepolis

Tectonic
Wall

Johnny's
Wall

Private
Drive

No Public
Access

Practice
Wall

Washboard
Wall

Joe Ponder
Hollow

P

Bruisebrother's
Wall

Rebel Camp
Hollow

Fin Castle Road

Sunnyside

2016

Donations and volunteer involvement are
encouraged and organized by
Friends of Muir Valley
For more information, please visit
http://www.friendsofmuirvalley.org

The Bowling
Alley

Hatton
Hollow

N
W E
S

1,000
Feet

Copyright 2010 Michelle Ellington

CLIFF	SUN / SHADE	HIKE	RAIN	ROUTES	GRADE RANGE	CLASSIC ROUTES
COYOTE CLIFF page 208	p.m. / shade	25 mins		9	5.6- .7 .8 .9 .10 .11 .12 .13 .14	*Centerfire* 11c
SLAB CITY page 210	all day	25 mins		9	5.6- .7 .8 .9 .10 .11 .12 .13 .14	
THE ARSENAL page 212	all day	25 mins	rain OK	7	5.6- .7 .8 .9 .10 .11 .12 .13 .14	*Relode* 12c
MIDNIGHT SURF page 214	shade	25 mins	rain OK	9	5.6- .7 .8 .9 .10 .11 .12 .13 .14	*Cell Block Six* 12c
THE BONEYARD page 216	a.m. / shade	25 mins		29	5.6- .7 .8 .9 .10 .11 .12 .13 .14	*Renegade* 11c
ANIMAL CRACKERS page 220	p.m.	20 mins		7	5.6- .7 .8 .9 .10 .11 .12 .13 .14	
BIBLIOTHEK page 222	a.m.	25 mins		20	5.6- .7 .8 .9 .10 .11 .12 .13 .14	
PERSEPOLIS page 225	p.m.	30 mins		5	5.6- .7 .8 .9 .10 .11 .12 .13 .14	
THE SOLARIUM page 226	a.m.	25 mins	rain OK	12	5.6- .7 .8 .9 .10 .11 .12 .13 .14	*Abiyoyo* 12b
THE GREAT ARCH page 228	a.m.	25 mins	rain OK	8	5.6- .7 .8 .9 .10 .11 .12 .13 .14	
SUNBEAM BUTTRESS page 230	all day	25 mins		17	5.6- .7 .8 .9 .10 .11 .12 .13 .14	
THE GREAT WALL page 232	p.m.	20 mins	rain OK	12	5.6- .7 .8 .9 .10 .11 .12 .13 .14	
SHAWNEE SHELTER page 235	shade	20 mins		6	5.6- .7 .8 .9 .10 .11 .12 .13 .14	
THE HIDEOUT page 236	all day / shade	15 mins		19	5.6- .7 .8 .9 .10 .11 .12 .13 .14	
INDY WALL page 240	p.m.	15 mins		13	5.6- .7 .8 .9 .10 .11 .12 .13 .14	
THE SANCTUARY page 242	a.m.	15 mins	rain OK	16	5.6- .7 .8 .9 .10 .11 .12 .13 .14	*Prometheus Unbound* 13a / *Jesus Wept* 12d / *Triple Sec* 12d
INNER SANCTUM page 246	a.m.	15 mins		11	5.6- .7 .8 .9 .10 .11 .12 .13 .14	
THE STADIUM page 249	all day	20 mins	rain OK	23	5.6- .7 .8 .9 .10 .11 .12 .13 .14	
TECTONIC/JOHNNY'S WALL page 252	p.m.	20 mins	rain OK	18	5.6- .7 .8 .9 .10 .11 .12 .13 .14	
WASHBOARD WALL page 256	a.m.	15 mins	rain OK	9	5.6- .7 .8 .9 .10 .11 .12 .13 .14	
PRACTICE WALL page 258	a.m.	15 mins	rain OK	23	5.6- .7 .8 .9 .10 .11 .12 .13 .14	
BRUISE BROTHERS WALL page 262	all day	15 mins	rain OK	24	5.6- .7 .8 .9 .10 .11 .12 .13 .14	
SUNNYSIDE page 265	p.m.	15 mins	rain OK	15	5.6- .7 .8 .9 .10 .11 .12 .13 .14	

COYOTE CLIFF

p.m. shade 25 mins

9 routes

5.6- .7 .8 .9 .10 .11 .12 .13 .14

Character

This tall, impressive cliff is a short distance around the corner from Slab City. It has a few existing gems and room for a few more. The two popular lines, *Golden Road* and *Buddhalicious*, stand side by side, yet due to the varied features of the wall climb completely different. They, along with *Thunderclinger*, are definitely worth a trip to this cliff.

Approach

Walk left from Slab City (page 210). Within five minutes you will reach a large ledge from which it is possible to descend a third-class gully on your left or continue another 50 feet to a short slot and make a fourth-class move onto a wide 15-foot-high ledge. You will soon reach an aesthetic cliff line and mossy rock garden. The first bolted route left of the mossy rock garden is *Golden Road*.

Conditions

Coyote Cliff is west- to northwest-facing, so expect afternoon sun and some shade. There are many pines in the area that shade the wall fairly well.

❶ Primortal Nonsence 5.4

Toprope. This and the next route are difficult to access but offer some great exposure above the valley. They are located approximately 100 feet above the sidewalk-sized traverse ledge mentioned in the directions to Coyote Cliff. To reach these routes you will need to backtrack past the third-class gully area and find a faint trail leading up to another exposed ledge above. Make a sketchy traverse high above the lower traverse ledge to reach a giant balcony above that contains more rock. This route is a few feet left of an obvious left-leaning flake. Bolted anchors.
40 ft. *FA Jared Hancock, Pete Hogaboam, 2005.*

❷ Hiking Boot Highway 5.5 ★

This is the obvious left-leaning flake mentioned in the previous route description.
40 ft. *Pete Hogaboam, Jared Hancock, 2005.*

❸ Golden Road 5.12a ★★★★

This is the first bolted line on the main wall after the mossy rock area. A tough start leads to fun moves before a blank section up higher. Stand in a giant hueco for a great view and some solid chain anchors.
90 ft. 9 bolts. *FA Jared Hancock, Tim Powers, 2005.*

❹ Buddhalicious 5.11a ★★★

This line follows the left edge of an obvious groove about 20 feet left of *Golden Road*. Finesse the first groove to a desperate crux just before the large ledge up high. From the ledge, slap and squeeze the striking golden Buddha bellies all the way to the chains.
60 ft. 7 bolts. *Karla Hancock, Jared Hancock, 2006.*

❺ MumMum 5.11a ★★

Begins on a flake 30 feet left of *Golden Buddha*. Climb up to a small roof and smack over it to reach a ledge. Continue up on decent sidepulls and edges to end with a nice sloping finale.
70 ft. 9 bolts. *FA Brad Combs, 2009.*

❻ Manteleer 5.9 ★★★

Move left a few feet to reach this bolted and flared obtuse dihedral. A reachy start on good jugs takes you to a ledge from which you can step left and cruise the crack above. First line put up at Coyote Cliff. The bottom tends to stay wet.
70 ft. 7 bolts. *Mark Ryan, Skip Wolfe, Jared Hancock, 2005.*

❼ Thunderclinger 5.10c ★★★★

This tricky line begins on a vertical face left of a large hemlock. If you're at a loss, remember this: fingers pointing down and palms against the rock. Sit back and watch your buddy try to onsight this one.
60 ft. 6 bolts. *Tom and Ines Truesdale, Jared Hancock, Karla Carandang, 2005.*

❽ Bombardier 5.10b ★★

Bombs away. Don't kill your belayer. This is the next line left of *Thunderclinger*. Climb at your own risk and beware of the blob.
50 ft. 5 bolts. *Jared Hancock, Pete Hogaboam, 2005.*

❾ Trundling Trolls 5.11a ★

Continuing left along the cliff you will soon reach a small amphitheater with a short, overhanging sport line. Blast through the steep lower section to reach a dramatic change in angle and grade.
40 ft. 4 bolts. *Karla Carandang, Ines Truesdale, Jared Hancock, Tom Truesdale, 2005.*

8
Thunderclinger

Golden Road **3**

Manteleer **6**

4
Buddhalicious

Trundling Trolls **9**

SLAB CITY

9 routes

25 mins   5.6- .7 .8   .9 .10 .11 .12 .13 .14

Character

The name says it all. If you don't like climbing on your toes, then you're not going to like climbing at Slab City. But if you do, this wall offers some of the best lines in Muir Valley. Bring good shoes and powerful legs, along with the ability to crank on minimal edges. Don't shy away too quickly though. Red River locals tend to call vertical routes "slabs." For the traddies, *Flashpoint* is a superb thin crack requiring hard cranking skills. More slightly overhanging than slabby, *Iron Lung*, with its smack-down boulder problem and solid edges, is guaranteed to make your visit to this wall worthwhile. And for anyone who enjoyed *Boltergeist, Thrillbillies* is the definite sequel.

Approach

Continue down the gravel access road past the Arsenal for two or three minutes until you see some steps and a signed trail leading uphill on your right. A couple of switchbacks later the trail meets the wall directly beneath the thin crack, *Flashpoint*.

Conditions

Slab City is primarily south facing, so expect to bake in the sun, especially on *Strip the Willows* or *Thrillbillies*.

Return to Balance

❶ Return to Balance 5.11a ★★★★

From the top of the trail, head left past several bolted lines to a vertical section of wall with several large flakes. This line is located on the left side of the wall near an arete. Begin by climbing up to a flake, then continue to a wide water-groove-like feature. Reach left around the arete for a sloper and a hidden pocket or crimp and edge straight up the groove to bigger and better holds.
50 ft. 5 bolts. *FA Jared Hancock, Skip Wolfe, Mark Ryan, 2005.*

❷ Child of the Earth 5.12a ★★★★

Move right a few feet from the previous line to the middle of the three sport routes on this section of wall. Reach through a thin and techy crux to gain the reward of jugs in the pocketed orange rock above.
60 ft. 6 bolts. *FA Jared Hancock, Karla Carandang, 2005.*

❸ The Middle Path 5.11 ★★★

Toprope. A wandering toprope face climb between *Child of the Earth* and *Sacred Stones.*
60 ft. *FA Jared Hancock, 2004.*

❹ Sacred Stones 5.11c ★★★★

This is the third bolted line from the left on this section of wall. Begin just left of the dihedral *Go West.* Balance, precise footwork, and flexibility are required to reach the first bolt, then enjoy easier but long moves to the anchors.
65 ft. 7 bolts. *FA Jared Hancock, Rob Copeland, James Case, 2005.*

❺ Go West 5.7 ★★★

The right-facing dihedral to the right of the previous bolted lines. Fun the whole way.
70 ft. *FA Joel Bruhn, Jared Hancock, Rob Copeland, 2004.*

❻ Strip the Willows 5.11b ★★★

This is the first bolted route right of the dihedral *Go West,* on the slabby section of the wall. It's called Slab City for a reason.
80 ft. 8 bolts. *FA Karen Clark, Kipp Trummel, 2006.*

❼ Thrillbillies 5.10b ★★★★

Begin just right of *Strip the Willows* on a small pedestal, then trend up and left to thin water grooves, sidepulls, deep horizontals, and plates. Find your way up the featured slab and finish on a large ledge. Take your shoes off at the anchors to relieve your toes. Check out the view, too!
90 ft. 9 bolts. *Karla Carandang, Jared Hancock, 2005.*

❽ Flash Point 5.12a ★★★★

This is the obvious thin and slightly overhanging crack at the top of the trail. Excellent, powerful, and technical climbing.
45 ft. *FA Josh Thurston, 2006.*

❾ Iron Lung 5.12c ★★★★

Head right from *Flash Point* to locate this impressive face climb. Begin just right of a large black hueco. Ride the right edge of the hueco, then contemplate the blank face from the last point of comfort. When ready, tiptoe out onto the face, hack a loogie, and crank hard on edges to the anchors.
50 ft. 6 bolts. *FA Ray Ellington, Kipp Trummel, 2006.*

Thrillbillies

Flash Point

Iron Lung

THE ARSENAL

all day | 25 mins | OK in rain | 7 routes

5.6- .7 .8 .9 .10 .11 .12 .13 .14

Character
Situated around the corner from the Solarium, this wall has a small collection of high-quality lines. *Bathtub Mary* is one of the best of its grade, and will challenge the 5.11 leader with tricky moves and a fierce pump. Side by side, *Bullfighter* and *Reload* deliver great tough moves on quality stone.

Approach
Follow the approach to the Solarium (page 226) but continue down the main road instead of turning right on the road leading to the Solarium and the Great Arch. After 100 feet you will see the trail for the Arsenal on the right. Follow the trail shortly uphill to end up just left of *Sacriledge*. The wall can also be accessed by hiking left and around the corner from the Solarium near *Air Ride Equipped* for about 300 feet.

Conditions
The Arsenal soaks up the sun, so it's a great place to climb during the winter. The routes are usually dry during heavy rain, except for the top section of *Reload*.

❶ Quicksilver 5.8 ★★★
The obvious dihedral just left and around the corner from *Sacriledge*. Lower from chain anchors.
70 ft. *FA Josh Thurston, Brian Boyd, DRC, 2006.*

❷ Sacriledge 5.10d ★★★
At the top of the approach trail are two bolted lines on a heavily pocketed wall with large huecos mid-height. This is the left line. Climb pockets to a damp ledge and better rock quality on the slightly overhanging face above.
60 ft. 8 bolts. *FA Jared Hancock, Rob Copeland, James Case, 2005.*

❸ Bathtub Mary 5.11a ★★★★
See description opposite.

❹ Bullfighter 5.12b ★★★★
The bolted line 20 feet right of *Bathtub Mary* is a ferocious opponent. Begin with a launch to a good hold, then remain graceful and confident while acting masterful over the cruxes. Duck into a large hueco for a breather, then emerge as a brave matador to battle again. Forgo

the bloody finale and clip the chains for victory. Ole!
65 ft. 6 bolts. *FA Kipp Trummel, Rob Hunter, Jared Hancock, 2005.*

❺ Reload 5.12c ★★★★★
Just right of *Bullfighter*. Climb increasingly harder moves to a roof. Reload the forearms, fight through it, and continue on less overhanging rock to the anchors.
70 ft. 7 bolts. *FA Brad Weaver, Eric Heuermann, 2006.*

❻ Freakin' Deacon 5.12a ★★★
Just right of *Reload*. Climb through large slots that quickly grow increasingly further apart and smaller. Tougher than it looks from the ground.
65 ft. 6 bolts. *FA Andrew Wheatley, 2009.*

❼ Chicken Little Loves Abubu 5.9 ★★
The obvious left-leaning dihedral right of the previous bolted lines. Climb a few easy ledges, follow the crack, then launch around the arete and onto an exposed alcove below the anchors.
50 ft. *FA Loren Wood, J.J., 2005.*

Bathtub Mary

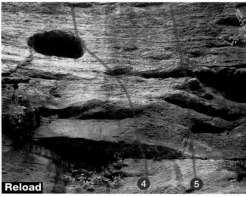
Reload

3 Bathtub Mary 5.11a ★★★★ ☐
Move 15 feet right from *Sacriledge* to the
next bolted line. Climb pockets to a slabby
section with interesting moves, then attack
the pumpy upper headwall.
70 ft. 9 bolts. *FA Kipp Trummel, Karen
Clark, 2005.*

Ashley Hamilton. Climber Photo Dan Brayack.

MIDNIGHT SURF

9 routes

shade   25 mins   rain OK

5.6- .7   .8   .9   .10 .11 .12 .13 .14

Character

This newly developed wall has quickly made it to near the top of the list of the best cliffs in the Red. The wall is big and intimidating, with most of the routes involving big throws to big square incuts. The right half of this wall is unique for the area; you'll find it hard to believe it's in the Red River Gorge. Be prepared to use your fast-twitch muscles and get dynamic here, especially if you're vertically challenged! Some climbers will find themselves with no option but to full-on dyno on a few of the lines. Standing side by side on the far right side of the cliff, *Cell Block Six* and *Iniquity* are quickly becoming two of the Red's most-wanted 5.12 lines. These routes, along with *Shiva* and *Tapeworm*, are must-dos. The left half of this wall is more pocketed and featured, like you would expect at the Red, yet still offers excellent steep pumpers such as *Vortex* and *The Crucible*.

Approach

Follow either approach to the Boneyard. Continue past the last routes on the right side of The Boneyard and follow the trail downhill. The trail heads back uphill and wraps around an ampitheater with a water-fall. Within a couple hundred feet and just right of the waterfall you'll reach a section of black lichen-covered boulders. Midnight Surf is the obvious overhanging wall right of the waterfall.

Conditions

Midnight Surf faces north and is a good warm-weather destination. The wall stays dry in a downpour, but after many days of rain it has been known to sweat.

❶ Starfish and Coffee 5.13a ★★

This is the first route encountered to the right of the large amphitheater and waterfall. Begin on a large ramp/ledge feature and trend up and left toward a giant hueco near the top on the severely overhanging pocketed face.
80 ft. *FA Greg Kerzhner, 2009*

❷ A Farewell to Arms 5.13a ★★★

Begin just right of *Jofish*. Climb a right-leaning flake to reach a hand ledge at the first bolt. Continue up on large holds to just before the body-length roof where hammer drops and things get serious. Bust over the roof to a ledge, then race up the severely overhanging wall on pockets and pinches to a big-move crux near the top.
80 ft. 12 bolts. *FA Ray Ellington, Kipp Trummel, 2007*

The Crucible

Vortex

Shiva

Mello Yellow

❸ The Crucible 5.12c ★★★★

Move about 20 feet right to the next line, which begins on a stack of boulders. Climb easy moves up to a three-foot roof. Make a big move to an edge, then slap for another good ledge. Take advantage of the rest, then move up the overhanging face through a series of pockets and sidepulls to a pump crux near the top.

80 ft. 9 bolts. *FA Ray Ellington, Kipp Trummel, 2007.*

❹ Vortex 5.12c ★★★★

Begin 10 feet right of *The Crucible*. Climb easy moves up to a large roof. Reach over the roof to good holds, then continue up the overhanging face on pockets and underclings to a good rest. Recover, then finish up the second half of the route, saving some juice for the brutal finger-cramming pocket crux just before the chains.

80 ft. 8 bolts. *FA John Cioci, Kipp Trummel, 2007.*

❺ Shiva 5.13b ★★★★

Move right from *Vortex* about 40 feet to the next bolted line. Begin 15 feet right of a tree. Boulder through the initial blank face to reach a series of long moves to large ledges. Power through a long undercling move to reach a decent edge. Match and throw, then finish up on less difficult moves.

80 ft. 8 bolts. *FA Brad Weaver, 2007.*

❻ Tapeworm 5.12d ★★★★

Begin by climbing a fragile flake 15 feet right of *Shiva*. Continue up the vertical face, passing some big moves, until the wall kicks out. Take a lay-down rest out left (if nobody's at the wall to see you) then move up to a good

ledge and head into the business – a full-on dyno if you can't use the bad sloper. Consider another chump rest out left near the top, then crank down on a pair of very bad holds and gun for a big hold just before the chains.

80 ft. 8 bolts. *FA Brad Weaver, Kipp Trummel, 2007.*

❼ Cell Block Six 5.12c ★★★★★

It doesn't get better than this! *Cell Block Six* begins 20 feet right of *Tapeworm*. Begin by climbing a short dihedral to reach the first bolt. Attack the overhanging grey stone with gorilla-swinging style and take advantage of every rest you get because you will need it for the redpoint crux run to the chains. Photo page 221.

80 ft. 9 bolts. *FA Brad Weaver, Kipp Trummel, 2007.*

❽ Iniquity 5.12b ★★★★

A complete classic. If you can't do the crux boulder problem, yard through (or start on *Cell Block*) just to experience the route. Boulder out the start to reach a good horn. Edge and throw to perfect ledges and hang on as the wall steepens dramatically near the middle. Take a squat rest on a ramp, then get dynamic again as you make the final push to the chains.

90 ft. 8 bolts. *FA Brad Weaver, Kipp Trummel, 2007.*

❾ Mello Yellow 5.11b ★

This is the last bolted line on the right side of the wall. This route is sometimes referred to as "caked mud." Nevertheless, talk it up to your friends who don't climb 5.12 yet so they'll head up to the Surf with you. Take on the arete, then move right at the roof near the middle of the route to reach the caked mud. Claw to the chains.

80 ft. 8 bolts. *FA Andrew Wheatley, Kipp Trummel, 2007.*

THE BONEYARD

a.m.   shade   25 mins

29 routes

5.6- .7 .8 .9 .10 .11 .12 .13 .14

Character

This wall contains a few mossy lines on not-so-great rock, but also a few excellent lines on solid rock. Named by the late Craig Luebben in remembrance of his buddy, the late Todd Skinner, *Renegade* would not disappoint him if he were still alive. The striking zig-zag hand crack sits high above the valley floor and offers a remarkable long ride to the anchors. If you lugged your gear up to climb *Renegade*, be sure to hike around to the left side and do the two mixed lines *The First Fast Draw* and *Son of a Wanted Man*. *Glide*, a recent addition at 5.12a, is an excellent face climb with a powerful crux that makes a trip to this wall worth the hike.

Approach

If you are headed to the Boneyard from the parking area, follow the road to the right, located near the entrance to the parking area, and find a short trail on the left that leads to another road. This road winds downhill to reach the valley floor near a stream. Take the first left on the road as it doglegs back left and immediately crosses the stream. Within a few minutes there will be a sign indicating Calvin Hollow/Boneyard/MN Surf on the left. This trail winds uphill to meet up with the cliff between Animal Crackers Wall and the Boneyard. For the Boneyard, hike to the right. The first routes you encounter with this approach will be *Lula Mae* and *Stealing Melinda*. Continue hiking right along the wall and you will eventually end up at Midnight Surf.

For the original approach, which begins directly across from Slab City, follow the marked trail across a creek and uphill to an impressive wooden staircase. Bail left at the top of the first set of stairs for routes 1-22 and continue to the top of the second set of stairs and walk right to reach the remaining routes and eventually Midnight Surf.

Conditions

The Boneyard is primarily a north- to northeast-facing wall, so expect a bit of early morning sun and good shade for the rest of the day. A few of the steeper lines stay dry in the rain, but better to go elsewhere if you're looking for a rainy-day crag.

❶ Armed Insurection 5.10d ★★★
This is the first sport route encountered left of where the original approach trail meets the cliff at the top of the first set of stairs. Bouldery start to short roof to dirty vertical face. Rap, don't lower, from the anchors to avoid twisting your rope.
80 ft. 9 bolts. *FA Jared Hancock, Rob Copeland, 2005.*

❷ Cindarella 5.9 ★★★
This is the second route to the left of the wooden stairs and is located 15 feet left of *Armed Insurection*. Begin on a flake and climb a low-angle, pocketed face to a steeper finish.
80 ft. 9 bolts. *FA Cinda Norton, J.J., 2005.*

❸ Lucy Goocy 5.10b ★★
Climb to a dirty ledge and continue on a dirty face to the chains.
80 feet. 11 bolts. *FA Barry Brolley, 2007.*

❹ One-Armed Bandit 5.9 ★★★
This line begins on the obvious arete 20 feet left of the previous line.
80 ft. 12 bolts. *FA Sarah Gross, 2006.*

❺ Captain Blondie Sinks the Ship 5.11a ★★★
Begin just left of the arete with an easy vertical section, which quickly leads to a left-angling, pumpy, overhanging face. Dig for heel-toes when you need them to recover.
75 ft. 11 bolts. *Craig Luebben, Kris Hampton, 2006.*

❻ Hoosierheights.com 5.11c ★★
Begin 30 feet left of *Captain Blondie Sinks the Ship*. Traverse in on a hand ledge from the left to start, then climb through large ledges to reach a no-hands rest. Once recovered, tackle the slightly overhanging but positive finish.
75 ft. 10 bolts. *FA Greg Martin, Josh Thurston, 2006.*

❼ Van der Waals Goo Open Project ★★★
Just around the corner from *Hoosierheights.com* is a nice-looking wall with a gold streak. This route takes on the line of bolts right of the streak. Climb through moderate terrain, then make a big move to a hueco. Move straight up out of the hueco, then trend left on small edges to reach a heinous and extremely difficult move on minuscule holds. Stretch and tiptoe the remainder to the chains.
50 ft. 7 bolts. *Equipped by Kipp Trummel.*

The Last Slow Draw

Hoosierheights.com

8 Gym Jones Approved 5.11b ★★★
Continue following the trail left. Eventually you will
reach an impressive wall containing this and the next
few lines. This is first route on the right side of this wall.
Pull up to a five-foot-high ledge, then tackle a roof
to gain another ledge near the first bolt. Continue on
pockets to the chains.
70 ft. *FA Barry Brolley, Craig Lubben, Mark Ryan, Jeff
Colombo, 2007.*

9 The Last Slow Draw 5.11d ★★★
Just five feet left is another line with a roof near the bottom. Pull over the small roof and continue up a pocketed
face past a few bulges.
70 ft. 9 bolts. *FA Craig Luebben, 2006.*

10 The First Fast Draw 5.11c ★★
Move 10 feet left to a mixed line, which begins as an
obvious crack but continues up a bolted face for the
second half.
75 ft. 4 bolts. *FA Craig Luebben, Kris Hampton, 2006.*

11 Son of a Wanted Man 5.10a ★★★
Another 10 feet left is a mixed line that begins with a
knobby face and leads to a horizontal where the crack
begins.
75 ft. 1 bolts. *FA Craig Luebben, Kris Hampton, 2006.*

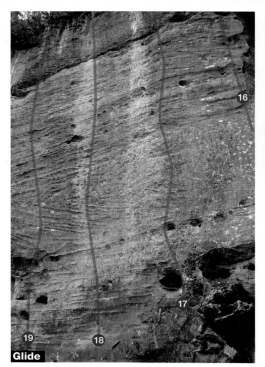

⑫ Jeff's Boneyard Project 5.12a ★

This bolted line begins 15 feet left of *Son of a Wanted Man*. Grab high crimps to start and pull up to a ledge. **Currently a closed project.**
70 ft. *Equipped by Jeff Columbo.*

⑬ Hijacked Project 5.9 ★★

This is the short bolted line left of *Jeff's Boneyard Project*. Pull through a six-foot-high roof to begin, then continue on crimps and plates to a slightly steeper finish to chains that come quicker than you'd like.
50 ft. 6 bolts. *FA Mark Ryan, Jenny Ryan, Jeff Colombo, Ashley Coll, 2007.*

⑭ Winona 5.7 ★

Locate a crack with a pod left of *Hijacked Project*. Follow a crack up to a cave with some strange formations. Squeeze through a hole at top of cave, then continue up to a set of chains.
45 ft. *FA Skip Wolfe, 2007.*

⑮ Oink! Oink! 5.8 ★★★

This line follows the thin finger crack beneath a roof 20 feet left of *Winona*.
40 ft. *FA Karen Clark, 2007.*

⑯ Surfin' the Whale's Back 5.10b ★★

This bolted line begins on a pocketed face 20 feet left of *Oink! Oink!* Climb the chimney for the first three bolts, make an awkward third clip, then step left on to the face for interesting pocket climbing.
55 ft. 7 bolts. *FA Jeff Colombo, Mark Ryan, 2008.*

⑰ Three-Toed Sloth open project ★★

Walk left from *Surfin' the Whale's Back* to locate a vertical wall hosting three bolted lines. This is the first line encountered. If *Black Mamba* in Hueco was a cake walk for you, give this a shot.
45 ft. 6 bolts. *Equipped by Kipp Trummel.*

⑱ Gorilla 5.12c ★★★

Left of *Three-Toed Sloth*. Climb up to a large pocket and make a big move left to a decent set of holds. Dive into two bolts worth of insanity, then try not to blow it for the remainder of this superb crimpfest.
45 ft. 6 bolts. *FA Ray Elliongton, Kipp Trummel, 2009.*

⑲ Glide 5.12a ★★★★

This excellent route begins just left of *Gorilla*. Climb easy moves to an undercling before the third bolt. Get powered up, then crank hard on edges to reach a knob up and left. Grab a quick shake, then dance up the face on solid edges interspersed with the occasional iron oxide jug.
45 ft. 6 bolts. *FA Kipp Trummel, 2008.*

⑳ Stealing Melinda 5.9 ★★

A short, bolted line 100 feet left of *Glide*. Surprisingly fun for its length. Pull a difficult start, then reach and step to the chains.
25 ft. 3 bolts. *FA Jeff Colombo, Mark Ryan, Skip Wolfe, Rick Weber, 2008.*

㉑ Lula Mae 5.6 ★

This route takes the twin flakes just left of a *Stealing Melinda*.
25 ft. *FA Eric Cox, 2007.*

The remaining lines are located to the right of the top of the second set of stairs.

㉒ Abby Gabby Doo 5.8
This route is the first bolted line about 100 feet right of the top of the second set of stairs.
30 ft. 5 bolts. *FA Mike Susko, Stacia Susko, 2006.*

㉓ Flying Serpents 5.12a ★★
Move right a few feet to the next overhanging wall with three bolted lines. This is the left line.
65 ft. 6 bolts. *FA Jared Hancock, Tim Powers, Karla Carandang, 2005.*

㉔ Tanduay Time 5.10d ★★★
The middle of the three sport routes.
60 ft. 5 bolts. *FA Jared Hancock, Tim Powers, Karla Carandang, J.J., 2005.*

㉕ Tao Bato 5.11a ★★
This is the right of the three lines on the pocketed face.
50 ft. 7 bolts. *FA Jared Hancock, J.J., 2005.*

㉖ Renegade 5.11c ★★★★★
Walk right about 40 feet to locate this obvious zig-zag crack. Start in an alcove under a bolt about 20 feet up. Take fingers to hands pro, with extra off-fingers and thin-hands sizes. Bolt anchors.
85 ft. 1 bolts. *FA Craig Luebben, 2006.*

㉗ Bangers and Mash 5.11c ★★★★
This and the next three routes begin right of *Renegade* and can be approached by traversing along the ledge near the base of the wall. For this line, keep a careful belay going to the third bolt. After the ledge rest at mid-height, watch your forearms turn to mash as you throttle for the chains.
70ft. 9 bolts. *FA Kipp Trummel, Karen Clark, 2007.*

㉘ Sweet Tater 5.11d ★★★
This is the next route right of *Bangers and Mash*. Named in honor of "Sweet Tater" Creech, a matriarch of the area. Casual climbing to a smack-down crux.
70 ft. 8 bolts. *FA Kipp Trummel, 2007.*

㉙ Hagis, Neeps and Tatties 5.11c ★★
Traverse the ledge to the righmost line. Climb to a roof, then pull over on large holds to encounter a line of edges and slopers with some way-right-of-the-bolts excitement.
85 ft. 9 bolts. *FA Kipp Trummel, 2007.*

Bangers and Mash

ANIMAL CRACKERS

7 routes

20 mins

5.6- .7 .8 .9 .10 .11 .12 .13 .14

Character

Animal Crackers Wall is just as it sounds: fun for the kids. It's a short section of slabby wall with a few fun slab climbs. If you enjoy slab climbing and you're on your way to Biblothek Wall, then stop and do the route named *Sam* when you pass it.

Approach

If you are headed to Animal Crackers Wall from the parking area, follow the road to the right, located near the entrance to the parking area, and find a short trail on the left that leads to another road. This road winds downhill to reach the valley floor near a stream. Take the first left on the road as it doglegs back left and immediately crosses the stream. Within a few minutes there will be a sign indicating Calvin Hollow/Boneyard/MN Surf on the left. This trail winds uphill to meet up with the cliff between Animal Crackers Wall and the Boneyard. Head left until you reach a small, slabby wall with several bolted lines. To reach *24-Hour Bug* and *Much Ado About Nothing*, continue walking past the main wall. If you reach an overhanging wall with several bolted lines you've walk too far and ended up at Biblothek.

Conditions

This wall will be wet when it rains. Sun hits from mid-morning until early afternoon.

Photo Elodie Saracco.

❶ Panda Bear 5.8 ★★★

This is the first route encountered on the slabby Animal Crackers wall. Crimps on a slab.
45 ft. 4 bolts. *FA Natasha Fischer, 2007.*

❷ Sam 5.10b ★★★★

Next route left of *Panda Bear*. If you approach this route with the mindset that nothing at a wall named Animal Crackers could quite possibly be difficult, then you may get smacked down by this tough little slab. Best route on the wall.
45 ft. 6 bolts. *FA Brett Stark, 2007.*

❸ Rikki Tikki Tavi 5.8 ★★★

Next line left of *Sam* and the third route from the right. It is what it looks like.
50 ft. 5 bolts. *FA Reese Nelson, 2007.*

❹ Harvey 5.7 ★★★

Next route left of *Rikki Tikki Tavi*. Stop at first anchors at 45 feet (six bolts) or continue past four more bolts to the second set of anchors for extended fun.
80 ft. 10 bolts. FA   *Rick Weber, 2007.*

❺ Casey 5.8 ★★★

This is the leftmost bolted route on the main Animal Crackers wall. Crimpy for 45 feet, then pure friction and balance for the next 30 feet to the top.
75 ft. 11 bolts. *FA Rick Weber, 2007.*

❻ 24-Hour Bug 5.8 ★★

To locate this crack, continue past the main Animal Crackers wall a couple hundred feet until just before the trail heads down a steep ravine beneath a large ampitheater. Begin jamming 10 feet off the deck and continue to the chains.
45 ft. *FA Josh Thurston, Rick Weber, 2007.*

❼ Much Ado About Nothing 5.11c ★★★

This left angling bolted line begins 10 feet left of *24-Hour Bug*. Climb through easy moves to a stopper crux at the fourth bolt. Continue on good handholds and bad feet to the chains.
45 ft. 5 bolts. *FA Josh Thurston, Ron Bateman, 2009.*

Katie Erickson, *Cell Block Six* 5.12c, Midnight Surf, page 215. Photo: Dan Brayack.

BIBLIOTHEK

a.m.   25 mins   20 routes

5.6- .7 .8 .9 .10 .11 .12 .13 .14

Character

If 5.11 is your grade, then this is your wall. Bibliothek boasts 15 decent-quality overhanging 5.11 lines all within just feet of each other. Most of the lines on the main wall climb similarly and feel about the same grade, so it was tempting to just give every route 5.11b/c. A couple of the lines do stand out though. *Everything That Rises Must Converge* is easily the best line on the main wall, but also probably the most difficult. Oh, and the names? They're all titles of books. If you can't remember any of them, you're not alone.

Approach

Follow the approach for Animal Crackers Wall but continue walking past Animal Crackers Wall for a few hundred feet until you reach a steep ravine near a large amphitheater. Walk down the sandy ravine and cross a small stream near the bottom. Hike a short distance up and around the corner to reach an overhanging wall with several bolted lines. The routes *Tea at the Palaz of Hoon* through *100 Years of Solitude* are located on this main wall, from left to right. To reach *American Psycho* through *A Confederacy of Dunces*, continue walking past the main wall for 100 feet.

Conditions

Most of these lines are overhanging so they're climbable in a decent rain. They're a bit tough on the skin due to the texture of the rock, but you'll like it when you're trying to hang on to the sloping holds. The wall gets sun from the morning until early afternoon.

Everything That Rises

① A Prayer for Owen Meany 5.6 ★★
Past Animal Crackers Wall and down a steep ravine is this short right-angling handcrack, located about 35 feet before rounding the corner to reach the main Bibliothek wall.
30 ft. *FA Ron Bateman, Josh Thurston, 2009.*

② 100 Years of Solitude 5.11a ★★★
Rightmost line on the main wall. Climb the asthetic face just right of a large scoop in the cliff. A bouldery start leads to comfortable stances and fun moves to a thinner finish.
55 ft. 5 bolts. *FA Ron Bateman, Josh Thurston, 2007.*

③ Who Pooped in the Park? 5.11c ★★★
Bolted line just left of *100 Years of Solitude.* Begin by either climbing the crack, if it's dry, or the face to the left. Leave the comfort of large holds and move right onto the face to make the second clip. Continue up to a rest, then bust through single-pad edges up the short but pumpy headwall. Sucker your partner into hanging the draws.
55 ft. 6 bolts. *FA Andrew Wheatley, Brad Combs, 2009.*

④ The Giver 5.6 ★
Climb the flake to the left of *Who Pooped in the Park?.* Reach for the first hold and continue up the left-angling flake, using hand-size gear. Shares anchors with *The Short Happy Life of Francis Macomber.*
45 ft. *FA Cleveland Wilson, Brad Combs, 2008.*

⑤ The Short, Happy Life of Francis Macomber 5.10b ★★
Short but sweet. Just left of the crack climb *The Giver* and the first route left of the large scoop. A steep, technical start leads to Creature-like climbing above.
45 ft. 4 bolts. *FA Ron Bateman, Josh Thurston, 2007.*

⑥ The Stranger 5.12a ★★
Next route left of *The Short, Happy Life.* Boulder through a short section of slopey, textured rock to reach a set of good sidepulls. Clip the second bolt, then bust through pockets and pinches to reach the mossy but easier upper section.
55 ft. 5 bolts. *FA Josh LaMar (L.J.), Josh Thurston, 2009.*

⑦ Everything That Rises Must Converge 5.11d ★★★★
This route has excellent movement and is likely the best on the wall. Begin just left of *The Stranger.* Grab high pinches on textured orange rock to start. Pump up through a sequential series of protruding edges and finger pockets while keeping an eye out for the occasional hidden hold.
60 ft. 6 bolts. *FA Josh Thurston, Ron Bateman, Josh LaMar, 2009.*

⑧ Resuscitation of a Hanged Man 5.11b ★★
Ten feet left of the previous line. A little sharp, but should dull out over the years. Medium-sized holds and no big resting jugs.
65 ft. 7 bolts. *FA Josh Thurston, Ron Bateman, 2008.*

⑨ All the Pretty Horses 5.11c ★★★
Take on the sustained and pumpy face just a few feet left of the previous line.
70 ft. 8 bolts. *FA Josh Thurston, Ron Bateman, TJ Halls, 2007.*

⑩ No Country for Old Men 5.11b ★★★
Start just left of *All the Pretty Horses.* Move through the pumpy lower section to a rest, then crank through a tough finish.
65 ft. 7 bolts. *FA Josh Thurston, Ron Bateman, 2008.*

⑪ The Unbearable Lightness of Being 5.11c ★★★★
Next bolted line left of *No Country for Old Men.* Move up the overhanging face, taking advantage of the occasional gargantuan jug rest. Scoot left near the top and make a big move before the chains.
70 ft. 7 bolts. *FA Josh Thurston, Ron Bateman, 2007.*

⑫ A Portrait of the Artist as a Young Man 5.11b ★★★
Twenty feet left of *The Unbearable Lightness.* Pinch and crimp up the overhanging face. Don't waste time searching for huge double-handed ledge jugs – the route to the right stole them all.
70 ft. 7 bolts. *FA Ron Bateman, Josh Thurston, Betsey Adams, 2008.*

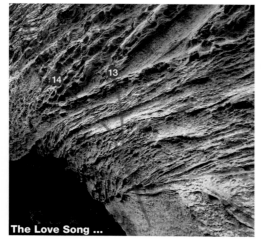

The Love Song ...

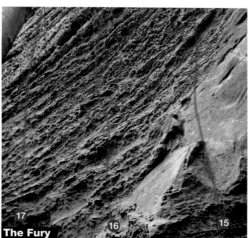

The Fury

East of Eden

⓭ The Love Song of J. Alfred Prufrock 5.11c ★★

Second bolted line on the left side of the main Biblio-thek wall, just before the trail heads down into a large ampitheater. Begin 10 feet left of the previous line. Sustained and technical climbing.

65 ft. 7 bolts. *FA Josh Thurston, Ron Bateman, 2008.*

⓮ Tea at the Palaz of Hoon 5.11b ★★

Shares the start with *The Love Song of J. Alfred Prufrock*, then angles left. Furthest left route on the main Bib wall. Pull the entrance moves on *Alfred Prufrock*, then move left to a large undercling near the second bolt.

60 ft. 5 bolts. *FA Josh Thurston, Ron Bateman, 2009.*

⓯ A Confederacy of Dunces 5.11c ★★

From the main Bibliothek wall, head left down a ravine for 50 yards to reach another section of the wall with a few bolted lines. This is the rightmost line on this section of the wall. If you can make it through the first three bolts of dirty and fragile rock, you'll be rewarded with slightly better climbing for the rest of the line.

70 ft. 7 bolts. *FA Joel Handley, Kipp Trummel, Ron Bateman, 2008.*

⓰ The Fury 5.11c ★★★

This line is just left of *A Confederacy of Dunces* and is much cleaner. Begin in a swampy mess to gain the face, then watch your forearms swell as you take on this overhanging monster of a route. If you're desperate for a rest, there are kneebars to be had.

70 ft. 8 bolts. *FA Kipp Trummel, 2008.*

⓱ The Sound 5.11c ★★

Just left of *The Fury*. If you climbed *A Confederacy of Dunces* and enjoyed it, then you've proved that your standards are low enough to have a good time on this route as well. Similar to its neighbors on the right.

65 ft. 8 bolts. *FA Kipp Trummel, 2008.*

⓲ East of Eden 5.11d ★★★

Walk left from the previous lines about 50 feet. Locate three short lines up on a ledge; this is the far right one. Crank a hard pocket problem to start and gain a good jug ledge. Launch onto the sustained face and bicep-curl your way to the chains.

40 ft. 5 bolts. *FA Kipp Trummel, 2008.*

⓳ Lolita 5.12a ★★★

Just left of *East of Eden*. This spicy route will keep your attention. Tell your belayer to bring his A game while you clip the third bolt.

40 ft. 4 bolts. *FA Kipp Trummel, 2008.*

⓴ American Psycho 5.11a ★★

Move left of *Lolita* a few feet for this one. It's longer than *Lolita* and *East of Eden*, but don't expect the same quality.

55 ft. 6 bolts. *FA Ron Bateman, 2008.*

PERSEPOLIS

p.m.   30 mins   5 routes

5.6- .7 .8 .9 .10 .11 .12 .13 .14

Character

The routes on this small section of cliff have strange names and strange moves. *Zendebad* is well worth the extra hike from Bibliothek if you're up for an amazingly unique and hard line. Do the line just left of it, *Rostam*, too. It's 50 feet of relentless slapping and sliding, where a high-friction day could mean the difference between sending and failing miserably. The lines here are hard!

Approach

Follow the approach for Animal Crackers Wall but continue walking past Animal Crackers Wall for a few hundred feet until you reach a steep ravine near a large amphitheater. Walk down the sandy ravine and cross a small stream near the bottom. Hike a short distance up and around the corner to reach an overhanging wall with several bolted lines which is Bibliothek. Continue hiking until you reach a wooden bridge. Cross the bridge and head down to a waterfall and a set of wooden stairs. Walk up the stairs and you'll end up just beneath *Zendebad*. See topo on page 223.

Conditions

The sun hits this wall in the late afternoon, but you'll probably want the shade for higher friction. Not a good candidate for a rainy day.

Zendebad

1 Zendebad 5.13a ★★★★

This is the first route encountered after the top of the wooden stairs. It begins left of a blunt arete. Make a difficult move to start, then continue through a series of bizarre and powerful moves on slopers, small crimps, and knobs to a more overhanging and pumpy finish on sidepulls and pinches.
55 ft. 7 bolts. *FA Ray Ellington, Kipp Trummel, 2007.*

2 Rostam 5.12c ★★★

This is the next line, 15 feet left of *Zendebad*. Bust through sloping holds and sequential moves, taking advantage of an occasional shake along the way. If you do this in the summer, give yourself a couple extra letter grades on your 8a.nu ticklist. It'll put you that much closer to Dave Graham.
55 ft. 5 bolts. *FA Kipp Trummel, 2007.*

3 Ferdowsi 5.11b

This route is not recommended. Per the FA, "Man, this makes my list of chop-able lines." Climb down a wooden ladder from the ledge that the previous two routes begin on, then head left about 50 feet to a taller wall with three lines. This is the first line from the right. Climb to a horizontal break midway, then take on the more overhanging second half of the route. Be careful making the next clip after leaving the midway ledge.
65 ft. 6 bolts. *FA Kipp Trummel, 2007.*

4 Paladine 5.12a ★★

Next route left of *Ferdowsi*. Climbs slanting, sloping crimps (yes, it's possible to have a sloping crimp) to a spicey run for a jug.
65 ft. 6 bolts. *FA Kipp Trummel, 2007.*

5 Apadana 5.12a ★★★

This is the last route on the wall and begins near a low crack. Start with a difficult opening move, then climb to a bulge beneath the second bolt. Make a tough move to reach a deep pocket near the bolt, then continue up the face on sequential, limestone-like finger pockets. If you aren't afraid of a little moss, then this route is actually pretty cool.
65 ft. 6 bolts. *FA Kipp Trummel, 2007.*

THE SOLARIUM

a.m. 25 mins OK in rain

12 routes

5.6- .7 .8 .9 .10 .11 .12 .13 .14

Character

This gold-striped wall seen from the main trail is as good as it looks. Most of the lines are within the 5.12 range and have hard moves near the bottom, leading to huge incuts on the upper "baked mud" section of the wall. Although it has a couple of epoxy-reinforced holds, *Banshee* still holds its weight as one of the most enjoyable and exposed 5.11s in the valley. If the epoxy bothers you, just branch left onto *Abiyoyo* for an epoxy-free and more difficult version of this excellent chunk of stone. It's hard to go wrong with any route on this wall.

Approach

This is the beautiful, brilliant-orange wall across from the Great Wall. From the creek crossing below the Great Wall near the hairpin curve, follow the road left and uphill until you reach a flat area with a large, mossy boulder and another logging road on your right that runs parallel to the Solarium. Walk along this level road for approximately 40 feet until you see a path marked with some wooden stairs leading uphill on your left. This will take you to the left end of the Solarium. Routes are listed from left to right.

Conditions

The Solarium gets sun early in the day and offers a great escape from the rain. Even if the upper section of the wall is getting sprinkled on, it's mostly incut jugs so you should still be able to climb through to the chains.

Manifest Destiny

❶ Air-Ride Equipped 5.11a ★★★★
Leftmost bolted line on the wall, just left of where the trail meets the cliff. Climb a tricky start up to a severely overhanging section with a number of tiered roofs. Heel hook and swing out the roofs, pulling a crux move just before the angle kicks back to vertical.
65 ft. 7 bolts. *FA Barry Broley, J.J., 2004.*

❷ Manifest Destiny 5.11d ★★★★
This excellent line is just right of *Air-Ride Equipped* and marked by a short roof midway up. Crank on crimps with poor feet to start, then fight the pump to reach the roof. Pull this with burly moves and keep it together for the ride to the chains.
70 ft. 8 bolts. *FA Jared Hancock, Tim Powers, J.J., 2004.*

❸ So Long Mr. Petey 5.12c ★★★
Next route right of *Manifest Destiny*. Bouldery, with a powerful section and a much thinner finish.
70 ft. 8 bolts. *FA Tim Powers, 2005.*

❹ Magnum Opus 5.12a ★★★★
Next sport route to the right. Fun and fingery pocket climbing, passing a couple of large huecos along the way.
90 ft. 10 bolts. *FA Jared Hancock, Tim Powers, Mike Susko, 2005.*

Summer Sunishine

Galunlati

5 Urban Voodoo 5.12d ★★★
Nice boulder problem to the third bolt. Deceptive roof crux, then mostly good holds to the anchors. Long draws recommended to eliminate rope drag from the roof.
95 ft. 10 bolts. *FA Greg Martin, Brian Boyd, Andrew Gehring, 2005.*

6 Super Best Friends 5.12b ★★★★
Begin left of a stack of large boulders on good holds. Climb to a large roof, passing a few big moves along the way. Take advantage of some good heel-hooks, then bust over the lip to reach the fun and easy juggy headwall.
95 ft. 10 bolts. *FA Brian Boyd, Greg Martin, 2005.*

7 Summer Sunshine 5.12b ★★★
Begin right of *Super Best Friends*, on the left side of a short arete. Trend right on good holds, then dig for power to sneak around the arete and reach the relaxing headwall.
95 ft. 10 bolts. *FA Greg Martin, Josh Thurston, Greg Purnell, 2005.*

8 Galunlati 5.12b ★★★★
This is the overhanging face that begins on the short arete feature right of the enourmous roof. Make thin, reachy moves past the second and third bolt, then fight your way through a few more cruxes to gigantic jugs at the top.
95 ft. 10 bolts. *FA Jared Hancock, Tim Powers, Josh Thurston, 2005.*

9 Mirage 5.12c ★★★★
This is the next route right on the gorgeous, overhanging orange face. Climb up between two huecos and enter into ultra-sustained crimping for 30-40 feet. As with most lines at the Solarium, relax on the comfortable incut jugs of the upper headwall.
95 ft. 10 bolts. *FA Chris Martin, 2005.*

10 Bundle of Joy 5.13a ★★★★
This project has finally been fully equipped and sent. Most of the routes at the Solarium mellow out toward the top, but this one just pours it on. Begin right of *Mirage* and start trying hard as soon as you step off the ground. A big flake that looks sketchy from the ground is actually very solid and will become a good friend when you need to shake out the pump. Have a stick clip or leaver biner ready if you can't pull the huge dyno guarding the chains!
90 ft. 7 bolts. *FA Andrew Wheatley, 2009.*

Abiyoyo

⑪ Abiyoyo 5.12b ★★★★★

Traverse to the right edge of the Solarium wall. Look for two gray Fixe hangers on a ledge above a 25-foot cliff, at the base of the dark orange overhanging wall. Once the belayer is anchored, stick clip the first bolt. Climb up and to the right, past four bolts, to a well-deserved sit-down rest in the leftmost of two large huecos. Exit the left side of the hueco. Moderate face climbing leads to an obvious crux, followed by 30 feet of pumpy face climbing. The crux may be more difficult for climbers under 5'8". Photo page 254. **60-meter rope recommended.**
95 ft. 10 bolts. *FA Eric Anderson, Mark Strevels, 2005.*

⑫ Banshee 5.11c ★★★★

Same start as *Abiyoyo*, but head up and right from the hueco rest after the fourth bolt. A tricky crux move leads to a second sit-down rest in a large hueco. Follow large jugs to the top. **60-meter rope recommended.**
100 ft. 11 bolts. *FA Eric Anderson, 2005.*

THE GREAT ARCH

a.m. 25 mins OK in rain 8 routes
.6- .7 .8 .9 .10 .11 .12 .13 .14

Character

The Great Arch is small, but due to one route, *Lip Service*, it receives a lot of attention. This route is an absolute must-do. While you're there, check out the 5.11 pumpers *Night Moves* and *Battery Life*. Cool down on *Black Powder*, then call it a day.

Approach

Follow the approach to the Solarium, but continue along the road past the trail heading up to that wall for a couple of minutes to the next trail on the left. Follow the trail shortly uphill to reach the cliff beneath *Lip Service*. If you look directly left at the opposing wall, you will be looking right at *Double Stuff*.

Conditions

The Great Arch receives morning sun, so if you want the friction you may need for *Lip Service*, visit in the afternoon. Most of the routes here are good candidates for rainy days.

❶ Double Stuff 5.12a ★★

Ascends the face just left of the dihedral *Ear Drops*, on the left side of the wall. Climb large ledges on steep stone to reach the first set of anchors. From the ledge, move left to tackle the airy second pitch via sidepulls and underclings. It is recommended to bring the belayer up to the first ledge and climb this route in multi-pitch style to avoid rope drag. The first ascentionist says a third pitch may be added.
90 ft. 11 bolts. *FA Josh Thurston, Jordan Garvey, 2006.*

❷ Ear Drops 5.8+ ★★★

Climb the wide dihedral in the left side of the *Great Arch* and continue to a set of anchors.
85 ft. *FA Jason Haas, Sarah Maclean, 2005.*

❸ Dyn-o-mite 5.9 ★★★

This is the leftmost sport route under the giant arch. It often appears wet, but can still be climbed. Fun movement with interesting features.
85 ft. 10 bolts. *FA Rick Weber, J.J., Tom Kwasny, 2005.*

Double Stuff ... 1

Lip Service ... 5

Night Moves

4 Black Powder 5.10a ★★★

More great climbing on fantastic features. Begin 15-20 feet right of *Dyn-o-mite* and angle up and right. There are several ways to make the thought-provoking moves at the third bolt.

85 ft. 10 bolts. *FA Rick Weber, Jared Hancock, Karla Carandang, J.J., 2005.*

5 Lip Service 5.11c ★★★★

This varied and unusual route starts as juggy roofs and becomes a technical face with big slopers.

80 ft. 9 bolts. *FA J.J., Josh Thurston, 2005.*

6 Beef Stick 5.12a ★★★

The obvious black streak 20 feet right of *Lip Service*. Mantel up on sloping holds to the chains. It looks like *Lip Service* but just isn't the same.

60 ft. 5 bolts. *FA Josh Thurston, Mike Uchman, 2006.*

7 Night Moves 5.11b ★★★

Stick clip the first bolt, then start on boulders left of the first bolt to begin. Casual moves on big holds to a lay-down rest. Soak it up before the bouldery finish.

80 ft. *FA Josh Thurston, 2005, Danny Rice, Mike Thurston, 2005.*

8 Battery Life 5.11c ★★★★

Share the first bolt of *Night Moves*, then move right into a tough move. Crank it out, then fight the pump on hand-over-hand sidepulls up the overhanging face. If you have an appetite for grungey cracks, you may feel this line is forced.

60 ft. 7 bolts. *FA Josh Thurston, Max Rodatz, 2005.*

SUNBEAM BUTTRESS

all day

25 mins

17 routes

5.6- .7 .8 .9 .10 .11 .12 .13 .14

Character

This sun-soaked wall has an abundance of enjoyable short lines and a few longer pumpers. A 5.11 climber can easily knock out every line on this wall in a day and have a great time doing it. The shorter lines begin on an exposed ledge, so they don't have that "quickie feel" to them. The starts of the lines have also been known to send climbers home crying. Bring a few extra ounces of *oomph* to get off the ground.

Approach

This wall is located just a few minutes up from the Great Arch. Continue along the main road accessing the Solarium and Great Arch. Pass through a grassy area, then look for an obvious trail to the left just as the road begins to head uphill.

❶ Sunbeam 5.10c ★★★

When the approach trail meets the cliff, there will be a ledge to the left with a fixed rope for access. This route is the first line to the right of the ledge that starts on the ground. Scramble to a fixed draw, tackle a difficult section near the second bolt, then continue on big holds to a set of anchors below the cave.

65 ft. 7 bolts. *FA J.J., Jared Hancock, Bram Bell, 2005.*

❷ Moonshine 5.10a ★★★

Move 15 feet right from *Sunbeam*. Climb to a large ledge beneath an intimidating roof. From the ledge, find the holds you want to use, then muscle over the roof. Larger holds lead to an interesting finish.

60 ft. 5 bolts. *FA Jared Hancock, J.J., Bram Bell, 2005.*

❸ Out of the Dark 5.10c ★★★★

The overhanging arete above the ledge to the right of *Moonshine*. Start as for *Moonshine*, then traverse right along the ledge to the high first bolt. Negotiate the roof, Tarzan up the overhanging arete, then get your focus back for the finish.

65 ft. 6 bolts. *FA Jared Hancock, J.J., 2005.*

❹ Revenge of the Sith 5.10 ★★

This is the short, overhanging hand crack directly beneath *Out of the Dark*. Boulder it, or stick clip the first bolt of *Out of the Dark* and do it as a direct start for that route.

20 ft. *FA Tom Kwasny, 2005.*

❺ Three Amigos 5.9+ ★★

This hand crack is found by following the cliff right for about 100 feet. As soon as you reach a small clearing with a tiny creek, look to your left and you will see this crack with a steep start. Bolted anchors.

70 ft. *FA Tim Powers, Tom Kwasny, Mike Susko, 2005.*

❻ Primordial Dissonance 5.10 ★★★

This route begins 20 feet right of the previous route. Climb up to the bolt and fight to reach a right-arching crack ending on a ledge. Clip another bolt, then pull over a roof to reach a crack leading to another ledge with anchors.

80 ft. 2 bolts. *FA Jared Hancock, 2005.*

LEDGE ROUTES: *Lines 7-12 begin on the ledge to the left of* Sunbeam.

❼ Predator 5.11b ★★★★

This excellent line is the leftmost route on the ledge, which is accessed via a short scramble with a fixed rope. Start with a reachy move, then continue up the vertical face with what few holds it has to offer. End with a mantel.

45 ft. 5 bolts. *FA Jared Hancock, J.J., Karla Carandang, 2005.*

❽ Prey 5.11b ★★★

Move 10 feet right from *Predator*. Dig into your bag of tricks to solve the roof at the start and be rewarded with less burly moves. Tape up if you plan to use the old hand-jam trick.

55 ft. 6 bolts. *FA Jared Hancock, J.J., 2005.*

❾ Universal Gravitation 5.10d ★★

The next route to the right follows the theme of tough starts. Fiddle around for holds, then commit and crank through the desperate beginning. Take a breather, then edge to the chains.

40 ft. 3 bolts. *J.J., Barry Brolley, 2005.*

❿ Backstabber 5.9 ★★★

The arete right of *Universal Gravitation*. Beware of the tree when cleaning.

40 ft. 4 bolts. *J.J., Karla Carandang, Jared Hancock, 2005.*

⑪ Radical Evolution 5.11a ★★★   ☐
The next overhanging route right of *Backstabber*. Fun,
steep climbing through several roofs.
45 ft. 4 bolts. *J.J., Jared Hancock, 2005.*

⑫ Morning Sun 5.11b ★★★   ☐
This is the furthest route right on the ledge. No tough
start here, but instead a longer, pumpy ride.
50 ft. 5 bolts. *J.J., Jared Hancock, 2005.*

⑬ Mossy Mayhem 5.1   ☐
This and the remaining lines are found by walking left
from the fixed rope used to access the ledge routes. This
line ascends the dirty third-class gully on the left side
of the pinnacle near the main wall. It can be used as an
access point for the ledge routes.
30 ft. *FA Jared Hancock (free solo), 2005.*

⑭ Trekker of the Treacherous 5.4   ☐
This line ascends the right side of the same pinnacle.
40 ft. *FA Jared Hancock (free solo), 2005.*

⑮ Stems and Seeds 5.11+ ★★★   ☐
Toprope. Continue left just around the corner from the
pinnacle. This difficult toprope problem ascends the
clean, short dihedral that ends beneath *Predator*. Use
friction, tension, smearing, and all the other techniques
you don't learn in the Red. There are anchors on the
ledge to toprope from.
30 ft. *FA Jared Hancock, J.J., 2005.*

⑯ Directed Panspermia 5.12 ★★   ☐
Toprope. Another enjoyable, difficult toprope. Power and
finesse up a thin face and flake just left of *Stems and Seeds*.
30 ft. *FA Jared Hancock, 2005.*

⑰ Where's My Chisel 5.9   ☐
One way to generate some controversy in the Red is to
bolt an artificial hold onto a route. Yes, that was done
on this route, but the hold has since been removed. The
natural remnants of the route can be found just left of
the previous toprope lines.
35 ft. 4 bolts. *FA Rizzo, 2005.*

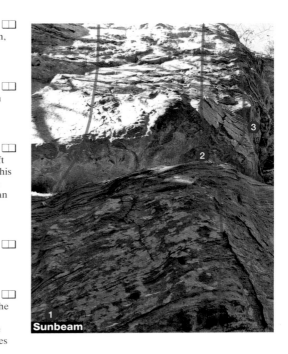
Sunbeam

THE GREAT WALL

 p.m.

20 mins — OK in rain — 12 routes

5.6- .7 .8 .9 .10 .11 .12 .13 .14

Character

The Great Wall is one of the more popular walls in Muir Valley. The routes are relatively short and very well protected, making it a great place for those wanting to bag their first 5.10 or 5.11. The climbing tends to be more technical than burly, with plenty of rests. The quality of the stone is high and the routes are all a lot of fun. However, the routes are a bit crammed, so expect a crowded feeling on good-weather days.

Approach

If approaching from the Hideout, walk left from *International Route of Pancakes* to the next bolted line, which will be *La Escalada*.

  If you are headed to The Great Wall Wall from the parking area, follow the road to the right, located near the entrance to the parking area, and find a short trail on the left that leads to another road. This road winds downhill to reach the valley floor near a stream. Take the first left on the road as it doglegs back left and immediately crosses the stream. Within a few minutes there will be a sign indicating Calvin Hollow/Bone-yard/MN Surf on the left. Continue past this sign and stay on the road, passing the approach for The Hide-out, until the road turns sharply right, just after crossing the stream again. Follow the road a few minutes longer and look for a wooden sign on the right pointing to the Great Wall, just before the road hairpins left and uphill toward the Solarium. Turn right on the trail, cross a creek, and continue through a marshy section. After a couple hundred feet the trail will wind uphill to meet up with the left side of the Great Wall.

Touch of Grey

Conditions

The lines at the Great Wall are slightly overhanging and broken up by small roofs, so it is possible to continue climbing here during a light rain. However, it is not a recommended rainy-day destination.

❶ **Weapons of Mass Deception** 5.9 ★★★
Follow an aesthetic, angling finger crack on the right side of the dihedral to a leftward roof traverse. Continue up the hand crack and arete feature to a large ledge with a roof. Take a moment to enjoy the view from the top.
85 ft. *FA J.J., Jared Hancock, 2004.*

❷ **Ledgends of Limonite** 5.8 ★★
The leftmost sport route on the Great Wall. Shares the start with *Glory ...*, then traverses left along an easy ledge to a slabby face loaded with limonite ledges. The direct start is 5.10.
55 ft. 6 bolts. *FA Jared Hancock, Mike Susko, 2004.*

❸ **Glory and Consequence** 5.7 ★★★
Very juggy face with many rests along the way.
50 ft. 5 bolts. *FA Jared Hancock, Toby Hamilton, 2004.*

❹ **Touch of Grey** 5.10d ★★★
Aesthetic and slightly pumpy climbing with a few small edges and a long move or two along the way.
60 ft. 7 bolts. *FA Jared Hancock, Karla Carandang, 2004.*

⑤ Bitter Ray of Sunshine 5.10c ★★★★
Great climbing! Start with a delicate mantel onto a ledge
right of *Touch of Grey*. Follow the rib to a series of surprisingly good jugs and two-finger pockets. Pull through
the tricky roof and jug up the left water groove.
65 ft. 8 bolts. *FA Karla Carandang, Jared Hancock, 2004.*

⑥ Dynabolt Gold 5.10a ★★★
Figure out the tough start and reap the reward of giant
plates the rest of the way.
70 ft. 7 bolts. *FA Jared Hancock, Karla Carandang, 2004.*

⑦ Little T-Bone 5.9 ★★★
Begin under the obvious hand crack splitting the Great
Wall. Boulder out the initial roof to an alcove with a
bolt. Plug a piece, make the mental move, protect in the
crack, and enjoy huge plates all the way to the end of the
crack and another bolt on the juggy face above.
75 ft. 2 bolts. *FA Tim Powers, Mike Susko, Jared Hancock,
2004.*

⑧ Momma Cindy 5.11a ★★★★
Technical and sustained. Pull the bouldery start with a
two-finger pocket, some edges, and a few crimps, then
enjoy several balancey and reachy sections with a few
fun slopers, edges, and sidepulls.
70 ft. 8 bolts. *FA Tim Powers, Mike Susko, Jared Hancock,
2004.*

⑨ Edge-a-Sketch 5.11a ★★★★
Best line on the wall. Begin left of a ramp on the far
right side of the wall. Solve the bottom boulder problem,
only to be confronted with a series of moves that will
keep you guessing to the chains.
70 ft. 8 bolts. *FA J.J., 2004.*

⑩ Ohio Arts 5.12a ★★★
An extension above *Edge-a-Sketch*. Continue past the
anchors, following three more bolts up a black slab and
over a fantastic overhanging flake feature to another
black slab with tiny crimps and slopers.
100 ft. 11 bolts. *FA Josh Thurston, 2004.*

⑪ Buccaneer 5.11b ★★★
Next route right of *Edge-a-Sketch*. Sharp crimps up a
slightly overhanging face.
70 ft. 6 bolts. *FA Tim Powers, 2006.*

⑫ La Escalada 5.6 ★★
Step up some easy ledges to a right-leaning ramp. Continue up the well-protected, plated face to the anchors.
Photo overleaf.
70 ft. 9 bolts. *FA J.J., Jane Maurer, 2004.*

Dynabolt Gold

Edge-a-Sketch

Jess Young on *La Escalada* 5.6 at the Great Wall (previous page). Photo: John Borland. www.morffed.com

SHAWNEE SHELTER

shade | 20 mins | 6 routes

5.6- .7 .8 .9 .10 .11 .12 .13 .14

Character

Until recently, this wall contained only one mystery line, but now has more to offer and potential for more. Expect to do a lot of cleaning, though, if you want to put up lines here. The wall is north facing and the uncleaned portions are coated with the infamous powder moss found on most north-facing sections of sandstone in the Red. Fortunately a couple of guys have scrubbed away some excellent lines, including *Kya*, 5.13a and *Noo-tha*, 5.11c. At around 100 feet tall, the only thing small at this wall are the holds. Be prepared to try hard.

Approach

Follow the approach for Great Wall, but continue hiking along the cliff for about 200 yards until you reach an enormous section of wall hosting these lines. Routes are listed from right to left.

Conditions

Even though these routes aren't extremely overhanging, they usually stay dry enough to climb on rainy days. The wall is north facing, so don't expect many sunny days here.

① Kya 5.13a ★★★★
Climb through somewhat sustained, powerful moves to reach a decent shake. Boulder some more, then enjoy a great finish. This ain't no jug haul.
90 ft. 10 bolts. *FA Andrew Wheatley, 2009.*

② Blue Jacket 5.13a ★★★
Pockets to a large roof, then finish on a fun upper headwall. Awkward bolt placements reduce the quality of the line.
90 ft. 10 bolts. *FA Thomas Cunningham, 2009.*

③ Black Hoof (Open Project)
This tall route has a short but very difficult crux section. Bolts may need to be moved depending which direction is taken through the hardness. Grade unknown.
110 ft. 9 bolts.

④ Tecumseh's Curse 5.11b ★★★★
Fun arete climbing. If it feels hard, you are doing it wrong.
60 ft. 9 bolts. *FA Andrew Wheatley, Brad Combs, 2009.*

⑤ Waterfall Ballet 5.10a ★★
Fun face left of *Tecumseh's Curse.*
50 ft. 6 bolts. *FA Mark Ryan, Jeff Columbo, 2009.*

⑥ Noo-tha 5.11c ★★★★
Fun and wandering adventure climbing with a nice little surprise after the hueco.
90 ft. 10 bolts. *FA Brad Combs, 2009.*

Photo Kelsey Gray

THE HIDEOUT

all day — shade — 15 mins

19 routes

5.6- .7 .8 .9 .10 .11 .12 .13 .14

Character

The Hideout lies between Indy Wall and the Great Wall in Main Valley Central. It is best known for its quality mixed lines, including *All Mixed Up, Bushwhacked,* and *Hoot and Holler.* For relief from the sun on hot days, duck into the shaded black corridor and climb *Old School, Special K,* and *Beware the Bear.* Also not to be missed is *Boltergeist,* 5.10b. At 100 feet long with 13 bolts, it is a classic for leaders breaking into the 5.10 grade.

Approach

If approaching from Indy Wall, walk left a couple hundred feet from *Parasite* until you reach the next bolted line, which should be *Apothesis Denied.* If approaching from the Great Wall, just head right and around the corner, where you will see the short three-bolt arete, *International Route of Pancakes.*

If you are headed to The Hideout from the parking area, follow the road to the right, located near the entrance to the parking area, and find a short trail on the left that leads to another road. This road winds downhill to reach the valley floor near a stream. Take the first left on the road as it doglegs back left and immediately crosses the stream. Within a few minutes there will be a sign indicating Calvin Hollow/Boneyard/MN Surf on the left. Continue past this sign a few hundred feet and you will see the sign for The Hideout on the right. The trail winds uphill to end up near *International Route of Pancakes.*

Conditions

The majority of this wall faces south to southwest, so expect a lot of sun, especially in the evening. There are no severely overhanging lines, so don't expect it to stay dry in a downpour.

❶ International Route of Pancakes 5.8 ★ ☐
This is the first route from the left at the Hideout, and can be found by walking right from the Great Wall to the next sport line. It follows three bolts up an arete with large holds.
35 ft. 3 bolts. *FA Karla Carandang, Carol Yates, 2004.*

❷ Roof Crack 5.8 ☐
Walk right from the previous line to locate this unappetizing chimney and roof crack beginning in the back of a narrowing corridor. Find tricky pro and chimney-traverse out and through the roof.
40 ft. *FA Bill Hebb, Loren Wood, 2004.*

❸ Earthsurfer 5.11d ★★★ ☐
Continue walking right from *Roof Crack* to locate a section of the wall with several bolted lines. This is the first route on the left side of the wall. Begin on large pockets, then fight through some bulges to reach a crimpy crux just before the relaxing water groove and slab run to the chains.
100 ft. 11 bolts. *FA Karla Carandang, Jared Hancock, 2005.*

❹ Cruisin' for a Bruisin' 5.10d ★★★★ ☐
Just right of *Earthsurfer.* Climb incut crimps up the gorgeous, vertical, orange face. A short crux at a perplexing bulge can be surmounted several different ways. May feel harder for the short climber.
60 ft. 7 bolts. *FA Jared Hancock, David Fromke, 2004.*

❺ Moots Madness 5.10a ★★★ ☐
Next bolted line right of *Cruisin' for a Bruisin'.* Begin with a reachy move below the first bolt and relax the rest of the way to the final overhanging section.
40 ft. 4 bolts. *FA Jared Hancock, Neal Schlatter, 2004.*

❻ Preemptive Strike 5.10c ★★★★ ☐
Start 15 feet right of *Moots Madness.* A thin, crimpy face leads to a technical slab and a finish on large overhanging plates. This route has it all.
90 ft. 11 bolts. *FA Mark Ryan, Jenny Wagner, JJ., Jared Hancock, Rick Weber, 2005.*

7 Shock and Awe 5.7 ★★★

A magnificent, bright-orange crack between *Moots Madness* and *Boltergeist*.
95 ft. *FA J.J., 2004.*

8 Boltergeist 5.10b ★★★★

This long route offers fun climbing and plentiful protection. Great for the beginning 5.10 leader. Start on positive crimps and follow large ledges up the never-ending slab with plenty of rests and enjoyable moves. Be sure to enjoy the great view of the valley from the chains.
100 ft. 13 bolts. *FA Jared Hancock, Tim Yates, Rick Weber, 2004.*

9 All Mixed Up 5.11a ★★★

Twenty feet right of *Boltergeist* is a wall with some low roofs, which ends just before the trail heads uphill to a narrow corridor. This mixed line is the first route on the left side of this wall. Bring a large piece or two for the exposed wide crack near the top.
85 ft. 4 bolts. *FA J.J., 2004.*

10 Bushwhacked 5.10c ★★★

This mixed line takes on the next path of least resistance right of *All Mixed Up*. Monkey through the low roof to reach a sporty face above, which eases up toward the chains.
60 ft. 4 bolts. *FA J.J., Jared Hancock, Tom Kwasny, 2004.*

11 Hoot and Holler 5.10c ★★★

This is the final mixed route on this section of the wall. Begin 15 feet right of *Bushwhacked*. Stick clip the high first bolt, then angle up toward a challenging bulge split by a handcrack. Jam through, then continue past a few long reaches on jugs to the chains.
60 ft. 4 bolts. *FA Jared Hancock, J.J., Tom Kwasny, 2004.*

12 Born Again Christian 5.8 ★★

Walk right and uphill from *Hoot and Holler* to a cool, black corridor that provides for some good air conditioning in the summer. This line takes on the crack system in back of the corridor. Climb past a chockstone and up into the squeeze chimney above. If you don't count your calories, then don't go too deep in the beginning! The chimney gets less green after the start.
50 ft. *FA Loren Wood, Bill Hebb, 2004.*

13 Old School 5.8+ ★★★

This fist-to-offwidth starts just right of *Born Again Christian* in the corridor. Be wary of the infamous 5.8+ grade. Bring a couple of large pieces and rap from anchors just before the last green section.
60 ft. *FA Loren Wood, Bill Hebb, 2004*

Earthsurfer

Boltergeist

Beware the Bear

Call of the Wild

⑭ Special K 5.11a ★★

In the corridor there are two sport lines. This is the one just right of *Old School*. Begin with a bouldery start, which leads to several sustained sloping pockets.
50 ft. 6 bolts. *FA Karla Carandang, Jared Hancock, 2004.*

⑮ Beware the Bear 5.10b ★★★

This fun corridor route takes on the line of bolts just right of *Special K*. Positioning yourself appropriately on the holds could make the difference between sending or falling. Be prepared for a tricky anchor clip.
50 ft. 5 bolts. *FA Jared Hancock, Tim Yates, 2004.*

⑯ Bourbon and Bluegrass 5.10c ★★★

Move right from the corridor to locate this right-arching crack that widens to a chimney after 30 feet. Ascend the crack until it is possible to escape out of the chimney onto the pretty, pocketed orange face to the left. Continue past a short boulder problem and three bolts to the top.
70 feet. 5 bolts. *FA Jared Hancock, 2005.*

⑰ Call of the Wild 5.7 ★★★★

Same start as *Bourbon and Bluegrass*. Climb the bolt-protected chimney and follow the arching crack up and right. You can clip the anchors on *Dance of the Druids*, or answer the call and journey upward past an easy overhang to the top where you will find another set of belay/rappel anchors above the final ledge.
80 feet. 2 bolts. *FA Jared Hancock, Karla Carandang, Any Moore, Jenny Wagner, 2005.*

⑱ Dance of the Druids 5.9 ★★

The slabby face right of the arching crack. Follow big holds to a grassy ledge, then dance up the thinning but well-protected slab above.
60 ft. 7 bolts. *FA Jared Hancock, Skip Wolfe, Mark Ryan, Karla Carandang, 2005.*

⑲ Apotheosis Denied 5.11c ★★★

Begins 30-40 feet right of *Dance of the Druids*. Crimp off the ground, then cruise moderate terrain to a bouldery blunt arete. Slap, squeeze, and smear up this mildly desperate section and finish up the heavily featured slab above.
80 ft. 9 bolts. *FA Jared Hancock, 2005.*

Adam Wisthoff gets through a *Mid-Life Crisis* 5.11c, Indy Wall overleaf. Photo Dan Brayack.

INDY WALL

p.m.

13 routes

15 mins   5.6- .7   .8   .9   .10 .11 .12 .13 .14

Character
Indy Wall, situated between the Sanctuary and Hideout, is a short, squared-off wall with lots of great lines and a nice flat base. The routes are vertical to slightly overhanging and each offers a unique experience. *Annie the Annihilator* is an area-favorite 5.10 and serves as a good warm-up for the other routes on the wall. For something hard, try the starting moves of *Stretcherous*. It is guaranteed to test the vertically challenged.

Approach
Follow the approach to the Sanctuary, but continue left and around the corner when the trail meets up with the cliff.

Conditions
Indy Wall faces southwest and gets sun in the later hours. Hit it early if you want to avoid the sun. The routes are slightly overhanging, so a light drizzle won't force you away.

Parasite

positive holds near the top. Bail at the first set of chains or continue to the second set for a great view.
60 ft. 9 bolts. *FA Karla Carandang, Jared Hancock, 2004.*

❸ Posse Whipped 5.12a ★★★
Begin 15 feet right of *Social Stigma*. Edge through a few bolts of nothing, passing a tough clip or two, to reach a short overhang up high. As with *Social Stigma*, you can stop at the first set of chains or continue on for a few more bolts of average climbing.
60 ft. 9 bolts. *FA Karla Carandang, Jared Hancock, 2005.*

❹ Drop the Hammer 5.12c ★★★
Previously a toprope line, this bolted crimpfest takes on the orange face right of *Posse Whipped*.
80 ft. *Equipped by Justin Riddel. FA Tim Powers, Mike Susko, 2004.*

❺ Owgli Mowgli 5.8 ★
Find this green and dirty crack system about 30 feet right of previous route. Begins as offwidth and ends as hand crack. Shares anchors with next route, or the crack can be climbed out the roof and taken to the top of the cliff.
40 ft. *FA Jared Hancock, Mike Susko, 2004.*

❻ Face Up to That Arete 5.8 ★★
This short route begins as a slab and climbs the left side of the arete to an anchor below the roof.
35 ft. 4 bolts. *FA Jared Hancock, Karla Carandang, 2004.*

❼ Makin' Bacon 5.10d ★★★
Next sport route right of *Face Up to that Arete* and the first route on the left side of the main short squared-off wall hosting the remaining lines. Bouldery start to positive crimps and rails, with one long thin move along the way. Harder than it looks.
40 ft. 5 bolts. *FA Jared Hancock, Karla Carandang, Tim Powers, 2004.*

❶ Parasite 5.11c ★★★
This is the leftmost line at Indy Wall and is located just left of a tree with a sign pointing toward the Hideout. To reach it, walk left about 50 feet past the obvious squared-off main wall of this crag to a taller wall containing several sport lines. Edge and crimp up to a difficult move, then dart left into a recovery zone before the final push toward the chains.
60 ft. 6 bolts. *FA Kipp Trummel, 2006.*

❷ Social Stigma 5.11d ★★★
Locate a line of bolts up a dark orange stain just right of *Parasite*. Pull a difficult start to reach sustained crimping on a steepening face. Make a couple of big moves on

Drop the Hammer

Owgli Mowgli

8 The Happy Fisherman 5.11d ★★★
Begin on a slab 10 feet right of *Makin' Bacon.* Follow five bolts up the thinning face to a bouldery pocket section. Enjoy surprisingly good holds on the overhanging finish.
40 ft. 5 bolts. *FA Tim Powers, Karla Carandang, Jared Hancock, 2004.*

9 Mid-Life Crisis 5.11c ★★★
Great climbing with crimps, edges, pinches, and an exciting finish. Begins as a steep slab, finishes as an overhang. Photo page 239.
40 ft. 4 bolts. *FA Tim Powers, Mike Susko, 2004.*

10 Stretcherous 5.12b ★★★
Crank through a height-dependent boulder-problem start, then enjoy reachy, technical 5.11 climbing to anchor.
40 ft. 4 bolts. *FA Jared Hancock, Mark McGarvey, 2004.*

11 Annie the Annihilator 5.10c ★★★
This slightly overhanging jug-haul is a great warm-up. Reachy start to pumpy climbing with a short technical crux. The first sport route in Muir Valley.
40 ft. 4 bolts. *FA Jared Hancock, Karla Carandang, 2004.*

12 Mentor Powers 5.11b ★★★
Begin left of the beech tree. Technical thin face climbing up a mildly overhanging orange wall, with a couple of cruxes and some jugs mixed in just when you want them. This route can be climbed to the left or to the right of the bolts in a few places. You decide.
40 ft. 4 bolts. *FA Jared Hancock, Tim Powers, 2005.*

13 The Muir the Merrier 5.11b ★★
Rightmost bolted route on Indy Wall. Harder than it looks. Sustained with back-to-back cruxes.
40 ft. 4 bolts. *FA Jared Hancock, Dave Hoyne, 2004.*

Annie the Annihilator

THE SANCTUARY

a.m. ☁ 🚶 15 mins ☔ OK in rain

16 routes

5.6- .7 .8 .9 .10 .11 .12 .13 .14

Character

This is one of the best walls in Muir Valley. It also contains some of the toughest lines. The wall is beautiful, the rock is solid, and the routes are stellar. Part of the wall is severely overhanging, while part of it is only slightly overhanging. Keeping the climbing consistent, the holds usually get smaller as the angle decreases. *Jesus Wept* and *Triple Sec* are two extremely popular lines, which are far from the average Red River jug haul. Bring your pocket-pulling power to this wall and crank them out.

Approach

If you are headed to The Sanctuary from the parking area, follow the road to the right, located near the entrance to the parking area, and find a short trail on the left that leads to another road. This road winds downhill to reach the valley floor near a stream. Skip the first left on the road as it doglegs back left and immediately crosses the stream and instead continue along the road until you reach a field on the left. Walk through the field to reach a stream crossing. Cross the stream then take the first left trail which winds uphill, ascends some stairs, and eventually meets the cliff between The Sanctuary and Indy Wall. Head to the right to be greeted by the stellar overhanging stone of The Sanctuary. The first bolted route you reach is *Cherry Red*.

Cherry Red

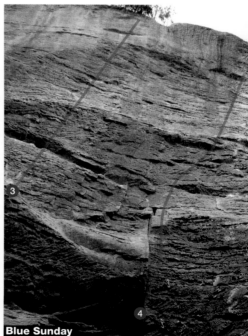

Blue Sunday

❶ **Perfidious Deciduous** 5.11b ★★
This overhanging crack is on the left side of the main wall just before walking around the corner to Indy Wall. Boulder up the initial overhanging crux to a good rest on a ledge. Layback and face climb on good holds to the chains.
55 ft. *FA Jason Haas, Sarah Maclean, 2004.*

❷ **Cherry Red** 5.14a ★★★★
This prominent red streak is the first line from the left on the main wall. Due to the line being rarely climbed, it may be slightly dirty, but after a good brushing it transforms to an excellent technical face climb. Begin by climbing through a series of sharp crimps to meet up with a tough boulder problem on very shallow pockets. Wish you had those crimps back now, huh?
80 ft. 7 bolts. *FA Andrew Gearing, Greg Martin, 2005.*

Elena Bakanova, *Jesus Wept* 5.12d, overleaf. Photo Dan Brayack.

❸ Name Dropper 5.13a ★★★★
This route follows a line 15 feet right of *Cherry Red*.
Begin on a low ledge, then traverse left to reach the
start. Launch up the overhanging face through bulges,
big moves, and shrinking rest holds.
70 ft. 7 bolts. *FA Kenny Barker, 2007.*

❹ Blue Sunday 5.13a ★★
An obvious mix of ledges and steep, switching dihedral/
aretes that splits the Sanctuary cave in the middle and
shares the last few bolts of *Peace Frog*. The start is extremely chossy but there is a possibility it may clean up in time.
70 ft. 8 bolts. *Equipped by Kenny Barker. FA Jason Forrester, 2008.*

❺ Peace Frog 5.12d ★★★
Begin just right of *Cherry Red*. Climb up to a ledge, then
move out a low roof to gain the overhanging, well-
featured face. Make several large moves to a decent rest
before the final steep run to the chains.
80 ft. 8 bolts. *FA Brian Boyd, Greg Martin, 2005.*

❻ Hoosier Boys 5.12d ★★
Begin just right of *Peace Frog*. Climb up to a roof and
move out over the lip to gain the steep face. Climb on
sharp pockets to a big sidepull move, then move on to
more pockets leading to a suspect flake. Carefully climb
the flake to gain a less-overhanging face leading to a
short roof just before the chains.
80 ft. 9 bolts. *FA Mike Kerzhner, Greg Martin, 2005.*

❼ Prometheus Unbound 5.13a ★★★★★
Boulder up and mantel the initial face right of *Hoosier
Boys*, then pull on crimps to reach the steeper section.
Continue up the steep face, passing a pocket crux near
the middle of the line. Grab a shake, then continue
through more sustained climbing and pull a small roof to
reach the chains.
95 ft. 10 bolts. *FA Greg Martin, Brian Boyd, Jeremy Stitch,
and Tommy Wilson, 2004.*

❽ Jesus Wept 5.12d ★★★★★
Hyper classic. Begin beneath the amphitheater. Boulder
through the initial section, trending right, to reach a steep,
pocketed face that quickly becomes more vertical with
fewer holds. Aesthetic climbing with several cruxes along
the way. Requires a 60-meter rope. Photo previous page.
95 ft. 11 bolts. *FA Tim Powers, Mike Susko, 2004.*
 A direct start climbs the arete and dihedral to the right,
meeting up with the normal route at the fourth bolt.
Dubbed ***Atlas Shrugged*** (5.12d).
2 bolts. *FA Kris Hampton, 2008.*

❾ Triple Sec (aka 50 Bucks) 5.12d ★★★★★
In between *Jesus Wept* and *Immaculate Deception* is
a beautiful, blank, yellow-and-black face with small
pockets and a few visible crimps. A no-hands-rest breaks
up the climb after a bouldery crux. Good face climbing
leads to a deceptive crux near the top of the wall. The
crux bolt has been moved slightly right, eliminating the

old crux of having to climb left to clip a bolt and bringing the grade down a notch.
95 ft. 9 bolts. *FA Andrew McDonald, Peter Maroni, Greg
Martin, Brian Boyd, 2004.*

❿ Buddha Slept 5.12a ★★★★
Climb the first three bolts of *Immaculate Deception*,
then continue up and left to a gor-
geous left-leaning crack. Enjoy fine finger-locking and
laybacking until you reach a thin dihedral below the
chimney. Crank on up and clip the anchors on *Triple Sec*
or continue up the chimney to an exposed ledge with
bolted anchors on the right.
100 ft. 3 bolts. *FA: Jared Hancock, 2005.*

⓫ Immaculate Deception 5.12a ★★★
Start from the ground or a ledge 10 feet up. Begin on two
undercling crimps and make a long move to a two-finger
pocket. Hang on through the thin crux, then relax on the
ledge before beginning the balancy, technical arete. Ride
the arete and then step left to finish via a sensational
overhanging jug haul to an anchor under the roof.
90 ft. 9 bolts. *FA Jared Hancock, Tim Powers, Mike Susko,
2004.*

⓬ Dirty Old Men 5.8+ ★★★
This right-facing dihedral is located right around the corner and uphill from *Immaculate Deception*. Climb a wide
hand crack to a slot. Layback and jam to an offwidth.
Slither up the offwidth to a good stance, then jam to a
large ledge and belay. Traverse the ledge left around a
corner to anchors. **90-foot rap!**
80 ft. *FA Tom Kwasny, Brad Truax, 2004.*

⓭ Cruxifixion 5.12d ★★★
The long and aesthetic vertical orange face right of *Dirty
Old Men*. Begin with a difficult direct-start boulder problem, then mellow out on 5.12b to the chains.
90 ft. 9 bolts. *FA Jared Hancock, 2006.*

⓮ Blue Collar 5.12b ★★★★
This route climbs the face left of *First Fall*. Make a big
move or a few thin moves to the first bolt, then crimp
and crank your way to a powerful, technical crux between the fourth and fifth bolts.
55 ft. 6 bolts *FA Jared Hancock, Tim Powers, 2004.*

⓯ First Fall 5.8 ★★★★
A must-do for the 5.8 trad leader. Start in a blocky left-
facing dihedral. Climb up, then step left to hand crack.
Continue up through a bulge to anchors.
60 ft. *FA Karla Carandang, Jared Hancock, 2004.*

⓰ Conquistador of the Crumbly 5.10+
(aka S-Crack)
Improvise a start to reach the high first bolt. Surmount
the bolted bulge, then crack climb to a bolt-protected
traverse. Follow the curving finger/hand/fist crack to a
set of anchors inside a high hueco.
75 ft. 2 bolts. *FA Jared Hancock, Karla Carandang, 2005.*

Peace Frog to Jesus Wept

Triple Sec

First Fall

INNER SANCTUM

a.m.

15 mins

11 routes

5.6- .7 .8 .9 .10 .11 .12 .13 .14

Character

Inner Sanctum is the section of cliffline right of the Sanctuary. The Inner Sanctum routes are mostly slabby to vertical. Two popular 5.10s, *Naughty Neighbors* and *Bad Company*, mark the beginning of the wall and the excellent crimpfest *Psyberpunk* marks the end.

Approach

Hike right from First Fall at the Sanctuary a few hundred feet until you reach a dip in the trail where the trail switches back. Head back uphill from the dip and look for the first bolted line which is *Tabernacle*.

If you are headed to The Sanctuary from the parking area, follow the road to the right, located near the entrance to the parking area, and find a short trail on the left that leads to another road. This road winds downhill to reach the valley floor near a stream. Skip the first left on the road as it doglegs back left and immediately crosses the stream and instead continue along the road until you reach a field on the left. Walk through the field to reach a stream crossing. Cross the stream and continue past the first trail on the left which leads to The Sanctuary and Indy Wall. Eventually you will reach another trail on the left which winds uphill to meet the cliff on the far right side of The Sanctuary. Walk right and down through a gully then head back up and look for the first bolted line which is *Tabernacle*.

Conditions

Most of the lines will be wet during even a light rain. *Naughty Neighbors* and *Bad Company* stay dryer than the rest.

Tabernacle

❶ Tabernacle 5.12a ★★★

This is the first line encountered at Inner Sanctum and begins on a ledge. Climb through cryptic moves on the gently overhanging wall on the right side of a corridor. Exciting runout to the third bolt.
80 ft. 8 bolts. *FA Justin Riddell, 2007.*

❷ Naughty Neighbors 5.10d ★★★★

Walk right from *Tabernacle* beneath an overhang and look for two bolted lines which begin on a ledge. This is the left line. Begin from the ledge and climb incut crimps, sidepulls, pockets, and plates up the slightly overhanging face.
55 ft. 5 bolts. *FA Jared Hancock, Karla Carandang, 2004.*

❸ Bad Company 5.10a ★★★

This is the bolted route 10-15 feet right of *Naughty Neighbors.* Fun vertical climbing on flakes, sidepulls, and jugs.
50 ft. 5 bolts. *FA Tim Powers, Mike Susko, 2004.*

❹ The Universe Next Door 5.8 R

Just to the right of *Bad Company* is a discontinuous crack system that jogs right and then back left after a short blank face section.
55 ft. *FA Greg Martin and Brian Boyd, 2004.*

Bad Company

Karmic Retribution

⑤ Karmic Retribution 5.10d ★★★★

The next sport route right of *Bad Company*. Begin with positive crimps on a moderate slab, up to a prominent rib. Reach left up the steepening face to good pockets and an interesting finish below the large ledge.
45 ft. 5 bolts. *FA Jared Hancock, Karla Carandang, 2004.*

⑥ Crack 'n Up 5.7 ★★

Ten to 15 feet right of *Karmic Retribution* is this easy crack. Walk up the initial wide section to a short offwidth layback followed by a few chimney moves, surmounting the occasional obstacle along the way.
50 ft. *FA Karla Carandang, Jared Hancock, 2004.*

⑦ Quaquaversal Crack 5.8+ ★★

Locate an obvious cave 40 feet up the wall. Begin on the easy, right-angling flake right of *Crack 'n Up* and climb up and right to a single bolt before entering the giant hueco. Stem, jam, and face climb up and out of the cave. Some exposed stemming will take you to the anchors.
65 ft. 1 bolts. *FA Jared Hancock, Karla Carandang, 2005.*

⑧ Netizen Hacktivist 5.9+ ★★★

Balance up the steepening slab right of the previous line until you reach an orange water groove. Ascend the sculpted shelves, edges, pinches, and pockets. Watch out for furry flying four-legged friends along the way.
60 ft. 7 bolts. *FA Jared Hancock, Karla Carandang, 2005.*

Netizen Hacktivist

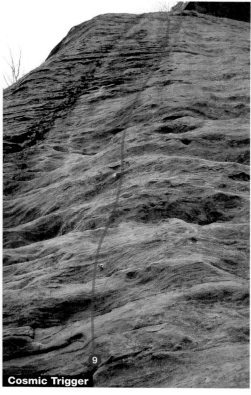

Cosmic Trigger

9 **Cosmic Trigger** 5.12b ★★★★

This is an obvious black arete with a golden bolted face to the right. Moderate climbing on jugs and pinches leads to a good bouldery crux. Mantel past the final bolt to anchors on roof.
70 ft. 7 bolts. *FA Greg Martin, Brian Boyd, 2004.*

10 **Cybersex** 5.7 ★

Just left of *Psyberpunk* is a large flake protected with large gear. Easy climbing leads to a ledge in the middle of the wall. A short crack leads to a large ledge. Put in a directional and belay off *Psyberpunk* anchors.
65 ft. *FA Greg Martin, Brian Boyd, 2004.*

11 **Psyberpunk** 5.11c ★★★★

This is the last route before the Stadium Area. Move 60 feet right of *Cybersex*, past a large boulder/flake leaning against the main wall, then up to a small ledge. Mostly jugs to two crimpy face sections to exit jugs.
65 ft. 7 bolts. *FA Greg Martin, Brian Boyd, 2004.*

Psyberpunk

THE STADIUM

all day · 20 mins · OK in rain · 23 routes

5.6- .7 .8 .9 .10 .11 .12 .13 .14

Character
The Stadium is primarily for trad climbers. Most of the lines at this area require at least one piece of gear. Start on the left side and do *Tradisfaction, Kentucky Waterfall, Dreamtheiver,* and *In a Pinch* and you will be one respected hard traddy. Each of the lines are stout and high quality. For non-masochists, two of the better sport 5.12s in Muir, *The Pessimist* and *Cheetah*, sit side by side on the far right edge of the Stadium.

Approach
If you are headed to The Stadium from the parking area, follow the road to the right, located near the entrance to the parking area, and find a short trail on the left that leads to another road. This road winds downhill to reach the valley floor near a stream. Skip the first left on the road as it doglegs back left and immediately crosses the stream and instead continue along the road until you reach a field on the left. Walk through the field to reach a stream crossing. Cross the stream and continue past the first trail on the left which leads to The Sanctuary and Indy Wall. Eventually you will reach another trail on the left which leads to Inner Sanctum. Continue past this trail and within a couple of minutes the trail will head left and uphill to meet up with the cliff just beneath the splitter crack *No Bones About It. Tradisfaction, Kentucky Waterfall,* etc. are about 300 feet left, past a rocky area.

Conditions
Tradisfaction and *Kentucky Waterfall* are good candidates for rainy days. Other routes in the area can be hit or miss.

① Kentucky Waterfall 5.11a ★★★★
Variation finish to *Tradisfaction*. Start on *Tradisfaction* and traverse left, following the thin arching flake.
80 ft. *FA Loren Wood, 2004.*

② Tradisfaction 5.10b ★★★★
Begin in large left-facing chimney. Continue up to a ledge to enjoy this satisfying dihedral. Stem, jam, and layback to a pumpy finish. Classic.
80 ft. *FA Jared Hancock, 2004.*

③ Dreamthiever 5.12a ★★★★
The striking roof crack above *Tradisfaction*. Climb *Tradisfaction* to the anchors, then traverse right and set a belay anchor in a cave. Crank out the roof and continue to the top of the wall.
35 ft. *FA Bart Bledsoe, 2006.*

④ In a Pinch 5.11b ★★★★
This climb is the next dihedral about 60 feet right of *Tradisfaction*. It starts as a thin left-facing dihedral and goes to a large roof (requires a small Slider nut for protection). Pull the awkward lip and belay from here on gear. A 5.8 second pitch goes to the top where you can rap off trees, but is not recommended. Anchors may now be in place above the first pitch.
80 ft. *FA Ken Thompson, Jeff Smith, 2004.*

⑤ Indecision 5.8 ★★★★
This route begins left of the approach trail near a chalk handprint. Climb the juggy face left of an arete. Step right to a crack and continue to top of cliff. Rappel from a tree.
95 ft. *FA Ed Griffiths, Jeff Smith, Ken Thompson, 2004.*

Tradisfaction

In a Pinch

No Bones About It

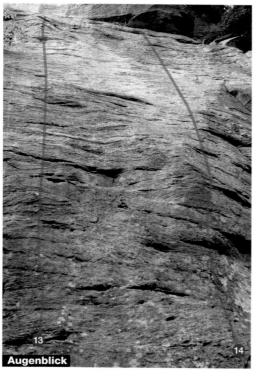

Augenblick

❻ Psycho Billy Cadillac 5.10+ ★★

Fifteen feet right of *Indecision* is another long mixed route up the main buttress. Jug up steep rock past two bolts to a tricky roof move. Pull the roof to gain an easy slab leading to a crack. Follow the crack until it ends and top out on the slab using a bolt for protection. Enjoy the great view from the top. Bolt anchor.

95 ft. 6 bolts. *FA J.J., Jared Hancock, 2006.*

❼ Walk the Line 5.9 ★★★

Begin five feet right of *Psycho Billy*. Climb overhanging rock past two bolts to a roof. Climb the left side of the roof to a soothing splitter crack. Follow the splitter to a slab top-out protected by a bolt.

100 ft. 3 bolts. *FA Jared Hancock, J.J., 2006.*

❽ Flying J 5.12b ★★★★

Begin on jugs near an obvious overhanging arete left of a big beech tree. A steep start will take you to the high first bolt. Go big or find the pinch undercling and then continue slightly up and left on the lower-angled face, with protection in horizontals. Finish on a sensational overhanging plated face protected by bolts.

80 ft. 5 bolts. *FA Nick Walker, Jared Hancock, 2006.*

❾ No Bones About It 5.10b ★★★

A steep thin-hands start leads to a widening, right-arching crack. Traverse slightly up and right at top of the arch and climb through soft rock to a short hand crack. Finish by traversing left to ledge with slings on tree. The first-ascent party found a lot of bones on the way up, hence the route name. It's possible to climb over to the anchors on Scrumbulglazer to avoid choss pushing for the last 30 feet.

90 ft. *FA Ken Thompson, Jeff Smith, Ed Griffiths, 2004.*

❿ Scrumbulglazer 5.10d ★★★

This route is located between *No Bones About It* and *ED*. Steep start with jugs and pockets. Good clipping holds with a thin, balancy crux, then sidepulls to the top.

60 ft. 6 bolts. *FA Gregg Purnell, 2005.*

⓫ Melancholy Mechanics 5.10d ★★★

The technical face right of *Scrumbulglazer* is slightly dirty but fun. It should clean up with more ascents.

60 ft. 6 bolts. *FA Gregg Purnell, Mark Ryan, J.J., Jared Hancock, 2005.*

⓬ ED 5.7 ★★★

A left-facing dihedral with large holds. Step right after approximately 50 feet to Fixe anchors above a ledge.

50 ft. *FA Ed Griffiths, Ken Thompson, 2004.*

⓭ Augenblick 5.10c ★★★

This line, previously a mossy and crunchy toprope named *Stadium Slab*, is the bolted route just right of *ED*.

80 ft. 8 bolts. *FA J.J., Jared Hancock, Karla Carandang, 2006.*

The Pessimist   21   22

⑭ Tug-o-War 5.11b ★★★★
The thin, techy, sustained slab on the face right of *Augenblick.*
80 ft. 9 bolts. *FA: Karla Carandang, Jared Hancock, J.J., 2006.*

⑮ Treetop Terror 5.10d ★★★
This route begins 20 feet right of an arete. Climb a fingery flake to reach a hand crack, which leads to a featured slab protected by bolts.
5 bolts. *FA Jared Hancock, Rob Copeland, Barry Brolley, J.J., Mark Ryan, 2006.*

⑯ Areterection 5.11c ★★★★
This is the obvious and aesthetic arete. Bouldery up to the third bolt.
80 ft. 9 bolts. *FA Jared Hancock, JJ, Gregg Purnell, 2005.*

⑰ Environmental Imperialism 5.8 ★★★
The obvious dihedral above *Arecterection.* Much easier than it appears.
35 ft. *Jared Hancock, 2005.*

⑱ Ascentuality 5.11a ★★★★
Follow the cliffline right past the previous line for about 100 feet to the start of this route. Climb a technical face past three bolts to reach a steep, striking, orange dihedral. Clean and classic.
80 ft. 3 bolts. *FA Jared Hancock, Karla Carandang, 2004.*

⑲ Black Tide 5.6 R Ⓢ
Gently climb the sandy and fragile flake 50 feet right of *Ascentuality.* Poor protection and poorer rock quality.
50 ft. *FA Yasmeen Fowler, 2004.*

⑳ High Times V0 ★★★
A quality highball boulder problem on the obvious triangular boulder below *Black Tide.* Clean and aesthetic with fun moves.
15 ft. *FA Unknown.*

㉑ The Pessimist 5.12c ★★★★
This impressive line starts 30 feet right of *Black Tide.* Climb a short flake system to reach an obvious bucket. Bust through an unlikely sequence to reach increasingly better holds. Move right and climb the striking and sustained orange streak to a horizontal break.
50 ft. 6 bolts. *FA Matt Hoffman, Bob Peterson, Peter Morone, 2006.*

㉒ Cheetah 5.12a ★★★★
The next bolted line on the orange-and-black streaked wall. Climb through powerful cruxes separated by good rests.
40 ft. 5 bolts. *FA Bob Peterson, Matt Hoffman, Paul Coover, 2006.*

㉓ El Patron 5.13a
Stunning overhanging orange streak 100 feet right of Black Tide. Last sport route to right before the twin falls. Currently missing the first few bolts but an extremely long stick clip makes it possible to climb.
80 ft. 11 bolts. *FA Gregg Purnell, Mike Duncan, 2005.*

TECTONIC AND JOHNNY'S WALLS

p.m. 20 mins OK in rain

18 routes

5.6- .7 .8 .9 .10 .11 .12 .13 .14

Characters

These two walls are great for climbers breaking into the 5.10 grade and looking to experience the infamous Red River forearm pump. They have some excellent 5.10s, including the extremely popular *Gettin' Lucky in Kentucky* and *Plate Tectonics*.

Approach

Follow the approach to the Sanctuary, but instead of taking the trail on the left after crossing the stream, take the trail on the right, which winds up the hill to the middle of Tectonic Wall and Johnny's Wall. If you walk to the right a few feet when the trail meets the cliff, you'll see a nice-looking wall with several bolted lines. This is Johnny's Wall and the first route you come to is *59" Drill Bitch*. The Tectonic Wall is to the left; the first bolted route you encounter walking left from where the trail meets the cliff is *Tall Cool One*.

Conditions

The slightly overhanging nature of these two walls provides for decent rainy-day climbing.

Gettin' Lucky in Kentucky

TECTONIC WALL

❶ LIDAR 5.8

Follow the cliffline 150 yards left of Tectonic Wall. Scramble up to a belay ledge below a vertical crack that gives way to horizontal features near the top. Protect the crux and pull into the first horizontal, then stem and chimney your way to the anchors.
80 ft. 6 bolts. *FA Brett Stark, Rob Copeland, 2008.*

❷ Gettin' Lucky In Kentucky 5.10b ★★★★

The left-most bolted route on the wall. Enjoyable, pumpy, technical climbing on jugs, pockets, sidepulls, and underclings to a steep finish. Classic.
60 ft. 6 bolts. *FA Jared Hancock, Karla Carandang, Tom & Ines Truesdale, 2004.*

❸ Plate Tectonics 5.10a ★★★★

The route right of *Gettin' Lucky*. A tricky start to enjoyable pumpy climbing on huge plates. Classic.
65 ft. 6 bolts. *FA Jared Hancock, Karla Carandang, Rick & Liz Weber, 2004.*

❹ 5th Bolt Faith 5.10c ★★★

Fifteen feet right of *Plate Tectonics*. This route follows an interesting variety of holds: pinches, slopers, plates, underclings – you name it. Fun moves.
55 ft. 6 bolts. *FA Jared Hancock, Mark Ryan, Karla Carandang, 2005.*

Tall Cool One

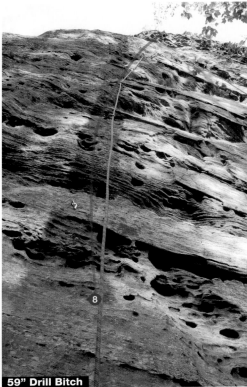

59" Drill Bitch

⑤ Continental Drift 5.8+ ★★

Mixed route between *Fifth Bolt Faith* and *Tall Cool One.*
80 ft. 3 bolts. *FA Harini Aiyer, 2008.*

⑥ Tall Cool One 5.9 ★★★

Located 10 feet right of *Fifth Bolt Faith*, on the left-facing wall. Move right from the first bolt on the face towards the crack to gain a ledge. Pull the small overhang to climb plates to the chains.
60 ft. 6 bolts. *FA Tim Powers, Jeff Neal, Mike Susko, 2004.*

⑦ Paraplegic Power 5.7 ★★

When walking to Tectonic Wall from where the approach trail meets up with the cliff, this is the first route you will encounter. It climbs the crack just right of *Tall Cool One*. Work left and pull the roof, protecting with a slung block and horizontals. Continue up a wide crack, then move left to the anchors on *Tall Cool One*.
60 ft. *FA Can Beck, Caleb Heimlich, 2007.*

JOHNNY'S WALL

⑧ 59" DrillBitch 5.10a ★★★

The left-most route on Johnny's Wall and the first bolted route encountered when walking right from where the approach trail meets the cliff between Tectonic and Johnny's Wall. Climbs vertical plates, edges, and pockets. Jug up and right to the interesting finish.
45 ft. 5 bolts. *FA Karla Carandang, Jared Hancock, 2004.*

⑨ Bethel 5.10a ★★★

Follow incut plates to a big move and juggy finish.
50 ft. 5 bolts. *FA Tim Powers, Jeff Neal, Mike Susko, 2004.*

⑩ Spinner 5.10a ★★★

Similar to *Bethel*, with a more difficult finish. Pull over the bulge on subtle holds to the anchors.
50 ft. 5 bolts. *FA Tim Powers, Mike Susko, 2004.*

Matt Fanning on *Abiyoyo* 5.12b, The Solarium, page 228. Photo Dan Brayack.

11

12

Mancala

⑪ Mancala 5.10a ★★★

Start on the boulder right of *Spinner*. Pick a path up the juggy plates to an interesting bulge and a fierce finish.
45 ft. 4 bolts. *FA Jared Hancock, Rob Copeland, J.J., Karla Carandang, 2006.*

⑫ Burning Bush 5.11a ★★★

Fifteen feet right of *Mancala* is another overhanging jug haul. You may want to place a piece of gear in the crack between the first and second bolt. Climb jugs to a well-defined crimp-and-crank crux just before the anchors.
50 ft. 4 bolts. *FA J.J., Rob Copeland, Jared Hancock, 2006.*

⑬ Climbing With Crowbars 5.7 ★

Move 50 feet right from *Burning Bush* to locate this chimney with a nice blocky dihedral and crack system. Bolted anchor.
50 ft. *FA: Mark Ryan, Jenny Ryan, J.J., 2006.*

⑭ Thanks Holly 5.8 ★★

Right of *Climbing With Crowbars* is this slabby arete. Follow big holds to anchors above a final ledge.
45 ft. 5 bolts. *FA Mike Trabel, Mike Susko, 2006.*

⑮ Two Chicken Butts 5.9 ★★

Twelve feet right of the arete is a slabby wall loaded with more huge holds.
45 ft. 5 bolts. *FA Mike Trabel, Mike Susko, 2006.*

⑯ Mental Affair 5.8 ★

Move right to this line, which begins eight feet right of a tree. Climb to a ledge and pull into a crack. Climb the crack to a face, then run it to the anchors.
45 ft. *FA JJ, Mike Susko, Holly Trabel, 2006.*

⑰ Brain Stem 5.7 ★

Move right to a short, striking dihedral. Shoot up the dihedral, then wander out a roof to locate a bolt on the slabby face above. Bolted anchors.
50 ft. 1 bolt. *FA J.J., Jane Maurer, Mark Ryan, Jenny Wagner, 2006.*

⑱ Grey Matter 5.10b ★

Toprope. Just right of *Brain Stem* is a thin, slabby arete. This toprope line climbs the face right of the arete. Make a few long reaches and enjoy some technical climbing to gain the juggy slab above.
40 ft. *FA Jared Hancock, J.J., Rob Copeland, 2006.*

WASHBOARD WALL

9 routes

a.m. · 15 mins · OK in rain · 5.6- .7 .8 .9 .10 .11 .12 .13 .14

Character

This overhanging wall has some great adventure sport climbing, as well as shorter pumpers in the 5.11 range. To fully enjoy what the wall has to offer, bring double ropes and some trad gear. If not, take a run up *Barenjager* and *Brushfire Fairytales* and be done with it.

Approach

Take the second approach trail from the main parking area, which begins at the far side of the parking lot near the kiosk and behind the garage. Follow the trail to the valley floor, cross the creek, and take the first trail on the left. Follow the trail north for a few minutes until you see the sign for Washboard Wall on the left. Follow the trail a couple of minutes to meet up with the main wall.

Conditions

Most of these lines stay dry in a downpour and can get great sun in the early hours of the day.

❶ Sierra's Travels 5.9- ★

Left-most route to the left of the big cave with a picnic table. Start directly under first bolt, left-hand slopey crimp to a sidepull, then stand up and follow the obvious line to the anchors.
45 ft. 2 bolts. *FA J.J. (free-solo), 2004.*

❷ Heard it on NPR 5.10d ★★★★

This long route is the left-most sport route on the Washboard Wall. Locate the high first bolt left of *Spider Crux*. You may want to place a piece of pro here. Follow five bolts up moderate terrain to a spacious ledge with anchors. Belay here to reduce rope drag or continue through the overhanging pocketed face past six more bolts to anchors. Use a 60-meter rope.
100 ft. 11 bolts. *FA Barry Brolley, J.J., 2004.*

❸ Spider Crux 5.10b ★★

Start under a small roof to gain this attractive, right-leaning hand-and-finger crack. Make a long move, then continue up easier ground to anchors on the ledge. Belay, rappel off here, or continue up *Heard it on NPR*.
50 ft. *FA J.J., Barry Brolley, 2004.*

❹ Cordillera Rojo 5.11a ★★★

Start immediately right of *Spider Crux*. Follow four bolts to the ledge system, then launch up the unrelenting and imposing headwall above. A 70-meter rope is not long enough to lower off, so use the intermediate anchor or figure out another way down.
115 ft. 12 bolts. *FA Barry Brolley, Keith Raker, 2006.*

❺ Barenjager 5.10d ★★★

This route ascends the overhanging face 10-15 feet right of *Spider Crux*. Follow a line of four bolts up pockets, flakes, and edges to a anchors.
40 ft. 4 bolts. *FA Jared Hancock, Rob Copeland, 2004.*

❻ Brushfire Fairytales 5.11a ★★★

Start 10-15 ft. right of previous route. Similar to *Barenjager* but slightly harder, with bigger, pumpier moves and a sequential crux.
40 ft. 4 bolts. *FA Rob Copeland, Jared Hancock, 2004.*

❼ Tradmill 5.7 ★★★

Climb the obvious left-leaning ramp. Step around this obstacle, then cruise up the left-leaning ramp over a small bulge. Clip the chain anchors on the left or continue into the cave. Build an anchor in the enormous cave and belay, or traverse left along the ledge to the *Spider Crux* anchors.
50 ft. *FA Dave Hoyne, Jared Hancock, Karla Carandang, Rob Copeland, 2004.*

❽ Sticks and Stones 5.11+ ★★★

Begin at base of *Tradmill*. Climb up to the roof and hand traverse 10-15 feet right to gain hand crack. Place some gear, then crank through the thinning and steepening crack to a good horizontal. Clip the bolt and make the move to the jug. Crimp your way to the anchors.
35 ft. 1 bolt. *FA Jared Hancock, Rob Copeland, 2004.*

❾ Bad Dentures 5.9 ★

Toprope. First recorded route done in Muir Valley. Walk 100 feet right of *Sticks and Stones*. Follow a ledge system up to an arete that is often wet. Climb the left side of the slabby arete to a large ledge with a tree.
70 ft. *FA Rick Weber, 2003.*

Barenjager

PRACTICE WALL

 a.m. 15 mins OK in rain

23 routes

5.6- .7 .8 .9 .10 .11 .12 .13 .14

Character

The name says it all. This is a great place to learn how to climb. An abundance of very short, easy, and well-protected routes awaits those with shiny new quickdraws and brand new ropes. You can bring your cams as well and learn placements on a couple of 20-foot cracks with bolted anchors.

Approach

Take the second approach trail from the main parking area, which begins at the far side of the parking lot near the kiosk and behind the garage. Follow the trail to the valley floor, cross the creek, and take the first trail on the left. Follow the trail north for a few minutes until you see the sign for Practice Wall on the left, just after the sign for Washboard Wall. You will arrive beneath the short wall containing *Low Exposure*.

Conditions

The routes here are short and most are less than vertical. A heavy rain could soak them, but the nature of the rock above them should keep the climbs tolerable in a light rain.

❶ Creeping Elegance 5.11a ★★
When the approach trail meets the wall just beneath *Slabalito*, continue walking left and slightly uphill, passing beneath a low roof for about 150 feet until you reach more short bolted lines and the obvious chimney that is *Dragon's Tail/Mouth*. This is the next bolted line, about 30 feet left of the Dragon routes. Surprisingly pumpy for how short it is.
45 ft. 5 bolts. *FA Jim Taylor, 2008.*

❷ Dragon's Tail 5.3 ★★★
The low-angle, right-leaning wide crack that begins 15-20 feet left of the *Dragon's Mouth* chimney. This route merges with the last two bolts of *Dragon's Mouth*. Continue to the top of cliff through a short third-class gully and rappel from a tree, or opt for the 5.6 finish to the anchors of *Dragon's Mouth*.
60 ft. 2 bolts. *FA Jared Hancock, Sierra Jones, J.J., 2005.*

❸ Dragon's Mouth 5.6 ★★
The obvious short, bolted, dirty chimney right of *Dragon's Tail*.
55 ft. 6 bolts. *FA Rick Weber, 2004.*

❹ Crescent Moon 5.10a ★★
The next sport route, 15 feet right of the *Dragon's Mouth* chimney. Ascends the featured face on good edges and pockets with a few reachy moves. The difficulty may vary depending on which way you go at the second bolt.
35 ft. 3 bolts. *FA J.J., Mark Ryan, Skip Wolfe, Jared Hancock, 2005.*

❺ Crescendo 5.8+ ★★
Right of *Crescent Moon* is another vertical face. Begin with a tough start and end with a short overhanging section.
40 ft. 3 bolts. *FA Jared Hancock, J.J., Skip Wolfe, Mark Ryan, Amy Moore, 2005.*

❻ Another One Fights the Rust 5.9- ★★
Fifty feet right of *Crescendo* is this slightly overhanging right-facing dihedral. The low crux is bolt protected. Finish by topping out on the ledge above.
35 ft. 1 bolt. *FA Jared Hancock, Skip Wolfe, Mark Ryan, J.J., 2005.*

❼ The Handout ★★
Short but steep line beginning beneath the head-height roof just right of *Another One Fights the Rust*. Closed project. Grade unknown.
30 ft. 4 bolts. *Equipped by Isaac Heacock.*

❽ Slabalito 5.7 ★
Walk back down to the trailhead routes to locate this short, bolted line that begins left of the two trees on the obvious short slab.
20 ft. 2 bolts.

❾ Shawty 5.8 ★
Another short, bolted line 15 feet right of *Slabalito*.
20 ft. 2 bolts.

❿ Low Exposure 5.8 ★★
Crimpy face 25 feet right *Shawty*. This short climb has a brief thin section before topping out onto the ledge. Shares anchors with the dihedral *Short and Sweet*.
25 ft. 3 bolts. F*A Jared Hancock, Sierra Jones, Mark Ryan, 2005.*

⓫ Short and Sweet 5.7 ★★
The short left-facing dihedral just right of *Low Exposure*.
20 ft. *FA Mark and Kate Calder, 2004.*

⓬ Slither and Squeeze 5.2 ★
A few feet right of *Short and Sweet* is this short, unremarkable squeeze chimney.
20 ft. *FA Jared Hancock (free-solo), 2004.*

Slabalito to Short and Sweet

Kate's First Trad Lead

Dragon's Mouth

⓭ Kate's First Trad Lead 5.1 ★★
The slabby crack in a right-facing dihedral with large face holds right of *Short and Sweet*.
20 ft. *FA Kate and Mark Calder, 2004.*

⓮ Acrophobiacs Anonymous 5.4 ★★
This may be the easiest sport line in the Red. The short slabby face right of *Kate's First Trad Lead* that trends up and left to shared anchors.
25 ft. 3 bolts. *FA Jared Hancock, Karla Carandang, Jane Maurer, Mark Ryan, 2005.*

19

Beta Spewer

20

22

Sheet Rock

⓯ Yu Stin Ki Pu 5.5 ★★
Approximately 20-30 feet right of the previous route is
another short novice climb.
20 ft. 3 bolts. *FA Jared Hancock, Skip Wolfe, Mark Ryan,
2005.*

⓰ Sweet and Sour 5.5 ★★
This thin, slabby, left-facing dihedral is sweet in that it is
good-quality climbing, but sour because it ends way too
early. Bolt anchor.
20 ft. *FA Jared Hancock, Skip Wolfe, Mark Ryan, 2005.*

⓱ Ai Bang Mai Fa Kin Ni 5.7 ★★
Another short route right of *Sweet and Sour.*
20 ft. 2 bolts. *FA Jared Hancock, Karla Carandang, Jenny
Wagner, Mark Ryan, 2005.*

⓲ Mercenary of the 5.9+ ★★
Mandarin Chicken
Short, right-leaning arete just right of the previous line.
25 ft. 2 bolts. *FA Karla Carandang, Jared Hancock, Skip
Wolfe, 2005.*

⓳ Beta Spewer 5.10b ★★★
Around the corner to the right is this short, overhanging
face with fun, flowing moves.
20 ft. 2 bolts. *FA Jared Hancock, Karla Carandang, Skip
Wolfe, Mark Ryan, 2005.*

⓴ BDSM 5.10b ★★★
This short, bouldery, overhanging crack can be found 30
feet right of *Beta Spewer.* Jam, crimp, and power your
way to the ledge. Bolted anchor.
25 ft. *FA J.J., Barry Brolley, Jared Hancock, 2005.*

㉑ Night Foxx 5.11d ★★★★
Start 20 feet right of *BDSM,* beneath a ramp. Power
through the overhang to gain the ramp, then make a
committing third clip. Tackle the crux between the third
and fourth bolts, then enjoy easier climbing to tough
moves guarding the chains.
60 ft. 6 bolts. *FA Isaak Heacock, Josh Thurston, 2009.*

㉒ Sheet Rock ★★★
Next route right of *Night Foxx.* Has a chain draw on the
first bolt and takes on a right-facing flake for the start,
then leads up to the overhanging face. **Closed project.**
Grade unknown.
60 ft. 7 bolts. *Equipped by Isaac Heacock.*

㉓ Beastly Traverse 5.11a ★★★
This line follows the left-leaning ramp, beginning as an
offwidth right of *Sheet Rock.* It resembles a 5.10 version of *Tradmill.* The route is 5.10 trad to the first set of
anchors. From there you can continue up bolt-protected,
overhanging ledges for a 5.11a finish to another set of
anchors.
90 ft. 6 bolts. *FA Loren Wood, J.J., 2005.*

Kathleen Kennedy, *CH4* 5.7, Bruise Brothers Wall, overleaf. Photo Dan Brayack.

BRUISE BROTHERS WALL

24 routes

all day | 15 mins | OK in rain | 5.6- .7 .8 .9 .10 .11 .12 .13 .14

Character

This popular wall has several great 5.10s. The left side of the wall contains shorter routes with more technical moves, while the far right side contains several long and sustained forearm pumpers on great stone. *Workin' for the Weekend* and *Return of Manimal* are two favorites that climb a gorgeous wall interspersed with big moves between blocky roofs and features. The shorter but fierce *Jungle Trundler* is on you at the start but quickly eases up to a relaxing ride.

Approach

Take the second approach trail from the main parking area, which begins at the far side of the parking lot near the kiosk and behind the garage. Follow the trail to the valley floor, cross the creek, and continue straight past the first trail on the left. (That trail leads to Practice and Washboard Walls.) Soon you will reach a fork in the trail. Follow the left fork uphill a few minutes and you will eventually see the area of cliff where *Jungle Trundler* is, to your left through the trees. An obvious short trail leads up to the wall. Staying on the mail trail for about 100 feet will bring you to *Workin' for the Weekend* and *Manimal*.

Conditions

This wall receives excellent sun and most of the routes will stay dry in the rain. Expect crowds.

❶ Dirt in Eye 5.7 ★
The first four routes are located about 30-40 feet uphill and left of the logging road, on the small buttress left of the main Bruisebrothers Wall. Climb the handcrack in the short dihedral to a ledge under the first overhang. Once on the ledge, step right behind a boulder and up to rap hangers on the left side of the heuco.
60 ft. *FA Mike Susko, Mike Trabel, 2005.*

❷ Pine Needle Shuffle 5.6
Right of *Dirt in Eye* is a broken and wandering crack system with some ledges along the way. Climb the crack to a ledge and traverse left to another crack. Continue up, then traverse to the right to the anchors on *Redeye Brew*.
50 ft. *FA J.J., Jared Hancock, 2005.*

❸ Redriveroutdoors.com 5.10a ★★
Bolted line right of *Pine Needle Shuffle*. Follows a small flake-like feature to anchors below the ledge.
40 ft. 4 bolts. *FA J.J., Jared Hancock, 2005.*

❹ Redeye Brew 5.8 ★★
Just right of *Redriveroutdoors.com* is another so-so bolted line. Climb up to a ledge, then follow pockets and edges to top out onto another ledge.
45 ft. 5 bolts. *FA Jared Hancock, J.J., 2005.*

❺ Flutterby Blue 5.9 ★★★
This is the first route on the left side of the main Bruise Brothers Wall. Continue hiking down the road from the previous lines to a set of wooden stairs marking the start of the main wall. This line follows an arete and begins with a tough start.
40 ft. 5 bolts. *FA Mike Susko, Stacia Susko, J.J., 2004.*

❻ Tomthievery 5.8 ★★
(aka The Sultan Returns)
Blocky right-facing dihedral 10-15 feet right of *Flutterby Blue*. No anchors; traverse off left.
50 ft. *FA Tom Kwasny, Dennis Rice, 2004.*

❼ Sweet Jane 5.8- ★★
Next right-facing dihedral right of *Tomthievery*.
50 ft. 1 bolt. *FA J.J., Jane Maurer, 2004.*

❽ Hey There, Fancy Pants 5.10c ★★★
This is the first sport route right of *Sweet Jane*. Follow an obvious fingery flake up the vertical face, making a couple of long moves along the way.
55 ft. 5 bolts. *FA J.J., Jared Hancock, 2004.*

❾ Jungle Trundler 5.11a ★★★
This is the middle of the three sport routes. A bouldery start soon eases to moderate climbing and a short layback finger-crack feature. Top out onto the large ledge and enjoy the view. May feel easier for tall climbers.
60 ft. 6 bolts. *FA Jared Hancock, J.J., 2004.*

Hey There, Fancy Pants

CH4

⓾ Little Viper 5.10b ★★★
Climb a right-facing flake to very small roof. Clip the fourth bolt, crank a boulder problem, and follow pockets and edges to the top.
50 ft. 6 bolts. *FA Tim Powers, Mike Susko, 2004.*

⓫ CH4 5.7 ★★
This is the first bolted route right of a wild-iris patch and intermittent waterfall. Short, fun climbing under a large roof. Photo previous spread.
30 ft. 3 bolts. *FA J.J. (free solo), 2004.*

⓬ Rising 5.11a ★★★
Steep roof route above *CH4*. Can be done from the ground in one pitch (then known as *Methane Rising*, six bolts). Follow bolts to a chain anchor.
30 ft. 3 bolts. *FA Barry Broley, J.J., 2004.*

⓭ A-Beano 5.7 ★★
Begin 10 to 15 feet right of *CH4*. Hard first move, heady last move.
30 ft. 3 bolts. *FA Mike Susko, J.J., 2004.*

⓮ Immodium AD 5.7 ★★
Crack right of *A-Beano*. Shares anchors with previous route.
30 ft. *FA J.J., 2004.*

⓯ Don't Take Yer Guns to Town 5.10c ★★★
Climb a short dihedral to an easy slab and big roof. Hand traverse right and make a long move to pull the roof. One-move wonder.
50 ft. 5 bolts. *FA Jared Hancock, Rob Copeland, 2004.*

⓰ The Offering 5.7 ★★★
Begin near right edge of the ledge. Follow easy crack system and ledges up and right to an exciting finish.
45 ft. 5 bolts. *FA Dennis Rice, Mike Susko, Tim Powers, 2004.*

⓱ The P. Heist Rockway to Heaven 5.6 ★★
Follow the crack system that begins from the base of *The Offering* up and right to the chain anchor on *Get on the Good Foot*.
60 ft. *FA Mike Susko, Stacia Susko, 2004.*

Workin' for the Weekend

⑱ Put the Best Foot Forward 5.8 ★★★
This route is a variation finish to *Get on the Good Foot*. Climb *GOTGF* until it is possible to step up and left to the bolted face. Follow two bolts up the juggy slab to anchors just below the ledge.
55 ft. 2 bolts. *FA J.J., Rick Weber, 2004.*

⑲ Get on the Good Foot 5.8 ★★★
Follow a right-angling crack and flake system 10-15 feet right of *The Offering* and *P. Heist* up and right to chain anchors under the large roof.
60 ft. *FA J.J., Tracy Crabtree, 2004.*

⑳ Send Me on My Way 5.9- ★★★★
Pluck and plunder the pleasantly plump and plentiful plates left of the leaning crack. Then juice the jugs as they send you on your way to the anchors. Much fun. Highly recommended for the novice leader.
75 ft. 9 bolts. *FA Jared Hancock, Karla Carandang, Jenny Wagner, Mark Ryan, 2005.*

㉑ Workin' for the Weekend 5.10c ★★★
Starts on easy slab. Make a couple of long, pumpy moves on a small flake feature. Crimp or undercling through another short crux and pull over a large flake to the anchors.
70 ft. 8 bolts. *FA Jared Hancock, Karla Carandang, 2004.*

㉒ Return of Manimal 5.10d ★★★★
Moderate slab with big reaches to a giant roof at the top.
85 ft. 10 bolts. *FA Tim Powers, Mike Susko, 2004.*

㉓ Critters on the Cliff 5.10d ★★★★
Begin 15 feet right of *Return of Manimal*. Balance up the moderate slab to steepening terrain. Reach through the overhanging finger-crack section and stroll past a few more bolts to the anchors.
75 ft. 9 bolts. *FA Jared Hancock, Tim Powers, Tony Panozzo, Karla Carandang, 2004.*

㉔ Rat Stew 5.10a ★★★★
The right-most route on Bruise Brothers Wall. Balance up the knobby face to a small ledge. Continue cranking up a slightly overhanging face on good holds, through two solid black sections to an anchor under the final roof. Good moves. Easier than it looks.
75 ft. 9 bolts. *FA Jared Hancock, Joel Bruhn, Tim Powers, 2004.*

SUNNYSIDE

p.m. 15 mins OK in rain

15 routes

5.6- .7 .8 .9 .10 .11 .12 .13 .14

Character

If the crowds at Bruise Brother's Wall have got you down, head over to Sunnyside. Here you'll find some more great routes in the 5.10 to 5.11 range, and even a 5.12. Begin on the highly recommended *Fear or Common Sense,* then head over to the tiered roofs of *Machete* and *Weed Eater.* If you've got mad edging skills, jump on the highly technical *Suppress the Rage.*

Approach

Take the second approach trail from the main parking area, which begins at the far side of the parking lot near the kiosk and behind the garage. Follow the trail to the valley floor, cross the creek, and continue straight past the first trail on the left (which leads to Practice and Washboard Walls). Soon you will reach a fork in the trail. Follow the right fork toward Sunnyside. (The left fork leads uphill to Bruise Brother's Wall.) Follow the trail downhill then uphill until you meet the cliff just beneath *Fear or Common Sense.* The rest of the routes are to the right.

Conditions

Don't let the name fool you. Sunnyside actually isn't sunny all day. The wall is mainly west facing, so if you're an early riser you can avoid the sun on hot days. The steeper routes on the far right wall will stay dry in a downpour.

❶ Dog Wars 5.12 ★★★★
This is the overhanging finger-and-hand crack that splits the middle of the main wall when the approach trail meets the cliff. It is about 20 feet left of the bolted line *Fear or Common Sense.*
90 ft. 3 bolts. *FA Ken Thompson.*

❷ Fear or Common Sense 5.11b ★★★
Begins from the right side of the ledge 15-20 feet right of the previous route. Follows the flake feature up the arete.
70 ft. 7 bolts. *FA J.J., Barry Broley, 2004.*

❸ Continental 5.12a ★★★
Toprope. Boulder-problem start to pocketed section resembling the Dark Continent. Long, sustained, pumpy moves up spaced-out slopers.
80 ft. *FA on TR Jared Hancock, JJ.*

❹ Mini Me 5.9+ ★★★
This short, gently overhanging finger-to-hand crack is right of the previous toprope line. Boulder the start, then follow the crack until it ends. Contine by climbing past chickenheads to anchors.
30 ft. *FA J.J., David Fromke, 2004.*

Dog Wars

Mini Me

7 Machete 5.10b ★★★

Next bolted line right of *Virgin Bolter Tag Team*. Climbs a pocketed face to a small alcove. Shake out and fight the pump up and over a few roofs.
65 ft. 7 bolts. *FA J.J., Jared Hancock, 2004.*

8 Weed Eater 5.11b ★★★★

The next sport route to the right of *Machete*. Climb slabby pockets to steep ledges to a steep finish on crimpy pockets.
75 ft. 8 bolts. *FA David Fromke, J.J., 2004.*

9 Velveteen 5.5 ★★★

Ascend the obvious chimney between the left side of the pinnacle and the main wall. Climb up through the cave and spiral around to a ledge near the top at the right side of the pinnacle. Fun.
40 ft. *FA J.J. (free-solo), 2005.*

10 Velvet Revolution 5.11d ★★★

Super steep route that continues out the rock house above the pinnacle. Fun and exposed with a few powerful moves.
100 ft. 9 bolts. *FA J.J., Jared Hancock, Tim Powers, 2005.*

11 Kokopeli's Dream 5.9 ★★★

This sport route climbs the pinnacle. It begins as a technical slab and angles up and left to the arete. Balance on up with some underclings, then finish by laybacking on the arete. Some harder variations can be toproped from the anchors.
40 ft. 4 bolts. *FA Jared Hancock, Karla Carandang, J.J., 2005.*

12 Baccaus Goes Climbing 5.8 ★★

Climb the wide, arching crack formed between the right side of the pinnacle and the main wall.
45 ft. *FA Chris Moratz, Cindy Simpson, J.J., 2005.*

13 Suppress the Rage 5.12a ★★★★

Walk right from the pinnacle to a small ledge with three bolted lines. This is the first line on the left and climbs the left-angling blunt arete.
50 ft. 6 bolts. *FA Kipp Trummel, Eric Heuermann, 2005.*

14 Some Humans Ain't Human 5.10c ★★★★

This technical line is the middle of the three bolted routes on the ledge. Begin with fun moves, then balance up solid sandstone on nice edges to the chains.
50 ft. 5 bolts. *FA Rob Copeland, Jared Hancock, James Case, 2005.*

15 Dingo the Gringo 5.10c ★★★

The last bolted line on the right side of the ledge. Solve the beginning sequence to reach easier slab climbing to the anchors.
45 ft. 5 bolts. *FA Jared Hancock, Karla Carandang, Mark Ryan, Jenny Wagner, 2005.*

To reach the remaining lines, walk right along the main trail for approximately 300 yards until you see a wooden sign marking the Sunnyside Wall. Follow the trail left and uphill to arrive near an overhang and left of Enganche.

5 Enganche 5.10b ★★

This route is 50 feet to the left of the entrance to a cave that forms a hidden arch. Wide layback crack with two roofs. The upper roof is fun and exposed. May still need some cleaning.
60 ft. *FA: Danny Rice, Chris Dent, 2004.*

6 Virgin Bolter Tag Team 5.10b ★★

Walk 50 feet right from the large cave near *Enganche* to a pocketed wall with some bolted lines and a pinnacle formation. This is the first of the bolted lines. Climb through the crux roof at the start, then cruise up moderate terrain to a steep finish.
65 ft. 6 bolts. *FA Jared Hancock, Mike Hatchett, Mark Ryan, Skip Wolfe, 2005.*

Virgin Bolter to Kokopeli's Dream

Enganche

Surpress the Rage

PENDERGRASS-MURRAY RECREATIONAL PRESERVE

Introduction

The Pendergrass-Murray Recreational Preserve (PMRP) is a 700-acre region owned and maintained by the Red River Gorge Climbers' Coalition. The PMRP contains over 300 sport and traditional rock climbs from 5.6 to 5.14, with the potential for hundreds more. This is the largest direct land acquisition ever made by climbers and permanently secures access to a significant amount of the climbing in the Red.

The Red River Gorge Climbers' Coalition is a nonprofit organization dedicated to ensuring quality climbing opportunities for the recreating public by promoting responsible climbing. The historic PMRP purchase represents the RRGCC's dedication to ensure quality climbing opportunities on public and private land. The purchase and operation of the PMRP is made possible solely through private donations and volunteer efforts. Current yearly expenses – including the property payment, property taxes, legal fees, and maintenance – are close to $30,000. The mortgage on the property will be paid off in 2013. All donations made in support of the RRGCC and the PMRP are tax deductible. Volunteer contributions in the form of trail work or pro-bono professional services are also welcome. You can download an RRGCC membership form from www.rrgcc.org. Please mail the completed form to RRGCC, PO Box 22156, Lexington, KY 40522-2156.

History and Vision

On March 28, 1908, Daniel Boone Pendergrass secured his first 530-acre parcel of land on Bald Rock Fork, which runs through the heart of the Pendergrass-Murray Recreational Preserve. Pendergrass bought three more tracts, including the 325-acre Coal Bank Hollow, eventually totaling over 1000 acres. The land stayed in the Pendergrass family for three generations, being passed finally to the granddaughter of Daniel Boone Pendergrass, Mattie Murray, and her husband, Lafayette. During the late 1990's, inspired by the discovery of the nearby Motherlode, climbers started exploring and developing the superb climbing potential of the many cliffs on this land. On January 20, 2004 the RRGCC officially purchased the surface rights to the 700 acres from the Murrays and secured climbing access for the future.

The vision of the PMRP is to create an outdoor recreational haven in Eastern Kentucky that encourages a love for the outdoors, facilitates human-powered recreation, and builds appreciation and a sense of stewardship for this unique and beautiful land. As a public-trust organization dedicated to responsibly ensuring open, public access to rock climbing, and other outdoor recreational opportunities, while encouraging conservation, the RRGCC plans to provide a variety of recreational opportunities, including hiking and mountain biking, with an emphasis on the "recreational experience" in this unique natural and geological environment.

Directions and Guidelines

All crags at the PMRP can be accessed from KY 11 south of Torrent via either Fixer Road or Bald Rock Fork Road, both of which are county roads maintained by Lee County. Charmane Oil Company, the current oil and gas lessee on the property, has constructed many other roads on the Preserve to access its oil wells. Thus it is important to look for and follow directional signs in the Preserve. **It is also absolutely imperative to park your vehicles in the designated parking areas only and follow all posted rules and guidelines.** Be sure to park off of any gravel road and away from any pipes, oil wells, or other oil production equipment, and always yield the right-of-way to any oil worker or truck. Stay clear of all oil production equipment – oil wells, injection sites, and storage tanks. They are dangerous and pose serious risk.

RULES OF THE PMRP

Climbing is a dangerous activity and should always be taken seriously. The RRGCC assumes no liability for your safety and personal property while visiting the PMRP. You climb and recreate on the PMRP at your own risk.

Before climbing at the PMRP you must sign a liability waiver. These are available at kiosks or on the www.rrgcc.org website. If you are interested in establishing any new sport routes or traditional routes with fixed anchors at the Preserve, please send an e-mail to rrgcc@rrgcc.org and the RRGCC will reply with contact information so that you can coordinate your activities with the PMRP property manager. Other rules and guidelines for the Preserve are as follows:

•Please climb responsibly and follow "Leave No Trace" practices.

•All dogs must be leashed or under control of their owners.

•Stay off all tagged projects and do not touch or use any project ropes, draws, or other gear.

•Stay on established trails and do not mark or damage trees or other vegetation. Approval by the RRGCC is required prior to the establishment of any new crags or trails.

•No hunting, trapping, digging for archaeological artifacts, or operation of motorized vehicles off established roads is permitted.

•No open fires are permitted due to the oil extraction activity in the area and the enormous threat a forest fire in a region of numerous oil wells would pose.

•Overnight camping (no long-term camping) is permitted as long as it is not in a climbing area, along a trail, or near any oil equipment. Please remove all refuse and bury human waste.

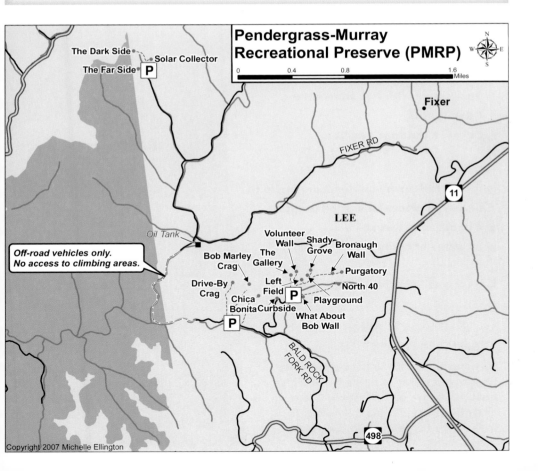

Pendergrass-Murray Recreational Preserve (PMRP)

Copyright 2007 Michelle Ellington

Lago Linda HIDEAWAY

CLIMBER friendly

*L*ago Linda Hideaway is nestled in the foothills of the Cumberland plateau in scenic Eastern Kentucky. Only 65 miles from Lexington, and 16 miles from the entrance to the Red River Gorge, we provide a hideaway for those who seek a quiet and relaxing experience.

Camping

- 35 sites with water and electricity, some 30 amp available
- Clean restrooms
- Bathhouse with hot showers and flush toilets
- Covered outdoor pavilion

Cabins

- 5 cozy hideaway cabins from basic to luxury at prices to suit all budgets
- 410 acres of forest
- 15 miles of trails

Cafe available for groups (seats 30)

Located Just 4 miles from "The Motherlode"

Directions: At Slade turn right onto Highway 11. Go 14 miles. Turn right onto Highway 498. Turn right again onto Highway 52. Go 2 ½ miles. Turn left onto Highway 399. Entrance ½ mile on left.

Lago Linda Hideaway
850 Black Ridge Road
Beattyville, KY 41311
606-464-2876

www.lagolinda.com

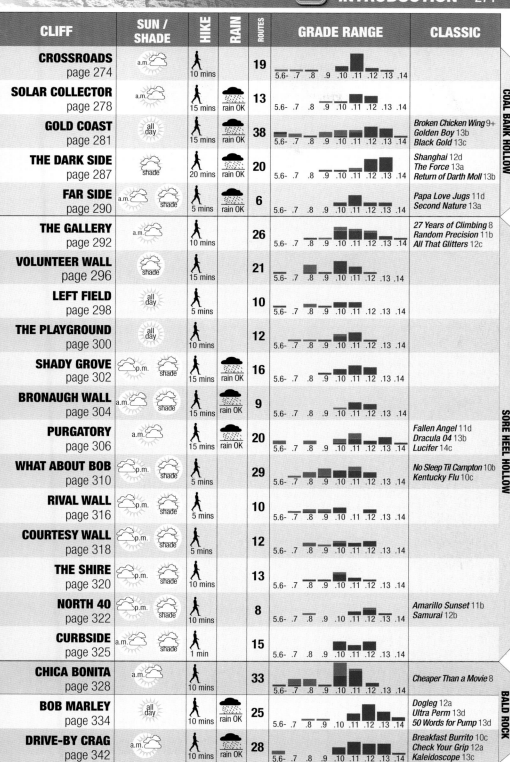

CLIFF	SUN / SHADE	HIKE	RAIN	ROUTES	GRADE RANGE	CLASSIC	
CROSSROADS page 274	a.m.	10 mins		19	5.6- .7 .8 .9 .10 .11 .12 .13 .14		COAL BANK HOLLOW
SOLAR COLLECTOR page 278	a.m.	15 mins	rain OK	13	5.6- .7 .8 .9 .10 .11 .12 .13 .14		COAL BANK HOLLOW
GOLD COAST page 281	all day	15 mins	rain OK	38	5.6- .7 .8 .9 .10 .11 .12 .13 .14	*Broken Chicken Wing* 9+ *Golden Boy* 13b *Black Gold* 13c	COAL BANK HOLLOW
THE DARK SIDE page 287	shade	20 mins	rain OK	20	5.6- .7 .8 .9 .10 .11 .12 .13 .14	*Shanghai* 12d *The Force* 13a *Return of Darth Moll* 13b	COAL BANK HOLLOW
FAR SIDE page 290	a.m. shade	5 mins	rain OK	6	5.6- .7 .8 .9 .10 .11 .12 .13 .14	*Papa Love Jugs* 11d *Second Nature* 13a	COAL BANK HOLLOW
THE GALLERY page 292	a.m.	10 mins		26	5.6- .7 .8 .9 .10 .11 .12 .13 .14	*27 Years of Climbing* 8 *Random Precision* 11b *All That Glitters* 12c	SORE HEEL HOLLOW
VOLUNTEER WALL page 296	shade	15 mins		21	5.6- .7 .8 .9 .10 .11 .12 .13 .14		SORE HEEL HOLLOW
LEFT FIELD page 298	all day	5 mins		10	5.6- .7 .8 .9 .10 .11 .12 .13 .14		SORE HEEL HOLLOW
THE PLAYGROUND page 300	all day	10 mins		12	5.6- .7 .8 .9 .10 .11 .12 .13 .14		SORE HEEL HOLLOW
SHADY GROVE page 302	p.m. shade	15 mins	rain OK	16	5.6- .7 .8 .9 .10 .11 .12 .13 .14		SORE HEEL HOLLOW
BRONAUGH WALL page 304	a.m. shade	15 mins	rain OK	9	5.6- .7 .8 .9 .10 .11 .12 .13 .14		SORE HEEL HOLLOW
PURGATORY page 306	a.m.	15 mins	rain OK	20	5.6- .7 .8 .9 .10 .11 .12 .13 .14	*Fallen Angel* 11d *Dracula 04* 13b *Lucifer* 14c	SORE HEEL HOLLOW
WHAT ABOUT BOB page 310	p.m. shade	5 mins		29	5.6- .7 .8 .9 .10 .11 .12 .13 .14	*No Sleep Til Campton* 10b *Kentucky Flu* 10c	SORE HEEL HOLLOW
RIVAL WALL page 316	p.m. shade	5 mins		10	5.6- .7 .8 .9 .10 .11 .12 .13 .14		SORE HEEL HOLLOW
COURTESY WALL page 318	p.m. shade	5 mins		12	5.6- .7 .8 .9 .10 .11 .12 .13 .14		SORE HEEL HOLLOW
THE SHIRE page 320	p.m. shade	10 mins		13	5.6- .7 .8 .9 .10 .11 .12 .13 .14		SORE HEEL HOLLOW
NORTH 40 page 322	p.m. shade	10 mins		8	5.6- .7 .8 .9 .10 .11 .12 .13 .14	*Amarillo Sunset* 11b *Samurai* 12b	SORE HEEL HOLLOW
CURBSIDE page 325	a.m. shade	1 min		15	5.6- .7 .8 .9 .10 .11 .12 .13 .14		SORE HEEL HOLLOW
CHICA BONITA page 328	a.m.	10 mins		33	5.6- .7 .8 .9 .10 .11 .12 .13 .14	*Cheaper Than a Movie* 8	BALD ROCK
BOB MARLEY page 334	all day	10 mins	rain OK	25	5.6- .7 .8 .9 .10 .11 .12 .13 .14	*Dogleg* 12a *Ultra Perm* 13d *50 Words for Pump* 13d	BALD ROCK
DRIVE-BY CRAG page 342	a.m.	10 mins	rain OK	28	5.6- .7 .8 .9 .10 .11 .12 .13 .14	*Breakfast Burrito* 10c *Check Your Grip* 12a *Kaleidoscope* 13c	BALD ROCK

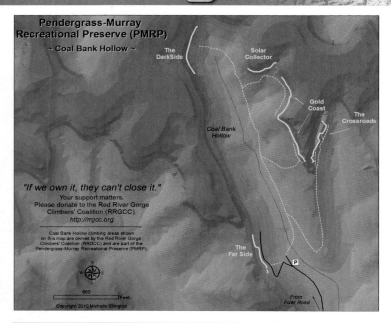

Pendergrass-Murray Recreational Preserve (PMRP)
~ Coal Bank Hollow ~

The DarkSide

Solar Collector

Gold Coast

The Crossroads

Coal Bank Hollow

"If we own it, they can't close it."
Your support matters.
Please donate to the Red River Gorge Climbers' Coalition (RRGCC).
http://rrgcc.org

Coal Bank Hollow climbing areas shown on this map are owned by the Red River Gorge Climbers' Coalition (RRGCC) and are part of the Pendergrass-Murray Recreational Preserve (PMRP).

The Far Side

P

680 Feet

From Fixer Road

Copyright 2010 Michelle Ellington

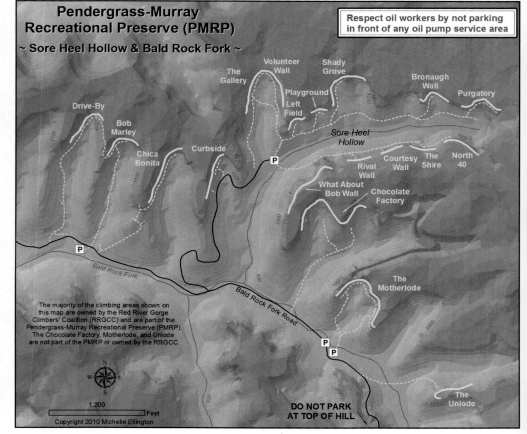

Pendergrass-Murray Recreational Preserve (PMRP)
~ Sore Heel Hollow & Bald Rock Fork ~

Respect oil workers by not parking in front of any oil pump service area

Drive-By

Bob Marley

Chica Bonita

Curbside

The Gallery

Volunteer Wall

Shady Grove

Playground

Left Field

Bronaugh Wall

Purgatory

Sore Heel Hollow

P

Rival Wall

Courtesy Wall

The Shire

North 40

What About Bob Wall

Chocolate Factory

P

Bald Rock Fork

Bald Rock Fork Road

The majority of the climbing areas shown on this map are owned by the Red River Gorge Climbers' Coalition (RRGCC) and are part of the Pendergrass-Murray Recreational Preserve (PMRP). The Chocolate Factory, Motherlode, and Unlode are not part of the PMRP or owned by the RRGCC.

The Motherlode

P

P

The Unlode

1,200 Feet

Copyright 2010 Michelle Ellington

DO NOT PARK AT TOP OF HILL

Be a Part of History

With your continued support, the RRGCC will secure the largest land acquisition by an organization of its kind on July 15, 2013.

Without your support, we will loose this land and thousands of classic routes

274 • PMRP

CROS...

Characte...

This crag
a full-se...
rumor...
ing...
Ho...

Pr vate
Playground

Shady
Grove

Purgatory
Bronaugh
Wall

Volunteer
Wall

The
Gallery

Bob Marley
Crag

Left Field

P

Chica Bonita

North 4
The Shire

Arena

Courtesy
Wall

Rival Wall

What About
Bob Wall

The following pages feature the Pendergrass-Murray Recreation Preserve. When this guidebook was published, the PMRP was home to over 25% of the routes at the Red River Gorge and that number is still growing. If you enjoy climbing here, please show your support www.rrgcc.org

~~ROADS

 a.m. 10 mins

19 routes

| 5.6- | .7 | .8 | .9 | .10 | .11 | .12 | .13 | .14 |

...has been around since the early 1990s but was only recently rediscovered and developed into ~~ice sport climbing venue hosting nearly 20 routes (versus the original four). Brian McCray is ~~d to be the equipper and FA of the original four routes on the left side of the wall. If you're look-~~ get your forearms pumped, keep walking past this cliff and head to Solar Collector or Dark Side. ~~ever, if you're looking to get your calves pumped then this is the place for you. Most of the lines are ~~abby to vertical and the quality of the rock is pretty good. One section of the cliff resembles an ocean ~~ave, where the crux of the lines is pulling over the crest. They're definitely worth checking out. For the beginning climber, one of the better 5.8 lines around, *Boilerplate*, can be found here.

Approach

Follow the directions to reach the Solar Collector/Gold Coast parking area. From the parking area, walk a few feet past the kiosk to locate the trail marker. Follow the trail down and across a small bridge then uphill along a dirt road for a short distance (just as you're walking to Solar Collector or Dark Side). Take the first right on an old oil/logging road. Follow this for about 75 yards, then continue left on the road at the fork. Take this to an old oil rig. Behind this road forks again. Take the left fork and follow it around until you can see the cliff. To reach the first routes, look for a trail branching off and uphill on the left. For *October Sky* and the routes right of it, remain on the road a bit longer, passing another old oil pump, then cross a small footbridge to end up just beneath *October Sky*.

Conditions

The routes here are less than vertical. Many of the routes are wet at the top for days after a period of heavy rain. The wall gets sun from morning until early afternoon. Not all of the lines are slabs, though, so you may luck out and find *Hippie Speed Ball*, *Cannabis Love Generator*, *Banjolero*, and *Boilerplate* dry during or after a good rain.

❶ Legalize It 5.12a ★★★
Take the first left off the main trail then head up to the cliff. Walk left along the cliff to an obvious section of the wall hosting two face climbs. This is the left line on the wall and the leftmost line at Crossroads at this time.
55 ft. 4 bolts. *FA Unknown.*

❷ Wake and Bake 5.11d ★★★
15 feet right of the previous line is another crimp fest but with more holds than its neighbor. Begin on a ledge and step and reach up the slightly less than vertical face. Shift slightly left just before the shuts.
55 ft. 4 bolts. *FA Unknown.*

❸ Hippie Speed Ball 5.11d ★★★
Just right of the slab wall is an overhanging section of the cliff with two nice-looking pocket lines. This is the first line on this wall. Clip a high first bolt to begin. Pull through long moves on deep pockets to a crimp crux just before the shuts. Watch out for the tree from the last bolt to the anchors.
60 ft. 5 bolts. *FA Unknown.*

❹ Cannabis Love Generator 5.11c ★★
Just right of the previous line is another overhanging pocketed line. Climb deep pockets to an obvious crux. Continue on jugs to the anchors or keep moving to the anchors on the previous line for more value.
50 ft. 5 bolts. *FA Unknown.*

❺ Praying Mantis 5.13 ★★★
Hugs the left leaning arete 15 feet right of *Cannabis Love Generator*. Currently a closed project.
7 bolts. 60 ft. *Equipped by Kipp Trummel. FA Unknown.*

❻ Happy Feet 5.11c ★★★
Thirty feet right of the previous lines is a less than vertical wall. This line begins left of a blunt arete. Climb an easy start, then tiptoe up the face while improvising your way through multiple blank sections of rock. Route photo overleaf.
65 ft. 7 bolts *FA Phil Wilkes, Josephine Neff, 2009.*

❼ Kung Fu Panda 5.12 ★★★
Climb the blunt arete right of *Happy Feet*. Currently not bolted but may be by the time this guide is out.
65 ft. 0 bolts. *FA Unknown.*

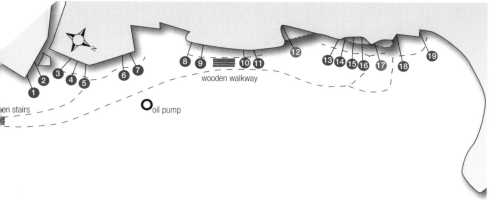

wooden walkway

en stairs

oil pump

Legalize It

Hippy Speed Ball

Happy Feet

8 Safety Meeting 5.11

Head back down to the main trail if approaching from the previous lines, then walk 120 feet right, passing a second oil pump, to locate a small wooden bridge branching left. You will meet the cliff at *October Sky* and this line is about 15 feet left of it. This adventurous line is either an unfinished sport route or an old sketchy mixed route. Details are unknown. There is some talk of adding more bolts to it so the bolt count may change by the time this guide is out. The grade is only a guess.

70 ft. 3 bolts. *FA Unknown.*

9 October Sky 5.11c ★★★★

This line is almost directly in front of the wooden walkway where the trail meets the cliff. Get your slab on for a brief session, then pinch and crimp through a crux to reach enjoyable face climbing. Reach into the bass mouth for the finale.
70 ft. 8 bolts. *FA Jeff Neal, 2009.*

10 Foot Jive 5.11d ★★★

Move right to locate two more bolted lines, which begin with jugs but turn to attractive stone after the first bolt. This is the first on the left. Solve the very difficult entrance moves to earn the ticket to sustained crimping and high stepping up this beautiful streak of sandstone.
65 ft. 8 bolts. *FA Matt Johns, Jeff Neal, 2009.*

11 Whippoorwill 5.11b ★★

Move 15 feet right for more slabby goodness. As with the previous line, you will be rewarded with holds you can feel between your fingers if you make it through the nerd gate.
65 ft. 7 bolts. *FA Jeff Neal, Theresa Neal, Matt Johns, 2009.*

12 Turkey Crossing 5.4 ★★

Head right along the cliff line to an incut area. This is the wide crack on the left side.
45 ft. *FA Jeff Neal, Theresa Neal, 2009.*

13 A1A 5.10a ★★★

Walk right a bit until you see a section of the cliff containing several bolted lines that surpass a roof shaped like a wave. This is the first of these routes on the left and borders the left edge of the wave roof. Take on a difficult start that quickly eases to fun climbing on solid stone.
50 ft. 5 bolts. *FA Don Mcglone, 2009.*

14 Yell Fire! 5.10d ★★★

The next route right of *A1A*. Climb a flake to a stance below the roof. Use thin seams to get high feet and gun for the lip. Continue on easier ground to reach the short, overhanging, pockety finale to the chains.
80 ft. 10 bolts. *FA Tania Allen, 2009.*

15 Severn Bore 5.11b ★★★★

Just right of *Yell Fire* is another slab-to-roof problem. Tiptoe up to a decent stance just before the roof, then use thin seams and edges to extend as far as possible to reach a good hold in the flake. Thug over the lip, then enjoy less stressful climbing to an enjoyable airy finish. Use a long draw for the roof bolt to save your rope.
60 ft. 7 bolts. *FA Kipp Trummel, Scott Brown, 2009.*

16 Red Tag Rape 5.11c ★★

This is the route on the far right of the wave. Climb a flake system to reach the crest of the wave. Make use of a pocket and a crimp to pull the lip, then fight for a stance. Move up on larger holds to another fun, pockety finish.
80 ft. 10 bolts. *FA Ray Ellington, 2009.*

17 Wrong Turn 5.7 ★★

Move right to locate this right-angling crack. Enjoy decent protection and a few slabby moves, then top it off with a nice set of anchors.
50 ft. *FA Jeff Neal, 2009.*

18 Banjolero 5.10c ★★

Around the corner from *Wrong Turn* is this heavily featured face. Climb to a ledge to reach the high first bolt, then continue up the face on pockets and pinches, staying left of a crack. Move left onto the face before the chains.
65 ft. 7 bolts. *FA Jeff Neal, Theresa Neal, 2009.*

19 Boilerplate 5.8 ★★★★

Excellent route for the grade. Head right 50 feet from *Banjolero* and walk up a steep section of the trail to find this enjoyable line on a northeast facing section of the wall. Begin on a small ledge, then pull on solid plates to a steeper run for the chains.
50 ft. 6 bolts. *FA Jeff Neal, Matt Johns, 2009.*

14

15

16

Severn Bore

19

Boilerplate

Scott Glasberg encounters *God's Own Stone* 5.14a, The Gold Coast, page 201. Photo Dan Brayack.

SOLAR COLLECTOR/GOLD COAST

 a.m. all day OK in rain 🚶 15 mins

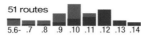
51 routes
5.6- .7 .8 .9 .10 .11 .12 .13 .14

Character

The Solar Collector and Gold Coast walls host a variety of routes of all grades and types. Solar Collector offers classic overhanging bucket hauls in the 5.11-5.12 range on a wall with several huecos large enough to crawl into and take a sit-down rest along the way. Each year, projects on the striking main wall of the Gold Coast are being sent, making for a collection of some of the most aesthetic and difficult sport lines in the Red, including *God's Own Stone* 5.14a and *True Love* 5.13d. Further right you will find several excellent traditional routes.

Approach

From Miguel's Pizza, drive 7.9 miles south on KY 11 and turn right on Fixer Road. Drive about 0.2 miles and take the first left. After a couple of miles on this road you will descend a steep, winding hill. At the bottom of the hill, the road turns to gravel. Drive 1.1 miles on the gravel road until you see a road on your right directly across from a black oil tank the size of a car. Turn right onto this road and head up a steep hill, then down another hill. Continue along the slightly rough road for about 0.5 miles staying left (do not turn right onto a road that heads down a steep hill where oil company equipment is located) until you reach an obvious parking area where an RRGCC kiosk is located. From the parking area, walk a few feet past the kiosk to locate the signed trailhead on the right. Follow the trail down and across a small bridge, then along an old dirt road for a few hundred yards, passing a road branching off to the right (the approach for Crossroads) until you see a trail to the right, marked by a wooden sign. This trail heads shortly uphill to end just beneath the bolted line *On the Prowl*. It is recommended to take this trail for routes 26-52. For the rest of the routes, remain on the main trail, negotiating a marshy area along the way, until you see another sign and a trail which doglegs back to the right and uphill. Take this trail, which winds uphill to end just beneath the main Solar Collector wall near *Super Pinch*. If you continue on the main trail past the dogleg it will take you to the Dark Side.

Conditions

Solar Collector is aptly named, blazing in the morning to midday sun. The sun leaves the wall in the afternoon but remains focused on the streaked walls of the Gold Coast until sundown. A number of the difficult lines on the main wall of the Gold Coast remain dry after periods of rain. The Solar Collector wall offers a dry escape from light rain, but will get wet in a downpour.

Access

Please fill out a waiver before climbing. Waivers are located on the RRGCC kiosk near the trailhead. Please obey any rules posted on the kiosk and pay special attention to parking concerns for the area.

---

❶ Super Pinch 5.10d ★★★
This is the first bolted route encountered when the trail meets the wall. It starts just left of a thin seam. Climb the slightly overhanging wall, with a long pull down low.
50 ft. 5 bolts. *FA Rob McFall, 1999.*

❷ Mona Lisa Overdrive 5.11b ★★★
This is the second bolted route from the left on the main wall. Start just right of the thin seam and boulder a tough start to better holds. Climb past the large hueco onto the face and continue to the anchors.
55 ft. 6 bolts. *FA Rob McFall, 1999.*

❸ Green Horn 5.11a ★★★
Move 10 feet right from *Mona Lisa Overdrive* to the next bolted line. Climb up to a large hueco, then negotiate a way out. Continue up the face to anchors.
55 ft. 5 bolts. *FA Hugh Loeffler, 1999.*

❹ Chickenboy 5.11b ★★★
This line is located a few feet right of *Green Horn*. Pull past a tough start, then contine up the sustained face to anchors.
70 ft. 6 bolts. *FA Neal Strickland, 2000.*

Solar Collector left side

Solar Collector right side

❺ Psychopathy 5.12c ★

Walk 10 feet right of *Chickenboy* and locate a line with a blank section about midway up. Climb the line just right of a brown streak and try clipping the bolt at the crux. If you can't clip it, you may have to skip it and run to the next one.

65 ft. 7 bolts. *FA Jason McClennan, 2000.*

❻ Ethics Police 5.11d ★★★★

Move a few feet right to the next line. Climb up to a large hueco, take a breather, then cross out of the hueco into the crux and a sustained pumpy headwall to the anchors.

75 ft. 7 bolts. *FA Rob McFall, 1999.*

❼ Buddha Hole 5.11d ★★★★

Move 15 feet right from *Ethics Police*. Climb up on slopers, then mantel into a hueco. Move out of the hueco and onto the face. Make a couple of tough moves to another big heuco, then enjoy jugs to the anchors.

75 ft. 8 bolts. *FA Neal Strickland, 2000.*

❽ Herd Mentality 5.12c ★★★★

Starts up a harder-than-it-looks thin crack right of *Buddha Hole*. Climb past the big heuco out left onto the face, continuing up through a long sustained section of crimps to easier but still pumpy moves at the top.

70 ft. 8 bolts. *FA Rob McFall, 1999.*

❾ Blue Eyed Honkey Jesus 5.12b ★★★★

Stand on a short, flat boulder 10 feet right of the previous line and reach up to deep two-finger pockets to start. Climb into a huge hueco at 15 feet, then continue up the overhanging face to the anchors.

70 ft. 8 bolts. *FA Hugh Loeffler, 2000.*

❿ Supafly 5.12a ★★★★

This is the last bolted route before the dihedral on the main wall. Begin on a large boulder and make a big move to the hueco. Shift left and tackle the sustained face to the last bolt. Take a rest, then make some steep, tough moves to the anchors.

70 ft. 7 bolts. *FA Chris Martin, 2000.*

⓫ Yakuza 5.9 ★★★

This is the obvious, overhanging, left-facing dihedral at the right end of the main wall, just past the bolted lines.

90 ft. *FA Barry Brolley, Clyde Stroman, 1997.*

⓬ Brambly Downslide 5.10a ★★★

Walk right from *Yakuza* to a slab wall with many water grooves before the black and tan Gold Coast wall starts. This route is the first bolted line on this wall. Enjoy fun and technical slab climbing.

75 ft. 6 bolts. *FA Bram Bell, Kevin Downs, JATD crew, 2007*

⓭ Spring Jammers and Widget Blocks 5.10d ★★

This line shares the first three bolts with the previous line, then heads right up a brown streak. Poor rock quality.

75 ft. *FA Dan Beck, Matt Kiroff, JATD Crew, 2007.*

16 **Black Gold** 5.13c ★★★★★
This great route follows a drainage line and requires
dry conditions. Move 30 feet right of the previous lines
to a taller section of the wall. Climb past shelves to a
large ledge 15 feet up, then head left up the striking dark
streak to anchors in a hueco just before the top.
60 ft. 8 bolts. *FA Bill Ramsey, 2001.*

Scott Glasberg has the rope under his leg! Photo Dan Brayack.

Gold Coast main wall

The Gold Coast

The remaining lines are located about 100 feet right. Follow the trail, beneath a large overhang with a crack, until you reach a striking golden wall. This is the Gold Coast.

⑭ Damascus 5.12b ★★

This route is the left-most bolted route and starts with a roof. Climb up loose rock to a shelf about 20 feet up to begin. Clip a fixed chain, then climb out of the short overhang. Continue up the slightly overhanging face to the anchors just before a large slopey ledge.
50 ft. 6 bolts. *Equipper: Jason McClennan. FA Gus Alexandropolus.*

⑮ Black Plague 5.12a ★★

This line shares the first three bolts with the previous line, then heads right up a brown streak. Poor rock quality.
50 ft. 6 bolts.

⑯ Black Gold 5.13c ★★★★★

See description opposite.

⑰ God's Own Stone 5.14a ★★★★★

Start the same as *Black Gold* but angle right after the first two bolts. Power up the golden face to the anchors just before a large horizontal. The crux is short lived; the route may feel easy for the grade if you have steel fingers. Photo page 277.
70 ft. 7 bolts. *Equipper: Hugh Loeffler. FA Ben Cassel, 2003.*

⑱ Gold Coast Project

Just right of *God's Own Stone* are two open projects. This is the one on the left, and climbs a golden face bordered by two black streaks that start halfway up the wall. **Open project.**
70 ft. 7 bolts. *FA Unknown. Equipper Jeff Moll.*

⑲ Gold Coast Project 2

This is the bolted line right of #16. **Open project.**
70 ft. 7 bolts. *Equipper Jeff Moll.*

⑳ 100 Ounces of Gold 5.14a ★★★★

Move about 30 feet right from the previous projects to the next line, which travels straight up a gold streak between two black streaks. Climb up to a large ledge to start. A critical hold broke in 2007, which may put the grade closer to 5.14a than 5.13d.
70 ft. 6 bolts. *Equipper: Rob McFall. FA Ben Cassel, 2003.*

㉑ Golden Boy 5.13b ★★★★★

This route tackles the next line of bolts about 15 feet right of *100 Ounces of Gold*. One of the best lines of its grade in the Red. Relentless sloping edges with not much for a shake. Lynn Hill flashed this line in 2008. Think of that while you're struggling on it. Check out Joe Hedge's video of Lynn's feat on Vimeo.
70 ft. 7 bolts. *Equipper: Chris Martin. FA Bill Ramsey, 2004.*

㉒ True Love 5.13d ★★★★★

Step just right of *Golden Boy* and embark on powerful crimping up the left margin of a black streak.
70 ft. 6 bolts. *FA Dave Hume, 2001.*

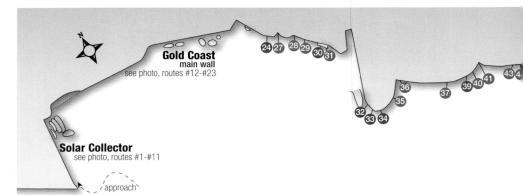

23 **No Fluff** 5.11d ★★★★

To the right of the main Gold Coast wall is a platform beneath three short steep routes. This is the first of the three. Angle left up to a large sloping shelf. Grab a horn and mantel up to the steeper face above, then run to the anchors. **45 ft. 5 bolts.** *FA Rob McFall, 2000.*

24 **Brilliant Orange** 5.13a ★★★★

This is the next route just right of *No Fluff.* Originally ended higher up on the wall but the anchors have been lowered, making it an excellent and doable line. Climb long moves between bad crimps to reach the well-worth-the-trip last move. Photo page 1. **70 ft. 8 bolts.** *Equipper Rob McFall.*

Gold Coast, main wall right

25 Mr. Roarke 5.12c ★★★

This is the last route on the gold-streaked overhanging wall. Belay from the platform as with the previous two routes. Climb a sustained face until you reach the last bolt. Lower from the last bolt for a grade of 5.12c or continue to the anchors to send an open project.
65 ft. 7 bolts. *Equipper Jeff Moll.*

26 Gecko Circus 5.13b ★★★

Walk around a blunt corner 100 feet right from the previous lines until the ground flattens. This is the first vertical bolted route you see, and lies about six feet left of the detached pinnacle climbed by *Erik's First.*
80 ft. 7 bolts. *FA Tony Lamiche 2007 Equipper: Josh Thurston.*

27 Erik's First 5.6 5.9- ★★

Just right of the previous line is a pair of nice-looking cracks ascending a small pillar and sharing the same anchors. This route ascends the crack on the left and gets a little wide towards the top.
35 ft. *FA Blake Bowling, 2000.*

28 Erik's Second 5.6 5.9+ ★★

This is crack just right of *Erik's First* and shares the same anchors. Climb a slabby start to a thin crack, which widens toward the top.
35 ft. *FA Blake Bowling, 2000.*

29 Smoothie Nut 5.10c ★★★★

This route ascends the striking, thin, left-facing dihedral 15 feet right of *Erik's Second.* Lower from bolted anchors.
60 ft. *FA Blake Bowling, Jason Tackett, 2000.*

30 Red Shift 5.11d ★★★★

Walk about 20 feet right from *Smoothie Nut* to locate this slab route, which begins on top of a boulder. Climb the less-than-vertical face, which gets steeper toward the top, and end beneath a block. **Hand Drills and Handgrenades** 5.10d R, climbs the finger crack above the anchors, past two bolts on the face to a second set of anchors.
50 ft. 4 bolts. *FA Blake Bowling, 2000.*

31 Dark Matter 5.11a ★★★

Ascends the crack just right of *Red Shift* to anchors on that route.
50 ft. *FA Blake Bowling, 2000.*

Smoothie Nut

Red Shift

Zone of Silence

Riptide Ride

32 Zone of Silence 5.12b ★★

Walk right from the previous lines about 75 feet, past a dirty dihedral to a downward-sloping portion of the trail. This contrived line wants to follow what would be an excellent 5.12c, but climbers are staying right, on the path of least resistance, making it a not-so-great 5.12a/b.
55 ft. 5 bolts. *FA Dave Hume, 2002.*

33 Amelia's Birthday 5.11c ★★

This line climbs the face just right of the previous route. Start either on the ground or from a small ledge, and climb the pocketed face past four bolts to a 15-foot runout before the anchors.
60 ft. 4 bolts. *FA Hugh Loeffler, 2003.*

34 Highway Turtle 5.11d ★★★

Step down around the corner from *Amelia's Birthday* to locate this line. Veer left up the overhanging face on holds that seem to all be facing the wrong way.
60 ft. 5 bolts. *FA Nate Heide, 2003.*

35 From the Ashes 5.8+ ★

Walk right and around the corner from *Highway Turtle* to locate this crack-and-face system right of the large leaning block. Use caution placing pro on this line, since there is a possible death block waiting to detach. Rappel from a tree.
65 ft. *FA Scott Hammon, Frank Waters, 2006.*

36 Futuristic Testpiece 5.4 ★★

Walk right from *Highway Turtle* until the trail heads down the hill and then back up to meet the cliffline again just beneath *Riptide Ride*. Walk left about 50 feet to locate this chimney system, which leads to the top of the buttress. Rappel from a tree for the descent.
50 ft. *FA Unknown*

37 Riptide Ride 5.10c ★★★★

This is the obvious thin dihedral that has a unique hueco about 20 feet up. It is located 50 feet right of *Futuristic Testpiece* where the trail meets up with the cliff. Enjoy excellent climbing with challenging gear placements.
55 ft. *FA Nate Heide, Matt Raymond, 2003.*

38 Sunny the Boxer 5.9 ★★

Walk right from *Riptide Ride* until you come to a slab wall with a couple of bolted lines sharing the first two bolts. This line moves up and left after the second bolt to end in a slot.
85 ft. 8 bolts. *FA Justin Elkins, Scott Hammon, Frank Waters, 2007.*

39 Lucky Duck Soup 5.5 ★★

This short route shares the first two bolts with the previous line but continues straight up to its own set of anchors.
45 ft. 4 bolts. *FA Scott Hammon, Stephanie Carson, 2003.*

40 The Perfect Pint 5.4 ★★

Climb the splitter crack mentioned in the previous route description to the same ring anchors.
45 ft. *FA Tony Panozzo, Jared Hancock, Curtis Williams, 2003.*

41 Chester Fried Chicken 5.4 ★★

Climb the arching dihedral eight feet right of the previous route to the same anchors.
45 ft. *FA Scott Hammon, Stephanie Carson, 2002.*

42 Fubar 5.10c ★★★

Steep lieback crack left of Rebar that eventually joins with it after the large hueco near the top.
60 ft. *FA Dustin Stephens, 2009.*

43 Rebar 5.11a ★★★★

Just right of *Chester Fried Chicken* you'll see two obvious cracks splitting the face. This route ascends the left crack. Begin by climbing *Broken Chicken Wing*, then step left when the crack splits into two.

60 ft. *FA Josh Thurston, Scott Lappin, 2002.*

Sarah Garlick. Photo Anne Skidmore.

Rebar

Slow Jack

On the Prowl

43 Rebar 5.11a ★★★★

See description on previous page.

44 Broken Chicken Wing 5.9+ ★★★★★

This route ascends the left-angling hand crack just right of *Rebar*. Climb hands and fingers to a nice rest, then tackle the last few feet for an exposed clipping stance. Chain anchors.

60 ft. *FA Josh Thurston, Scott Lappin, 2002.*

45 Green Tea 5.10a ★★

This curving crack can be found just right of *Broken Chicken Wing*. Start by pulling a tricky boulder problem, then follow the path of least resistance to the chains.

50 ft. *FA Josh Thurston, Mike Thurston, 2005.*

46 Norway on My Mind 5.8 ★★

Move right and just around the corner to this bolted line, which ascends a slabby face left of *Slow Jack*.

45 ft. 4 bolts. *FA Don Byrd, Josh Thurston, 2006.*

47 Slow Jack 5.7 ★★

Climb the clean dihedral just right of *Norway on My Mind*. Stop at the chains just beneath a roof.

45 ft. *FA Josh Thurston, Mike Thurston, 2005.*

48 Should've Known Better 5.7 R

Walk right from *Slow Jack* to locate this line, which begins 30 feet left of the bolted line *On the Prowl*. Climb a ramp with no protection to a tree just before the start of the crack. Continue up the dihedral on soft rock until you reach a ledge where it is possible to traverse 20 feet right to bolted anchors.

65 ft. *FA Scott Brown, Mason Allen, 2006.*

49 On the Prowl 5.10a ★★★

Walk right to reach this bolted route, which is located just left of the obvious arete where the alternate approach trail meets the cliff. Begin from a small ledge 10 feet above the trail and continue up an enjoyable slab, making use of the arete when possible.

50 ft. 5 bolts. *FA Jared Hancock, Mark Ryan, Jenny Ryan, 2006.*

50 Peer Review 5.10b

50 feet right of the trailhead and *On the Prowl* are two short, bolted lines. This is the first of the two and ascends a featured face. This route has become popular due to the fact that it may be a top contender for the worst route in the Red.

35 ft. 4 bolts. *FA Mike Cole, JATD Crew, 2007.*

51 7-11 5.7 ★★

Just right of Peer Review is another short, bolted line on an arete. Although a blank-looking face, it's possible to stem off to the left.

45 ft. 4 bolts. *FA Scott Brown, JATD crew, 2007.*

THE DARK SIDE

shade · 20 mins · OK in rain · 19 routes

5.6- .7 .8 .9 .10 .11 .12 .13 .14

Character

The Dark Side has proven to be one of the Red's most popular cliffs for strong sport climbers. Only the Motherlode has more 5.13s. Like the Motherlode, the Dark Side doesn't offer much in the way of moderate climbing. The lines are steep, sustained, and more pocketed than most at the Red. Many have distinct cruxes, often located in the wall's unique "pocket band." Some of the pockets in this band can feel sharp – especially if you're weak, tired, or flailing. *Shanghai* is a five-star classic, finishing with a series of long throws between perfect incuts on an otherwise blank face. *Tuskan Raider* is another classic, with a slopey boulder-problem start and a stout crux lunge. Less bouldery, but packing a mighty pump, *The Force* is probably the most popular route on the wall.

Approach

Park in the same parking area as Solar Collector. Follow the approach to Solar Collector but instead of turning right to head uphill to that area, continue straight on the trail, which crosses a creek and winds uphill to meet the lower buttress near the first two routes listed below. The approach trails are signed.

Conditions

As its name implies, the Dark Side is a well-shaded area – it almost never sees the sun. The pockets on the routes here are notoriously sharp, so bring some tape and calloused fingers.

Dark Side ramp routes

❶ Redneck Jedi 5.11a ★★★

Head left about 100 feet when the approach trail first reaches rock to locate this dihedral with two bolts. Climb the dihedral and slab to a set of chains.
60 ft. 2 bolts. *FA Blake Bowling, 1999.*

❷ Young Jedi 5.11b ★★

The technical slab 15 feet right of *Redneck Jedi*. The most difficult moves are reaching the first bolt. The quality decreases reaching the second bolt, but the climbing is fun the rest of the way.
60 ft. 5 bolts. *FA Blake Bowling, 1999.*

❸ Grippy Green 5.12a ★★★★

As you reach the wall on the approach trail, head right. This slabby climb is the first route reached. Boulder up a blind left-leaning flake for a few bolts, then continue up the slab to a hueco. Pull around the hueco, then climb more slab to reach a slightly overhanging headwall.
70 ft. 8 bolts. *FA Neal Strickland, 2002.*

❹ Small Fry 5.9 ★★

Lies on a short buttress just right of *Grippy Green* and before the main Dark Side wall.
40 ft. 4 bolts. *FA Rob McFall, 1999.*

❺ Padawan 5.10a ★

Another short warm-up. Climb the plated face 20 feet right of *Small Fry*.
40 ft. 4 bolts. *FA Nick Walker, Jared Hancock, Karla Hancock, 2006.*

❻ Techulicous 5.12a ★★★

Walk right from *Small Fry* to reach the main overhanging wall of the Dark Side. On the left side of the wall you will see a ramp leading up and left to a number of lines on a high section of the wall. Walk left beneath this ramp to locate tree stairs leading up to the start of this route.
50 ft. 4 bolts. *FA Hugh Loeffler, 2002.*

❼ Mama Benson 5.12a ★★★

Starts at the highest point and leftmost edge of the ramp mentioned in the previous route description. Climb up the ramp, clipping and unclipping bolts along the way to protect a fall, until you reach the start. Climb the steep wall with big moves at the top.
50 ft. 6 bolts. *FA Rob McFall, 2000.*

8 Shanghai 5.12d ★★★★★　　　　☐

This classic route begins on the ramp and is located just right of *Mama Benson*. A pumpy start leads to the archetypal "cruel joke" finish.
50 ft. 6 bolts. *FA Chris Martin, 2000.*

9 Big Burley 5.13b ★★★★　　　　☐

This route lies just right of *Shanghai* and is the third route from the left on the ramp. Power through pumpy moves to a bouldery finish.
60 ft. 6 bolts. *FA Dave Hume, 2002.*

10 American Dream 5.12b ★★★　　　　☐

This is the last route that begins on the ramp and climbs a faint groove feature. Most people preclip the second bolt. Pull a tough move at the second bolt, then continue through wicked cross moves and sustained pumpy climbing to the anchors.
65 ft. 5 bolts. *FA Chris Martin, 2000.*

11 Vader project　　　　☐

This is the first route from the left on the main wall that does not begin on the ramp. Begin with a tough boulder problem, which leads to another tough boulder problem, which leads to insanely difficult boulder problems, to a very tough boulder problem guarding the chains. Currently an open project.
70 ft. 9 bolts. *Equipped by Brad Weaver.*

12 The Return of Darth Moll 5.13b ★★★★★ ☐

One of the best and stiffest 13b lines in the Red. Begin just right of the previous insane project. Climb straight up, then angle left and up through difficult cruxes.
65 ft. 8 bolts. *FA Bill Ramsey, 2001.*

13 Jedi Mind Trick 5.13b ★★★　　　　☐

Same start as the previous route but move right. Rarely done due to a tweaky shutdown move. Crank up to a dyno off a small pocket then continue up easier ground to the anchors.
75 ft. 7 bolts. *Equipper: Neal Strickland. FA Dave Hume, 2002.*

14 The Force 5.13a ★★★★★　　　　☐

Classic. This route begins a few feet right of *Jedi Mind Trick* and climbs past a cool-looking stone embedded in the wall at about 25 feet. A jumpy start and some long pocket pulls gain the stone. Continue up the pumpy bulging wall; may the force be with you for the redpoint crux at the top.
75 ft. 7 bolts. *FA Chris Martin, 2000.*

15 Mind Meld 5.12d ★★★　　　　☐

This route begins just right of *The Force*. More bouldery but less sustained than that route. Boulder through sharp bowling-ball-grip pockets, make a difficult third clip, and continue on progressively easier terrain. Stout for the grade.
75 ft. 7 bolts. *FA Hugh Loeffler, 2000.*

16 Elephant Man 5.13b ★★★★　　　　☐

Step a few feet right from *Mind Meld* to locate this beast. Start on slopey holds, then crank sustained hard boulder problems for the first five bolts.
75 ft. 9 bolts. *FA Rob McFall, 2000.*

17 Tuskan Raider 5.12d ★★★★　　　　☐

Start on the same slopey holds as *Elephant Man* but traverse steeply right. Climb the bulging wall and make a difficult move to gain a huge hueco. Take a rest, then move left and up to an easier finish.
75 ft. 9 bolts. *FA Rob McFall, 2000.*

18 Straight Outta Campton 5.13a ★★★★　　　　☐

Dave Graham is roumored to have fallen on this line, making it his first fall on a 13a in several years. That should tell you something about the grade for this beast. Starts right of *Tuskan Raider* and climbs into and out of the right side of the big round hueco.
75 ft. 6 bolts. *Equipper: Chris Martin. FA Bill Ramsey, 2002.*

If you've nothing left to do at this cliff, then check out the Euro-style linkup starting on *Tuskan Raider,* then moving right out of the large hueco to finish on this route. Dubbed **Straight Outta Locash** 5.13a.
FA Jason Forrester, 2009.

19 Swingline 5.13d ★★★★　　　　☐

This line has become one of the most sought-after 5.13d lines at the Red. Same start as *Straight Outta Campton* but breaks right. Begins with 5.13a climbing to a very difficult boulder problem. Continue up the sustained face to the anchors.
75 ft. 7 bolts. *Equippers: Rob McFall, Chris Martin. FA Tony Berlier, 2003.*

20 Non starter 5.13b ★★★　　　　☐

This is the furthest route on the right. Aid up to the first bolt to begin, then step up to the steep wall and power to the anchors.
75 ft. 7 bolts. *Equipper Hugh Loeffler. FA Bill Ramsey, 2003.*

Paul Vidal on *The Force* 5.13a. Photo Wes Allen.

Dark Side main wall

THE DARKSIDE
8. Shanghai 5.12d
9. Big Burley 5.13b
12. The Return of Darth Moll 5.13b
13. Jedi Mind Trick 5.13b
14. The Force 5.13a
15. Mind Meld 5.12d
16. Elephant Man 5.13b
17. Tuskan Raider 5.12d
18. Straight Outta Campton 5.13a
19. Swingline 5.13d
20. Non Starter 5.13b

FAR SIDE

a.m. shade OK in rain

12 routes

5.6- .7 .8 .9 .10 .11 .12 .13 .14

Character

This small crag only has a handful of routes, but they include some amazing lines. *Papa Love Jugs* hucks moves between three sinker huecos. *Second Nature* powers through an extremely difficult boulder problem to reach a protruding lightning-bolt feature that runs the length of the wall. These lines alone make the Far Side a worthy destination.

Approach

Follow directions to Solar Collector and park in the same area. If you are facing the RRGCC kiosk, the Far Side is directly uphill to your left. Avoid bushwhacking up the hill by walking back in the direction you drove in and head up the dirt road to your right. Follow the dirt road as it winds up the hill to the cliff, then walk right until you reach an obvious notch in the rock formed by two closely spaced walls. The first route listed ascends the striking arete on the left wall.

Conditions

North facing, steep, and sheltered, *Papa Love Jugs*, *Second Nature*, and *Quantum Narcissist* are good in hot or wet weather. The other climbs receive morning sun and little shelter.

Second Nature

❶ Dirty Sanchez 5.12c ★★★
This route ascends the striking and seemingly featureless arete on the wall forming the left side of the notch. Pull over a small overhang to reach to the bald arete and climb it until the bolts force you left onto the face, where a few troublesome bulges lead to the anchors.
50 ft. 4 bolts. *FA Laban Swaford*

❷ Subject to Change 5.10d ★★★
Walk about 100 feet right from *Dirty Sanchez*, but do not hike down to the road to a wall on the right side of the notch facing the parking lot. This route ascends the short face via small crimps and fingery underclings.
40 ft. 4 bolts. *FA Jack Hume, 2004.*

❸ Far Side Project #1 5.12 ★★
Five feet right of *Subject to Change* is a set of anchors that may eventually blossom into a line of bolts. Hopefully it will then evolve from a closed project to an open line we can all fall on. Grade and quality are estimates.
50 ft. 5 bolts.

❹ Nameless 5.10d ★★★
Step 20 feet right to the next line, which begins behind a large tree. Climb past a crimpy start, then continue up the face on slopey ribs and the occasional good pinch.
40 ft. 5 bolts. *FA Jack Hume, 2004.*

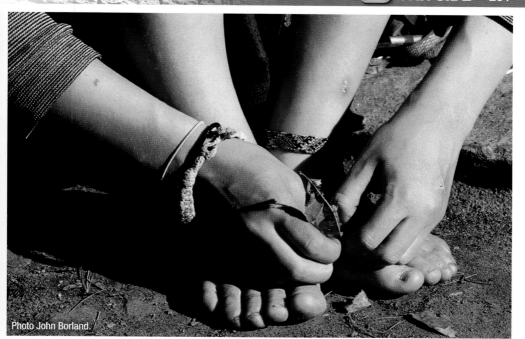

Photo John Borland.

5 Digitalgia 5.11c ★★

Right of *Nameless* is another crimpy line. Beware of the biting pocket.
50 ft. 5 bolts. *FA Arthur Cammers, 2007.*

6 Papa Love Jugs 5.11d ★★★★★

Pure fun. Walk back down to the road and follow it for 100 feet to the right. Look for a north-facing overhanging wall with a lightning-bolt-shaped feature. This route is on the left and links three huecos. Scramble up to an overhang to start.
45 ft. 5 bolts. *FA Nick Reuff, 2003.*

7 Second Nature 5.13a ★★★

This rarely traveled yet excellent line ascends the lightning-bolt-shaped feature just right of *Papa Love Jugs*. Make a big move to a good right hand jug, then power through the obvious crux. Continue up the feature with zig-zagging sidepulls to an exciting finish. Stout for the grade. People now dyno through the crux. The route is much harder if you do it statically as it was originally climbed.
50 ft. 6 bolts. *FA David Hume, 2003.*

8 Quantum Narcissist 5.13a ★★★

Just right of *Second Nature* is another difficult and technical line angling right as it follows the margin of a slanting arete. Very tough opening moves.
50 ft. 6 bolts. *FA David Hume, 2003.*

9 NAMBLA RAMBLA 5.11 ★

Thirty feet right of *Quantum* and *Second Nature* is a vertical wall containing four vertical lines. Not much is known about these lines and only *ATM* is being climbed currently. None of them appear to be closed projects and the grades and quality are estimated.
50 ft. 6 bolts. *Probably equipped by Joe Haynes. FA Unknown.*

10 Nose Ring 5.11 ★

Next route right of *NAMBLA RAMBLA*.
50 ft. 6 bolts. *Probably equipped by Joe Haynes. FA Unknown.*

11 French Fighter 5.11 ★

Just right of *Nose Ring*.
50 ft. 6 bolts. *Probably equipped by Joe Haynes. FA Unknown.*

12 ATM 5.11d ★★★

This is the fourth line right of *Quantum Narcissist* on the vertical face. Begin with a big move to a good edge, then continue up the crimpy face interspersed with a few more big moves on small edges to the chains.
50 ft. 6 bolts. *FA Johnny Vagabulla, 2007.*

THE GALLERY

a.m. | 10 mins | 26 routes | 5.6- .7 .8 .9 .10 .11 .12 .13 .14

Character

This excellent wall is the first of the Sore Heel Hollow areas described. It is easily accessible and hosts a unique blend of striking lines. As you approach the wall you will see one of the most aesthetic cracks in the Red, *All That Glitters*, a Red River Gorge classic and must do for the elite trad climber. If your technical face-climbing skills are up to par, put them to work on the amazing slab climb of *Random Precision*.

Approach

Drive 12.4 miles south on KY 11 from Miguel's toward Beattyville. Turn right on KY 498. Drive 1.2 miles to a sharp right curve. Just beyond this curve, take a sharp right on Bald Rock Road, a good gravel road, and follow it slowly, staying left at the first intersection, as it curves left toward a house. After 0.3 miles the road turns to gravel and descends a steep hill. **The steep hill is usually drivable in a regular car but you may have trouble getting back out in wet or muddy weather. If you have doubts, climb somewhere else – do not park at the top of the hill, as this area is used for access to oil company equipment and you are liable to be towed.** Pass the Motherlode parking area and turn right on the first gravel road 0.3 miles past the Motherlode parking. There is a "Sore Heel Parking" sign at the turn off. Follow the road up the hill past a row of large, bright-blue storage tanks, make a sharp right turn (0.2 mile after turn-off), and follow the road for another half mile, eventually descending a short hill to the Sore Heel Hollow parking area at the bottom of the hill on the right.

From the Sore Heel Hollow parking area, instead of hiking the trail that leads to the main Sore Heel Hollow areas (the Playground, Shady Grove, Purgatory, etc.), walk back up the road you drove down to the top of the final hill. At the top of the hill, take a sharp right and follow a road until it begins to head downhill 100 feet past some oil equipment on the right. Just as the road heads downhill, look for an old overgrown road on the left. Follow the road, which quickly narrows to a well-defined trail leading to the wall. The first route you encounter will be the obvious right-slanting crack of *All That Glitters*. The routes are listed from the far left side of the wall just before a drainage.

Conditions

The wall receives morning sun and afternoon shade.

❶ Thin Skin 5.10b ★★

Climb the short dihedral just left of *Blank Canvas* on the left far side of the Gallery. Rap from webbing.
35 ft. 7 bolts. *FA Danny Rice, 2007.*

❷ Blank Canvas 5.12c ★★★

This is the first bolted line on the far left side of the wall. Follow an arete and mini-dihedral through multiple boulder problems separated by good rests.
60 ft. 7 bolts. *FA Jason Forrester, 2005.*

❸ Crude Awakening 5.10b ★★★

Walk 100 feet right from *Bank Canvas* to locate this enjoyable face climb with an oil-soaked start.
60 ft. 8 bolts. *FA Kipp Trummrl, Brent Dupree, 2008.*

❹ DaVinci's Left Ear 5.10b ★★★

Walk 50 feet right from *Crude Awakening* to locate the next bolted lines. This is the left line. Climb the face on fragile holds, making use of inconspicuous underclings along the way.
60 ft. 7 bolts. *FA Blake Bowling, 2001.*

❺ Smack Dab 5.11b ★★

Climb the vertical face 10 feet right of the previous line. The top is often wet.
50 ft. 6 bolts. *FA Blake Bowling, 2001.*

❻ Different Strokes 5.11c ★★★★

Move 30 feet right from *Smack Dab* to this line, which begins left of a wide chimney. Climb the pumpy face, making use of sidepulls and pinches the whole way. If you find a horizontal hold, you must be on a different route.
50 ft. 6 bolts. *FA Terry Kindred, 2001.*

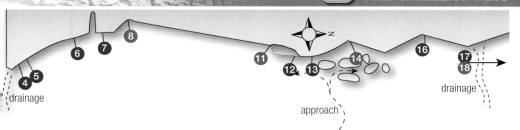

drainage

drainage

approach

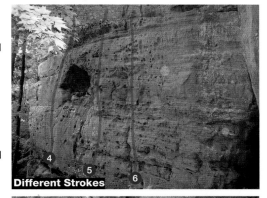

Different Strokes

⑦ Random Precision 5.11b ★★★★

Move 30 feet right to locate this amazing technical line that begins 15 feet right of a wide chimney. Begin with a tough and balancey start and continue up the face, making use of precise foot placements and the random good hold along the way. An extra bolt has been added after the fifth bolt, eliminating the original run out.
60 ft. 7 bolts. *FA Terry Kindred, 2001.*

⑧ Stucconu 5.11+ ★★★

This route ascends the obvious dihedral 15 feet right of *Random Precision*.
60 ft. *FA Florian Gritzer, 2004.*

⑨ Zen and the Art 5.12d ★★★★
of Masturbation

This is the first of two lines on the striking, gold, slightly overhanging face right of *Stucconu*. Begin with an easy start, then quickly transition to heinous crimping interspersed with mellow pocket cimbing, to reach the upper headwall. Try to get a shake, then tackle the overhang to reach a jug. Trend left to hide in a large hueco for a bit, then creep out to take the finishing jugs to the chains.
70 ft. 7 bolts. *FA Eric Stevenson, 2007.*

⑩ The Shocker 5.14b ★★★★

This is the next line right of *Zen and the Art of Masturbation*. Begin left of the large hueco in the middle of the wall. Apparently this line has some stopper moves on it but these didn't seem to thwart the freakish strength of James Litz.
70 ft. 7 bolts. *FA James Litz, 2008.*

⑪ Darkside of the Flume 5.9 ★★

Climb the chimney and hand crack 50 feet right of the previous line. Lower from bolted anchors.
70 ft. *FA Danny Rice 2006.*

⑫ Gold Rush 5.11d ★★★★

Walk right and around the corner from the wide crack to an overhanging and well-featured face. This line is on the left side of the face and begins with a low roof and dirty start. Pull over the roof on good jugs to gain the plated face. Pull on plates and good edges to a less featured and more overhanging section near the top. Get a good shake and crank through big moves on smaller edges to a surprise ending.
70 ft. 8 bolts. *FA Terry Kindred, 2003.*

Random Precision

Gold Rush

Calm Like a Bomb

The Tribute

⑬ Mosaic 5.12c ★★★★

This line begins on a low ledge 20 feet right of *Gold Rush*. Follow a thin seam, then angle right and continue up the face near the left margin of a black-and-orange streaked wall. Photo page 311.
60 ft. 6 bolts. *FA Blake Bowling, 2003.*

⑭ All That Glitters 5.12c ★★★★★

Walk right and around the corner from *Mosaic* to this striking right-angling crack which has a bolt near the beginning. Crank through the lower crux move, then enjoy aesthetic crack climbing to the anchors.
70 ft. 1 bolt. *FA Blake Bowling, 2006.*

⑮ Calm Like a Bomb 5.13a ★★★

Walk right from *All That Glitters* to the next bolted line, which takes on a thin seam up an overhanging section of the wall. Begin on steep and slightly fragile rock to reach the seam. Sidepull and crimp through powerful moves to a decent rest. Get a shake and pull the difficult ending to reach the anchors on *Break the Scene*. If you suffer from this strange disease some locals catch, then you will not use the incredibly obvious no-hands rest near the end of the route.
70 ft. 7 bolts. *FA Ben Cassel, 2006.*

⑯ Break the Scene 5.12a ★★★★

The bolted dihedral just right of *Calm Like a Bomb*. Pull a difficult start to the crack, followed by pumpy stemming to a sloping ledge near the top. Creep left into the overhang, trying not to lose your feet, and gun for the anchors. Don't cheat the last move by hanging 10 foot draws on the anchors!
55 ft. 8 bolts. *FA Terry Kindred 2004.*

⑰ The Tribute 5.13 ★★

The next bolted line right of *Break the Scene*. Climb mungey rock to an impossible move. Work magic, then continue up to the anchors on eroding jugs. The beginning boulder problem on this line kept it as an open project for several years until Litz easily did it and called the line 12d/13a.
55 ft. 5 bolts. *FA James Litz, 2009.*

⑱ All That Quivers 5.10b ★★

Hike right from *The Tribute* to the bottom of a gully, and locate an offwidth crack beginning halfway up the face. Start in the mud and climb the face to reach the crack. Take on the offwidth to a large ledge 15 feet from the top. Rappel from the ledge.
100 ft. *FA Danny Rice, Paul Coover, 2006.*

⑲ Happy Trails 5.10d ★★★

Move up from the gully until you reach an iron cable extending from the top of a cliff to the ground. Step over the cable and walk about 50 feet further to locate the next bolted line left of a rounded corner. Climb past a low overhang on fragile rock to start. Pump up the face past many eyebrow-like holds and feet that disappear when you get above them.
75 ft. 9 bolts. *FA Terry Kindred, 2005.*

⑳ The King Lives On ... 5.10b ★★★

Just right of *Happy Trails*. Climb through edges to start, then enjoy rounded, sloping holds for most of the way to the anchors.
70 ft. 9 bolts. *FA Gary Drexler, Jared Hancock, 2004.*

Happy Trails 19

27 Years of Climbing

20 22

24

21 Johnny B. Good 5.11a ★★★

Move right from the previous line to locate this route, which begins with a bulge leading to a low-angled section. Tread lightly on low-angle rock past thin sidepulls to a severely overhanging section near the top. Crank out the roof on big jugs to a pocketed section before the anchors.
85 ft. 9 bolts. *FA Gary Drexler, Tim Powers, 2004.*

22 27 Years of Climbing 5.8 ★★★★★

Possibly the best 5.8 sport line in the Red! This is the next bolted line right of *Johnny B. Good*. Climb through a low-angle face to an interesting feature just before an overhang. Desperado past the feature, then crank through large pockets in the overhang to reach the anchors.
65 ft. 7 bolts. *FA Unknown.*

23 Closed Project

The bolted line right of *27 Years of Climbing*, just past the wide crack. Several hangers are currently missing. **Project.**
65 ft.

24 Murano 5.10b ★★★

Step just right from the previous line. Climb over a low roof to reach a series of plates. Continue up to an enjoyable slab at the top.
75 ft. 9 bolts.

A Brief History of Climb 25

25 A Brief History of Climb 5.10c ★★★

Walk right from *Murano* to the next bolted line. Scramble up slightly suspect rock to reach the first bolt. Boulder past the next two bolts, then enjoy fun, steep climbing on good holds.
75 ft. 9 bolts. *FA Blake Bowling, 2006.*

26 A Briefer History of Climb 5.10b ★★★

Climb a direct start or the first several bolts of *A Brief History of Climb* to reach a ledge with bolted anchors. Clip a high bolt, then run with the difficult crack to a higher set of chains.
75 ft. 1 bolt. *FA Blake Bowling, 2007.*

VOLUNTEER WALL

shade · 15 mins · 21 routes · 5.6- .7 .8 .9 .10 .11 .12 .13 .14

Character

Just before John Bronaugh's death, he placed red tags at the base of this wall in the locations where he planned on drilling routes. In 2005, a group of volunteers got together and continued where John left off. This took the number of routes here from nine to 21. This wall is one of the few in the Red with a good selection of excellent 5.10 lines.

Approach

Approach from the Sore Heel Hollow parking area (for details, see approach notes for the Gallery). Walk uphill on a cleared dirt road a few hundred feet to the marked trailhead on the right. Take this trail and then take the first trail on the left, which is marked with a wooden sign. Follow the trail a few minutes until you reach the first bolted line, which should be *Generosity*. There is also another way to reach the wall. Instead of taking the first marked trailhead on the right, continue along the dirt road a few hundred more feet to the next trail on the right, which is also marked with a wooden sign. When the trail meets up with the wall, follow it to the left until you reach the first bolted line, which should be *Swap Meet*.

Bleed Like Me

Hurt

❶ **Bleed Like Me** 5.12b ★★★
This line is the leftmost on the wall before a large ampitheater. Climb past a dirty start to reach tough crimping through the first few bolts. Ease up for a bit, then bear down again at the last bolt. Currently there is a long runout between the last bolt and the chains. Another bolt may be added in the future.
65 ft. 9 bolts. *FA Blake Bowling, 2006*

❷ **Same Way** 5.11b ★★★
Next bolted line 20 feet right of *Bleed Like Me*. Pull past a sequence of large plates to a ledge. From the ledge, step up into pumpy pockets through a series of subtle bulges.
65 ft. 8 bolts. *FA Matt Tackett, Blake Bowling, 2006.*

❸ **Hurt** 5.10c ★★★
Begin on a boulder 50 feet right of the previous line. Climb around a large plate, which leads to pockets and edges on a more featured section of the wall.
65 ft. 8 bolts. *FA Blake Bowling, Matt Tackett, 2006.*

❹ **A Chip Off the Old Sturnum** 5.8 ★★
The right-facing dihedral around the corner from *Hurt*. Climb up to a ledge underneath a roof. Traverse underneath the roof via face holds, and continue up the crack to chain anchors. Be sure to inspect the anchor situation on this route before lowering. There has been a stress fracture surrounding them for a few years.
80 ft. *FA Jason Haas, Sarah Maclean, 2005.*

❺ **Darwin Loves You** 5.9+ ★★★
This is the next bolted line 100 feet right of the dihedral. Begin with a reachy start, then continue up a short but fun face to a time-bomb clipping jug.
50 ft. 4 bolts. *FA Wes Allen, 2004.*

❻ **Johnny on Roofies** 5.11a ★★★
Move right from *Darwin Loves You* to the next bolted line. Pull a small opening roof to easy moves leading to a tricky bulge. Continue on incut shelves to the top.
65 ft. 6 bolts. *FA Unknown, 2004.*

Darwin Loves You

Donor

7 Donor 5.11b ★★★★

Pull a small opening roof in the center of the wall, just right of the previous routes start. Consistent climbing on crimps and plates, through a bulge midway, to sidepulls and open grips.

55 ft. 6 bolts. *FA Unknown, 2004.*

8 The Wal-Martification of Trad 5.8 ★★

Move right from the previous line, past a large crack in a corner, to this route, which begins as a finger crack and shares anchors with *Family Tradition*.

50 ft. *FA Steve Kaufmann, Jill Messer, 2004.*

9 Family Tradition 5.10b ★★

Move a few feet right from the previous crack climb to the next bolted line on the wall. It starts as a bolted crack, then leads to rounded bulges.

50 ft. 7 bolts. *FA Alex Yeakley, 2004.*

10 Tong Shing 5.10d ★★★★

Right of *Family Tradition* is this fun, bolted line on a featured face with grooves near the top.

55 ft. 6 bolts. *FA Andy Pense, Sam Watson, J.J., Jared Hancock, 2005.*

11 Anger Management 5.8+ ★★

The offwidth dihedral right of *Tong Shing*. Rap from a tree or walk off to the right.

65 ft. *FA Jason Haas, Sarah Maclean, 2005.*

12 Nice to Know You 5.10b ★★★★

This is the next bolted line right of *Anger Management*. Tiptoe past the first bolt, pull through the bulge, and launch into the slab moves and crimps. High quality, technical moves, interspersed with "thank you" pockets, keep the route interesting.

40 ft. 6 bolts. *FA John Bronaugh, Ryan Adams, 2004.*

Nice To Know You

⑬ Helping Hands 5.10d ★★★

Another fun line located right of *Nice to Know You*.
40 ft. 5 bolts. *FA John Bronaugh, Ryan Adams, 2004.*

⑭ Swap Meet 5.6 ★★

This short sport route is just right of *Helping Hands* on a corner. Climb past a dirty start, then continue up the face, passing a perfectly spherical hold along the way.
35 ft. 4 bolts. *FA Ryan Adams, Tina Bronaugh, 2004.*

⑮ Farley's Folley 5.10a ★★

Walk right from *Swap Meet* to the next bolted line, 10 feet left of *Haas Memorial Route*. Boulder out the roof to start, then move up to and out another roof on large holds.
40 ft. 5 bolts. *FA Curt Farley, 2007.*

⑯ The Haas Memorial Route 5.10a ★★★★

Walk right from *Swap Meet* to locate this excellent off-width dihedral. Start back in the cave and traverse out the roof crack to gain the wide dihedral. Leavittate up the offwidth to a ledge, then chimney to the top.
90 ft. *FA Jason Haas, Sarah Maclean, Mark Johnson, 2005.*

⑰ Stephanie's Cabaret 5.11c ★★

Walk right from *The Haas Memorial Route* to the next bolted line just before a cave. Climb through a dirty start, then crank through long moves and a couple of fingerlocks to the first set of anchors. The route continues to a second set of anchors.
50 ft. 6 bolts. *FA Joe Leismer, 2005.*

⑱ Four Shower Tokens, 5.8- ★★
a Guinness, and My Girl

Start back in the cave just right of *Stephanie's Cabaret*. Work up the face to gain the thin roof crack. Pull through a low crux, then enjoy large holds and ledges up the face. When you've had enough of the dihedral, bail to the right-leaning crack on the main face. Follow it to the anchors of *First Time*.
50 ft. *FA Mark Johnson, Jason Haas, 2005.*

⑲ Normalised Bramapithecus 5.10d ★★★★

Ascends the slightly overhanging face just right of the previous trad line. Reach high for the start holds, then surmount a roof to gain the face.
65 ft. 8 bolts. *FA Unknown.*

⑳ First Time 5.8+ ★★★

Walk 25 feet right from the previous line to this enjoyable route that ascends black rock just left of a corner. Begin on a boulder and climb through surprisingly good holds to the anchors.
50 ft. 5 bolts. *FA Bill Strachan, 2004.*

㉑ Generosity 5.10d ★★★

Just around the corner from *First Time*. Grab sandy holds to start and climb to a bulge. Crank over the lip and gain a stance. Continue up the slightly overhanging face, enjoying the improving quality of the rock with each move.
55 ft. 6 bolts. *FA Paul Vidal, 2005.*

LEFT FIELD

all day · 5 mins · 10 routes
5.6- .7 .8 .9 .10 .11 .12 .13 .14

Character

This small wall is signed off the main Sore Heel Hollow trail. It is just left of and around the corner from the Playground.

Directions

Park in the Sore Heel Hollow parking area (for details, see approach notes for the Gallery). Walk uphill on a cleared dirt road a few hundred feet to the marked trailhead on the right. Follow the trail for a few minutes and take a trail on your left signed Left Field.

❶ Lowered Expectations 5.5 ★★

See description opposite.

❷ Apoplectic Chick from Missouri 5.10b ★★★

Begin right and around the corner from the previous line and climb through an overhanging section to a blank face. Negotiate the blank section, then continue on larger holds to the anchors.
45 ft. 4 bolts. *FA John Bronaugh, 2004.*

❸ Autograph 5.11a ★★★

Begin a few feet right of the previous line. Climb to a large and comfy sidepull, then make a big move to a jug. Pump through the overhanging remainder past a couple of bulges to the anchors.
60 ft. 6 bolts. *FA John Bronaugh, 2004.*

❹ Come to Me, Marie 5.8

Walk right about 20 feet to a wide dihedral leading to a squeeze chimney. Stem the dihedral until you are forced to dive into the chimney. Descend from chains.
80 ft. *FA Mark Johnson, Jason Haas, Chris Nowak, 2005.*

❶ Lowered Expectations 5.5 ★★
As the approach trail meets the wall, walk left of the blunt arete a few feet to locate this line on a less-than-vertical face. Climb through large holds, angling right to the anchors. Chossy and dirty, but everyone does it. **45 ft. 5 bolts.** *FA John Bronaugh, 2004.*

❺ If Trango Could Whistle 5.8 ★
Locate a wide crack splitting the face 20 feet right of *Come to Me, Marie*. Ascend the crack using mainly face holds and the occasional chicken wing. Walk off left following the old pipelines down the slab.
100 ft. *FA Matt Tackett, Jason Haas, 2005.*

❻ Hopscotch 5.11a ★
Twenty feet right of the previous line is a slabby to vertical wall with numerous bulges. This is the first bolted line on the wall. Begin by climbing to a ledge 15 feet up, passing one bolt along the way. Climb the slab to a perplexing bulge near the top.
60 ft. 8 bolts. *FA John Bronaugh, 2004.*

❼ No Love for Charlie 5.10c ★★
Start the same as the previous line, but move right five feet once you reach the ledge. Fight the pump past sustained edge climbing to the anchors.
60 ft. 7 bolts. *FA John Bronaugh, 2004.*

❽ Jet Lag 5.9 ★★
Walk right from the previous lines under a large overhang to a set of three routes that begin on the right side of the overhang. This is the first route encountered and begins by climbing a fat flake leading to a small bulge. Pull the bulge and continue on big ledges to the anchors.
60 ft. 6 bolts. *FA Unknown.*

❾ Thru Space & Time 5.10a ★★★
Step right from the previous line a few feet uphill to locate the next bolted line, which begins beneath a small roof feature 10 feet up. Balance up to the feature, then tech your way up the remaining enjoyable face to the anchors.
65 ft. 8 bolts. *FA Unknown.*

❿ Jack Move 5.11b ★★
Move right from the previous line about 15 feet uphill to the next bolted line beginning with two slopey holds. Grab the slopers, find a foot, and move up left to a jug. Tiptoe up the face to a tough long move midway. Finesse a bulge, then run to the anchors on larger holds.
65 ft. 8 bolts. *FA Unknown.*

Terri Lloyd. Photo: Wes Allen.

THE PLAYGROUND

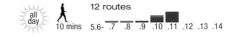

all day · 10 mins · 12 routes · 5.6- .7 .8 .9 .10 .11 .12 .13 .14

Character
The Playground is a small wall with several great short lines on nice orange-and-black rock. Bolted primarily by John Bronaugh before his passing in 2004, it was one of the last crags he developed. This is a fun area with good bolted moderates.

Approach
Park in the Sore Heel Hollow parking area (for details, see approach notes for the Gallery). Walk uphill on a cleared dirt road a few hundred feet to the marked trailhead on the right. Follow the trail for a few minutes and take a trail on your left signed "The Playground." The first route you reach is *Red Rover.*

Conditions
Routes 1-7 are sightly overhanging, so they stay fairly dry in the rain. Avoid 8-12 if is raining, as they are slabs. These routes get great sun.

❶ Red Rover 5.11b ★★
The first route encountered where the trail meets the wall. Pumpy sidepulls lead to anchors.
65 ft. 6 bolts. *FA John Bronaugh, 2004.*

❷ Steal the Bacon 5.11a ★★
Right of *Red Rover* is another bolted line. Climb up through some bulges to the anchors.
65 ft. 6 bolts. *FA John Bronaugh, 2004.*

❸ Chickenhawk 5.10d R ★★
Tough lead. Right of *Steal the Bacon* is an intermittent crack. Follow the crack, making liberal use of face holds along the way.
45 ft. *FA John Bronaugh, 2004.*

❹ Jungle Gym 5.10b ★★★
Move a few feet right from *Steal the Bacon* to locate this bolted line. Fun ending with a funky lip move.
50 ft. 4 bolts. *FA John Bronaugh, 2004.*

❺ Monkey Bars 5.10a ★★★★
This route begins just right of *Jungle Gym.* Climb up through nice pockets and jugs to big moves on steep rock toward the top.
50 ft. 5 bolts. *FA John Bronaugh, 2004.*

❻ Capture the Flag 5.11b ★★★★
This fun and powerful route begins just right of *Monkey Bars.* Climb through great moves on small edges and pockets to the anchors.
50 ft. 5 bolts. *FA John Bronaugh, 2004.*

❼ Crack the Whip 5.11d ★★★
This powerful crimpfest begins right of *Capture the Flag.*
50 ft. 5 bolts. *FA Jason Haas, 2004.*

❽ Octopus Tag 5.7 ★★★
On the right side of the main wall is a clean chimney. Climb the chimney to anchors. Despite appearances, no large gear is needed to protect the line.
60 ft. *FA Ryan Adams, 2004.*

❾ Balance Beam 5.11a ★★★★
Just right of *Octopus Tag* is a slabby section of the wall. This is the first bolted line on the wall. Climb the technical slab to anchors.
65 ft. 7 bolts. *FA John Bronaugh, 2004.*

❿ Teeter Totter 5.11c ★★★★
This is the second route from the left on the slab wall. Sustained and desperate edging leads to the anchors.
65 ft. 8 bolts. *FA John Bronaugh, 2004.*

⓫ Slide 5.9 ★★★
This is the second-to-last route from the left on the slab wall. Start down the hill a bit from *Teeter Totter.* Climb reachy moves through knobs and edges to the anchors.
65 ft. 8 bolts. *FA Bob Matheny, 2004.*

⓬ Tire Swing 5.10a ★★★
This is the furthest right route on the slab wall, just right of *Slide,* and has a bouldery, somewhat chossy start. Climb the slab to the anchors.
70 ft. 8 bolts. *FA Ryan Adams, 2004.*

SHADY GROVE

 p.m. shade OK in rain 15 mins

16 routes

5.6- .7 .8 .9 .10 .11 .12 .13

Character
Shady Grove is located a short way beyond and around the corner from the Playground. It offers long, steep, pocketed climbs of varying difficulty. *Citizen's Arete* and *Girls Gone Wild ...WOO!* have quickly become popular moderate lines on the wall.

Approach
Park in the Sore Heel Hollow parking area (for details, see approach notes for the Gallery). Walk uphill on a cleared dirt road a few hundred feet to the marked trailhead on the right. Follow the trail for a few minutes, past the Playground, and take a trail on your left signed "Shady Grove."

Conditions
Shady Grove was named for obvious reasons. It offers good relief from the hot Kentucky sun during the summer. Although the routes have been around for several years now there still may be some questionable rock on a few of them, so climb with caution.

❶ Citizen's Arete 5.11b ★★★
This route begins just right of the obvious arete on the left side of the wall. Climb the face until you run out of holds, then make a big move left to the arete. Make another big move, then ride the arete to the anchors.
60 ft. 6 bolts. *FA Shannon Stuart-Smith, 2004.*

❷ Girls Gone Wild ... WOO! 5.10d ★★★
Step five feet right from *Citizen's Arete* to locate this route. Grab a shelf and pull up and through a bulge. Continue up the face, staying just right of a flake. Photo overleaf.
60 ft. 6 bolts. *FA Terry Kindred, 2004.*

❸ Crucify Me 5.11c ★★★
Step 10 feet right from *Girls Gone Wild* and look for a high first bolt. Climb up the steep face, making use of jugs and hidden pockets along the way. Tackle the crux toward the top and finish off on jugs to the anchors.
70 ft. 6 bolts. *FA Terry Kindred, 2004.*

❹ Who Knows? 5.11d ★★
This route is located 20 feet right of *Crucify Me*. Climb steep rock for two bolts to gain a large ledge. Continue up past a fat flake to another ledge then up steeper rock to the anchors.
70 ft. 8 bolts. *FA Blake Bowling, 2004.*

❺ Which is Which? 5.11c ★★
Step 10 feet right of *Who Knows*. Crank through a steep start to a hand ledge. Continue up a more vertical face to the overhanging headwall. Conquer the headwall and clip the chains.
70 ft. 8 bolts. *FA Chris Martin, 2004.*

❻ Who is Who? 5.11d ★★★
Start five feet right of *Which is Which?* on the same steep section of the wall. Crank through four bolts of pocket pulling to gain a vertical section. Climb past the vertical section, then deal with steepening rock to the anchors.
70 ft. 9 bolts. *FA Blake Bowling, 2004.*

❼ Coming Out Party 5.11d ★★★
This unique line is located 25 feet right of *Who is Who?*, just past an overhanging crack in a dihedral. Boulder out extremely steep rock to gain a large ledge. Climb the overhanging face past a few pods along the way.
75 ft. 9 bolts. *FA Shannon Stuart-Smith, 2004.*

❽ Far From God 5.12b ★★★★
Shares the first bolt of *Coming Out Party*. Power out the start of *Coming Out Party* to gain a ledge. Then veer right and climb the sustained, overhanging face to anchors.
75 ft. 8 bolts. *FA Chris Martin, 2004.*

❾ False Idol 5.12b ★★★
Walk 30 feet right from *Far From God* to locate this route. Boulder out a steep, pocketed start to gain a ledge. Continue up the sustained, overhanging face to the anchors.
90 ft. 10 bolts. *FA Blake Bowling.*

❿ Irreverent C 5.12b ★★
Just right of the previous route is a hueco 25 feet up. This route begins just left of the hueco and meets up with a water groove toward the top.
90 ft. 8 bolts. *FA Shannon Stuart-Smith.*

⓫ Imagine There's No Heaven
This **closed project** takes on the next line of bolts to the right of *Irreverent C*. Please do not climb on it until it has been done.
90 ft. 8 bolts.

⓬ Taste the Rainbow 5.13a ★★★
Walk right from *Imagine There's No Heaven* to locate this extremely overhanging, adventurous line. If *Pile Driver* leaves a bad taste in your mouth, just taste the rainbow and you'll feel much better.
14 bolts. 100ft. *FA Bentley Bracket 2009.*
Equipped by Mark Stevenson.

Shady Grove right side

13 **Pile Driver** 5.12d ★
Put your beer goggles on for this one! Next line right of *Taste the Rainbow*. Climb through several epoxied jugs and botched bolt placements to the chains.
11 bolts. 80 feet. *Equipped by Mark Stevenson. FA Greg Kerzhner, 2008.*

14 **Listerine Girl** 5.9
Walk right from *Pile Driver* and head uphill about 30 feet to locate this line.Climb to a dish then move out onto a tongue feature before tackling the roof. Finish on a well-featured slab to the chains.
75 ft. 9 bolts. *FA Jason Burton, Ron Snider, Ben Cassel, 2006.*

15 **Shaved Squirrel** 5.10d ★★★
Up the steep hill from *Listerine Girl* is a flat spot with two routes. This is the left route. Begin with a thin start, then move up into a good stance on the left side of a large hueco. Leave the comfort zone by tiptoeing left onto the face where the holds disappear and the climbing gets tough. Make a few thin moves, then enjoy larger holds all the way to the chains.
60 ft. 7 bolts. *FA Ron Snider, Brian Clark, Jason Burton, 2006.*

16 **Street Fight** 5.10a ★★★
Shares the beginning moves of *Shaved Squirrel* but heads right from the hueco out into the business. Pull a few delicate moves, then run to the chains on Disneyland jugs.
65 ft. 6 bolts. *FA Ron Snider, Jason Burton, James Street, 2006.*

Citizen's Arete

BRONAUGH WALL

a.m. | shade | 15 mins | OK in rain

9 routes

5.6- .7 .8 .9 .10 .11 .12 .13 .14

Character

This small wall is situated between Shady Grove and Purgatory. Right off the trail, *Jingus* and *Collision Damage* are good warm-ups for the harder lines at Purgatory. A few must-do lines exist at this wall, including *Little Teapot*, *Belly of the Beast*, and *Like a Turtle*. Each climbs completely differently, yet are within several feet of each other.

Approach

Follow the approach to Shady Grove, but continue along the main trail a few minutes until you see the wooden sign marking the trail to Bronaugh Wall on the left. The trail heads slightly uphill and wraps around the cliff ending just beneath *Little Teapot*.

Conditions

This wall faces east, making for a good summer retreat in the afternoon. The overhanging section of the wall is quite steep and routes 3-6 stay dry in the rain.

❶ Unnamed Grade Unknown
This route is currently a closed project and still in the state of being bolted. It is the first line encountered on the left side of the wall. Don't count on it being bolted any time soon since it has been in the project state for over 5 years.
50 ft.

❷ Little Teapot 5.12a ★★★★
This fun little line takes on the short black face that begins on a high sloping ledge. Reach through a series of crimp ledges to a bouldery crux just before the anchors.
45 ft. 3 bolts. *FA Blake Bowling, 2005.*

❸ Jingus 5.11b ★★★★
Move right from the previous line about 15 feet to the first line on the overhanging section of the wall. Pull through the steep beginning, then continue up on coarse pinches and ledges to the anchors.
55 ft. 7 bolts. *FA Alex Yeakley, 2004.*

❹ Collision Damage 5.11d ★★★
Move right to the next line. Pump through pinches and pockets to reach the more vertical and slightly licheny finish.
50 ft. 6 bolts. *FA John Bronaugh, 2004.*

❺ Crumblies 5.12a
Step about five feet right from the previous line to locate this adventure. Shoot for a high pinch to start, then move up to a 50-pound flake waiting to blow. Tread lightly around the flake, then continue up the right-angling face on holds that magically disappear when you're done or while you are using them.
55 ft. 7 bolts. *FA John Bronaugh, 2004.*

❻ Belly of the Beast 5.12c ★★★★
This is the fifth line from the left side of the wall and the last line on this section of the wall. Begin under a roof and yard out on jugs to gain the overhanging face. Climb through long moves on good holds to a well-defined crux. Keep it together for the rest of the route because it ain't over.
60 ft. 9 bolts. *FA Shannon Stuart-Smith, 2005.*

❼ Two Women Alone 5.11a ★★★
From *Belly of the Beast*, step down to the other side of the wall to locate this and the next route. Climb through thin holds and plates on a vertical wall.
50 ft. 7 bolts. *FA Julia Fain, 2005.*

❽ Like a Turtle 5.11b ★★★★
Move down the hill 15 feet right from *Two Women Alone*. Boulder through the start on thin incuts to reach a series of large plates. Ponder the moves on the thin face from the last jug, then shoot for the iron oxide turtle head feature. Navigate through long reaches to a welcoming jug at the anchors.
55 ft. 7 bolts. *FA Julia Fain, 2005.*

❾ Unnamed 5.10d R ★★★
Climb the face just right of the previous line. Begin by climbing through a plated bulge to reach an intermittent crack, which increases in protectability near the top. Lower from chain anchors.
55 ft. *FA Shannon Stuart-Smith, 2005.*

Callie Rennison on *Girl's Gone Wild ... WOO!* 5.10d, Shady Grove, previous spread. Photo: Wes Allen.

Little Teapot   2

7   8

Like a Turtle

PURGATORY

 a.m. OK in rain 15 mins

21 routes

5.6- .7 .8 .9 .10 .11 .12 .13 .14

Character

Purgatory has some excellent, difficult sport lines including one of the toughest in the Red, *Lucifer*. During the winter of 2006, Canadian Mike Doyle spent several weeks working *Lucifer*, a severely overhanging power-endurance climb that had been an open project before his send. On the last day of his trip, he sent the line and rated it 5.14c. During the same period, Kenny Barker sent the extension to his already difficult *Paradise Lost*, which he named *Paradise Regained*. It was a good winter for Purgatory, which now hosts some of the hardest new and challenging lines in the Red. 5.13b seems to be the popular grade at this wall, but don't expect them all to come easy as each one packs a powerful series of cruxes.

Directions

Purgatory is the last cliff on the main Sore Heel trail. To reach it, park in the main Sore Heel parking area and walk up a dirt road past the kiosk. Take a small trail on the right, which leads up to the main trail. Turn left on the main trail, then hike for about 10 minutes, passing Left Field, the Playground, Shady Grove, and Bronaugh Wall. Continue past Bronaugh Wall for a few more minutes on the main trail and look for the next trail on the left, which leads slightly uphill to Purgatory.

Routes 1-4 are located left of the arch leading to the main wall.

❶ Butterfly Gangbang 5.8+ ★★

Just before going through the arch to reach the main sport routes of *Purgatory*, walk left 50 feet to locate this left-leaning flake that starts as a hand crack and has a tree 50 feet up on a ledge. Climb the widening hand crack, past the tree, to the top of the cliff. Rap from a tree to descend.
80 ft. *FA Matt Tackett, Jason Haas, 2005.*

❷ Looking Through the 5.6 ★★
Devil's Window

This wide, left-leaning ramp up a green face begins 30 feet left of *Butterfly Gangbang*. Layback up the clean crack to bolted anchors near the entrance of a cave.
40 ft. *FA Jason Haas, Matt Tackett, 2005.*

❸ Mist of Funk 5.10b ★★★

Walk 30 feet left of *Looking Through the Devil's Window* to a left-facing dihedral with two roofs. Boulder up to a ledge, then layback up and around the first roof to a no-hands rest in a large hueco. Continue to a higher ledge and belay. Tackle the surprisingly short second roof and top out.
90 ft. *FA Jason Haas, Matt Tackett, 2005.*

❹ Skunk Love 5.11b ★★★★

Move 20 feet left of *Mist of Funk* to this excellent slab. Begin in a wide crack, then tiptoe onto the face to encounter a difficult crux. Continue up the quality rock, negotiating more funkified moves along the way.
65 ft. 8 bolts. *FA Kipp Trummel, 2006.*

The remaining routes are located on the main wall, which is accessed by walking through the small arch.

❺ Believer 5.11b ★★★★

This is the first bolted route encountered after walking through the arch. Look to your left 10 feet after you walk through the arch for a face with a few bolted lines. Climb finger pockets to a sit-down rest, then take on the overhanging headwall above.
60 ft. 6 bolts. *FA Tony Reynaldo, 2005.*

❻ Special Boy 5.11c ★★★★

Move right from *Believer* to the next bolted line. Begin with a thin start, which leads to better holds and fun climbing with a nice hueco rest midway. Keep it together for the long run to the anchors.
75 ft. 7 bolts. *FA Kenny Barker, 2004.*

❼ Fallen Angel 5.11c ★★★

Locate a beautiful crack splitting the face right of the previous lines. Crank through sporty moves to reach an expanding right-facing dihedral near the top, which offers a bit of relief. Rap anchors. Bouldery.
70 ft. *FA: Kenny Barker, 2004.*

❽ Gluttony 5.12a ★★★★

Step right from *Fallen Angel* to locate this bolted line. Climb up a slab and crack, then move out onto the face at the third bolt. Crank through a shoulder-busting move to gain better holds. Continue up the overhanging face on perfect pockets to reach the vertical run to the anchors.
75 ft. 5 bolts. *FA Kenny Barker, 2005.*

ARE YOU A BADASS?

Well come on, prove it. Below is a list of the Red's most outstanding open projects. Each of these lines are impressive, proud… and desperate. Many have tried, but no one has delivered the right combination of power, precision, and passion. Could you be the one?

• **Line left of Take That Katie Brown**, page 351, Motherlode

• **Honeycomb**, page 364, Chocolate Factory

• **Iron Mike**, page 321, the Shire

• **Van Der Waals Goo**, page 216, Boneyard

• **Vader Project**, page 288, Darkside

Peter is. Photo Dawn Kish.

⑨ Fat Man's Misery 5.4 ★★

Climb the start of *Gluttony* to a ledge and build a belay. Crawl through the cave on the belay ledge for 30 feet to reach the anchors of *Looking Through the Devil's Window* on the opposite side of Purgatory and rappel. Bring a #5 Camalot for the belay.
40 ft. *FA Jason Haas, Matt Tackett, 2005.*

⑩ The Proverbial Donkey 5.11a R ★

Start in an alcove 20 feet left of *Dracula*, behind a large boulder. Work up the face to gain a fist crack in a roof. Be careful not to fall as you have a good chance of hitting the boulder beneath. The second is also in danger of swinging into the boulder, as it isn't possible to protect the low section. Work up the crack system, over several ledges, to reach a comfy belay ledge directly under a 15-foot roof. Bail out here for a higher quality climb at 5.10b R, or continue out the roof on shaky jams and bad feet to chain anchors just past the lip of the roof.
100 ft. *FA Jason Haas, Jordan Wood, 2005.*

Fallen Angel

⓫ Dracula '04 5.13b ★★★★★ ☐
Move right from *The Proverbial Donkey* to the next
bolted line, marked by a sharp corner. Power through
the initial technical and brutal moves to reach a decent
clipping hold. Climb a crack for a few feet, then bust left.
Hold your breath for the clip, then make your way to
the next bolt. Recharge for the long run to the anchors.
Great climbing!
60 ft. 6 bolts. *FA Kenny Barker, 2005.*

⓬ Lucifer 5.14c ★★★★★ ☐
This may well be the most difficult line at the Red. Begin
just right of *Dracula '04*. Climb relatively easy moves to
the third bolt, then bust left through a v7 boulder problem to reach a quick shake at the fourth bolt. Recharge,
then boulder through a more difficult section to reach a
moderate rest at the fifth bolt. From the fifth, endure the
redpoint run to the break. At the break, ponder on what
a bad ass mofo you are, then finish it up.
100 ft. 9 bolts. *FA Mike Doyle, 2006.*

⓭ The Castle Has Fallen 5.13b ★★★★ ☐
Climb the first three bolts of *Lucifer,* then head straight
up the thin seam with a wicked-hard boulder problem
at the top.
60 ft. 6 bolts. *FA Unknown.*

⓮ Paradise Lost 5.13a ★★★★★ ☐
Formerly a 5.13b but the FA downgraded to 5.13a since
everyone was choosing to stand on the obvious ledge
which he avoided. Regardless this line is the must-do
route at Purgatory. It's a classic. Begin by climbing the
flake marking *The Castle Has Fallen* then traverse right
to reach a sit down rest on the notorious ledge or avoid
it for nostalgia. Recruit your fast twitch muscles to work
through powerful movements up the striking overhanging arête. Save a few grunts for the final crux after the
last clip.
65 ft. 6 bolts. *FA Kenny Barker, 2004.*

⓯ Paradise Regained 5.13b ★★★★ ☐
From the anchors of *Paradise Lost,* continue up the
sustained and overhanging headwall. 70-meter rope
necessary. Stiff for the grade!
40 ft. 5 bolts. *FA Kenny Barker, 2006.*

⓰ Hellraiser 5.12c ★★★★★ ☐
Walk right from *Paradise Lost* past a large amphitheater.
This is the next sport line and follows a distinct line of
pockets through grey rock. Climb through fragile holds
a few feet to reach a good hold. Reach hard through the
crux, then flow to the anchors on large holds.
65 ft. 7 bolts. *FA Kenny Barker, 2005.*

⓱ The Gimp 5.10a ★★★ ☐
Walk right from *Hellraiser* to the next bolted line. Pull
on plates to reach a slab. Start up the vertical section,
then make a tricky move to the next clip. Continue on
larger holds to the anchors.
60 ft. 6 bolts. *FA Tony Renaldo, Drew, 2005.*

⓲ Back in the Days of Bold 5.11c R ★★★ ☐
Step right around the corner from *The Gimp* to locate
this broken finger crack. Work your way up the low finger
crack on the left, then boulder up and right to regain the
crack. Follow the flaring crack until it ends, then friction
on an easy but sparsely protected slab to the chains.
85 ft. *FA Jason Haas, Matt Tackett, 2005.*

⓳ Jumbo Shrimp 5.10a ★ ☐
To the right of *The Gimp* starts a slightly dirty route
that moves up through some technical vertical face and
surmounts a small bulge before continuing on big holds
to chain anchors.
50 ft. 5 bots. *FA Tony Renaldo, 2008.*

⓴ The Seventh Circle of Dante 5.10a R ★ ☐
Walk 60 feet right of the previous crack to find this route
at the end of the ledge. Start in a large hueco and climb
the face to a wide crack. Work up the crack until it flares,
then fades. Protect out of a pocket and continue up the
slab to reach a rappel tree.
65 ft. *FA Jason Haas, Sarah Maclean, 2005.*

Dracula 04

WHAT ABOUT BOB WALL

   p.m. | shade | 5 mins

29 routes
5.6- .7 .8 .9 .10 .11 .12 .13 .14

Character

What About Bob Wall is the easily accessible stretch of cliffline situated above the main Sore Heel Parking area. A unique blend of lines can be found on this cliff, from man-eating roof cracks to calf-blowing slabs. Most of the bolted lines are from slabbly to slightly overhanging, so don't go here expecting typical steep, pumpy pocket climbing.

Approach

From the main Sore Heel Parking Area, walk south (opposite the main road leading to the Gallery) toward the edge of the parking lot, near a stream, to locate a trail leading off to the right (west) into the woods. The trail that immediately crosses a wooden footbridge heading east onto a wide dirt road leads to Rival and Courtesy Walls. The What About Bob Wall trail is opposite that trail. Follow the trail for about five minutes, crossing a small stream along the way, until the trail heads uphill and forks near a large boulder directly in front of the cliff. Routes 1-16 can be found by taking the right fork uphill about 30 feet. The remainder of the routes are just left of the large boulder.

Conditions

This wall faces mainly northwest to west, so expect a mixture of shade and afternoon sun.

❶ Pongosapien 5.11d ★★★★

As the approach trail meets the main wall near a large boulder, the trail forks left and right. If you take the right fork and head up to the cliff about 30 more feet you will arrive beneath a cluster of three cracks (routes 5-8). Left of these cracks is a ramp leading to a ledge. *Pongosapien* is the leftmost bolted line on this ledge. Climb to a low ledge, grab a flake, and dig through your bag of tricks to reach a pair of small crimps on the face. Crimp hard for a few bolts, then relax on easier fun climbing, passing through a body-sized hueco just before the chains.
50 ft. 6 bolts. *FA Kipp Trummel, 2008.*

❷ Gild the Lily (Closed Project) ★★★

Right of *Pongosapien* is another crimpfest on black rock. Currently a closed project. Grade is unknown.
50 ft. 5 bolts.

❸ Running in Place (Open Project) ★★★

Right of the previous line is a crack system leading to a vertical face. Begin by climbing the crack, clip a bolt, then plug gear up to a bulge where the crack ends and the face climbing begins. Grade is unknown. Open project.
40 ft. 3 bolts. *Equipped by Kipp Trummel in 2008.*

❹ Hirsute (Open Project) ★★★

This is the next bolted route right of *Running in Place*. Begin on large holds and make a few long moves to reach a three-bolt blank section. Have fun figuring it out. Open project.
60 ft. 8 bolts. *Equipped by Kipp Trummel in 2008.*

Maximus

❺ Gluteus 5.9 ★★

Move right from *Hirsute* to the leftmost crack of a trio. Climb an offwidth pod to a wide hand crack and improvise a way down.
45 ft. *FA Jason Haas, Matt Tackett, 2006.*

❻ Maximus 5.9 ★

This is the middle crack. Climb a hand crack in a right facing dihedral over a few ledges to a fixed piece. Lower from fixed anchors.
40 ft. *FA Jason Haas, Matt Tackett, 2006.*

Carlo Nasisse on *Mosaic* 5.12c, The Gallery, page 294. Photo Dan Brayack.

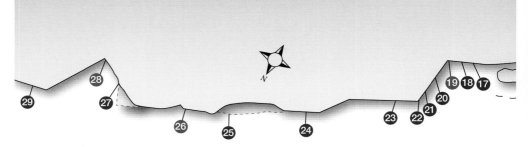

7 Hole 5.8 ★★

This is the rightmost crack. Begin in a wide, left-facing dihedral that quickly pinches down. Ascend the arching crack to the shared anchors of *Maximus*.
40 ft. *FA Matt Tackett, Jason Haas, 2006.*

8 Optical Rectitus 5.11a ★★★★

This is the bolted line just right of the previous cracks. Climb the blunt arete, making use of what little holds it has to offer.
50 ft. 6 bolts. *FA Matt Tackett, Aaron Tackett, Amy Tackett, Steph Meadows, Morgain Sprague, 2006.*

9 Tumble Dry Low 5.12b ★★★★

From the previous lines walk right to a scramble with a fixed rope. Scramble up to the ledge then walk left to the end of the ledge to reach the start of this line. Crimp up the vertical face past some tough moves.
45 ft. *FA Kipp Trummel, Matt Tackett 2008.*

10 Weathertop Stings 5.10b ★★

Next line right of *Tumble Dry Low* and also begins on the ledge. Grab a high iron oxide ledge, then scoot out left. Head up on friable holds to the chains located just above a large hueco. Currently there is a set of anchors just right of this line that may evolve into a route by the time this guide is released.
45 ft. 5 bolts. *FA Matt Tackett, Jared Hancock, Jeremy Egleston, Don McGlone, 2006.*

11 Tobacco Crack Ho 5.8 ★

This line ascends the face 20 feet right of *Weathertop Stings*, making use of natural protection. Climb pockets to a fragile ledge, then step right to get a placement. Move left at the top to belay and rap from bolted anchors.
45 ft. *FA Don McGlone, Jeremy Egleston, 2006.*

12 Stem Cell 5.10a ★★

This is the next bolted line 25 feet right of *Tobacco Crack Ho*. Stem between the boulder and face or traverse in from the left to start. Continue up the arete while occasionally sneaking out left onto the featureless black rock when you need to clip bolts.
55 ft. 4 bolts. *FA Don McGlone, Jeremy Egleston, 2006.*

13 Cultural Wasteland 5.9 ★★

Walk right from *Stem Cell* to locate this short, fun crack.
35 ft. *FA Jason Haas, Jeremy Egleston, Jared Hancock, Don McGlone, Matt Tackett, 2006.*

14 Threat Level Blue 5.9 ★★

Move right from *Cultural Wasteland* to the next short, bolted line. Pull over a low overhang at the start to reach a high jug. Leave the comfort of the jug behind for the funk movement that lies ahead. Make a committing move to clip the chains, then move left for better quality routes.
35 ft. 3 bolts. *FA Jared Hancock, Don McGlone, Jeremy Egleston, Matt Tackett, 2006.*

15 Stuck Buckeye 5.8 ★★

Hike right from the previous lines about 200 yards to locate two enormous roof cracks about 40 feet apart. This line tackles the left roof crack. Climb hands to a squeeze chimney in an overhanging dihedral. If you don't get stuck, rap from a tree to descend. Otherwise wait for the buzzards.
75 ft. *FA Ken Thompson, 2006.*

16 Farewell Drive 5.11a ★★★
with a Spit in the Eye

This is the right roof crack. Work up the initial handjams and maneuver yourself into the chimney. Carefully traverse the roof until you can turn the lip. Rap from a tree to descend.
50 ft. *FA Jason Haas, Matt Tackett, 2006.*

The following routes are reached by taking the left fork near a large boulder in the approach trail.

17 Project 5.12+/5.13- ★★★★

As the approach trail meets the main wall near a large boulder, the trail forks left and right. If you take the left fork, this is the first bolted slab line just past a large boulder. Currently an open project.
80 ft. 9 bolts.

18 Kentucky Flu 5.10c ★★★★

Begin 15 feet left of the previous line. Edge up to a large hueco, then shift left out onto the face to begin this enjoyable ride. Tiptoe up the left edge of a water groove on little black knobs and the occasional incut crimp. Pull onto a large ledge near the top and scramble up and left for the chains. Make sure to turn around and soak in the view.
80 ft. 9 bolts. *FA Matt Tackett, Don McGlone, 2005.*

19 Adventures of the Leper Nurse 5.9 ★★★

Twenty-five feet left of *Kentucky Flu* is an obvious clean dihedral. Fight to the top and lower from anchors.
50 ft. *FA Matt Tackett, Jeremy Egleston, 2005.*

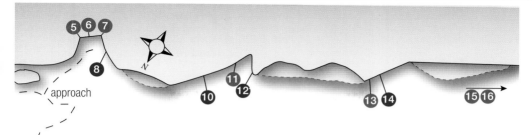

Code Red

20 **Code Red** 5.12d ★★★★
This line takes on the vertical face 10 feet left of the dihedral. Bust through the blank start and keep it together for the next few bolts. Bring lots of shoe rubber.
80 ft. 9 bolts. *FA Kevin Todd, 2005.*

21 **Duputyren's Release** 5.12b ★★★★
10 feet left of *Code Red* is another spectacular face climb.
80 ft. 9 bolts. *Equipped by Kipp Trummel. FA Justin Riddel, Colleen Reed, 2009.*

22 **GSW** 5.12a ★★★★
This line ascends the slabby arete 10 feet left of the previous line.
80 ft. 9 bolts. *FA Brad Weaver, Eric Heuermann, 2006.*

Kentucky Flu

28

27

Brothel Doc

23 **Drip Wire** 5.11a ★★★

Move 20 feet left from the arete to the next bolted line, which has a high first bolt. Climb through a slightly dirty start to reach a roof. Hyper-extend or heel-hook and lock-off to surmount the roof. Claw up to the chains on small to non-existent edges.
7 bolts. 80 ft. *FA Kipp Trummel, 2005*

24 **Dr. Synchro (Project)** 5.12a ★★★

Move left from *Drip Wire* to locate this bolted slab line with long, difficult movements. Grade is an estimate.
95 ft. 13 bolts. *Equipped by Matt Tackett.*

25 **No Sleep Till Campton** 5.10c ★★★★

Walk left 70 feet from *Dr. Synchro* until you reach a dip in the trail. This sport route starts when the trail starts back up hill, and just above a low overhang. Traverse in from the left and make a long move to reach a jug. Continue up the vertical face, passing through a couple of long reach moves to decent-sized holds. Midway up, enjoy the change in scenery when the rock becomes orange and pockety for a few moves. Reach far left to a crack, which will lead you to a well-deserved monster jug beneath a roof. Heave over the roof and enjoy the grand finale of fun moves to the chains.
80 ft. 11 bolts. *Don Mcglone, Matt Tackett, 2005.*

26 **Alternative Medicines** 5.7 ★★★

Twenty-five feet left of *No Sleep Till Campton* is this long and enjoyable crack system. Shares anchors with *No Sleep Till Campton.*
75 ft. *FA Matt Tackett, Jeremy Egleston 2005*

27 **Brothel Doc** 5.11a ★★

Walk left about 100 feet until you reach an overhanging, featured arete where the trail heads sharply uphill. This line begins 15 feet left of the arete. Stick clip the first bolt and begin with a bouldery start, then enjoy the tricky moves that follow. The first set of anchors is for *Kindred Spirits;* this sport line goes to the top.
75 ft. 10 bolts. *Matt Tackett, Amy Tackett, Jason Haas, 2006.*

28 **Kindred Spirits** 5.11a ★★

Inside the cave 20 feet left of *Brothel Doc* is a wide crack that gradually pinches down as you near the lip. Work out the dihedral and roof to a no-hands rest in a pod. Emerge from the pod to a handcrack that leads to bolted anchors.
60 ft. *FA Jason Haas, Matt Tackett, Terry Kindred, 2006.*

29 **Bowling Pain** 5.11c ★★★

Move 50 feet left of *Brothel Doc* to the next bolted line. Climb a slab past a small roof at the third bolt. Continue up and over a right-angling arete to take on a heavily featured overhanging headwall.
80 ft. 10 bolts. *Blake Bowling, 2006.*

Kipp and Karen.
Photo Kipp Trummel collection.

KIPP TRUMMEL

PROFILE: The guy with the drill

It's rare that we know who the first ascensionist of a route if we haven't seen some super-human rock star's thwarted attempts at it in the latest Dosage video. Even more rare is knowing who took time away from climbing to jug up and down the ropes to drill and bolt the routes we love to play on. But if you bolt enough quality lines, people will eventually catch on to who you are and may even thank you for what you're doing. Kipp Trummel has done just that. During the past five years, Kipp has bolted nearly 80 lines including classics such as *Amarillo Sunset, Samurai, Iniquity,* and *Zendebad*.

Kipp, with his wife Karen, moved to Lexington, KY, from Illinois in 2005 and immediately jumped into the bolting scene with his first route in the Red, *Supress the Rage*. Immediately afterwards he was greeted by the late and colorful local legend, Terry Kindred, who asked him, "what's up with the crappy anchor placement?" Not long after that incident Kipp had one of his red-tagged projects snagged by a local (which turned out to be a misunderstanding). It wasn't a great introduction to developing in the Red, but Kipp's thick skin helped him to shrug it off and keep drilling away.

Kipp's biggest task was in the winter of 2007 when Rick Weber, the owner of Muir Valley, offered to provide all of the hardware if Kipp would put some routes up at what came to be known as *Midnight Surf*.

Not many people would jump at the "opportunity" to bolt a north-facing, severely overhanging wall using mostly glue-in bolts in the dead of winter. After 80 hours in a matter of a few weeks, and a near miss when descending a rope which had turned into an ice-covered deathtrap, Kipp had bolted some of the most unique and classic new routes in the Red. But if you look at the first ascensionists of these routes you'll notice Kipp is only on one of them. Why? Because Kipp is known to give his buddies a shot at his routes even if he's close to sending them. It is apparent that his joy comes from envisioning and bolting the line, and, in the words of Kipp, "leave the sending to those who actually train."

Most people say route developers only bolt for themselves and other climbers just reap the benefits of their selfish endeavors. Kipp is the exception. He bolts routes as a creative outlet with no regard for whether the line is within his ability or not. So if you're ever out climbing and hear the sound of a hammer drill and the clank of a five-piece Rawl being pounded into sandstone, stroll on over and drop a six pack of Avalanche Ale at the base of the static line and yell thanks to the guy with the drill. ∎

RIVAL WALL

 p.m. shade 🚶 5 mins

10 routes

5.6- .7 .8 .9 .10 .11 .12 .13 .14

Character:

Situated between Courtesy Wall and What About Bob Wall, and just uphill from the main trail, Rival Wall is definitely worth a visit. *Lobster Claw* is an excellent pumper guaranteed to make your forearms explode. Just left of the main approach trail are the long and surprisingly moderate sport lines *Delayed Gratification* and *Hatfield*.

Approach:

From the Sore Heel parking lot, cross the footbridge on the left to reach a wide dirt road. Follow the road uphill and take the first trail to the right. The cliff is about 50 feet uphill from the main trail. Lines 1-8 are to the right of the approach trail; the remaining lines are just left of where the approach trail meets the cliff.

Conditions:

This wall, as others on this side of the Sore Heel parking area, is north- to northwest-facing, so expect shade or some afternoon sun. The corridor containing *Lobster Claw* and the project to its left is a great shady spot in the summer. Most of the sport lines stay dry in a light rain.

Epic Indicator

Monobrow

❶ Epic Indicator 5.9+ R ★★

Walk right 100 feet from where the approach trail meets the cliff, then take the left trail, which leads to a ledge. Walk out onto the ledge to the left of the following two sport lines to locate a short, overhanging hand crack that starts about five feet off the deck. Work up the crux hand crack and onto the face above on good holds. Continue to work up the crack with questionable gear to the top of the wall. Rap from tree to descend.
70 ft. *FA Matt Tackett, Jason Haas 2006.*

❷ Rorschach Inkblot Test 5.8+ ★★

This is the first bolted line right of the approach trail and is located just right of *Epic Indicator*. Begin on a ledge and surmount the low overhang, making use of whichever holds you can find. Continue on larger holds to the anchors.
50 ft. 5 bolts. *FA Yasmeen Fowler, Don McGlone, JATD crew 2006.*

❸ Monobrow 5.10a ★★★

Move a few feet right from *Rorschach Inkblot Test* to the next bolted line, just left of an arete. Climb the face, making use of the arete when you're at a loss for holds.
50 ft. 5 bolts. *FA Brad Combs, Don McGlone, JATD crew 2006.*

❹ The Cheerleader Catch 5.6 X ★★

This is the wide, left-facing dihedral just right of *Monobrow*. Chimney up the dihedral to an anchor at the top. Fiddle in a small cam or nut at about one-third height, then run it to the top. Top out or lower from the anchors on *Monobrow*.
55 ft. *FA Jason Haas, Matt Tackett 2006.*

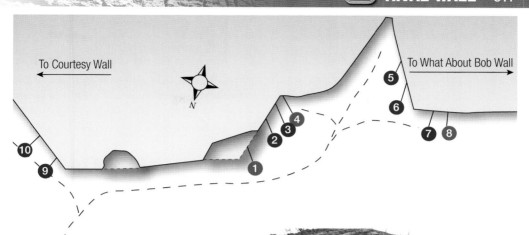

Hatfield

⑤ **Cork Eye** 5.12a ★★★

Fifteen feet right from *Cheerleader Catch* is a corridor. On the right side of the corridor is a pocketed and slightly overhanging face, which hosts this and the following sport lines.
55 ft. 7 bolts. *FA Kipp Trummel, 2007.*

⑥ **Lobster Claw** 5.12a ★★★★

Move a few feet right from *Cork Eye* to the next bolted line. Begin just right of a low hueco. Climb large pockets to reach the first bolt, then precisely stab your way through tiny pockets to a breather near the top. Don't get too confident because you still have to make it to the chains.
55 ft. 7 bolts. *FA Kipp Trummel 2006.*

⑦ **Days of Thunder** 5.9

Move right and just around the corner from *Lobster Claw* to the next bolted line. Climb a dirty start to gain better rock above. Take on a slopey crux near the top, then run it on jugs to the anchors.
60 ft. 5 bolts. *FA Mark Ryan, Jenny Ryan, Jared Hancock, Karla Hancock 2006*

⑧ **May as Well** 5.7

This line follows the crack system just right of *Days of Thunder.* Climb the initial wide crack that starts on top of a small roof, then traverse left to another crack. Work up the cracks and pods to a ledge with several small trees. Continue up to a higher ledge and larger trees to rappel, or bail from the anchors on *Days of Thunder.*
80 ft. *FA Matt Tackett, Jason Haas 2006.*

The last two lines are located just left of where the approach trail meets the cliff.

⑨ **Delayed Gratification** 5.10c ★★★★

Step left a few feet from the end of the approach trail to a tall wall with two bolted lines. This is the right line. Begin by climbing up to a right-leaning flake. Use the flake to reach up to a good edge, then skate up to a large horizontal. Continue up the face, staying just left of a blunt arete, making long moves between solid iron-oxide horizontals.
80 ft. 9 bolts. *FA Bram Bell, Bill Strachan, JATD crew 2006.*

⑩ **Hatfield** 5.10d ★★★★

Just left of *Delayed Gratification* is another long and sustained pumper. However, this one doesn't offer as many tasty iron oxide jugs. Your forearms might be screaming as you clip the chains.
80 ft. 9 bolts. *FA Jared Hancock, Matt Tackett 2006.*

COURTESY WALL p.m. shade 5 mins

12 routes

5.6- .7 .8 .9 .10 .11 .12 .13 .14

Character:

Located between the Shire and Rival Wall, Courtesy Wall contains some excellent bolted lines, a nice trad line, and a few projects that should end up being very difficult technical lines. The sport lines are not severely overhanging but still pack the power to deliver a wicked pump. If you want to test it out, jump on *Tweaked Unit*.

Approach:

From the Sore Heel parking lot, cross the foot bridge on the left to reach a wide dirt road. Follow the road past the first trail to the right (which leads to Rival Wall) and look for the next trail on the right. Follow the trail a short ways to reach the main wall near *Welcomed Guest*. This wall may also be reached by hiking 200 feet left from Rival Wall past a breakdown in the cliff.

Conditions:

This wall, as others on this side of the Sore Heel parking area, is north- to northwest-facing, so expect shade or some afternoon sun.

❶ Welcomed Guest 5.11d ★★★★
From the approach trail, walk right a few feet to reach an attractive wall with three sport lines. This is the first route encountered and begins on an arete. Climb the blank arete to a small, pocketed roof. Work over the roof then move up and right to the anchor.
85 ft. 10 bolts. *FA Jason Haas, 2006.*

❷ Wearing Out My Welcome 5.12a ★★★
Move 15 feet right from *Welcomed Guest* to the next line. Climb a technical face to reach a breather in a gigantic hueco. Continue up and right to reach an overhanging dihedral leading to the anchors.
80 ft. 8 bolts. *FA Jason Haas, 2006.*

❸ Go Home Yankee 5.12a ★★
This line ascends the overhanging arete 45 feet right of *Wearing Out My Welcome*.
75 ft. 7 bolts. *Matt Tackett, 2007.*

❹ Kiss It All Better 5.8 ★★
From the approach trail, walk left to locate this obvious, wide, right-facing dihedral. Climb through easy but slightly dirty climbing and enjoy a great view at the top. Rap from slings on a tree.
90 ft. *FA Dan Beck, Catherine Harrison, 2006.*

❺ STD 5.10a ★★★
Move left 20 feet around the corner from *Kiss It All Better* to a section of the wall hosting three sport lines. This is the right line. Climb large iron oxide jugs to a blank section. Make a long reach, then continue on with the reach and step routine.
70 ft. 7 bolts. *FA Sandy Davies, Tina Bronaugh, Dana Weller, 2006.*

❻ Tweaked Unit 5.11b ★★★★
This is the bolted line 10 feet left of *STD*. Begin with a high left sidepull and pull up to a couple of jugs. From the jugs, pull a tough move to get past a blank section. Enjoy the last few large holds as you approach the sequential pumpfest that lies ahead. Clip the chains from a big comfy hueco. As this route cleans up it will definitely earn another star.
70 ft. 9 bolts. *FA Wes Allen, Stephanie Meadows, JATD crew, 2006.*

❼ Aural Pleasure 5.11a ★★★
Shuffle 10 feet left of *Tweaked Unit* to the next sport line. Climb jugs up a left-leaning arete. At the third bolt, move sharply left into the business half of this route. Flexibility will help the shorties get through the well-defined crux.
70 ft. 7 bolts. *FA Wes Allen, JATD crew, 2006.*

❽ The Climbing Corpse Cometh 5.10d ★★★
Walk 70 feet left of *Aural Pleasure* to find this appealing finger-and-hand crack splitting the face next to a large black streak. Work your way up the initial grungy face to a large pod, then tackle the splitter crack. Lower from chains.
60 ft. *FA Jason Hass, Matt Tackett, Don McGlone, 2006.*

❾ Jackie the Stripper 5.12b ★★★
This line takes on the left-facing dihedral just left of *The Climbing Corpse Cometh*. Work through mellow moves, then let the stemming madness begin. Formerly an aid climb called *Zombie Sloth*. Lower from chain anchors to descend.
70 ft. 2 bolts. *FA John "Fred" Aragon, Mike Cole, 2006. FFA Jordan Wood, 2008.*

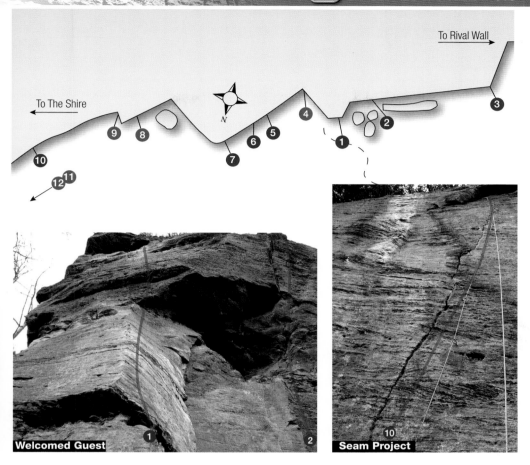

To Rival Wall

To The Shire

N

Welcomed Guest

Seam Project

The Climbing Corpse

⑩ Project 5.12+ ★★★

Walk 50 feet left from the previous line to locate this gently overhanging bolted seam. Project. **90 ft. 8 bolts.** *Equipped by Wes Allen.*

⑪ Trad is His Son 5.9 ★★

Walk left from the previous line about 150 to 200 feet until you reach a small dip in the trail. This line starts with a broken face and moves left into a right-leaning crack. Lower from bolted anchors near a small tree. **65 ft.** *FA Matt Tackett, Jeremy Egleston, 2006.*

⑫ And They Called It a Route 5.8

This discontinuous crack system begins about 20 feet left from *Trad is His Son.* Begin on iron-oxide jugs to gain a thin crack, which quickly fades. Traverse right to more cracks and fiddle in some gear. Pull a layback move to reach a ledge with anchors. The first ascentionists of this route do not provide a money-back guarantee. **50 ft.** *FA Matt Tackett, Jason Haas, 2006.*

THE SHIRE

p.m. shade 10 mins

13 routes

5.6- .7 .8 .9 .10 .11 .12 .13 .14

Character:
The Shire is a small wall containing a handful of decent moderates and a couple of tough lines.

Approach:
Follow the main dirt road that leads to Rival and Courtesy walls until the road narrows to more of a trail. Eventually you will reach a large fin-shaped boulder on the left, at which point the trail veers right and uphill to the main wall. Do not take the left fork at the large boulder.

Conditions:
The main wall, on which routes 1-7 are located, can be quite cold. As with most walls in this area, it is north- to northwest-facing, so expect a bit of afternoon sun.

❶ My Name is Earl 5.11d ★★★
As the approach trail nears the cliff you will see four bolted lines on a slightly overhanging plated face. This line ascends the short arete on the adjacent wall, just left of a dihedral. It's short, but give it a chance.
30 ft. 3 bolts. *FA Josh Thurston, 2007.*

❷ Pee-Wee 5.7 ★★
This is leftmost route on the main face and begins just left of a large rock shelter. Fun final moves!
35 ft. 4 bolts. *FA Ron Bateman, Josh Thurston, Betsey Adams, 2006.*

❸ Audie 5.8 ★★★
This route follows the line of bolts beginning just above the rock house. Start in the rock house or left of it, and traverse in to the first bolt. Continue on plates and pockets to the anchors.
35 ft. 4 bolts. *FA Ron Bateman, Jared Hancock, Matt Tackett, 2006.*

❹ Miranda Rayne 5.9 ★★★★
Move right a few feet from *Audie* to step it up a grade and gain some more height to the anchors.
60 ft. 7 bolts. *FA Ron Bateman, Eric Cox, 2006.*

❺ The G-Man 5.10c ★★★
Once you've graduated from the previous three lines, move right to take on the toughest line on the wall. Begin just left of an arete and stick clip the first bolt. Climb through pumpy moves on sloping pinches to the anchors.
40 ft. 6 bolts. *FA Ron Bateman, 2006.*

❻ Significant Other 5.10b ★★
Move right a few feet and around the corner from *The G-Man* to locate this and the next line. Climb a mossy start to gain a ledge, then continue up the fingery face to the anchors.
40 ft. 4 bolts. *FA Josh Thurston, Bob Peterson, 2006.*

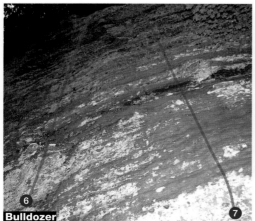

Bulldozer ❻ ❼

Iron Mike 9

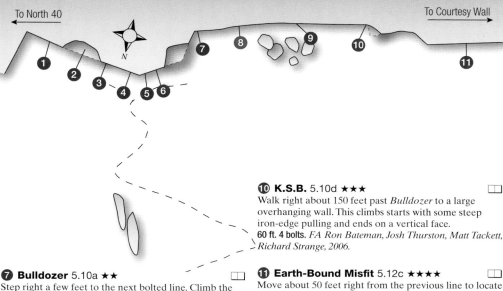

To North 40 ←

To Courtesy Wall →

N

① K.S.B. 5.10d ★★★
Walk right about 150 feet past *Bulldozer* to a large overhanging wall. This climbs starts with some steep iron-edge pulling and ends on a vertical face.
60 ft. 4 bolts. *FA Ron Bateman, Josh Thurston, Matt Tackett, Richard Strange, 2006.*

⑦ Bulldozer 5.10a ★★
Step right a few feet to the next bolted line. Climb the slabby face past thought-provoking moves.
40 ft. 4 bolts. *FA Ron Bateman, Betsey Adams, 2006.*

⑧ Buffalo Crickets 5.10b R ★★
Twenty feet around the corner from *Bulldozer* is this left-facing dihedral. Crank past a tough start, then continue up the crack. Near the top, the crack widens and becomes extremely dirty. Protect out of horizontals on the arete to the left. Descend from bolted anchor.
45 ft. *FA Josh Thurston, Betsey Adams, 2006.*

⑨ Iron Mike (Open Project) 5.13+ ★★★★
Twenty-five feet right of *Buffalo Crickets* is a striking line of isolated shallow pockets and crimpers. Start up the first four bolts of easy iron rails and get a quick rest. While recovering, scope the path of least resistance and try your luck with the sustained and heady crux.
90 ft. 8 bolts.

⑪ Earth-Bound Misfit 5.12c ★★★★
Move about 50 feet right from the previous line to locate this striking thin dihedral, which begins about 20 feet off the deck and ends on a perch. Contains some difficult clips and a little bit of spice.
50 ft. 4 bolts. *Kris Hampton, 2007.*

⑫ Team Wilander 5.11+ ★★★
Twenty-five feet right of the dihedral is this bolted line, which begins in a cave. Crank through the initial cave moves, then emerge to the first bolt and enjoy gymnastic moves to the finish.
40 ft. 4 bolts. *FA Ron Bateman, 2007.*

⑬ Mis-Conception 5.12b ★★
Twenty-five feet right from the previous route is this deceptively difficult line. Climb through sloping holds to a redpoint crux just before the anchors.
60 ft. 5 bolts. *FA Mike Uchman, Josh Thurston, Ron Bateman, 2007.*

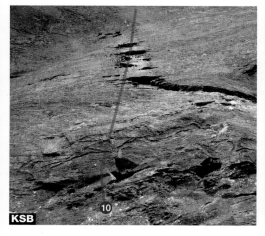

KSB   10

Earth-Bound Misfit   11

NORTH 40

p.m. shade 10 mins

8 routes

5.6- .7 .8 .9 .10 .11 .12 .13 .14

Character:

This crag has only a handful of routes but the percentage of excellence is very high. *Amarillo Sunset* (5.11b) and *Samurai* (5.12b) are two of the Red's best lines of their grades, so put them on your must-do list. Get ready for big reaches and hard pulls, because as you may know, a classic can never be a gimme for the grade!

Approach:

To reach North 40, follow the approach to the Shire, but continue walking past the last line at the Shire for a few minutes until you see an obvious large amphitheater. *Amarillo Sunset* will be on the right just before the trail heads sharply downhill.

Conditions:

North 40 is primarily a north- to northwest-facing cliff, so expect at most a bit of afternoon sun.

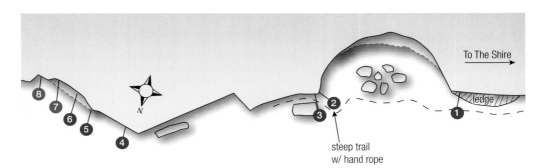

To The Shire

ledge

steep trail
w/ hand rope

N

❶ Amarillo Sunset 5.11b ★★★★★

One of the best for the grade. Start from a ledge just right of a large ravine. Gorilla swing through monster holds while savoring the excellent exposure. Photo overleaf.
50 ft. 7 bolts. *FA Kipp Trummel, 2006.*

❷ Swine Flew 5.13 ★★★★

Hike down from *Amarillo Sunset*, through the ravine, and up to the other side with help of a hand rope. Begin by climbing the steep arete that hovers above the ravine to reach an intimidating blank headwall above.
80 ft. 8 bolts. *FA Bentley Bracket, Kipp Trummel, 2006.*

❸ Samurai 5.12b ★★★★★

Step left a few feet from the arete, look up, and bow to the opponent. Take a stance, breath, then slice through a series of difficult and unique moves along a striking feature. Claim victory at the chains.
55 ft. 6 bolts. *FA Ray Ellington, Kipp Trummel 2006.*

❹ Barbed Wire 5.12b ★★★

Walk left from *Samurai* a few hundred feet to the next bolted line, which begins just right of a blunt arete. Step hard through a difficult start, then power-smear through the crux and jet for larger holds up high.
55 ft. 6 bolts. *FA Kipp Trummel, 2006.*

❺ Yosemite Sam 5.12a ★★★

Move left and downhill a bit from *Barbed Wire* to the next bolted line. Grab the best holds you can find, then power through the tough start. Pump out for the rest of the line and don't lose it up high.
55 ft. 7 bolts. *FA Kipp Trummel, 2006.*

❻ Outlaw Justice 5.11d ★★★

Move left a few feet from *Yosemite Sam* to the next bolted line. Make some tricky moves around a feature to gain fun climbing above.
55 ft. 8 bolts. *FA Kipp Trummel, 2006.*

❼ Pistol Gripped 5.12a ★★★

Technical face-climbing skills will be rewarded with a perfect hand crack above.
55 ft. 4 bolts plus gear. *FA Kris Hampton, Justin Riddell, Kipp Trummel, 2006.*

❽ Summer Breeze 5.8 ★★

Twenty-five feet left of *Pistol Gripped* is this obvious crack system. Follow the crack up and right until it fades to chains.
50 ft. *FA Josh Thurston, Jordan Garvey.*

Amarillo Sunset 1

Swine Flew 2

Samurai 3

Barbed Wire 4

CURBSIDE

a.m.   shade 1 min

15 routes

5.6- .7 .8 .9 .10 .11 .12 .13 .14

Character:
The proximity of this wall to the road makes it a great place to get a warm up for other walls, or bag a few new lines at the end of the day. The first ascentionists at Curbside have tried to make the names of the routes a play on the Roadside route names. So, for bonus points on your sends, match the route name of the line you send with the Roadside route it is named after. Most of the lines at Curbside can deliver a good pump, and some require a good bit of power to reach the chains.

Approach:
Curbside is a very accessible wall bordering the left side of the road on the way to the main Sore Heel Hollow parking area for the Gallery, Volunteer Wall, etc. When you turn right off of Bald Rock Road onto the road leading to the Sore Heel Parking area, follow it for 0.5 miles to a hairpin curve to the right near an oil pump. The trail to the main wall is on the left side of the road 50 feet behind the pump. Routes 1-4 are best reached by hiking back up the road in the direction you came in, and locating another short trail angling left up to the wall.

Conditions:
Most of the routes at Curbside stay dry in the rain. The wall is east- to northeast-facing, so expect morning to afternoon sun and shade.

❶ Waltz the Deal 5.10a ★★
Walk 40 feet left from the arete where the approach trail meets the wall to locate this route. Scramble up a short low-angle slab and pull over a bulge to reach the first bolt. Continue up the face, staying just left of a wide crack.
50 ft. 8 bolts. *FA Kipp Trummel, Karen Clark, 2006.*

❷ Sudoku 5.10a ★★
This line begins on the northeast facing buttress directly at the head of the trail. Climb large holds to the anchors.
50 ft. 5 bolts. *FA Kipp Trummel, Karen Clark, 2006.*

❸ Action over Apathy 5.10b ★★★
Begin five feet right of the previous line, on pockets. Move up to a short roof, don't wuss out left, and crank hard to a good ledge. Continue up, angling right, on pumpy underclings and sidepulls.
60 ft. 5 bolts. *FA Kipp Trummel, 2006.*

❹ The Return of Frank Byron 5.12c ★★★★
Move 20 feet right from the corner to a line of bolts beginning with a horizontal shelf. The holds are there but they're tough to spot. Grab the shelf to start, then trend left on pockets and edges. Veer back right to the second bolt, clip it, then crank a few more moves to reach an incut slot. Shake, then follow easier ground to the anchors. Bouldering on a rope.
55 ft. 5 bolts. *FA Ray Ellington, Kipp Trummel, 2007.*

Return of Frank Byron

Ben Davis on *Amarillo Sunset* 5.11b, North 40, previous spread. Photo Jonathan Vickers.

9
Conscription 10 11 12 13

5
Curbside No Traction 6

5 **Curbside No Traction** 5.10c ★★★ 　　□□
This is the first line on the main Curbside wall. It's possible to head right from the previous lines but easier to walk back down to the road, then follow the trail to the left near the next oil pump. From where the approach trail meets the wall, walk about 100 feet left and up to a ledge from which this and the next route can be accessed. This is the line on the left of the clean slab and begins left of a rounded flake-like feature. Burn rubber. **35 ft. 5 bolts.** *FA Kipp Trummel, 2006.*

6 **The Ankle Brute** 5.11a ★★★ 　　□□
This is the next slab line right of *Curbside No Traction.* **35 ft. 4 bolts.** *FA Kipp Trummel, 2006.*

7 **The Second Labor of Hercules** 5.10c ★★□□
The next two lines are located just left of the corner of the main Curbside wall. This is the line on the left and climbs the featured wall, using pinches and underclings. **50 ft. 7 bolts.** *FA Josh Thurston, Ron Bateman, 2006.*

8 **Single Finger Salute** 5.10c ★★ 　　□□
Move right a few feet to the next line. Begin with a tough start, then move up through pumpy moves to the chains. Better rock quality than the previous line. **55 ft. 5 bolts.** *Ron Bateman, Josh Thurston, 2006.*

9 **Ghost in the Machine** 5.10d ★★★ 　　□□
This enjoyable line begins 10 feet right and around the corner from the previous two lines. It is the first line on the main east face of Curbside. Climb up through sloping holds to a large ledge. Pull off the ledge into a short section of steeper rock to reach the chains. **60 ft. 7 bolts.** *FA Ron Bateman, Rosanna Bateman, 2006.*

Wildfire   13   14   15

⑩ Subtle Thievery 5.11c ★★

Step right about 15 feet to the next line. Climb the sequential lower face to a good rest and contemplate the final boulder problem below the chains.
65 ft. 6 bolts. *FA Josh Thurston, Ron Bateman, 2006.*

⑪ Conscription 5.11c ★★★

This excellent pumper is just right of the previous line. Climb sustained pockets and edges, passing a tough move or two along the way. Beach onto a sandy ledge, finagle a rest, reach high to find the best holds you can get, then high-step and heel-hook over the roof to a relieving finish.
65 ft. 6 bolts. *FA Ron Bateman, Josh Thurston, Kipp Trummel, 2006.*

⑫ Avalanche Run 5.11d ★★★

This line is marked by an obvious large roof with a fixed draw. Pull on positive holds to reach the intimidating roof. Locate key holds, release the feet, and hope the barndoor doesn't pull you off. Hang on to reach the chains.
65 ft. 6 bolts. *FA Kipp Trummel, 2006.*

⑬ Wildfire 5.12a ★★★★

The next few lines are on the steeper and less featured righthand side of the wall. Begin about 10 feet right of the previous line, on a boulder. Step out into a right-angling traverse. Bust straight up through the fingery face, make the last clip, then blast through the final moves to the chains.
50 ft. 5 bolts. *FA Paul Vidal, Kipp Trummel, 2006.*

⑭ Outbreak 5.12b ★★

This is the next route right of *Wildfire* on the overhanging orange wall. Begin with a steep move to reach a sloping ledge. Trend right up the face using bullet pockets and finger slots to a reach-around move near the top.
55 ft. 5 bolts. *FA Kevin Todd, Kipp Trummel, 2006.*

⑮ Thunder 5.12c ★★

Last route on the main overhanging Curbside wall at this time. Begin 10 feet right on sandy holds. Blast through small edges on a blank section of the wall to reach a band of pockets. Gain relief on the pockets, then bear down for another blank run to the anchors.
60 ft. 6 bolts. *FA Brian Arnold, 2008.*

CHICA BONITA WALL

a.m. 10 min | 33 routes | 5.6- .7 .8 .9 .10 .11 .12 .13 .14

Character:

Chica Bonita Wall is a recently developed wall on the Pendergrass Murray Recreational Preserve property. The east-facing wall is best known for the trio of excellent slab routes, *Brown-Eyed Girl*, *Baby Blue Eyes*, and *Bessie*, as well as the up-and-coming classic, long, arching crack, *Cheaper Than a Movie*. The routes are easy to locate and, except for *Sorostitute*, they are within a short distance of one another.

Approach:

Park in the parking area for Drive-By Crag and Bob Marley Wall, and walk back down the road toward the Motherlode for a couple hundred feet until you reach two roads forking off uphill on the left. Take the road that veers right up the hill. There will be a sign near its intersection with the main road indicating the wall. Follow the dirt road uphill, passing a short road with an oil pump on the right, and then another road on the right. When you reach the third road on the right, follow it uphill a short ways to reach an oil pump near a cliff. The trail heads down the hill on the right side of the cliff and shortly wraps around to the main wall.

Conditions:

Chica Bonita Wall faces directly east, so expect morning to early afternoon sunshine. Routes 1-4 are situated inside a large rockhouse, so they are climbable in a heavy rain. The other lines are slabby for the most part so they won't stay as dry.

1 Laying Pipe Under the Bridge 5.7 ★★★
Instead of taking the trail that drops down to the right from the oil pump, take a trail on the left. After roughly 300 feet you will come to this obvious line that has an old oil pipeline coming down from the top of the cliff near it. This line ascends the hand crack right of the pipe to the top of an arch.
70 ft. *FA Dan Beck, Matt Tacket, 2008*

2 Darling Dirtbag 5.8 ★★
As you walk in to Chica Bonita, this is the arete, crack, and face system immediately before the rockhouse hosting *Quicky* through *The Dude Abides*. Climb the arete, then move into a hand crack. Stay in the hand crack to reach a slab leading to the top. Bring small cams for the top.
90 ft. *FA Dan Beck, Nicole Bunda, 2008.*

3 Quicky 5.8 ★
This line ascends the first short dihedral on the left side of the rockhouse. There are no anchors – down-climbing is the only possible descent.
25 ft. *FA Jason Haas (Free Solo), 2005.*

4 Mary Pop-Parazzi 5.5 ★★
The first short, bolted line just right of *Quicky*. Another short-attention-span type of route.
25 ft. 3 bolts. *FA Jenny Ryan, Mark Ryan, Keith Raker, Neil Arnold, 2009.*

5 Pocahontas Path 5.7
The next short line just right of *Mary Pop-Parazzi*. Bored yet?
25 ft. 3 bolts. *FA Jenny Ryan, Mark Ryan, Keith Raker, 2009.*

6 The Spice of Life 5.10b ★★★
Locate a wide crack 30 feet right of *Quicky*. Climb the face next to the crack to a ledge. It is possible to get a piece of pro in a pocket on the face. From the ledge, traverse out the massive roof to another ledge with chain anchors. Entertaining, to say the least.
70 ft. *FA Jason Haas, Matt Tackett, 2005.*

7 Raindancer 5.10a ★★
This short sport route takes the line of bolts just left of the next dihedral on the right side of the rockhouse. Negotiate a tough start to reach good pockets above.
30 ft. 3 bolts. *FA Jared Hancock, Matt Tackett, Mike Cole, Mark Ryan, 2006.*

8 Rinse and Repeat 5.7 ★
Climb the short dihedral to a set of anchors.
30 ft. *FA Jesse New, Mike Cole, Jared Hancock, 2006.*

9 The Dude Abides 5.11a ★★★★
Just right of *Rinse and Repeat* is another bolted line. Climb to a ledge, then continue up a pocketed face to the chains.
65 ft. 7 bolts. *FA Don McGlone, John "Fred" Aragon, 2006.*

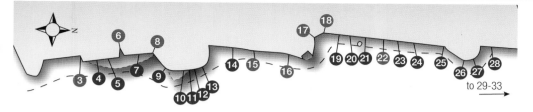

10 Blake's Route 5.12a ★★★
Next bolted line right of *The Dude Abides*. Bouldery with rests. Could use another bolt at the top.
90 ft. 9 bolts. *FA Blake Bowling, 2009.*

11 Hot Drama Teacher 5.11a ★★★
Next route right of *Blake's Route*. Climb through a series of plates and horizontals to a short roof. Jam or claw through the roof, then continue to the chains.
90 ft. 9 bolts. *FA Merrick Schaefer, Matt Tackett, 2005.*

12 Ridin' the Short Buzz 5.9 ★★★
Climb the short, plated face just right of *Hot Drama Teacher*. Climb slow and the buzz will last longer than Salvia.
35 ft. 4 bolts. *FA Jared Hancock, Karla Hancock, Mark Ryan, Jenny Ryan, 2006.*

13 When Rats Attack 5.10b ★★
Move right 30 feet to the arete. Climb up through a series of bulges and ledges. Photo page 333.
55 ft. 5 bolts. *FA Mark Ryan, Jenny Ryan, 2006.*

14 Flying the Bird 5.11a ★★★
Right of *When Rats Attack* is a large dirty chimney. This bolted line climbs the slab 20 feet right of the chimney. Not for the mantelly disabled.
50 ft. 5 bolts. *FA Aika Yoshida, Barry Brolley, Mark Ryan, JJ, 2008.*

15 Honduran Rum 5.10c ★★
Move 50 feet right to a section of the cliff separated by a large ledge midway up. This line ascends the thin crack system starting 15 feet up and behind a tree. End on the middle ledge at bolted anchors.
70 ft. *FA Jason Haas, Cory Weber, 2005.*

The Dude Abides

Honduran Rum

Be My Yoko Ono   16

Cheaper Than a Movie   17   18   19

16 Be My Yoko Ono 5.8 ★★★

The abundance of large face holds on this line makes for a great beginning lead. Move 40 feet right to a crack system surrounded by large plates. Climb jugs to a higher handcrack. Rap from a tree or traverse the ledge to the bolted anchors above *Honduran Rum*.
70 ft. *FA Jason Haas, Matt Tackett, 2005.*

17 Let's Get Drunk 5.10a ★★★ and Think About It

She looks good now but wait until you climb her. This next line is cursed with good looks but a whole lot of mud. Walk about 200 feet right from the previous line to a section of wall with two impressive-looking cracks. This line ascends the crack on the left. Climb the dihedral to a ledge with a tree and belay. Ascend the cleaner right arching flake to the top. Rap from a tree to descend.
80 ft. *FA Jordan Wood, Jason Haas, 2005.*

18 Cheaper Than a Movie 5.8 ★★★★★

This line, one of the best and longest in its class, is definitely worth a visit to Chica Bonita Wall. Climb the gorgeous right-angling crack until it ends at a solid set of rap anchors. A 60-meter rope barely gets you to the ground, so tie a knot in the end.
100 ft. *FA Matt Tackett, Jason Haas, 2005.*

19 Brown-Eyed Girl 5.10a ★★★★

Immediately right of *Cheaper Than a Movie* is a wide slab of sandstone containing a few incredible calf burners. This is the first line on the wall and thins out near the top.
70 ft. 6 bolts. *Nick Walker, Jared Hancock, Mark Ryan, 2006.*

20 Baby Blue Eyes 5.10c ★★★★

Climb the next bolted line just right of *Brown-Eyed Girl*. Begin on a small flake, then head straight up the clean section of rock, passing a large horizontal slot along the way.
75 ft. 7 bolts. *FA Amy Tackett, Matt Tackett, 2006.*

21 Bessie 5.11c ★★★★

Walk 20 feet right from *Baby Blue Eyes* to the next bolted line on the slab. This is the best, but also the most difficult and beta intensive, of the lines on this wall. Keep pressure on your toes for the runouts near the top.
100 ft. 10 bolts. *FA Matt Tackett, Amy Tackett, 2005.*

22 Sexy Sadie 5.10b ★★

This heady line is recognized by the short crack system that starts about 20 feet or so off the ground right of *Bessie*. Climb through a well-protected crux near the end of the initial crack, then continue up the slab, passing the occasional horizontal placement.
100 ft. *FA Don McGlone, 2007.*

23 You Take Sally 5.11d ★★★★

Locate the obvious hueco about 25 feet up right of the previous lines, with routes going out the left and right side. This line climbs up and left of the hueco. Pure slab climbing and probably the hardest on the wall.
80 ft. 9 bolts. *FA Matt Tackett, Don McGlone, 2007.*

24 I'll Take Sue 5.11a ★★★★

An easier version of *You Take Sally*. Climb up to the hueco, then crux out of it. Get the friction on.
80 ft. 9 bolts. *FA Don McGlone, Matt Tacket, 2006.*

Cheaper Than a Movie

Sally and Sue

25 Size Doesn't Matter 5.11a ★★★★

Another tough-to-onsight, no-holds line right of *I'll Take Sue*. If those holds were just a bit bigger, then you would've gotten up a little quicker. I guess size does matter in this case.

80 ft. 8 bolts. *FA Natasha Fischer, Reece Nelson, Ron Batemen, Matt Tackett, 2007.*

26 That's What She Said 5.10c ★★★

A great intro route for the slab shy. Begin just right of *Size Doesn't Matter* on the ledge near where the trail cuts downhill. Climb through stop-and-go terrain with bolt placements just where you want them.

90 ft. 12 bolts. *FA Matt Tackett, Don McGlone, 2007.*

27 She Might Be a Liar 5.11b ★★★★

End the day with some spice. Begin on the same ledge as the previous line and take on awkward movements requiring full commitment.

75 ft. 8 bolts. *FA Dan Beck, Matt Tackett, 2007.*

28 Motor Booty Pimp Affair 5.10d ★★

This is the next route right of *She Might Be a Liar* but must be approached by heading downhill on the trail and cutting around the outcropping that forms the ledge from which the previous lines begin. May be a disappointment after the phenomenal lines on the main wall.

95 ft. 12 bolts. *FA Dan Beck, Matt Tackett, Don McGlone, 2007.*

29 Thunda Bunda 5.10d ★★

Look for an offwidth beginning in a low roof right of the previous lines. Get your ass off the ground and continue up to a large hueco where it's possible to traverse left to another wide crack and set a belay. Thrash up to another hueco, move left, and take the face to the top. It is possible to climb over to the anchors on *Motor Booty Pimp Affair*. A 60-meter rope will get you down from the tree above the anchors, though, if you don't want to commit to reaching them.

110 ft. *FA Ben Strohmeier, Dan Beck, 2008.*

30 Falkor 5.10d ★★★

Begin with the same tough start as *Thunda Bunda*, but head straight up instead of moving left. Continue up a sparsely protected face to the top. Rap from a tree above the anchors on *Motor Booty Pimp Affair* if you've only got a 60-meter rope.

110 ft. *FA Dan Beck, Matt Tackett, 2008.*

31 Marriage Counseling 5.11c ★★★

Follow the trail to the right and head downhill around a buttress for about 100 feet to reach the next line. Locate a less-than-vertical crack beginning on a flat boulder just right of a low overhang. Climb through easy moves to reach a large hueco about 30 feet up. Move left out of the hueco on good holds to a stance beneath an overhanging, right-angling crack system in black rock. Pump up through the overhanging crack to bolted anchors at a large ledge.

80 ft. *FA Sam Elias, Beck Kloss, 2005.*

32 Sister Catherine the Conqueror 5.12b ★★

Hike right from *Marriage Counseling* across a drainage, then back up to the cliff. Look for a line of bolts near some small boulders with a large roof at mid-height. If you aren't afraid of commitment to the choss, you may find some enjoyment in this route. Gets pumpy near the top if you can just hang in there mentally to reach it.

95 ft. 10 bolts. *FA Dan Beck, 2008.*

33 Sorostitute 5.7 ★

This dirty line can be found about 300 feet right of *Marriage Counseling*. Climb the dihedral in the back of an amphitheater to a sandy ledge, then rap from fixed gear to descend.

50 ft. *FA Jason Haas, Cory Weber, 2005.*

Arthur Cammers on When Rats Attack 5.10b, Chica Bonita, page 329. Photo Scott James.

BOB MARLEY CRAG

all day | 10 mins | OK in rain | 25 routes | .7 .8 .9 .10 .11 .12 .13 .14

Character

Once a ghost crag full of unfinished routes, hanging ropes, impossible projects, and a handful of short, awkward roof climbs, this crag has now matured into one of the best in the Red for difficult, pumping rock climbs. The attention started with the Petzl Rock Trip in 2007 where the longstanding project *50 Words for Pump* was listed as the men's ultimate route. Some of the best climbers in the world threw themselves at this beast, and Mickaël Fuselier ended up with the win, confirming a stiff grade of 5.14c. During the trip, surrounding routes including *No Redemption* (5.13b), *Ultra Perm* (5.13c), and *Sugar Magnolia* (5.13d) received more ascents in a week than they usually see in a year. A project was sent (*MILF Money*, 5.13b) and a new tough line was bolted by Daniel DuLac (*El Encuentro*, 5.13b). In 2008, visiting climber Joe Kinder established a new line between *50 Words* and *Ultra Perm* named *Southern Smoke* (5.14c) and even left behind a direct start that is now one of the hot open projects in the Red.

The once-considered-awkward roof routes are now some of the most popular 5.11s and 5.12s around. *Dogleg* still stands as the toughest 5.12a in the Red for the vertically challenged, but is now being over-shadowed by a better-quality line that branches left after the original novelty start (*Demon Seed*, 5.12c). As for easy lines, there's still not much to be had. However, you probably have a better shot at convincing your partner to come belay you on *Ultra Perm* just one more time, since a new trail now puts Drive-By crag just a five-minute hike away. It's safe to say that Bob Marley is no longer a ghost crag.

50 WORDS FOR PUMP

How about 50 words for drama! A project for more than a decade, this high-quality pumpfest finally saw a first ascent during the 2007 Petzl Rock Trip. The route reportedly has a scary and tough clip in the crux section, which is how it was originally climbed. Shortly after the FA, Mike Doyle added two bolts slightly right of the original which prevented having to shift over to make the scary clip.

Some climbers thought this new sequence brought the route down a letter grade and was unnecessary, while others argued it now follows the line of least resistance and the crux of a route should not be clipping the bolt. This is similar to what happened with *50 Bucks* (*Triple Sec*) at Muir Valley (is there something with the number 50 going on!?).

Adam Taylor of Lexington, KY, added even more controversy to this route by smashing the new hangers after his project draws were removed and not replaced from the original bolts for a supposed photo shoot. The climbing blogs exploded and rap artist Odub even put out a song expressing his strong opinion on the situation. As Steve Petro once said, "Welcome to Ol' Kentuck."

Approach

Drive 12.4 miles south on KY 11 from Miguel's toward Beattyville. Turn right on KY 498. Drive 1.2 miles to a sharp right curve. Just beyond this curve, take a sharp right on Bald Rock Road, a good gravel road, and follow it slowly as it curves left toward a house, staying left at the first intersection. After 0.3 miles the road turns to gravel and descends a steep hill. **The steep hill is usually drivable in a regular car but you may have trouble getting back out in wet or muddy weather. If you have doubts, climb somewhere else – do not park at the top of the hill as this area is used for access to oil company equipment and you are liable to be towed.** At the bottom of the hill you will pass the parking area for the Motherlode on the right. Remain on the road for a total of 1.4 miles (0.6 miles past the Motherlode parking) until you see a wooden sign indicating the RRGCC parking area on the left. Park here and walk back out to the road. Cross the road and head straight up a gravel road for 0.2 miles to reach a trail that cuts left and uphill to the wall.

Conditions

This crag is a dry, sandy beach. If it's raining and you can climb 5.12 or above, you'll have a full day of great climbing ahead of you here. The sun shines directly on this wall, but the steep nature of most of the routes puts you in the shade and your belayer in the sun.

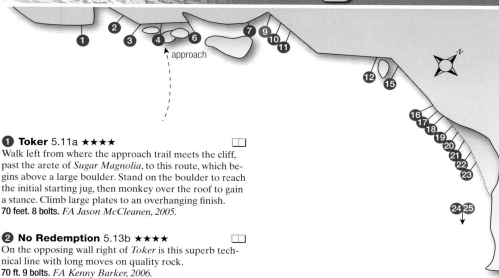

approach

1 Toker 5.11a ★★★★
Walk left from where the approach trail meets the cliff, past the arete of *Sugar Magnolia*, to this route, which begins above a large boulder. Stand on the boulder to reach the initial starting jug, then monkey over the roof to gain a stance. Climb large plates to an overhanging finish.
70 feet. 8 bolts. *FA Jason McCleanen, 2005.*

2 No Redemption 5.13b ★★★★
On the opposing wall right of *Toker* is this superb technical line with long moves on quality rock.
70 ft. 9 bolts. *FA Kenny Barker, 2006.*

3 Sugar Magnolia 5.13d ★★★
This prominent orange arete is just right of *No Redemption*. Crank through small edges, then angle left to the arete and continue up the extremely thin face.
85 ft. 10 bolts. *Andrew Gearing, 2006.*

4 Demon Seed 5.12c ★★★★
This excellent new addition shares the first five bolts and long moves of *Dogleg*, then branches left when *Dogleg* doglegs right. Climb through continuous long moves on small holds using the ramp for feet. Requires full attention and a big set of balls. You'll need a 60-meter to get down.
105 ft. 9 bolts. *FA Andrew Wheatley, 2009.*

5 Dogleg 5.12a ★★★★★
Twenty feet right of *Sugar Magnolia* is a tall, vertical, orange face with an obvious line of pockets marking the beginning of this line and *Demon Seed*. Begin with gigantic moves between horizontals to reach the sequential face above. Angle right to the anchors. The line of bolts leading off left halfway up does not have a finish.
90 ft. 10 bolts. *FA Unknown.*

6 Beeper 5.11d
About 20 feet right of *Dogleg* is an arete with a high dihedral. Begin on the large boulders near its base. Grab the arete and follow it over soft rock and up into a thin crack. Continue up the crack to the anchors. Caution! Rock turns to crap up high.
70 ft. 8 bolts. *FA Keith Moll, 1996.*

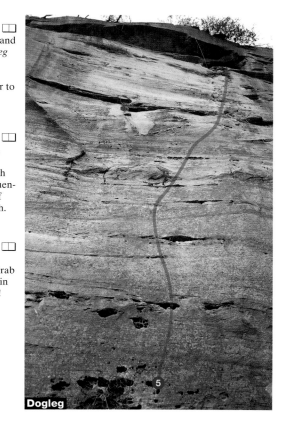

Dogleg

Tony's Happy Christmas Crack

50 Words for Pump

❼ MILF Money 5.13b ★★★
See description opposite.

❽ Granny Panties 5.12c ★★
The bolted line just left of *Tony's Happy Christmas Crack*.
Boulder through several bolts of quality moves, and finish
on easier choss to the chains. Bolt count approximate.
70 ft. *FA Kenny Barker, 2007.*

❾ Tony's Happy Christmas Crack 5.8 ★★★
Just right of the previous line is an obvious hand crack in
a dihedral. Climb the crack to a set of anchors 35 feet up,
or continue over suspect rock and 5.11 climbing to the
anchors on *Mas Choss*.
80 ft. *FA Jack Hume, Tony Tramontin, Steve McFarland,
Gene Hume, David Hume, 1994.*

❿ Mas Choss 5.11c ★★★
About 15 feet right of *Tony's Happy Christmas Crack*
is this slab route with striated holds. Climb some tough
moves to a small roof. Move left at the roof and reach up
to a large flake. Continue up the face to the anchors.
80 ft. 7 bolts. *FA Kellyn Gorder, 1996.*

⓫ Route 22 5.12a ★★★
Move 15 feet right from *Mas Choss* to the next slab
line. Climb the small edges and ledges up and right to a
reasonable stance. Angle a little left to a small overhang,
then power over thinning holds to the anchors.
80 ft. 7 bolts. *FA Dave Hume, 1996.*

⓬ Fifty Words for Pump 5.14c ★★★★★
See introduction for the controversy surrounding this route.
Hike down and around the corner from the previous lines
and you'll be standing directly beneath this huge, intimidating, steep beast. Good luck.
90 ft. 10 bolts. *Equipped by Hugh Loeffler. FA Mickaël
Fuselier 2007.*

⓭ Southern Smoke Direct ★★★★★
Project. Climbs straight up through a desperate boulder
problem to join *Southern Smoke* at its second bolt. Currently an open project. Grade estimated at 5.14c or d.
100 ft. 11 bolts. *Equipped by Joe Kinder.*

⓮ Southern Smoke 5.14c ★★★★★
This ultimate stamina route begins on the slab on which
Ultra Perm starts, but immediately transitions left onto
the face for 5.14a climbing up the relentlessly overhanging face to meet up with *Ultra Perm* just where the hard
climbing begins.
90 ft. 10 bolts. *FA Joe Kinder, 2008.*

7 MILF Money 5.13b ★★★

Tough boulder problem to 5.9 choss. The line begins with tough pulls on very shallow pockets, then cuts directly right to meet up with climbing on sand for the remaining two-thirds of the route. The bolts may feel awkwardly placed if they haven't been shifted around yet.

60 ft. 7 bolts. *FA Sean McColl, 2007.*

Greg Kerzhner. Photo Dan Brayack.

15 Ultra Perm 5.13d ★★★★★
One of the best routes east of the Mississippi (or west, for that matter). Begin on a boulder 20 feet right of the previous line. Climb the initial face, then move left to an overhanging wall. Enjoy a few bolts of confidence-building moves on big holds to prepare for the smackdown that awaits. Dive into a tough boulder problem that doesn't seem to let up until you turn the lip. The size of your fingers may be the difference between you marking this "hard" or "soft" on your scorecard.
90 ft. 9 bolts. *FA Dave Hume, 1997. Equipper: Chris Martin.*

Dahlia Ojeda. Photo Keith Ladzinsky.

15 Ultra Perm 5.13d ★★★★★
See description above.

16 Horn 5.11d ★★★★
Walk 30 feet around the corner to the next set of steep lines in a large overhang. This is the first route encountered and begins on a boulder. Grab pockets on the heavily featured face and move left. Continue up the face to anchors above the lip of a small roof.
50 ft. 5 bolts. *FA Chris Martin, 1997.*

17 Flush 5.11d ★★★
Start the same as the previous line but head straight up and over the lip.
50 ft. 4 bolts. *FA Chris Martin, 1997.*

18 Velvet 5.11d ★★★★
Ten more feet right is another steep line of pockets with anchors just past the lip.
50 ft. 5 bolts. *FA Chris Martin, 1997.*

Horn to ... Beef

19 Tacit 5.12a ★★★★

This route climbs a lot better than it looks. Move five feet right of *Velvet* to the next line, which begins near a crack above a boulder. Crank up the steep, pocketed face to a roof. Creep out the roof on large holds and pull past the lip to a good horizontal. Continue up past a bulge to the anchors.
50 ft. 6 bolts. *FA Porter Jarrard, 1997.*

20 Reticent 5.12d ★★

Five feet right of *Tacit* is the start to another pocketed line leading to the large roof. Begin on a boulder and climb through slightly sharp holds to the roof. Power through a sequence of pockets in the roof to great holds just over the lip. Move up the face on small edges to the anchors.
50 ft. 6 bolts. *FA Porter Jarrard, 1997.*

21 Blood Bath 5.12c ★★★★

Step 10 feet right from the previous climb to some small boulders marking the beginning of this climb. Grab pockets and head up the steep wall to a horizontal just below the roof. Shake out and move through the roof to good holds just past the lip. Continue up over a bulge on the headwall to the anchors.
50 ft. 5 bolts. *FA Chris Martin, 1997.*

22 Where's the Beef? 5.12c ★★★★

Move 10 feet right to the last route in this area of the wall. Climb through steep pockets and crimps to a horizontal roof. Pull the roof, making use of sharp pockets, then crank over the lip to a jug. Continue up easier face to the anchors.
50 ft. 5 bolts. *FA Chris Martin, 1998.*

23 Bettavul Pipeline 5.12a ★★★★

Next route right of *Where's the Beef.* Begin near a pipeline that was drilled from the top of the crag and missed by a couple of feet at the bottom. Race up the steep wall on jugs.
55 ft. 5 bolts. *FA Mark Johnson, Drew Cronan, 2006.*

24 El Encuentro 5.13b ★★★

If only it weren't a water streak. Hike right about 150 feet from last route listed on the main wall. You'll drop down into the lowest part of the valley and up the other side a bit until you see this gorgeous, slightly overhanging bolted face. Often wet. Bolted and climbed during the Petzl Rock Trip 2007.
90 ft. 11 bolts. *FA Daniel Du Lac, 2007.*

25 Tikka Chance 5.9+ ★★★★

Hike right about 150 feet from the last route listed on the main wall. You'll drop down into the lowest part of the valley and up the other side a bit until you see the first reasonable crack. Climb the crack and face to the lip of the wall.
90 ft. *FA John Bronaugh, Jason Burton, 2002.*

DRIVE-BY CRAG

a.m. 10 mins OK in rain   28 routes   5.6- .7 .8 .9 .10 .11 .12 .13 .14

Character

This excellent crag has something to offer climbers at all levels. You'll find several excellent 5.13 lines, including one of the best 5.13c pumpfests in the Red, *Kaleidoscope*. As a warm up for *Kaleidoscope*, jump on one of the best 5.12 lines in the Red, *Check Your Grip*. After getting spanked on *Kaleidoscope*, cool down on two of the best 5.10 lines around, *Breakfast Burrito* and *Fire and Brimstone*.

The harder lines at Drive-By tend to be slopey and steep, while the rest of the lines tend to be slightly overhanging and crimpy. Expect to wait in line for almost every route here during peak season.

Approach

Use the same approach as Bob Marley Crag (page 334) and park in the signed RRGCC parking area. Walk out onto the approach road, turn left, and hike for about 100 feet to the next dirt road on the right. Hike up the dirt road until it intersects with another road. Stay right and continue uphill for about seven minutes (do not turn left on the next road) until the road curves around to the right. About 100 feet after the curve, look for a small wooden ladder on the left, which leads up a short, steep bank and ends directly beneath *Check Your Grip* and *Whipper Snapper*. It's also possible to approach this crag from Bob Marley by walking left past *Toker* and following the trail which leads through a notch and heads downhill to meet up with Drive-By near *Kaleidoscope*.

Conditions

The slightly overhanging walls of this area provide good shelter from the rain. The wall receives morning to mid-afternoon sun, so arrive late if you're climbing here in the summer. Expect large crowds including babies, dogs, beginner groups, and arguing couples.

Breakfast Burrito

❶ **Slick and the 9mm** 5.10b ★★★
This is the farthest left route on the wall, located about 35 feet left of the bolted seam of *Hakuna Mata*. Climb over a bulge and up to the anchors in the middle of the face. From the anchors, it is possible to traverse right to a left-facing dihedral and continue to another set of anchors about 40 feet up. This pitch goes at 5.9.
60 ft. 7 bolts. *FA Kellyn Gorder, 2000.*

❷ **Slut Men** 5.11d ★★
About 10 feet left of *Hakuna Mata* is the next line, which begins under an overhang.
70 ft. 8 bolts. *FA Danita Whelan, 1996.*

❸ **Hakuna Matata** 5.12a ★★★★
This sustained route follows a thin crack/seam system on the left side of a gently overhanging golden face. Boulder up to a small ledge, then climb crimps and fingertip locks to the anchors.
85 ft. 9 bolts. *FA Kellyn Gorder, 1996.*

❹ **Extra Backup** 5.12a ★★★
A shorter climb on the golden face right of *Hakuna Matata*. Climb small crimps past well-spaced bolts to the anchors.
70 ft. 6 bolts. *FA Dave Hume, 1997.*

⑤ Fire and Brimstone 5.10d ★★★★★ ☐☐

This route begins in an obvious dihedral. Climb the funky dihedral to a stance. Pull through a series of good edges, then head right for the saddle sit-down on the arete. Continue up through easier moves to the anchors. **90 ft. 10 bolts.** *FA Kellyn Gorder, 1997.*

⑥ Breakfast Burrito 5.10d ★★★★★ ☐☐

Classic. About 40 feet left of the approach trail is an attractive plated face with an alcove about 60 feet up. Climb up to the alcove, take a deep breath, then brave the exposed arete and steep face to the anchors. The famous "flexi-hold" finally broke, making for a tough crux clip. **80 ft. 8 bolts.** *FA Gene Hume, 1995.*

⑦ Make a Wish 5.10b ★★★ ☐☐

Walk left from the approach trail about 20 feet to find this line. Boulder up to good holds, move right around a flake/overhang, then surmount a ledge. Climb pockets and small edges, then jugs to the top of a point of rock. **75 ft. 8 bolts.** *FA John Bronaugh, Christina Bronaugh, 1999.*

⑧ Whipper Snapper 5.12b ★★★ ☐☐

At the end of the approach trail is an overhanging face with many bolted lines. This route is the first line encountered and begins just right of a crack. Climb up to a tough move near the third bolt, then save some steam for more hard moves higher up. **80 ft. 9 bolts.** *FA Unknown.*

⑨ Check Your Grip 5.12a ★★★★★ ☐☐

This route starts about 10 feet right of *Whipper Snapper*. Mantel the start and climb up to a ledge beneath an overhanging face. Pull a bouldery sequence, then continue rapidly up the sustained face to anchors. **80 ft. 7 bolts.** *FA Neal Strickland, 1998.*

⑩ Big Sinkin' Breakdown 5.11c ★★★ ☐☐

Move 10 feet right from *Check Your Grip* to the next line. Crank out a difficult boulder problem to a shelf, then continue up the overhanging face to a nice sit-down rest above the last bolt. Check out the view, then gun to the anchors. **85 ft. 7 bolts.** *FA Hugh Loeffler, 1998.*

⑪ Primus Noctum 5.12a ★★★★ ☐☐

This route begins 10 feet right of *Big Sinkin' Breakdown* and is marked by an obvious slab section near the beginning of the route. Climb up past the slab, pull a roof, then continue up the face to a long, exciting runout before the anchors. **75 ft. 8 bolts.** *FA Porter Jarrard, 1998.*

⑫ Spirit Fingers 5.11c ★★★★ ☐☐

Scramble up to a large ledge just right of *Primus Noctum* to start. Climb edges and pockets up the enjoyable face. **70 ft. 7 bolts.** *FA Craig Smith, 1997.*

Primus Noctum

Spank

㉕ Kaleidoscope 5.13c ★★★★★ ⬜

Walk right of *The Business* until you come to the large
amphitheater. This overhanging arete is on the left side
of the amphitheater. Begin by climbing through delicate
and spicey moves to gain the steeper right-angling arete.
Battle through big moves and a couple of difficult clips
while fighting the relentless Red River pump.
80 ft. 8 bolts. *FA Monique Forestier, 2006.*

⑬ Whip-Stocking 5.11a ★★★★ ⬜
This is the next bolted line right of *Spirit Fingers*, around a blunt corner. There is a large alcove near the top and to the left of the line. Climb the plated face to anchors just above a roof.
80 ft. 8 bolts. *FA Porter Jarrard, 1997.*

⑭ Yadda Yadda Yadda 5.11b ★★★ ⬜
This route ascends the arete about 15 feet right of *Whip-stocking* with interesting and reachy moves.
50 ft. 6 bolts. *FA Kellyn Gorder, 1997.*

⑮ Head and Shoulders 5.11d ★★★★ ⬜
This route ascends the bolted flake system just right of *Yadda Yadda Yadda* and on the adjacent wall.
70 ft. 8 bolts. *FA Kellyn Gorder, 1997.*

⑯ Knees and Toes 5.12b ★★★ ⬜
This is an extension to *Head and Shoulders.* From the anchors on *Head and Shoulders,* continue up past two long bolt runs on tough, powerful terrain. Stacked on top of *Head and Shoulders* these moves will feel hard!
90 ft. 11 bolts. *Equipped by Mike Doyle. FA Audrey Sniezek, 2007*

⑰ Beer Belly 5.13a ★★★★ ⬜
Begin on *Head and Shoulders.* Climb to the fifth bolt, clip it, then traverse right. Be prepared to get gymnastic at the crux, which meets you pretty quickly into the traverse. Keep gunning to the right and give it all you got for the final pop move before the chains.
90 ft. 12 bolts. *FA Mike Doyle, 2007.*

⑱ Super Charger 5.13d ★★★★ ⬜
The beginning of this route was toproped for years as a short problem named *Maizy Mae.* It now goes to the top, thanks to Joe Kinder. Climb the powerful, slant-ing face right of *Head and Shoulders* to reach a ledge beneath the main overhanging wall. Move up through increasingly difficult-to-hold slopers, pinches, and the occasional hand-sized hueco.
11 bolts. 90 ft. *Equipped by Joe Kinder. FA Tobias Wolf, 2009.*

⑲ Dirty, Smelly Hippie 5.13b ★★★★ ⬜
Begin by climbing the right arete of the 30-foot block to the right of *Head and Shoulders.* From the ledge, continue up a flake, then leave its comfort to battle the steepness while aiming for the butt crack above where you will meet the crux. Pull the lip to gain a stance, look up, and ask yourself why the anchors are "up there" and not "right here."
90 ft. 10 bolts. *FA Dave Hume, 1997.*

⑳ Spank, aka Tika Monster 5.13a ★★★ ⬜
This route ascends the overhanging face a few feet right of *Dirty, Smelly Hippie* and just right of a dihedral. Begin by climbing left of the dihedral, then move right at the good stance to take on the severely overhanging face. Shake it out at the obvious jug near the top, then slap and pinch to the anchors. Most people skip the last bolt, but be careful if you decide to!
70 ft. 8 bolts. *FA Chris Martin.*

㉑ The Nothing 5.14a ★★★ ⬜
This route starts up a faint crack system about 15 feet right of the previous route. Hard boulder problem!
90 ft. 10 bolts. *FA Dave Hume, 1999*

㉒ The Galaxy Project ⬜
This line is currently being bolted. Follows the fat flake 30 feet right of *The Nothing*.
90 ft. *Equipped by Strange.*

㉓ The Business 5.11d ★★ ⬜
This route is located about 15 feet right of *The Nothing*. Climb pockets to the left side of a hueco, then continue through more pockets to the anchors.
65 ft. 8 bolts. *FA Eric Lowe, 1998.*

㉔ Easy Rider 5.13a ★★ ⬜
Walk right of *The Business* until you come to the large ampitheater. This line begins about 30 feet left of the ampitheater and climbs to the top of the cliff. Begin on the ledge and head up a ramp to gain consistent climbing with decent rests. Pace yourself and save enough juice to enjoy the last 20 feet of excellent climbing that makes it all worthwhile. Join the crowd if you fall on the very last move.
100 ft. 12 bolts. *FA Mike Doyle, 2007.*

㉕ Kaleidoscope 5.13c ★★★★★ ⬜
See route description opposite

㉖ The Sharma Project ⬜
This line climbs out the insanely steep amphitheater 50 feet right of *Kaleidoscope*. Not finished. The question of the day: Where does he plan to start this thing?
Equipped by Chris Sharma.

㉗ Mud on the Rug 5.11d ★★ ⬜
Walk right from *Kaleidoscope* several hundred feet to locate this dihedral. Climb through 15 feet of dirty rock to reach the good stuff. When the dihedral ends move left through an overhang to be rewarded with a great topout.
100 ft. *FA Barry Little, Kerry Gorder, 1996.*

㉘ George of the Jungle 5.6 ★★ ⬜
25 ft. right of *Mud on the Rug* is a crack that starts about 20ft off the ground. Climb the initial part of *Mud on the Rug* then traverse right to a ledge. Follow the crack and face to top.
100 ft. *FA Jason Haas, 2004.*

MOTHERLODE REGION

Elodie Saracco on *Resurrection*, the Motherlode, page 356. Photo Dan Brayack.

Character

Until the 2004 purchase of the Pendergrass Murray Recreational Preserve by the Red River Gorge Climber's Coalition, the "Southern Region" of the Red included most of the crags now on that property. With those crags now covered in their own chapter, the only areas remaining in this guide's "Motherlode Region" are the Motherlode, the Unlode, and the recently developed Chocolate Factory. However, since the Motherlode is the Mecca of sport climbing in the Red, maybe it is fitting that it has a chapter almost entirely to itself.

Approach

All the crags in this region are approached from the Motherlode parking area. To reach it, drive 12.4 miles south on KY 11 from Miguel's toward Beattyville. Turn right on KY 498. Drive 1.2 miles to a sharp right curve. Just beyond this curve take a sharp right on Bald Rock Road, a good gravel road. Follow it for 0.8 miles, driving slowly, staying left at an intersection, past some houses with dogs, down a steep hill, alongside a small cliff on your left, to a clearing on the right at the bottom. **The steep hill is usually drivable in a regular car but you may have trouble getting back out in wet or muddy weather. If you have doubts, climb somewhere else – do not park at the top of the hill as this area is used for access to oil company equipment and you are liable to be towed.** If you think you can make it back up the hill, park at the bottom of the hill in the well-worn parking area on the right or in a smaller gravel pulloff on the right a few yards farther on. Do not park next to the oil derick on the other side of the road.

Access

The cliffs are located on private property, so please respect the wishes of the landowners, which may include parking restrictions, donation boxes, leash laws, etc. Also, be careful not to block access to any machinery which appears to be owned or used by the oil companies that lease mining rights to this land.

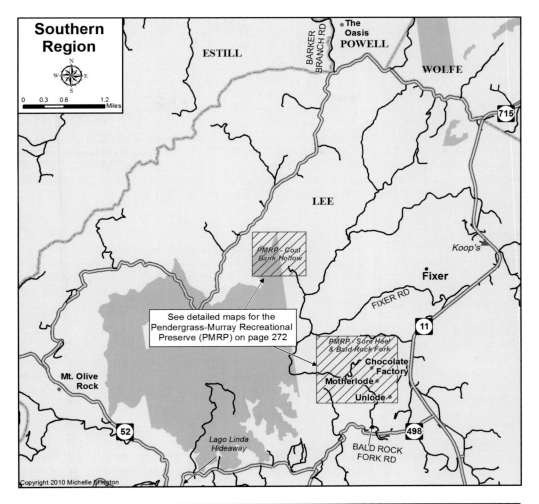

Southern Region

0 0.3 0.6 1.2 Miles

ESTILL

BARKER BRANCH RD

•The Oasis
POWELL

WOLFE

715

LEE

Koop's

•Fixer

PMRP - Coal Bank Hollow

FIXER RD

11

See detailed maps for the Pendergrass-Murray Recreational Preserve (PMRP) on page 272

PMRP - Sore Heel & Bald Rock Fork

Chocolate Factory

Motherlode

Unlode

Mt. Olive Rock

52

Lago Linda Hideaway

BALD ROCK FORK RD

498

Copyright 2010 Michelle Ellington

CLIFF	SUN /	HIKE	RAIN	ROUTES	GRADE RANGE	CLASSIC
THE MOTHERLODE page 348	shade / a.m. p.m.	10 mins	rain OK	60	5.6- .7 .8 .9 .10 .11 .12 .13 .14	*Ale-8-One* 12b *Stain* 12c *Tuna Town* 12d *Snooker* 13a *BOHICA* 13b *The Madness* 13c
THE UNLODE page 359	a.m.	5 mins	rain OK	3	5.6- .7 .8 .9 .10 .11 .12 .13 .14	
CHOCOLATE FACTORY page 360	all day	10 mins		30	5.6- .7 .8 .9 .10 .11 .12 .13 .14	*Loompa* 10c *Malice* 12c *The Golden Ticket* 14c

THE MOTHERLODE

62 routes

 a.m. p.m. shade 10 mins OK in rain

.9 .10 .11 .12 .13 .14

Character

Weighing in with thirty 5.12s, sixteen 5.13s, and three 5.14s, the Motherlode is the hard-sport-climbing Mecca of the Red and one of the best sport crags in the world. If you don't like taking big whips on steep rock, "The Lode" is not the place for you. Some people climb in the Red for years and don't go anywhere else. The Lode is a place to get fit, see the best climbers, and gawk at freakish displays of strength.

The western side of the huge amphitheatre offers technical face climbing on solid, slightly overhanging streaked walls. The central curve of the amphitheatre forms the Madness Cave and has some of the steepest routes in the Red. The Undertow Wall forms the eastern side of the ampitheatrer. One hundred and fifty feet long, 75 feet tall, and overhanging at a solid 25-degree angle, the Undertow hosts a slew of the most classic pumpfests in the Red. Although there are a few 5.11 lines at the Lode, to get the most from the place you need to climb solid 5.12.

Approach

Locate the obvious approach trail that leads uphill from the back of the big muddy, dirty pulloff. If you are headed to the Madness Cave or the Undertow Wall, stay right at the major fork in the trail; this branch meets the cliff at the left side of the Undertow Wall, beneath *Team Wilson*. If you are headed to the western side of the cliff, including Buckeye Buttress, Warm-up Wall, or GMC Wall, stay left at the major fork and follow a trail that reaches the cliff just right of Buckeye Buttress.

Conditions

Next to Roadside Crag, The Motherlode is one of the best wet-weather destinations in the Red. The overhanging walls offer great shelter from the rain. It is possible to climb all day at the Lode and escape or follow the sun, depending on which side of the amphitheatre you climb. The walls on the left side of the cave – Buckeye Buttress, Warm-Up Wall, and the GMC Wall – get morning to midday sun. The Madness Cave starts getting sun in the early afternoon. The Undertow Wall is a good warm-weather destination; it stays in the shade most of the day, receiving only an hour or two of evening sun.

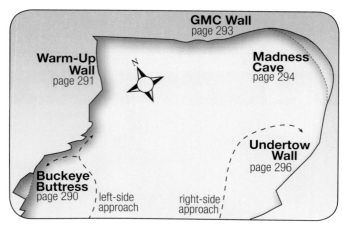

Access

The Motherlode is privately owned. Although there have been no access problems reported recently, its inclusion in this book does not imply that climbers have the right to climb there. If you chose to climb at the Motherlode, please act and behave with respect toward the landowners. During the past few years, a number of vehicles in the Motherlode parking area have been broken into. It it is highly recommended that you remove valuables from your car.

METOLIUS
www.metoliusclimbing.com

New Hampshire public defender Justin Hayes self-sentencing himself on, *40 ounces to Justice* (5.13a, Motherlode), Red River Gorge, Kentucky © Hayes Collection

Buff the Wood

Twisted

BUCKEYE BUTTRESS

❶ One-Eyed Willy Up the Back 5.11c ★★
From the end of the approach trail for the western side of the wall, walk left past a few bolted lines and scramble up and around some boulders beneath a large overhang. Just left of the overhang is a bolted line on the arete, which is *Trad Sucker*. The route is just around the corner left of *Trad Sucker*. Climb just left of the arete, pull over the roof, and climb through small finger pockets at the top.
50 ft. 5 bolts. *FA Keith Moll, 1994.*

❷ Trad Sucker 5.11b ★★★
This route ascends the line of bolts just right of the arete. Start on a large boulder. Be careful clipping the first bolt.
40 ft. 4 bolts. *FA Keith Moll, 1994.*

❸ The Chronic 5.12b ★★
The start of this route faces *Trad Sucker* and is on the right of the overhanging back wall. Climb a slab left of the arete until you reach a crack, then make a big move left to the overhanging headwall.
50 ft. 6 bolts. *FA Jeff Moll, 1994.*

❹ Twisted 5.11b ★★★
Start as for *The Chronic* but follow the crack a little longer, then make a big move left. Crank up through the overhanging wall to a ledge.
50 ft. 5 bolts. *FA Tim Cornette, 1994.*

❺ The Reacharound 5.12c ★★★
Start the same as the previous two routes but move right around the arete, then continue up the seam and face to the anchors.
60 ft. 5 bolts. *FA Brian McCray, 1994.*

❻ Stain 5.12c ★★★★★
This route begins around the corner 15 feet to the right of *The Reacharound*. Blast through the first few bolts, then make an exciting move to a jug out right. Gain a shake, then head left on pockets and straight up through sequential moves on slopers and edges. Save some juice for the last move to the anchors.
50 ft. 6 bolts. *FA Chris Snyder, 1994.*

❼ Buff the Wood 5.12b ★★★★
This route begins just right of *Stain* and is marked by a short finger crack about 15 feet up. Boulder up to the finger crack and make the clip. Take a rest, then move right on crimps and deadpoint to a crimp rail. Launch for a jug, then continue up the face to a pocket problem. Make some big moves, then clip the chains.
50 ft. 5 bolts. *FA Jeff Moll, 1994.*

❽ Golden Touch 5.13b ★★★★
This beautiful line follows a golden streak just right of *Buff the Wood*. Power up to a delicate crux requiring the use of a credit-card-sized edge for most. Keep it together for the final moves before the anchors.
45 ft. 5 bolts. *FA David Hume, 1995.*

❾ Heart Shaped Box 5.12c ★★★★
This line starts about 15 feet right of *Golden Touch*, on a ledge. Scramble up to the ledge to make the first clip. Crank through on decent edges and make the move to the heart-shaped box. Shake out and climb smaller crimps to the anchors.
50 ft. 5 bolts. *FA Brian McCray, 1995.*

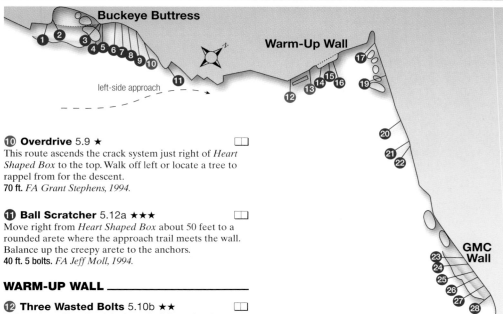

Buckeye Buttress

Warm-Up Wall

left-side approach

GMC Wall

⑩ Overdrive 5.9 ★
This route ascends the crack system just right of *Heart Shaped Box* to the top. Walk off left or locate a tree to rappel from for the descent.
70 ft. *FA Grant Stephens, 1994.*

⑪ Ball Scratcher 5.12a ★★★
Move right from *Heart Shaped Box* about 50 feet to a rounded arete where the approach trail meets the wall. Balance up the creepy arete to the anchors.
40 ft. 5 bolts. *FA Jeff Moll, 1994.*

WARM-UP WALL

⑫ Three Wasted Bolts 5.10b ★★
Follow the trail to the right from *Ball Scratcher* for about 100 feet. This route begins where the trail meets a rock patio. Climb juggy plates to a large ledge, using natural protection to reach the beginning of the route. Continue up the face from the ledge to the anchors.
50 ft. 3 bolts. *FA Unknown, 1996.*

⑬ Crescenta 5.9 ★★
The obvious wide crack a few feet right of the previous route. Walk off left or locate a tree to rappel from for the descent.
70 ft. *FA Grant Stephens, 1994.*

⑭ Breathe Right 5.11c ★★★
This is the first bolted line on the main Warm-Up Wall, just right of *Crescenta*. Climb large holds up and through a fairly sequential section. Relax on large holds again to the anchors.
60 ft. 7 bolts. *FA Brian McCray, 1995.*

⑮ Injured Reserve 5.11a ★★★
Just right of *Breathe Right* is another bolted line. Follow large holds to a slopey crux. Negotiate this section then continue to the anchors on more forgiving holds.
60 ft. 5 bolts. *FA Chris Martin, 1994.*

⑯ Trust in Jesus 5.11b ★★★
The last bolted route on the Warm-up Wall. This route angles up and right through sharp plates and tough moves.
50 ft. 5 bolts. *FA Keith Moll, 1994.*

⑰ Purdy Mouth 5.12b ★★★
Walk right from *Trust in Jesus* to a route that begins just right of a chimney in a corner. Begin on a ledge and pull a difficult, sharp start.
70 ft. 6 bolts. *FA Hugh Loeffler, 1997.*

⑱ Open Project
10 feet left of *Take That, Katie Brown*. Look for the many bail biners.

⑲ Take That, Katie Brown 5.13b ★★★★
This reachy route ascends a line of pockets just right of a brown stain on the wall 50 feet right of *Purdy Mouth* and near a small drainage. Named with Katie Brown's consent as a tongue-in-cheek tribute to her kicking everyone's ass — as in, "thank God we finally found a route she can't onsight."
70 ft. 8 bolts. *FA Hugh Loeffler, 1997.*

⑳ Swahili Slang 5.12b ★★★★★
This picturesque line just begs to be climbed but is rarely traveled due to its less-than-vertical nature. Walk right from *Take That, Katie Brown* for 50 feet to locate a line of bolts near an arching ramp with bright orange stains. Follow the line up through very technical moves and over a small roof just before the anchors.
80 ft. 8 bolts. *FA Jeff Moll, 1995.*

㉑ So Low 5.12b ★★★
Another rarely traveled line that it features technical and enjoyable edging. Move right about 20 feet from *Swahili Slang* to the next bolted line, which begins near a large hueco close to the ground. Climb the plated face right of the hueco to a slab finish.
70 ft. 9 bolts. *FA Brian McCray, 1995.*

㉒ Techno Destructo 5.12b ★★★
Yet another vertical edging challenge that doesn't see much traffic. This route begins just right of a large tree a few feet right of *So Low* and climbs similarly.
80 ft. 10 bolts. *FA Brian McCray, 1995.*

GMC Wall

GMC WALL _____

23 Thanatopsis 5.14a ★★★★★
Move right from *Techno Destructo* about 100 feet to a sandy ledge. This route is the first encountered on an obvious, steep, blank-looking face.
60 ft. 6 bolts. *FA Dave Hume, 1996.*

24 Cut Throat 5.13b ★★★★★
Tough for the grade. This route moves up through crimps on steep rock a few feet right of *Thanatopsis*. Begin by grabbing a shelf about six feet up, then fire up the face and crank through a small overhang just before the anchors.
70 ft. 8 bolts. *FA Jeff Moll, 1995.*

25 8 Ball 5.12d ★★★★★
See description opposite.

26 Snooker 5.13a ★★★★★
This is the next bolted line, eight feet right of *8 Ball*. Begin with a bouldery start to a ledge. Mantel the ledge, then climb slanting crimps to a pocketed section. Make a desperate move left to a jug beneath the roof. Get a shake and climb small crimps on the headwall to the anchors.
70 ft. 8 bolts. *FA Dave Hume, 1995.*

27 Hot For Teacher 5.12c ★★★
Right of Snooker is a gigantic hueco. This line starts by traversing right on the ledge where *Snooker* begins. Climb up a blank face to reach the bottom right side of the hueco. Traverse the edge of the hueco, then pull up right and over a roof to the headwall above. Continue over bulges to the anchors.
80 ft. 7 bolts. *FA Chris Snyder, 1995.*

28 White Man's Overbite 5.13c ★★★★
This is the next bolted line just right of *Hot For Teacher*. Solid for the grade. Using a semi-permanent stack of cheater stones, reach up and grab a jug. Boulder out a steep section and up to a mantel. Continue up the overhanging wall on crimps and sloping holds to a relief jug just before the finishing moves.
80 ft. 9 bolts. *FA Dave Hume, 1995.*

29 White Man's Shuffle 5.13d ★★★★
Begin by climbing *White Man's Overbite*, then move right after the sixth bolt. Longer, more slopey, and substantially harder than *White Man's Overbite*. Solid for the grade.
80 ft. 11 bolts. *FA Bill Ramsey, 2003.*

30 Cosmic Sausage 5.13a ★
This is the last line encountered before the Madness Cave. Begin near the right edge of a large overhang and climb out the overhang on flakes. Turn the lip and bushwhack up the face to a large hueco near the top. Continue up the final and cleaner section of the face to the anchors.
100 ft. 11 bolts. *FA Jeff Moll, 1995.*

25 8 Ball 5.12d ★★★★★

This route begins below a right-facing dihedral 10 feet
right of *Cut Throat*. Start by grabbing a somewhat slopey
hold about six feet up. Crank up to a ledge, then move
left to a flake. Climb the flake for a few moves, prepare
your guns, then race up the vague dihedral and left face
before your arms melt.

70 ft. 7 bolts. *FA Chris Snyder, 1995.*

Climber: Christian Leblanc. Photo: Benjamin Goodpasture.

Madness Cave (starts)

MADNESS CAVE

31 Transworld Depravity 5.14a ★★★★★
Walk right from *Cosmic Sausage* to the beginning of the obvious overhang of the Madness Cave. This is the first line encountered. Begin by climbing through roughly 60 feet of 5.12c moves to a rest. When recovered, power through a hard move to reach sustained tough climbing, which leads to another hard move. Finish by romping up a relaxing 5.13a section to the anchors. It is possible to lower from the route with one 70-meter rope.
110 ft. 14 bolts. *FA Bill Ramsey, 2001.*

32 BOHICA 5.13b ★★★★★
This is the second bolted route in the Madness Cave, just right of *Transworld Depravity*. The first third of the route is a high quality steepish .12a or so, to a good rest. Milk it because the next section is extremely steep — *a la* your basic 45-degree training woody. Power endurancy, body tensiony, big moves. This one stays with you all the way to the anchors. It's a blast!
100 ft. 13 bolts. *FA Jeff Moll, 1995.*

33 Last of the Bohicans 5.13d ★★★★★
The direct finish to *BOHICA*. Continue to the second set of anchors. Low in the grade.
125 ft. 15 bolts. *FA Bill Ramsey, 1998.*

34 Flour Power 5.13b ★★★★★
A bit harder than *BOHICA*, this route begins by climbing through a roof eight feet right of *BOHICA* to reach a steep face. Climb through the steep face to a more vertical section and a good rest on a small ledge before the overhanging headwall. Climb the steep headwall, heading toward a faint dihedral near the top. Rest as well as you can at the base of the dihedral, then punch right and up to the anchors.
100 ft. 14 bolts. *FA Chris Martin, 1997.*

35 Pushin' Up Daisies 5.13c ★★★★★
This extension to *Flour Power* takes the route to the top of the cliff! From the chains above the original ending, make a hard move off a slopey ledge to reach easier climbing. Then make a committing deadpoint move off of two crimps to reach the jug at the top of the cliff. Two additional bolts to *Flour Power*.
FA Brad Weaver, 2008.

36 Omaha Beach 5.14a ★★★★★
One of the best routes of its grade in the country. Begins a few feet right of *Flour Power*, climbs up to the left side of a large alcove, then takes on the steeply overhanging headwall. The lower two-thirds of this route was originally a project named *Ice Cream Man* until Bill Ramsey extended it and made the first ascent in 1999. Shortly after, this line was onsighted by then-local climber Katie Brown! Several holds have since broken, upping the grade from 5.13d to 5.14a. The name comes from "the Beach," a slopey and somewhat sandy poor "rest"at two-thirds height. The crux is getting off the Beach — just like on D-Day.
130 ft. 13 bolts. *FA Bill Ramsey, 1999.*

37 The Madness 5.13c ★★★★★
This line is located 25 feet right of *Omaha Beach*. Move through a low roof to a no-hands rest in an alcove before the headwall. Race up the steep headwall and crank past a bulge near the top to reach the anchors.
120 ft. 13 bolts. *FA Brian Toy, 1997.*

38 Fourty Ounces of Justice 5.13a ★★★★
See description opposite.

38 Fourty Ounces of Justice 5.13a ★★★★

This route gives mortals a taste of the angle of the Madness Cave, but with the penalty of a decrease in quality. Step right from *The Madness* about 15 feet to the next line of bolts, near a small tree. Tram up to the first bolt to reach the starting jug. Power out the steep wall on increasingly larger holds to reach a decent stance just before the less steep but slightly more difficult finish. 110 ft. 14 bolts. *FA Porter Jarrard, 1997.*

Steve McClure thinks on his feet. Photo Keith Ladzinsky.

The Undertow

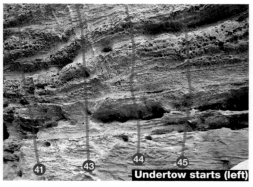

Undertow starts (left)

UNDERTOW WALL

39 The Sauce 5.12b ★★★
Walk right from the Madness Cave to a shorter and less overhanging wall hosting an abundance of lines. *The Sauce* is the first route encountered on the wall and begins to the right of a large tree growing up into the wall. Climb the face to a good stance just before the wall takes a turn for the steep. Pump up the steep face and save some sauce for the roof before the anchors.
60 ft. 6 bolts. *FA Chris Martin, 1995.*

40 Leave It to Beavis 5.12d ★★★★
This is the bolted line 15 feet right of *The Sauce*. Climb up and through a large hueco, then continue up the steep face on big jugs to some challenging pulls on smaller holds right at the top.
90 ft. 8 bolts. *FA Chris Martin, 1995.*

41 Tuna Town 5.12d ★★★★
This route begins near the right side of the large, low hueco that the previous line climbs through. Pump up the steep wall on incredibly big holds to a runout and exciting crux section at the top. Blow the finishing moves and you're going for a huge ride!
85 ft. 10 bolts. *FA Jeff Moll, 1995.*

42 The Flux Capacitor 5.12d ★★★
You'll either love it or hate it. Begin just right of *Tuna Town* on a flake. Climb up to a ledge, then take on a vertical rib system to a decent stance. Continue up past a bulge to reach the anchors.
95 ft. 10 bolts. *FA Chris Martin, 1995.*

43 Harvest 5.12d ★★★★
This route ascends the next line of bolts about 10 feet right of *The Flux Capacitor* and follows some distinctive rib-like features. It can be mossy and green after rain, so try to catch it in dry weather. Begin on a slopey ramp. Interesting moves up the groove and ribs lead to a rest on the right. One more hard move leads to an easier finish.
85 ft. 11 bolts. *FA Jeff Moll, 1994.*

44 Hoofmaker 5.13a ★★★★
Move 10 feet right from *Harvest* to the next line, which begins on a boulder. Climb up to a horizontal shelf, then crank out past a roof to some decent holds. Recover for an endurance haul on the sustained face to the anchors.
90 ft. 10 bolts. *FA Porter Jarrard, 1997.*

45 Team Wilson 5.12d ★★★★★
Tough for the grade. Move right from *Hoofmaker* to locate this route, which begins left of a large stack of boulders. Climb up to a horizontal, then take on a blank face to reach another horizontal. Rest here, then race up the long, strength-sapping headwall to the anchors.
85 ft. 9 bolts. *FA Chris Martin, 1995.*

46 Resurrection 5.12c ★★★★
This route begins on top of a large boulder to the right of *Team Wilson*. Power through the start, then move left through horizontals and continue up through pockets to the anchors. Photo page 346.
80 ft. 7 bolts. *FA Chris Martin, 1995.*

47 Subman 5.12d ★★★★
(aka The High Hard One)
Locate the line of bolts 10 feet right of *Resurrection*. Grab a shelf, then head up and left on sloping holds to a jug rest. Continue up the face on crimps to a corner-like feature. Continue up this feature and over a final bulge. Clipping the chains is often interesting!
80 ft. 8 bolts. *FA Jeff Moll, 1995.*

Undertow starts (center)

Undertow starts (right)

48 Crime Time 5.12d ★★★
Move five feet right from *The High Hard One* to a line of bolts with red hangers. Climb up to a mouth-like feature that is often damp. Make some tough moves and continue up the pumpy face, staying left of a faint dihedral.
75 ft. 7 bolts. *FA Brian McCray, 1995.*

49 Skin Boat 5.13a ★★★★
This route starts a few feet right of *Crime Time*. Climb ledges for a few feet, then make a move to a half-moon-shaped jug that is often damp. Crank through edges and small pockets to the second bolt. Move up to two opposing jugs, then hang on for as long as you can, hopefully all the way to the anchors.
80 ft. 7 bolts. *FA Jeff Moll, 1995.*

50 Convicted 5.13a ★★★★★
This route begins about 15 feet right of *Skin Boat*. It is less sustained but more cruxy than other climbs hereabouts. Boulder the initial section to a small flake, then continue up through pinches and sidepulls to powerful moves on sloping holds at the top.
70 ft. 7 bolts. *FA Jeff Moll, 1995.*

51 Ale-8-One 5.12b ★★★★
Begin just right of *Convicted* and to the left of a low, flat boulder. Climb a flake up to the first bolt, then traverse right and make a tough move to gain a jug. Get a shake and traverse back slightly left to begin the business. Make big moves up the overhanging face to a tough finish on edges and gastons.
65 ft. 7 bolts. *FA Brian McCray, 1995.*

52 Chainsaw Massacre 5.12a ★★★★
Classic enduro-climbing. This route provides a good introduction to the Undertow Wall and the steeper routes at the Lode. Begin on top of the low boulder mentioned in the description of *Ale-8-One*. Climb up, then make a tough move left to a good shake. Paddle up on good edges in a groove between two blank walls, keeping enough energy in reserve to clip the anchors.
60 ft. 7 bolts. *FA Jeff Moll, 1994.*

53 The Verdict 5.12b ★★★
This often-wet route begins on the right side of the low, flat boulder that provides the start for *Chainsaw Massacre,* and takes a line of pockets just left of a large brown streak. If you find it dry, it's worth climbing.
70 ft. 8 bolts. *FA Jeff Moll, 1995.*

54 Sam Krieg Will Bolt Anything 5.11d ★★
(SKWBA)
This line begins just right of *The Verdict*. Unpopular due to the poor rock quality compared to the other lines on this wall.
70 ft. 8 bolts. *FA Sam Krieg, 1997.*

55 Kick Me in the Jimmie 5.12a ★★★★
This route begins slightly uphill and about 30 feet right of *SKWBA*. Start on top of a small boulder, then move up and left to a big sloper move before the anchors.
60 ft. 7 bolts. *FA Jeff Moll, 1994.*

56 Burlier's Bane 5.12a ★★★
This route begins just right of *Kick Me in the Jimmie*, beneath a large hueco. Climb up through pinches and sucker jugs to the anchors.
60 ft. 6 bolts. *FA Roxanna Brock, 1995.*

57 Rocket Dog 5.12b ★★★★
This route begins just right of *Burlier's Bane* and moves up through an obvious black stain. Grab a high ledge and step up to the slopers. Climb slopey pinches for about 10 feet, then make a move right to a jug. Continue up through the groove on pockets to the anchors.
50 ft. 5 bolts. *FA Chris Martin, 1995.*

MOTHERLODE GRADED LIST

HARD

5.14a
Thanatopsis ☐☐
Transworld Depravity ☐☐
Omaha Beach ☐☐

5.13d
White Man's Shuffle ☐☐
Last of the Bohicans ☐☐

5.13c
White Man's Overbite ☐☐
The Madness ☐☐
Pushing' Up Daisies ☐☐

5.13b
Flour Power ☐☐
Take That, Katie Brown ☐☐
Cut Throat ☐☐
Golden Touch ☐☐
BOHICA ☐☐

5.13a
Convicted ☐☐
Hoofmaker ☐☐
Fourty Ounces of Justice ☐☐
Skin Boat ☐☐
Snooker ☐☐
Cosmic Sausage ☐☐

5.12d
8 Ball ☐☐
Team Wilson ☐☐
Subman ☐☐
Crime Time ☐☐
The Flux Capacitor ☐☐
Harvest ☐☐
Leave It to Beavis ☐☐
Tuna Town ☐☐

5.12c
Resurrection ☐☐
The Reacharound ☐☐
Heart Shaped Box ☐☐
Hot For Teacher ☐☐
Stain ☐☐

5.12b
So Low ☐☐
Swahili Slang ☐☐
Techno Destructo ☐☐
The Sauce ☐☐
The Verdict ☐☐
Ale-8-One ☐☐
Purdy Mouth ☐☐
The Chronic ☐☐
Buff the Wood ☐☐
Rocket Dog ☐☐

EASY

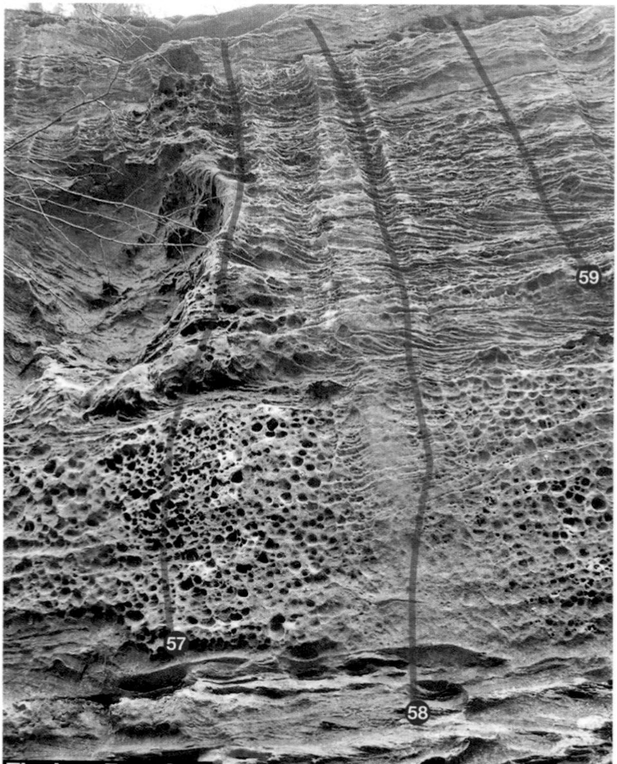

The Low Easy One

58 The Low Easy One 5.12b ★★★ ☐
Walk down some boulders right of *Rocket Dog* to a route with red hangers. Climb pockets to a pointy brown shelf. Get a shake, then continue up on pockets to the anchors.
50 ft. 5 bolts. *FA Roxanna Brock, 1995.*

59 Stella 5.11d ★★★ ☐
This is the next bolted line, about 10 feet right of *The Low Easy One* and just before an arete. Start by grabbing a low shelf and pull up into the business. Crank on gastons and pinches to the anchors.
50 ft. 6 bolts. *FA Roxanna Brock, 1995.*

60 Snapper 5.11a ★★★ ☐
This route begins about 30 feet to the right and around the arete near *Stella*. Climb the near-vertical face on small holds just left of a wide dihedral.
50 ft. 7 bolts. *FA Jeff Moll, 1995.*

61 Stabbed in the Back 5.10a ★ ☐
Yes, this is a crack climb. Climb the wide dihedral just right of *Snapper* to the top. Rappel from a tree to descend.
80 ft. *FA Jeff Moll, 1995.*

62 Scrambled Porn 5.12a ★ ☐
Begin just right of *Stabbed in the Back*. Climb the blank face to a hand ledge about 15 feet up. Continue up the vertical face, passing another horizontal break, to anchors.
60 ft. 6 bolts. *FA Terry Kindred, 2003.*

THE UNLODE

a.m. 5 mins | OK in rain | 3 routes

5.6- .7 .8 .9 .10 .11 .12 .13 .14

Photo: Elodie Saracco

Character

This little wall has a short approach and offers a couple of short, steep alternative warm-ups for climbers headed to the Motherlode.

Approach

Park in the Motherlode parking area, but hike back up the gravel road in the direction you drove in for a few minutes until you see an old and very over-grown logging road heading down the slope on your left. Follow the road a few hundred feet until you see the cliff to your right.

Conditions

The quality of the routes isn't stellar, but they should clean up with more traffic. Beware wasps in the summer.

❶ Undesirable 5.11c ★★★
This bolted route begins just right of a large tree. Climb overhanging rock to the anchors. Short but pumpy.
45 ft. 5 bolts. *FA Kellyn Gorder, 1996.*

❷ Unworthy 5.11a ★★
This is the next route left of *Undesirable*. Climb steep rock on larger holds to the anchors. Beware of swinging into the large tree while cleaning.
45 ft. 4 bolts. *FA Kellyn Gorder, 1996.*

❸ Unbridled 5.10c ★★★
Locate this route by walking left from *Unworthy* for about 200 feet to a less steep face.
55 ft. 6 bolts. *FA Kellyn Gorder, 1996*

Undesirable

THE CHOCOLATE FACTORY

30 routes

5.6- .7 .8 .9 .10 .11 .12 .13 .14

all day 10 mins

Character

The Chocolate Factory is best known for what may possibly be the most difficult sport line in the Red, *The Golden Ticket*. The route spit off some of the strongest climbers in the world who visited during the 2007 Petzl Rock Trip. Cameras were rolling while Chris Sharma made an attempt at the line, which later appeared in the climbing video *The Players*. Although a few of the climbers stuck around to give it some more attempts, none of them was successful. Two years later it was no surprise to locals that Adam Taylor of Lexington, KY, had finally put this line to sleep. However, just left of this line is another line nearly as striking but supposedly more difficult. Time will tell if it's even possible.

Photo: Keith Ladzinsky.

Aside from the insanely difficult, this wall still has plenty to offer. One of the best new 5.10 pumpfests, *Loompa,* and its brother *Oompa,* are well worth a trip to this cliff. There's even a lot for the traddies, including a couple of difficult lines: *Charlie,* 5.13b, and *Through the Looking Glass,* 5.11d. The routes here tend to involve more crimping and face climbing than overhanging jug hauling, so bring your finger strength in full force.

If you want to view one of the largest hornet's nest you'll ever see, take a hike up and look up and left of *The Golden Ticket,* in a large hueco near the top of the cliff.

Approach

Park in the Motherlode parking area and walk down the road toward Sore Heel Hollow parking area until you see a dirt road on the right. Walk up the dirt road about 100 yards until it turns right. Don't follow the road, but continue straight onto a path that will lead directly to the Chocolate Factory. Hiking time is approximately five minutes from the Motherlode parking area. To reach routes from *The Mad Hatter's Tea Party* through *Chocolate River,* take the left logging road visible shortly before you reach the cliff. To reach *Peaches and Cream* and the routes right of it, do not take the first left logging road. Stay on the trail for about 50 more feet until you see a cliff visible just up on the left with a short trail leading to it.

Conditions

There's plenty to do here on a light rainy day, as most of the routes are slightly overhanging. *Oompa* and *Loompa* will more than likely remain dry during the heaviest rains. Due to the extensive length and changing direction of the cliff, you're bound to find sun or shade when you need it.

to *routes #1 to 9*

to *Crimp My Ride*

❶ The Mad Hatter's Tea Party 5.9 ★★★
As the approach trail nears the cliff, look for an old logging road on the left. Follow the road/trail for about 100 yards until it turns uphill and ends at a section of the cliff containing some bolted lines. This is the obvious crack about 30 feet left of those lines. A stiff start leads to a stance, then jam or use limited face holds to reach the widening crack. Grab a welcomed rest before a featured section, then pull over the roof to a last move before the anchors.
70 ft. *FA Russ Jackson, Scott Hammon, Arnoldo Hutchinson, Frank Waters, Kipp Trummel, 2009.*

❷ Wobbler 5.11d ★★★★
This is the first bolted line right of *Mad Hatter's*. Begin with a few big moves, then race through sequential pockets and small crimps with no good rest to be had. Pull a small roof to gain the chains and throw a huge wobbler if you fall at this point because you have to do it all over again.
55 ft. 6 bolts. *FA Ray Ellington, Kipp Trummel, 2009.*

❸ Stalker 5.11d ★★★
Just right of *Wobbler*. Start with the comfort of a pair of good holds, which quickly diminish to relentless crimping up the slightly overhanging face. Grab a good shake on a decent set of slots, then crimp even harder through the obvious crux near the top. As with *Wobbler*, don't blow it going for the chains.
55 ft. 6 bolts. *FA Ray Ellington, Kipp Trummel, 2009.*

❹ One Side Makes You Taller 5.11a ★★★
Begin 10 feet right of *Stalker*, in a short flake. Climb a short section of flake, then exit up on large plates and knobs, trending left to a decent rest. Step off the rest and crimp a little harder on smaller edges to reach the chains.
55 ft. 6 bolts. *FA Russ Jackson, 2009.*

Wobbler

⑤ Through the Looking Glass 5.11d ★★★★ ☐
This is the overhanging acute dihedral right of the bolted lines. Climb through 35 feet of large blocks to reach a ledge. Take a deep breath then dive into relentless stemming and body smearing with difficult placements along the way.
75 ft. *FA Russ Jackson, 2009.*

⑥ Malice 5.12c ★★★★★ ☐
Right of the previous dihedral is a concave, gold and black streaked wall with two bolted lines. This is the left line and is a must do. Climb up a short, easy slab section to reach the overhang. Pop over to a large jug feature that may have some chalked X marks, but don't let them scare you. Many climbers have yarded on this feature and it hasn't broken. Reach hard for slopers, then leave the safety of the jugs for some of the best moves and holds the Red has to offer. A surprise route awaits you after the steep section is over.
60 ft. 8 bolts. *FA Kipp Trummel, 2009.*

⑦ Hookah 5.12b ★★★ ☐
Start the same as *Malice*, but move up and right instead of going to the jug feature at the start of the overhang. Pull a tough cross move, then bust up and right past a sloper crux. You're racing the pump clock on this one, so move quick. End with easier climbing near a crack to the chains.
60 ft. 8 bolts. *FA Ray Ellington, Kipp Trummel, 2009.*

⑧ Wonderland 5.10b ★★★★ ☐
This mixed line is about 50 feet right of *Hookah* and begins with a short crack. Pass a small section of face climbing, then up to a nice-looking thin dihedral. Maneuver around a bulge at the top of the dihedral, then continue up the crack to the chains.
80 ft. 1 bolt. *FA Russ Jackson, 2009.*

⑨ Down the Rabbit Hole 5.9 ★★ ☐
Walk right from *Wobbler*, then up and around the corner to a small clearing just past a large boulder. Thrash your way up the obvious offwidth until you can gain the face when the crack narrows. Get a last good piece, then run out the dirty slab to the top.
85 ft. *FA Russ Jackson, Scott Brown, 2009.*

⑩ End of the Innocence 5.10b ★★★ ☐
This and the following three routes are right of *Down the Rabbit Hole*, at the head of the main trail where it meets the cliff. Walk back down to the trail, then head back toward the fork near the top of the main trail. Look for a large boulder on your left with a trail bordering its left side. Head uphill to meet up with three bolted slab climbs. Walk 25 feet left from these lines to a crack at the left end of a roof 10 feet up. Scramble up to reach the crack. Place some small gear above your head, then crank through the initial layback moves to easier climbing above.
80 ft. *FA Phil Wilkes, Art Cammers, 2009.*

⑪ Sugar Rush 5.10a ★★★ ☐
This is the leftmost of the three bolted slab climbs mentioned above. Climbs well. Check out the view from the chains.
65 ft. 6 bolts. *FA Jeff Neal, Russ Jackson, 2009.*

⑫ Augustus Gloop 5.9 ★★★ ☐
Right of *Sugar Rush*. Start on large ledges or traverse in from the right. Fun slabbing on solid stone.
60 ft. 5 bolts. *FA Jeff Neal, Russ Jackson, Rick Estes, 2009.*

⑬ Chocolate River 5.9 ★★ ☐
Just right of *Augustus Gloop*. Begin on a reachy mantel and then climb a technical, slabby face to a finish over a bulge.
50 ft. 5 bolts. *FA Sam Cervantes, Dave Strawser, 2009.*

⑭ Peaches and Cream 5.10b ★★★ ☐
As the approach trail nears the cliff, continue past the logging road that leads left to *Wobbler*. Take the next trail on the left, which leads straight up to a vertical wall containing several bolted lines. This crack is just left of *J-Rat's Back* and starts with a low roof.
60 ft. *FA Mike Conley, Ron Snider, 2009.*

⑮ J-Rat's Back 5.12a ★★★★ ☐
This is the leftmost bolted route on the vertical wall visible as you approach the cliff. Climb slotted pockets to reach a distinct crux section. Continue up to a short overhanging pockets section just before the chains.
70 ft. 10 bolts. *FA Dario Ventura, 2007.*

⑯ Mike Teavee 5.12a ★★★ ☐
Fifteen feet right of *J-Rat's Back*. Climb a few bolts to reach a tough crux guarding the prominent flake feature, which leads to easier climbing for the rest of the route.
70 ft. 10 bolts. *FA Kenny Barker, 2007.*

⑰ Violet Beauregarde 5.12a ★★ ☐
Rightmost line on the vertical wall. Begin on the left edge of a low hueco. The first bolt is extremely high for some strange reason.
70 ft. 10 bolts. *FA Nate Auk, 2007.*

⑱ Willy Wonka 5.11a ★★★ ☐
This slab line can be found 50 feet right of the previous lines and is just off the main trail. Shorties will have a tough time with the opening moves. Tiptoe up the slab past several distinct cruxes.
60 ft. 8 bolts. *FA Karen Clark, Joel Handley, Kipp Trummel, 2008.*

⑲ Fickelgruber 5.8 ★★★ ☐
Obvious chimney offwidth to the right of *Willie Wonka*. Climb the chimney and offwidth to a roof. Pull the roof to get 30 feet of hand crack to a ledge.
60 ft. *FA Greg Humburg, Don McGlone, 2009.*

J-Rat's Back

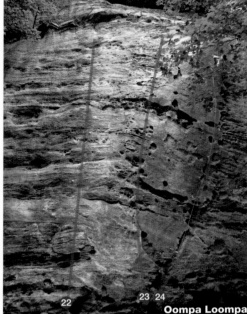

Oompa Loompa

Charlie

⓴ The Andy Man Can 5.10d ★★★ ⬚
Walk right from *Willy Wonka* to locate this crack, situated up and left above a large ledge. Continue through the thin-hands crack in a steep dihedral to a sit-down rest in a large hueco. From the hueco, continue up an offwidth, making use of good face holds to the top. **65 ft.** *FA Andy Davis, Rachel Melville, 2007.*

㉑ Veruca Salt 5.12a ★★★ ⬚
This bolted line is just right of *The Andy Man Can* and also begins on a high ledge. Battle dual aretes and shoot for a jug. Crux out onto the face, then continue up and left around the arete to the chains. **55 ft. 6 bolts.** *FA Kipp Trummel, 2008.*

㉒ The Glass Elevator 5.10d ★★★ ⬚
Fifty feet right of *Veruca Salt* is a featured wall hosting three bolted lines. This is the leftmost line on the wall. **65 ft. 6 bolts.** *FA Nick Redinger, 2007.*

㉓ Oompa 5.10a ★★★ ⬚
Next line right of *Glass Elevator*. Match and cross through an excellent line of sequential pockets and edges. A great line, but doesn't deliver the pump you'll get from *Loompa*. **55 ft. 6 bolts.** *FA Kenny Barker, Julie Smith, 2008.*

㉔ Loompa 5.10c ★★★★★ ⬚
One of the better 5.10 lines in the Red. Pump up the overhanging wall on incuts and pockets to reach a crux just where you don't want it. Dive for a gigantic horn and chill to the chains. **55 ft. 6 bolts.** *FA Kenny Barker, Julie Smith, 2008.*

The Golden Ticket

Open Projects

25 Charlie 5.13b ★★★★
See description opposite.

26 Honeycomb 5.14? ★★★
Begin just right of *Charlie* on the large boulder. Climb overhanging stone on good holds, which diminish near the third bolt. Currently an **open project**. Grade is estimated.
75 ft. 9 bolts.

27 The Golden Ticket 5.14c ★★★★★
50 feet right of the previous route is this striking line, which served many during the 2007 Petzl Rock Trip. Climb this slightly overhanging face, passing accuracy stabs and near-double-digit boulder problems, to a brutal showdown at the chains. Quite possibly the most difficult line in the Red at this time.
75 ft. 9 bolts. *FA Adam Taylor, 2009.*

28 Taffy Puller 5.13? ★★★
Right of the previous line is a prow-like feature hosting two lines. This is the left-most line and angles right to take on a short and steep arete, then finishes on a more vertical face. Currently an **open project**. Grade is estimated.
70 ft. 10 bolts.

29 The Syndicate 5.13? ★★★
This is the next route taking on the prow feature. Begin beneath the prow, then launch up to the right edge of a V-shaped hueco. Finish on a long and more vertical face. Currently an **open project**. Grade is estimated.
65 ft. 8 bolts.

30 Crimp My Ride 5.12a ★★★
Continue walking past the previous lines, crossing a ledge, until you reach a vertical wall. This is the first line encountered on the wall. Climb small edges into pockets to reach a no-hands rest on a ledge.
70 ft. 7 bolts. *FA Mike Conley, Ron Snider, 2009.*

25 Charlie 5.13b ★★★★

Just around the corner from *Loompa* is
this striking dihedral, which received an
attempt by Lynn Hill during the Petzl
Rock Trip in 2007. After her attempt, the
FA team all sent on preplaced gear the
same day.
75 ft. *FA Steve McClure, Mike Doyle,
Daniel DuLac, Sonnie Trotter, 2007.*

Climber: Steve McClure. Photo: Keith Ladzinsky.

SOUTHERN OUTLYING CLIFFS

Character
This short chapter features two small cliffs, The Oasis and Mount Olive Rock. These cliffs are located in the southwest of the Red River Gorge region, but are not part of the PMRP on Motherlode groups of crags.

Approach
The Motherlode Region map on page 347 shows the location of The Oasis and Mount Olive Rock. For detailed approach information, see the descriptions for each cliff.

MOUNT OLIVE ROCK

4 routes

all day | 5 mins | OK in rain | 5.6- .7 .8 .9 .10 .11 .12

Character
Although this small roadside area has only a few routes, all of them are worth doing, especially if you want to escape the crowds. *South Side of the Sky* is a must-do for any crack climber. Save it for a rainy day; due to the massive roof, it never sees a drop of rain.

Approach
This crag is located beyond the turnoff from KY 498 to the Motherlode. To find it, drive a full two miles down KY 498 past the Motherlode turnoff until you reach a T-intersection. Turn right on KY 52 and drive 2.8 miles to a small pulloff on the right between guard rails. Walk down the road 150 feet and look for an obvious left-facing dihedral on the cliff to your left. This is *South Side of the Sky*.

South Side of the Sky

❶ **South Side of the Sky** 5.11a ★★★★★
Climb the obvious, thin, left-facing dihedral to anchors under the roof. Watch for poison ivy around the anchors.
60 ft. *FA Martin Hackworth, Ron Martin, 1986.*

❷ **South Central** 5.11a ★★
Climb the line of obvious pockets around the corner 20 feet right of *South Side of the Sky* to chain anchors.
50 ft. 6 bolts. *FA Chris Snyder, 1996.*

❸ **Sprout's Climb** 5.10c ★★★
This route ascends the dihedral 50 feet left of *South Side of the Sky*. Climb the dihedral, then continue out the roof. Pull around the lip, then continue up to the anchors above *Palm Friction*.
50 ft. *FA Tom Fyffe, Matt Flach, 1997.*

❹ **Palm Friction** 5.10a R ★★
Climb the face 15 feet left of *Sprout's Climb*. Be careful of the long runout between the second and third bolts. The climbing is relatively easy in that section, but the fall would be close to a grounder.
65 ft. 6 bolts. *FA Kellyn Gorder, Barry Brolley, 1997.*

THE OASIS

all day · 10 mins · 5 routes

5.6- .7 .8 .9 .10 .11 .12 .13

Character

This small, obscure sport crag offers a few worthwhile lines. *Paddy O'Keefe's Walking Shoes* is the best route here. It begins with precise pocket stabbing on bullet-hard sandstone and ends with fun moves on an overhanging runout to the anchors.

With slopey moves up a short but powerful face, *Finnegan's Ladder* has the dubious distinction of being the shortest route in the Red.

Approach

From Miguel's Pizza, drive about seven miles south on KY 11 to the town of Zachariah, just before the Lee County line. Turn right onto 1036 and drive 2.0 miles. Just after a fenced-in oil-drilling yard, you'll see Big Bend Road. Drive past this road for 0.1 miles until you see the Sun Oil parking lot to your right. Depending on the condition of the gravel road and the quality of your 4WD vehicle, you can park here or head down the gravel road that descends from the parking lot. Walk or drive down the steep gravel road for 0.4 miles until you see an obvious cliff to your right. Head up a swampy drainage to reach the wall.

Conditions

This wall bakes in the sun. Avoid it at all costs during the summer. If the heat doesn't keep you away, the wasps will. The rock on the middle two routes is of poor quality, but the quality improves on the left and right sides of the wall.

❶ Finnegan's Ladder 5.11b ★★★
Walk to the left side of the wall to locate this short but powerful line. Climb the face via pinches and slopers to reach anchors 25 feet up.
25 ft. 3 bolts. *FA Mike Riegert, 1998.*

❷ Buzz 5.11b ★★
Move back right and over the swampy drainage to the next bolted line on the middle section of the cliff. Climb the steep face via pockets and edges with a big move before the anchors.
50 ft. 5 bolts. *FA Neal Strickland, 1998.*

❸ Hum 5.11a ★★★
Step right a few feet to the next line, which climbs similarly but is a bit easier than *Buzz*. Beware of bats and wasps in the huecos and on ledges.
50 ft. 5 bolts. *FA Mike Riegert, 1998.*

❹ Paddy O'Keefe's 5.11d ★★★★
Walking Shoes
This route alone will make your visit worthwhile. Walk right about 30 feet to the next line, which begins with an obvious section of pockets. Boulder through the pockets, then pull up onto the face. Creep over to a steep section, then gun for the anchors.
50 ft. 5 bolts. *FA Mike Riegert, Neal Strickland, 1998.*

❺ Manzanita 5.12b ★★★
Just right of the previous line is this long endurance route. Climb to the anchors, being careful of loose rock along the way.
85 ft. 9 bolts. *FA Mike Riegert, 1998.*

GRADED LIST OF SPORT CLIMBS

PROJECTS

Southern Smoke Direct	★★★★★ 336
Iron Mike (Open Project)	★★★★ 321
Beer Trailer Project 1	★★★ 202
Gild the Lily (Closed Project)	★★★ 310
Honeycomb	★★★ 364
Sheet Rock	★★★ 260
Van der Waals Goo	★★★ 216
The Handout	★★ 258
Three-Toed Sloth	★★ 218
Black Hoof (Open Project)	235
Closed Project	295
Gold Coast Project 1	281
Gold Coast Project 2	281
Imagine There's No Heaven	302
Open Project	351
The Galaxy Project	345
The Sharma Project	345
Unnamed Grade Unknown	304
Vader project	288

5.14c

Fifty Words for Pump	★★★★★ 336
Lucifer	★★★★★ 308
Southern Smoke	★★★★★ 336
The Golden Ticket	★★★★★ 364

5.14b

The Shocker	★★★★ 293

5.14a

God's Own Stone	★★★★★ 281
Omaha Beach	★★★★★ 354
Thanatopsis	★★★★★ 352
Transworld Depravity	★★★★★ 354
Cherry Red	★★★★ 242
100 Ounces of Gold	★★★★ 281
The Nothing	★★★ 345

5.13d

Last of the Bohicans	★★★★★ 354
Nagypapa	★★★★★ 45
True Love	★★★★★ 281
Ultra Perm	★★★★★ 338
Super Charger	★★★★ 345
Swingline	★★★★ 288
White Man's Shuffle	★★★★ 352
Sugar Magnolia	★★★ 335

5.13c

Black Gold	★★★★★ 280
Kaleidoscope	★★★★★ 344
Pushin' Up Daisies	★★★★★ 354
The Madness	★★★★★ 355
White Man's Overbite	★★★★ 352

5.13b

BOHICA	★★★★★ 354
Cut Throat	★★★★★ 352
Dracula '04	★★★★★ 308
Flour Power	★★★★★ 354

Golden Boy	★★★★★ 281
Table of Colors Direct	★★★★★ 55
The Legend	★★★★★ 45
The Return of Darth Moll	★★★★★ 288
Shiva	★★★★ 215
Big Burley	★★★★ 288
Dirty, Smelly Hippie	★★★★ 345
Elephant Man	★★★★ 288
Falls City	★★★★ 202
Golden Touch	★★★★ 350
No Redemption	★★★★ 335
Paradise Regained	★★★★ 308
"Take That, Katie Brown "	★★★★ 351
The Castle Has Fallen	★★★★ 308
The Wheel of Time	★★★★ 179
El Encuentro	★★★ 340
Gecko Circus	★★★ 283
Jedi Mind Trick	★★★ 288
MILF Money	★★★ 336
Non starter	★★★ 288
Paranoia	★★★ 195
Sam's Line	197

5.13a

Table of Colors	★★★★★ 55
Appalachian Spring	★★★★★ 155
Convicted	★★★★★ 357
Paradise Lost	★★★★★ 308
Prometheus Unbound	★★★★★ 244
Snooker	★★★★★ 352
Table of Colors	★★★★★ 55
The Force	★★★★★ 288
Beer Belly	★★★★ 345
Brilliant Orange	★★★★ 282
Bundle of Joy	★★★★ 227
Fourty Ounces of Justice	★★★★ 354
Hoofmaker	★★★★ 356
Kya	★★★★ 235
Name Dropper	★★★★ 244
Skin Boat	★★★★ 357
Straight Outta Campton	★★★★ 288
Zendebad	★★★★ 225
A Farewell to Arms	★★★ 214
Blue Jacket	★★★ 235
Calm Like a Bomb	★★★ 294
Chunnel	★★★ 189
Quantum Narcissist	★★★ 291
Second Nature	★★★ 291
"Spank, aka Tika Monster "	★★★ 345
Taste the Rainbow	★★★ 302
Starfish and Coffee	★★ 214
Blue Sunday	★★ 244
Easy Rider	★★ 345
Cosmic Sausage	★ 352
El Patron	251
Revival	48

5.13

Swine Flew	★★★★ 322
Praying Mantis	★★★ 274
Taffy Puller	★★★ 364

The Syndicate	★★★ 364
The Tribute	★★ 294

5.12d

8 Ball	★★★★★ 353
Jesus Wept	★★★★★ 244
Shanghai	★★★★★ 288
Stunning the Hog	★★★★★ 54
Team Wilson	★★★★★ 356
Triple Sec (aka 50 Bucks)	★★★★★ 244
Phantasia	★★★★ 103
Tapeworm	★★★★ 215
Code Red	★★★★ 313
Harvest	★★★★ 356
Leave It to Beavis	★★★★ 356
Mad Porter's Disease	★★★★ 201
Racer X	★★★★ 195
Seppuku	★★★★ 155
Subman	★★★★ 356
Tuna Town	★★★★ 356
Tuskan Raider	★★★★ 288
Wicked Games	★★★★ 182
Zen and the Art of Masturbation	★★★★ 293
Urban Voodoo	★★★ 227
Better Than Homemade	★★★ 203
Crime Time	★★★ 357
Cruxifixion	★★★ 244
Mind Meld	★★★ 288
Peace Frog	★★★ 244
The Flux Capacitor	★★★ 356
Hoosier Boys	★★ 244
Reticent	★★ 339
Pile Driver	★ 303

5.12c

Cell Block Six	★★★★★ 215
Super Slab	★★★★★ 50
Hellraiser	★★★★★ 308
Malice	★★★★★ 362
Orange Juice	★★★★★ 155
Reload	★★★★★ 212
Stain	★★★★★ 350
Steelworker	★★★★★ 194
Super Slab	★★★★★ 51
Wild Gift	★★★★★ 187
The Crucible	★★★★ 215
Vortex	★★★★ 215
Belly of the Beast	★★★★ 304
Blood Bath	★★★★ 340
Demon Seed	★★★★ 335
Earth-Bound Misfit	★★★★ 321
Hang Over	★★★★ 203
Heart Shaped Box	★★★★ 350
Herd Mentality	★★★★ 279
Iron Lung	★★★★ 211
Mirage	★★★★ 227
Mosaic	★★★★ 294
Mule	★★★★ 45
Resurrection	★★★★ 356
Science Friction	★★★★ 183

Route	Rating	Page
The Dinosaur	★★★★	55
The Pessimist	★★★★	251
The Return of Frank Byron	★★★★	325
Where's the Beef?	★★★★	340
Dirty Sanchez	★★★	290
So Long Mr. Petey	★★★	226
Blank Canvas	★★★	292
Drop the Hammer	★★★	240
Gorilla	★★★	218
Hardman	★★★	89
Hot For Teacher	★★★	352
Into the Mystic	★★★	195
Mr. Roarke	★★★	283
Out on a Limb	★★★	146
Rostam	★★★	225
The Reacharound	★★★	350
Daisychain	★★	51
Granny Panties	★★	336
Thunder	★★	327
Psychopathy	★	279
Torrential	★	195
Flashlight		155
Hydro Shock		195
Impossible Choss		197
Thirsting Skull		50

5.12b

Route	Rating	Page
Abiyoyo	★★★★★	228
Gung Ho	★★★★★	46
Mercy, the Huff	★★★★★	55
Reliquary	★★★★★	46
Samurai	★★★★★	322
Soul Ram	★★★★★	148
Swahili Slang	★★★★★	351
Tissue Tiger	★★★★★	46
Galunlati	★★★★	227
Super Best Friends	★★★★	227
Ale-8-One	★★★★	357
Big Money Grip	★★★★	195
Blue Collar	★★★★	244
Blue Eyed Honkey Jesus	★★★★	279
Buff the Wood	★★★★	350
Bullfighter	★★★★	212
Cosmic Trigger	★★★★	248
Deep Six	★★★★	180
Duputyren's Release	★★★★	313
Far From God	★★★★	302
Infectious	★★★★	53
Iniquity	★★★★	215
Jersey Connection	★★★★	185
Nicoderm	★★★★	48
Rocket Dog	★★★★	357
Sex Farm	★★★★	54
Tic-Tac-Toe	★★★★	186
Tumble Dry Low	★★★★	312
American Dream	★★★	288
Barbed Wire	★★★	322
Beer Trailer	★★★	203
Bleed Like Me	★★★	296
Etrier	★★★	51
False Idol	★★★	302
Gladiator	★★★	64
High Life	★★★	203
Hookah	★★★	362
Knees and Toes	★★★	345
Liquid Courage	★★★	203
Manzanita	★★★	367

Route	Rating	Page
Purdy Mouth	★★★	351
So Low	★★★	351
Special Impetus	★★★	51
Stretcherous	★★★	241
Strevels Gets In Shape	★★★	187
Summer Sunshine	★★★	227
Techno Destructo	★★★	351
The Low Easy One	★★★	358
The Rifleman	★★★	149
The Sauce	★★★	356
The Verdict	★★★	357
Whipper Snapper	★★★	343
Damascus	★★	281
Headwall	★★	183
Irreverent C	★★	302
Luck's Up	★★	103
Mis-Conception	★★	321
Outbreak	★★	327
Seeker	★★	180
Sister Catherine the Conqueror	★★	332
The Chronic	★★	350
Zone of Silence	★★	284
Aviary	★	191
Coexistence		42

5.12a

Route	Rating	Page
Bare Metal Teen	★★★★★	195
Check Your Grip	★★★★★	343
Dogleg	★★★★★	335
Hippocrite	★★★★★	191
Ro Shampo	★★★★★	186
The Gift	★★★★★	61
Twinkie	★★★★★	102
Are the Pies Fresh?	★★★★	62
Bettavul Pipeline	★★★★	340
Break the Scene	★★★★	294
Chainsaw Massacre	★★★★	357
Cheetah	★★★★	251
Child of the Earth	★★★★	211
Glide	★★★★	218
Glory Be	★★★★	156
Gluttony	★★★★	306
Go Easy Billy Clyde!	★★★★	153
Golden Road	★★★★	208
Grippy Green	★★★★	287
GSW	★★★★	313
Hakuna Matata	★★★★	342
J-Rat's Back	★★★★	362
Kick Me in the Jimmie	★★★★	357
Little Teapot	★★★★	304
Lobster Claw	★★★★	317
Magnum Opus	★★★★	226
Morning Wood	★★★★	202
Nicorette	★★★★	48
Pine	★★★★	188
Primus Noctum	★★★★	343
Scar Tissue	★★★★	191
Stay the Hand	★★★★	186
Supafly	★★★★	279
Suppress the Rage	★★★★	266
Tacit	★★★★	339
Too Many Puppies	★★★★	52
Us and Them	★★★★	198
Way Up Yonder	★★★★	187
Wildfire	★★★★	327
Straightedge	★★★	68
Posse Whipped	★★★	240

Route	Rating	Page
Apadana	★★★	225
Ball Scratcher	★★★	351
Beef Stick	★★★	229
Blake's Route	★★★	329
Burlier's Bane	★★★	357
Campfire Crank	★★★	137
Continental	★★★	265
Cork Eye	★★★	317
Crimp My Ride	★★★	364
Denial	★★★	62
Dr. Synchro (Project)	★★★	314
Evening Wood	★★★	202
Extra Backup	★★★	342
Freakin' Deacon	★★★	212
Frugal Chariot	★★★	152
Hardcore Jollies	★★★	156
Immaculate Deception	★★★	244
Legalize It	★★★	274
Lolita	★★★	224
Mama Benson	★★★	287
Mike Teavee	★★★	362
Nolo Contendere	★★★	146
Ohio Arts	★★★	233
Route 22	★★★	336
Slip It In	★★★	62
Sluts are Cool	★★★	203
Tabernacle	★★★	246
Techulicous	★★★	287
The Frayed Ends of Sanity	★★★	180
Veruca Salt	★★★	363
Wearing Out My Welcome	★★★	318
What's Right With the Underling?	★★★	146
"Wild, Yet Tasty "	★★★	55
Yosemite Sam	★★★	322
Black Plague	★★	281
Double Stuff	★★	228
Flying Serpents	★★	219
Go Home Yankee	★★	318
Nothing For Now	★★	50
Paladine	★★	225
The Bulge	★★	176
The Stranger	★★	223
Violet Beauregarde	★★	362
Grunge Face	★	149
Jeff's Boneyard Project	★	218
Scrambled Porn	★	358
Crumblies		304
Rad Boy Go		50
Right Turret		50

5.12

Route	Rating	Page
Kung Fu Panda	★★★	274
Far Side Project #1	★★	290
Directed Panspermia	★★	231

5.11d/5.12a

Route	Rating	Page
Forearm Follies	★★★★	44

5.11+

Route	Rating	Page
Stems and Seeds	★★★	231
Team Wilander	★★★	321

5.11d

Route	Rating	Page
All Things Considered	★★★★★	51
Papa Love Jugs	★★★★★	291
Seek The Truth	★★★★★	200
The Infidel	★★★★★	153

370 • SPORT ROUTES GRADED LIST

The Return of Chris Snyder	★★★★★	188
Buddha Hole	★★★★	279
Camp	★★★★	158
Dave the Dude	★★★★	148
Ethics Police	★★★★	279
Everything That Rises ...	★★★★	223
Gold Rush	★★★★	293
Head and Shoulders	★★★★	345
Hemisfear	★★★★	183
Horn	★★★★	338
Manifest Destiny	★★★★	226
Martin Rides Again	★★★★	149
My How Things Have Change	★★★★	201
Night Foxx	★★★★	260
No Fluff	★★★★	282
Paddy O'Keefe's Walking Shoes	★★★★	367
Pongosapien	★★★★	310
Recoil	★★★★	193
Red Shift	★★★★	283
Velvet	★★★★	338
Welcomed Guest	★★★★	318
Wobbler	★★★★	361
You Take Sally	★★★★	330
Social Stigma	★★★	240
ATM	★★★	291
Avalanche Run	★★★	327
Collision Damage	★★★	304
Coming Out Party	★★★	302
Corpus Delicti	★★★	145
Crack the Whip	★★★	300
Earthsurfer	★★★	236
East of Eden	★★★	224
Fire and Finesse	★★★	62
Flush	★★★	338
Foot Jive	★★★	276
Government Cheese	★★★	50
Highway Turtle	★★★	284
Hippie Speed Ball	★★★	274
Hoosier Buddies	★★★	200
My Name is Earl	★★★	320
Onaconaronni	★★★	200
Outlaw Justice	★★★	322
Physical Graffiti	★★★	149
Scissors	★★★	186
Sport for Brains	★★★	200
Stalker	★★★	361
Stella	★★★	358
Sweet Tater	★★★	219
The Happy Fisherman	★★★	241
The Last Slow Draw	★★★	217
Velvet Revolution	★★★	266
Wake and Bake	★★★	274
Whip It Out	★★★	59
Who is Who?	★★★	302
Wreaking Havoc	★★★	180
Down by Law	★★	180
Mud on the Rug	★★	345
Sam Krieg Will Bolt Anything	★★	357
Slut Men	★★	342
The Adventure	★★	186
The Business	★★	345
Who Knows?	★★	302
The Snatch	★	64
Beeper		335
Jac Mac		50
Sand		187
The Route Goes Where!?		147

5.11c

No Place Like Home	★★★★★	175
Areterection	★★★★	251
Lip Service	★★★★	229
Bangers and Mash	★★★★	219
Banshee	★★★★	228
Battery Life	★★★★	229
Bessie	★★★★	330
Bozo's Bogus Booty Biner	★★★★	50
Centerfire	★★★★	193
Different Strokes	★★★★	292
Disappearer	★★★★	180
Game Boy	★★★★	62
Noo-tha	★★★★	235
October Sky	★★★★	276
Psyberpunk	★★★★	248
Sacred Stones	★★★★	211
Sex Show	★★★★	198
Sick Puppies	★★★★	149
Special Boy	★★★★	306
Spirit Fingers	★★★★	343
Teeter Totter	★★★★	300
The Love Shack	★★★★	90
The Unbearable Lightness of	★★★★	223
There Goes the Neighborhood	★★★★	155
Livin' in the UK	★★★	201
All the Pretty Horses	★★★	223
Apotheosis Denied	★★★	238
Big Sinkin' Breakdown	★★★	343
Bowling Pain	★★★	314
Breathe Right	★★★	351
Conscription	★★★	327
Crucify Me	★★★	302
Flying Monkeys	★★★	174
Happy Feet	★★★	274
L'Ile au Ciel	★★★	156
Lynx Jinx	★★★	191
Mas Choss	★★★	336
Mid-Life Crisis	★★★	241
Minimum Creep	★★★	48
Much Ado About Nothing	★★★	220
Oz	★★★	174
Parasite	★★★	240
Relaxed Atmosphere	★★★	54
Stand and Deliver	★★★	59
The Fury	★★★	224
The Poacher	★★★	92
Third-World Lover	★★★	54
Undesirable	★★★	359
Who Pooped in the Park?	★★★	223
A Confederacy of Dunces	★★	224
Amelia's Birthday	★★	284
Cannabis Love Generator	★★	274
Digitalgia	★★	291
G'sUs	★★	200
"Hagis, Neeps and Tatties "	★★	219
Hoosierheights.com	★★	216
On Beyond Zebra!	★★	191
One-Eyed Willy Up the Back	★★	350
Red Tag Rape	★★	276
Stephanie's Cabaret	★★	298
Subtle Thievery	★★	327
The Love Song of J. Alfred ...	★★	224
The Sound	★★	224
Which is Which?	★★	302
Hurricane Amy		48

5.11b

Amarillo Sunset	★★★★★	322
King Me	★★★★★	146
Another Doug Reed Route	★★★★	44
Believer	★★★★	306
Capture the Flag	★★★★	300
Count Floyd Show	★★★★	104
Delusions of Grandeur	★★★★	89
Donor	★★★★	297
Electric Cowboy	★★★★	91
Eye of the Needle	★★★★	154
Fuzzy Undercling	★★★★	46
Geezers Go Sport	★★★★	190
Hen-ry!	★★★★	54
Jingus	★★★★	304
Like a Turtle	★★★★	304
Out for Justice	★★★★	180
Predator	★★★★	230
Prime Directive	★★★★	156
Random Precision	★★★★	293
Receiver	★★★★	193
Severn Bore	★★★★	276
She Might Be a Liar	★★★★	332
Skunk Love	★★★★	306
Tecumseh's Curse	★★★★	235
Tug-o-War	★★★★	251
Tweaked Unit	★★★★	318
Weed Eater	★★★★	266
Yellow Brick Road	★★★★	176
Parting Gift	★★★	50
Night Moves	★★★	229
A Portrait of the Artist ...	★★★	223
Aquaduck Pocket	★★★	54
Buccaneer	★★★	233
Cannonball	★★★	191
Chickenboy	★★★	278
Citizen's Arete	★★★	302
Del Boy	★★★	198
Fear or Common Sense	★★★	265
Finnegan's Ladder	★★★	367
Gym Jones Approved	★★★	217
Left Turret	★★★	50
Lollipop Kids	★★★	174
Mentor Powers	★★★	241
Mona Lisa Overdrive	★★★	278
Morning Sun	★★★	231
No Country for Old Men	★★★	223
Prey	★★★	230
Same Way	★★★	296
Smokin' Joe	★★★	153
Strip the Willows	★★★	211
Trad Sucker	★★★	350
Trust in Jesus	★★★	351
Twisted	★★★	350
Yadda Yadda Yadda	★★★	345
Jack Move	★★	299
Red Rover	★★	300
About Five Ten	★★	196
Buzz	★★	367
Ode to Poopie Head	★★	200
Resuscitation of a Hanged Man	★★	223
Smack Dab	★★	292
Tea at the Palaz of Hoon	★★	224
The Muir the Merrier	★★	241
Whippoorwill	★★	276
Young Jedi	★★	287
Mello Yellow	★	215
Ferdowsi		225

5.11a

☐ Air-Ride Equipped	★★★★	226
☐ Balance Beam	★★★★	300
☐ Bandolier	★★★★	193
☐ Bathtub Mary	★★★★	212
☐ Edge-a-Sketch	★★★★	233
☐ I'll Take Sue	★★★★	330
☐ Momma Cindy	★★★★	233
☐ Monkey in the Middle	★★★★	191
☐ Optical Rectitus	★★★★	312
☐ Return to Balance	★★★★	211
☐ Size Doesn't Matter	★★★★	332
☐ Super Dario	★★★★	149
☐ The Dude Abides	★★★★	328
☐ Toker	★★★★	335
☐ Whip-Stocking	★★★★	345
☐ Injured Reserve	★★★	351
☐ 100 Years of Solitude	★★★	223
☐ Aural Pleasure	★★★	318
☐ Autograph	★★★	298
☐ Brushfire Fairytales	★★★	256
☐ Buddhalicious	★★★	208
☐ Burning Bush	★★★	254
☐ Captain Blondie Sinks the Ship	★★★	216
☐ Commencement	★★★	145
☐ Cordillera Rojo	★★★	256
☐ Drip Wire	★★★	314
☐ Edgehog	★★★	190
☐ Flying the Bird	★★★	329
☐ Green Horn	★★★	278
☐ Hot Drama Teacher	★★★	329
☐ Hum	★★★	367
☐ Johnny B. Good	★★★	295
☐ Johnny on Roofies	★★★	296
☐ Jungle Trundler	★★★	262
☐ Kazi and Mito	★★★	62
☐ Maypop	★★★	53
☐ One Side Makes You Taller	★★★	361
☐ Radical Evolution	★★★	231
☐ Rising	★★★	263
☐ Skin the Cat	★★★	190
☐ Snapper	★★★	358
☐ The Ankle Brute	★★★	326
☐ Two Women Alone	★★★	304
☐ Willy Wonka	★★★	362
☐ Steal the Bacon	★★	300
☐ Creeping Elegance	★★	258
☐ Rectal Exorcism	★★	200
☐ American Psycho	★★	224
☐ Brothel Doc	★★	314
☐ Cold Shot	★★	136
☐ MumMum	★★	208
☐ South Central	★★	366
☐ Special K	★★	238
☐ Tao Bato	★★	219
☐ Unworthy	★★	359
☐ Hopscotch	★	299
☐ Trundling Trolls	★	208

5.11

☐ The Middle Path	★★★	211
☐ French Fighter	★	291
☐ NAMBLA RAMBLA	★	291
☐ Nose Ring	★	291
☐ Safety Meeting		276

5.10d

☐ Breakfast Burrito	★★★★★	343
☐ Fire and Brimstone	★★★★★	343
☐ Creep Show	★★★★	104
☐ Critters on the Cliff	★★★★	264
☐ Cruisin' for a Bruisin'	★★★★	236
☐ Hatfield	★★★★	317
☐ Heard it on NPR	★★★★	256
☐ Karmic Retribution	★★★★	247
☐ Naughty Neighbors	★★★★	246
☐ Normalised Bramapithecus	★★★★	298
☐ Pulling Pockets	★★★★	184
☐ Return of Manimal	★★★★	264
☐ Ruby Slippers	★★★★	174
☐ Tong Shing	★★★★	297
☐ Toxic Avenger	★★★★	138
☐ Shaved Squirrel	★★★	303
☐ Nameless	★★★	290
☐ Subject to Change	★★★	290
☐ Armadillo	★★★	190
☐ Armed Insurection	★★★	216
☐ Barenjager	★★★	256
☐ Circa Man	★★★	180
☐ Dragonslayer	★★★	184
☐ Family Values	★★★	196
☐ Generosity	★★★	298
☐ Ghost in the Machine	★★★	326
☐ Girls Gone Wild ... WOO!	★★★	302
☐ Happy Trails	★★★	294
☐ Helping Hands	★★★	298
☐ It's Alive	★★★	196
☐ Jack in the Pulpit	★★★	149
☐ Jailbird	★★★	190
☐ Just Duet	★★★	188
☐ K.S.B.	★★★	321
☐ Makin' Bacon	★★★	240
☐ Melancholy Mechanics	★★★	250
☐ Pocket Pussy	★★★	198
☐ Possum Lips	★★★	46
☐ Red Hot Chili Pepper	★★★	156
☐ Sacriledge	★★★	212
☐ Scrumbulglazer	★★★	250
☐ Super Pinch	★★★	278
☐ Tanduay Time	★★★	219
☐ The Glass Elevator	★★★	363
☐ Touch of Grey	★★★	232
☐ Yell Fire!	★★★	295
☐ Motor Booty Pimp Affair	★★	332
☐ Universal Gravitation	★★	230

5.10c

☐ Loompa	★★★★★	363
☐ Baby Blue Eyes	★★★★	330
☐ Bitter Ray of Sunshine	★★★★	233
☐ Crazyfingers	★★★★	184
☐ Delayed Gratification	★★★★	317
☐ Diamond in the Rough	★★★★	174
☐ Kentucky Flu	★★★★	312
☐ No Sleep Till Campton	★★★★	314
☐ Out of the Dark	★★★★	230
☐ Preemptive Strike	★★★★	236
☐ Some Humans Ain't Human	★★★★	266
☐ Store	★★★★	158
☐ Thunderclinger	★★★★	208
☐ 5th Bolt Faith	★★★	252
☐ A Brief History of Climb	★★★	295
☐ Annie the Annihilator	★★★	241

☐ Augenblick	★★★	250
☐ Back Door to Paris	★★★	62
☐ Coffee Talk	★★★	88
☐ Curbside No Traction	★★★	326
☐ Dingo the Gringo	★★★	266
☐ Don't Take Yer Guns to Town	★★★	263
☐ Hey There, Fancy Pants	★★★	262
☐ Hurt	★★★	296
☐ In the Light	★★★	46
☐ One Brick Shy	★★★	190
☐ Poopie Head	★★★	200
☐ Stool Sample	★★★	200
☐ Sunbeam	★★★	230
☐ Sundance	★★★	67
☐ That's What She Said	★★★	332
☐ The G-Man	★★★	320
☐ Unbridled	★★★	359
☐ Workin' for the Weekend	★★★	264
☐ No Love for Charlie	★★	299
☐ Banjolero	★★	276
☐ Last Resort	★★	196
☐ Single Finger Salute	★★	326
☐ The Second Labor of Hercules	★★	326

5.10b

☐ Boltergeist	★★★★	237
☐ Come in Your Lycra	★★★★	89
☐ Funkadelic	★★★★	154
☐ Gettin' Lucky In Kentucky	★★★★	252
☐ Nice to Know You	★★★★	297
☐ Sam	★★★★	220
☐ Thrillbillies	★★★★	211
☐ Apoplectic Chick from Missouri	★★★	298
☐ Action over Apathy	★★★	325
☐ Beta Spewer	★★★	260
☐ Beware the Bear	★★★	238
☐ Boom! Boom! Out Go the Lights	★★★	59
☐ Chimp	★★★	190
☐ Crude Awakening	★★★	292
☐ Danita Dolores	★★★	48
☐ DaVinci's Left Ear	★★★	292
☐ Jungle Gym	★★★	300
☐ Little Viper	★★★	263
☐ Loosen Up	★★★	180
☐ Machete	★★★	266
☐ Make a Wish	★★★	343
☐ Murano	★★★	295
☐ Overlord	★★★	104
☐ Reanimator	★★★	196
☐ Reserved Seating	★★★	68
☐ Slick and the 9mm	★★★	342
☐ The King Lives On ...	★★★	294
☐ You Can Tune a Piano, but ...	★★★	188
☐ A Way of Life	★★	88
☐ Bombardier	★★	208
☐ Family Tradition	★★	297
☐ Lucy Goocy	★★	216
☐ Significant Other	★★	320
☐ Surfin' the Whale's Back	★★	218
☐ The Short, Happy Life ...	★★	223
☐ Thin Skin	★★	292
☐ Virgin Bolter Tag Team	★★	266
☐ Weathertop Stings	★★	312
☐ When Rats Attack	★★	329
☐ Grey Matter	★	254
☐ Peer Review		286
☐ The Hook and the Pendulum		151

☐ Camel Toe Jockey	★ 187
☐ Eclipse	★ 161
☐ Just Another Trad Route	★ 153
☐ Maximus	★ 310
☐ Overdrive	★ 351
☐ Smoke Screen	★ 197
☐ Spinning Marty	★ 90
☐ Testosterone Testpiece	★ 136
☐ Things That Go Bump in the Night	★ 44
☐ Trad Wagon	★ 154
☐ Trident	★ 70
☐ Cindy Lou's Left Tube	79
☐ Don't Break the Edge	87
☐ Feltch Me	64
☐ Fox in Locks	80
☐ Guideline	151
☐ Icarus	151
☐ Never Again	42
☐ Punkin Head	69
☐ Route 52	96
☐ Sailing Shoes	48
☐ Suckers at the Top	91

5.9-

☐ Autumn	★★★★★ 60
☐ Blue Runner	★★★★ 98
☐ Attack of the Sand Shark	★★★ 104
☐ Broken Arrow	★★★ 66
☐ When Gravity Fails	★★★ 77
☐ Another One Fights the Rust	★★ 258
☐ Erik's First 5.6	★★ 283
☐ Exhibition	★★ 40
☐ On the Road	★★ 42
☐ Meteor Fall	★ 161
☐ Sierra's Travels	★ 256
☐ Xanthic Dance	★ 59
☐ Five Easy Pieces	59
☐ Outback	146
☐ Sugar Daddy	65

5.8+

☐ Dicey at Best	★★★★★ 121
☐ Rocket Man	★★★★★ 76
☐ Dog Days	★★★★ 118
☐ Good Times	★★★★ 148
☐ Lunatic Fringe	★★★★ 128
☐ Muscle Shoals	★★★★ 75
☐ The Shining	★★★★ 176
☐ Big Top	★★★ 40
☐ Bitchmobile	★★★ 72
☐ Dirty Old Men	★★★ 244
☐ Ear Drops	★★★ 228
☐ Green Grease	★★★ 116
☐ Jaws	★★★ 76
☐ Old School	★★★ 237
☐ Scared As a Virgin	★★★ 134
☐ Texas Tea	★★★ 65
☐ Anger Management	★★ 297
☐ Blood on the Nuts	★★ 84
☐ Butterfly Gangbang	★★ 306
☐ Continental Drift	★★ 253
☐ Devine Climb	★★ 124
☐ Invasion of the Love Queens	★★ 120
☐ It Ain't Over Yet	★★ 161
☐ Quaquaversal Crack	★★ 247
☐ Break the Edge	★ 87
☐ From the Ashes	★ 284

☐ G2 the Friction	★ 85
☐ Veldhaus Route	★ 154
☐ Courtesy Cringe	115
☐ Poison Ivy	120

5.8

☐ Arachnid	★★★★★ 118
☐ Cheaper Than a Movie	★★★★★ 330
☐ Arachnid	★★★★ 118
☐ Curving Crack	★★★★ 116
☐ Dancing Outlaw	★★★★ 119
☐ First Fall	★★★★ 244
☐ Five-Finger Discount	★★★★ 183
☐ Frenchburg Overhangs	★★★★ 100
☐ Hot Licks and Rhetoric	★★★★ 90
☐ Indecision	★★★★ 249
☐ Into the Purple Valley	★★★★ 90
☐ Snake	★★★★ 98
☐ Whiteout	★★★★ 175
☐ Zambezi Plunge	★★★★ 67
☐ Be My Yoko Ono	★★★ 330
☐ Bombs Bursting	★★★ 97
☐ Burcham's Folly	★★★ 195
☐ Carnivorous	★★★ 75
☐ Curiosity	★★★ 87
☐ Environmental Imperialism	★★★ 251
☐ Fickelgruber	★★★ 362
☐ Get on the Good Foot	★★★ 264
☐ Hung Jury	★★★ 169
☐ Jake Flake	★★★ 179
☐ Nautical Twilight	★★★ 64
☐ Oink! Oink!	★★★ 218
☐ One Fist, Two Fist, Red Fist ...	★★★ 80
☐ Put the Best Foot Forward	★★★ 264
☐ Quicksilver	★★★ 212
☐ Right Crack	★★★ 128
☐ Right On, Solid, and Far Out	★★★ 146
☐ Sassafras Tease	★★★ 105
☐ The Hangover Problem	★★★ 133
☐ Tony's Happy Christmas Crack	★★★ 336
☐ Wrong Crack	★★★ 128
☐ Berlin Wall	★★ 69
☐ 24-Hour Bug	★★ 220
☐ A Chip Off the Old Sturnum	★★ 296
☐ Baccaus Goes Climbing	★★ 266
☐ Bloody Fingers	★★ 77
☐ Born Again Christian	★★ 237
☐ Cruising for a Bruising	★★ 75
☐ Darling Dirtbag	★★ 328
☐ Hole	★★ 312
☐ Joe Camel	★★ 153
☐ Kiss It All Better	★★ 318
☐ Mailbox	★★ 61
☐ Rock Lobster	★★ 107
☐ Shipwrecked	★★ 164
☐ Sideshow	★★ 40
☐ Small Change	★★ 68
☐ Spiderweb Tearoom	★★ 124
☐ Star-Bellied Sneeches	★★ 80
☐ Stuck Buckeye	★★ 322
☐ Summer Breeze	★★ 322
☐ The Rampart	★★ 96
☐ The Wal-Martification of Trad	★★ 297
☐ Tomthievery	★★ 262
☐ If Trango Could Whistle	★★ 299
☐ Apehouse	★ 136
☐ Face Farce	★ 162

☐ Finger Filet	★ 163
☐ Gizmo	★ 85
☐ Lost Dart Crack	★ 120
☐ Mental Affair	★ 254
☐ Mole Vision	★ 169
☐ Old Friends	★ 149
☐ One Thing Leads to Another	★ 107
☐ Owgli Mowgli	★ 240
☐ Purple Cleaning Company	★ 79
☐ Quicky	★ 328
☐ Route 49	★ 96
☐ Second Thoughts	★ 107
☐ Seibert Route	★ 112
☐ Southern Comfort	★ 132
☐ Stratocaster	★ 121
☐ Suction Lipectomy	★ 58
☐ The Green Wombat	★ 120
☐ Thought it was Bubbles	★ 50
☐ Tobacco Crack Ho	★ 312
☐ Trunkline	★ 83
☐ You Got Served	★ 104
☐ And They Called It a Route	319
☐ Come to Me, Marie	298
☐ Cranky	132
☐ Eggshell	119
☐ LIDAR	252
☐ Made Me Sweat	85
☐ Must Dihedral	138
☐ Roof Crack	236
☐ The Bushman	91
☐ The Universe Next Door	246

5.8-

☐ Face Up to That Crack	★★★ 52
☐ Horny Bitch	★★★ 96
☐ Four Shower Tokens, Guinness...	★★ 298
☐ Grunt	★★ 90
☐ NEPA This	★★ 59
☐ Sweet Jane	★★ 262
☐ Tinker's Toy	★★ 134
☐ Madagascar	★ 118

5.7

☐ Roadside Attraction	★★★★★ 184
☐ Call of the Wild	★★★★ 238
☐ Casual Viewing	★★★★ 180
☐ Environmental Impact	★★★★ 67
☐ Full Moon	★★★★ 161
☐ Funhouse	★★★★ 138
☐ G.I.	★★★★ 51
☐ Good Tang	★★★★ 121
☐ Party Time	★★★★ 96
☐ Vision	★★★★ 179
☐ Alternative Medicines	★★★ 314
☐ Calypso I	★★★ 98
☐ Caver's Excitement	★★★ 117
☐ ED	★★★ 250
☐ Father and Son	★★★ 179
☐ Flaring Crack	★★★ 90
☐ Foxfire	★★★ 132
☐ Go West	★★★ 211
☐ Green Eggs	★★★ 80
☐ Ham	★★★ 80
☐ I Didn't Know This Was the End	★★★ 189
☐ Investigator	★★★ 123
☐ Laying Pipe Under the Bridge	★★★ 328
☐ Long Wall Chimney	★★★ 59

☐ Mama Told Me Not to Come	★★★ 77
☐ Octopus Tag	★★★ 300
☐ Off Width Your Head	★★★ 91
☐ Pink Panties Pulldown	★★★ 137
☐ Ride 'em Cowboy	★★★ 72
☐ Shock and Awe	★★★ 237
☐ Slimy Creatures	★★★ 85
☐ St. Alfonso's	★★★ 104
☐ Synergy	★★★ 107
☐ The Arrowhead	★★★ 66
☐ The Spider Squat	★★★ 121
☐ Tradmill	★★★ 256
☐ Two Step	★★★ 59
☐ Bobsledding	★★ 104
☐ Check Canopy	★★ 164
☐ Crack 'n Up	★★ 247
☐ Cussin' Crack	★★ 96
☐ God Save the Queen	★★ 80
☐ Grand Illusion	★★ 77
☐ Immodium AD	★★ 263
☐ Last Wave	★★ 76
☐ Paraplegic Power	★★ 253
☐ Ralph and Bob's	★★ 59
☐ Short and Sweet	★★ 258
☐ Slow Jack	★★ 286
☐ Theodor Seuss Geisel	★★ 80
☐ Wrong Turn	★★ 276
☐ Blade Runner	★ 48
☐ Brain Stem	★ 254
☐ Chimney Direct	★ 164
☐ Climbing With Crowbars	★ 254
☐ Cybersex	★ 248
☐ Decay's Way	★ 46
☐ Dirt in Eye	★ 262
☐ Pain is a Spice	★ 180
☐ Rinse and Repeat	★ 328
☐ Sorostitute	★ 332
☐ Take Off, Eh	★ 150
☐ Welcome to Bosnia	★ 72
☐ Winona	★ 218
☐ Woman Trouble	★ 75
☐ Hang Over	42
☐ Crude Boys	133
☐ Dirty Crack	164
☐ Five Tree	83
☐ May as Well	317
☐ Over Easy	84
☐ Should've Known Better	286
☐ Southern Hospitality	133
☐ The Integral	132

5.6

☐ Bedtime for Bonzo	★★★★★ 99
☐ Diamond in the Crack	★★★★★ 112
☐ Bongo	★★★ 137
☐ Calypso II	★★★ 98
☐ Copperhead	★★★ 112
☐ Groundhog	★★★ 116
☐ Motha	★★★ 184
☐ Nose Traverse	★★★ 117
☐ Salad Days	★★★ 116
☐ Sparky Goes Crack Climbing	★★★ 154
☐ The X Files	★★★ 70
☐ A Prayer for Owen Meany	★★ 223
☐ Big Crack	★★ 90
☐ Buckeye Testpiece	★★ 138
☐ Casual Corner	★★ 75

☐ Caterpillar Crack	★★ 120
☐ Cliff Hanger	★★ 124
☐ George of the Jungle	★★ 345
☐ Golden Fleece	★★ 163
☐ Looking Through the Devil's Window	★★ 306
☐ Razorback	★★ 67
☐ Ripp-Off	★★ 162
☐ Surfin With Grizz	★★ 77
☐ Suspended Sentence	★★ 169
☐ The Cheerleader Catch	★★ 316
☐ The P. Heist Rockway to Heaven	★★ 263
☐ Whoville	★★ 78
☐ Double Helix	★ 72
☐ Indian Castle	★ 85
☐ Lula Mae	★ 218
☐ Scared Shitless	★ 161
☐ Shattered	★ 120
☐ The Giver	★ 223
☐ Black Tide	251
☐ Land of the Glass Pinecones	71
☐ Mickey Mantle	124
☐ Pine Needle Shuffle	262
☐ Ron's Garden	161
☐ The Misadventures of Nabisco County	70
☐ Zig-Zag	164

5.5

☐ Big Country	★★★ 64
☐ Calypso III	★★★ 98
☐ Route 48	★★★ 97
☐ The Turret	★★★ 99
☐ Velveteen	★★★ 266
☐ Le Petite Bazaar	★★ 104
☐ Sweet and Sour	★★ 260
☐ Tomfoolery	★★ 104
☐ Father's Day	★ 175
☐ Hiking Boot Highway	★ 208
☐ Mindy	★ 127
☐ Oozing Couth	★ 99
☐ Stacy's Farewell	★ 44
☐ Another Grunge	118
☐ Bumblebee Junction	124
☐ Delirium Tremors	119
☐ Fungus Fantasy	149
☐ Leo	107
☐ Tunnel Route	164

5.4

☐ Laceration	★★★★ 107
☐ American Crack	★★★ 97
☐ Mighty Eidson	★★★ 116
☐ Beachcomber	★★ 66
☐ Chester Fried Chicken	★★ 284
☐ Fat Man's Misery	★★ 307
☐ Fortress Grunges	★★ 99
☐ Futuristic Testpiece	★★ 284
☐ Heartbreak of Psoriasis	★★ 107
☐ No Doz	★★ 40
☐ The Perfect Pint	★★ 284
☐ Turkey Crossing	★★ 276
☐ Bonzo's Revenge	★ 99
☐ The Grinch	★ 78
☐ Rockhouse	161
☐ Trekker of the Treacherous	231

5.3

☐ Caver's Route	★★★★★ 117
☐ American Wall	★★★ 97
☐ Double Caves Crack	★★★ 120
☐ Dragon's Tail	★★★ 258
☐ Tower Backside	★★★ 117
☐ Gumby Land	★ 188
☐ Initiation	★ 161
☐ Armed Forces	51
☐ Green Gully	51
☐ Joe's Route	100
☐ Seuss Seuss Sudio	79
☐ Tom's Route	100

5.2

☐ Minas Ithil	★★ 74
☐ Hmmm	★ 192
☐ Slither and Squeeze	★ 258
☐ Top-Roper's Route	46
☐ Chimney's Chimney	164
☐ DAB Chimney	121
☐ Get Outta My Way	99
☐ Lost Dart	120
☐ The Grunges	116

5.1

☐ Primordial Dissonance	★★★ 230
☐ Kate's First Trad Lead	★★ 259
☐ Revenge of the Sith	★★ 230
☐ Beginner's Nightmare	★ 162
☐ Pogue's Path	★ 121
☐ Mossy Mayhem	231
☐ People Gully	70

4th Class

☐ Ellen's Descent	★ 160

INDEX